Insights to Performance Excellence 2006

Also available from ASQ Quality Press:

Charting Your Course: Lessons Learned During the Journey Toward Performance Excellence
John G. Conyers and Robert Ewy

Business Performance through Lean Six Sigma: Linking the Knowledge Worker, the Twelve Pillars, and Baldrige
James T. Schutta

From Baldrige to the Bottom Line: A Road Map for Organizational Change and Improvement
David W. Hutton

There is Another Way!: Launch a Baldrige-Based Quality Classroom
Margaret A. Byrnes with Jeanne C. Baxter

The Path to Profitable Measures: 10 Steps to Feedback That Fuels Performance
Mark W. Morgan

The Certified Manager of Quality/Organizational Excellence Handbook, Third Edition
Russell T. Westcott, editor

The Quality Toolbox, Second Edition
Nancy R. Tague

Making Change Work: Practical Tools for Overcoming Human Resistance to Change
Brien Palmer

The Process-Focused Organization: A Transition Strategy for Success
Robert A. Gardner

Inside Knowledge: Rediscovering the Source of Performance Improvement
David Fearon & Steven A. Cavaleri

Quality Makes Money: How to Involve Every Person on the Payroll in a Complete Quality Process (CQP)
Pat Townsend and Joan Gebhardt

Everyday Excellence: Creating a Better Workplace through Attitude, Action, and Appreciation
Clive Shearer

To request a complimentary catalog of ASQ Quality Press publications, call 800-248-1946, or visit our Web site at http://qualitypress.asq.org.

Insights to Performance Excellence 2006

An Inside Look at the 2006 Baldrige Award Criteria

Mark L. Blazey

ASQ Quality Press

Milwaukee, Wisconsin

American Society for Quality, Quality Press, Milwaukee 53203
© 2006 by ASQ
All rights reserved. Published 2006
Printed in the United States of America

12 11 10 09 08 07 06   5 4 3 2 1

ISBN-13: 978-0-87389-685-6
ISBN-10: 0-87389-685-8

Publisher: William A. Tony
Acquisitions Editor: Annemieke Hytinen
Project Editor: Paul O'Mara
Production Administrator: Randall Benson

ASQ Mission: The American Society for Quality advances individual, organizational, and community excellence worldwide through learning, quality improvement, and knowledge exchange.

Attention bookstores, wholesalers, schools, and corporations: ASQ Quality Press books, videotapes, audiotapes, and software are available at quantity discounts with bulk purchases for business, educational, or instructional use.
For information, please contact ASQ Quality Press at 800-248-1946, or write to ASQ Quality Press, P.O. Box 3005, Milwaukee, WI 53201-3005.

To place orders or to request a free copy of the ASQ Quality Press Publications Catalog, including ASQ membership information, call 800-248-1946. Visit our Web site at http://www.asq.org or http://qualitypress.asq.org.

 Printed on acid-free paper

Quality Press
600 N. Plankinton Avenue
Milwaukee, Wisconsin 53203
Call toll free 800-248-1946
Fax 414-272-1734
www.asq.org
http://qualitypress.asq.org
http://standardsgroup.asq.org
E-mail: authors@asq.org

This book is dedicated to the memory of my father, Everett,
who taught me the value of continuous improvement,
and to my family members, who provide support for the
continuous search for excellence: my mother, Ann L. Blazey,
who at 78 continues to strive to improve
everything she does; my brothers Scott, Brian, and Brent;
my children Elizabeth and Mark; and most of all,
my lifelong partner and loving wife Karen.

Contents

CD-ROM Contents

Insights to Performance Excellence 2006 contains a companion CD-ROM, located on the inside back cover, with the following contents:

2006 CD-ROM Contents *(PDF and Word)*

2006 Baldrige Process Calendar *(PDF and Word)*

Baldrige Award Recipients and State Award Contact Information
1988-2005 Baldrige Award Recipients (PDF and Word)
State Award Contacts (PDF and Word)

2006 Business
2006 Baldrige Business Criteria and Applications
2006 Baldrige Business Criteria Booklet (PDF)
2006 Baldrige Business Criteria – Categories only (PDF and Word)
2006 Baldrige Award Application Forms (PDF)
2006 Eligibility Certification Forms (Word)
2006 Optional Worksheet - Business (PDF and Word)
2006 Baldrige Business Scoring Calibration Guide *(PDF and Word)*
2006 Baldrige Application Development Templates for Business *(PDF and Word)*
2006 Shingo and Baldrige 2006 Comparison
2006 Shingo and Baldrige Comparison Matrix (PDF and Word)
Baldrige or Shingo Prize for Excellence in Manufacturing (PDF)
ISO 9001 and Baldrige 2006 Comparison
Baldrige or ISO 9001 (PDF)
ISO 9001 and Baldrige 2006 Comparison Matrix (PDF and Word)

2006 Education
2006 Insights to Education Performance Excellence *(PDF)*
2006 Baldrige Education Criteria and Applications
2006 Baldrige Education Criteria Booklet (PDF)
2006 Baldrige Award Application Forms (PDF)
2006 Eligibility Certification Forms (Word)
2006 Optional Worksheet - Education (PDF)
2006 Baldrige Education Application Development Templates *(PDF and Word)*
2006 Baldrige Education Scoring Calibration Guide *(PDF and Word)*
Middle States Accreditation and Baldrige Education Comparison *(PDF and Word)*

2006 Health Care
2006 Insights to Health Care Performance Excellence *(PDF)*
2006 Baldrige Health Care Criteria and Applications
2006 Baldrige Health Care Criteria Booklet (PDF)
2006 Baldrige Award Application Forms (PDF)
2006 Eligibility Certification Forms (Word)
2006 Optional Worksheet Health Care (PDF)
2006 Baldrige Health Care Application Development Templates *(PDF and Word)*
2006 Health Care Scoring Calibration Guide *(PDF and Word)*
JCAHO and Baldrige Comparison
Baldrige or JCAHO (PDF)
JCAHO and Baldrige Introduction and Comparison Matrix (PDF and Word)

2006 Nonprofit Pilot
2006 Baldrige Award Application Forms *(PDF)*
2006 Eligibility Certification Forms *(Word)*
2006 Nonprofit Pilot Supplemental Eligibility Certification Form *(Word)*

A Global View of Quality *(PDF)*

Alignment of Baldrige With Six Sigma, Lean Thinking, and Balanced Scorecard *(PDF)*

Additional Materials from the Baldrige Award Web Site
Baldrige Frequently Asked Questions *(PDF and Word)*
Getting Started *(PDF)*
Improvement Act of 1987 *(PDF)*
Why Apply *(PDF)*
Why Baldrige *(PDF)*

Some files on this CD-ROM require Microsoft Word or Microsoft Excel.

PDF files may be opened using Adobe Reader 6.0 or higher or Adobe Acrobat® 6.0 or higher. Adobe Reader may be downloaded free of charge from the Adobe Web site at http://www.adobe.com/products/acrobat/readermain.html.

To place orders or to request a free copy of the ASQ Quality Press Publications Catalog, including ASQ membership information, call 800-248-1946. Visit our Web site at http://www.asq.org or http://qualitypress.asq.org.

Foreword

LEADERSHIP CHALLENGES

A lot of time and energy is put into answering the question, "What drives success in organizations?" It's as much a function of the people and the value the organization brings to the marketplace as it is the approaches chosen to deliver them. It takes more than being able to articulate the lessons learned by the successful—the trick is being able to help others incorporate and leverage those lessons in their own approaches, whether in the private sector, education, healthcare, or government. Dr. Mark Blazey is the leading expert in the application of the Baldrige Criteria to help organizations improve. He provided extremely valuable insight—through his writings and personal consulting—to help us at Xerox develop world-class management systems that led to Xerox Business Services being recognized as a 1997 recipient of the Baldrige Award. Dr. Blazey provides many valuable insights to help leaders make the changes needed to achieve the highest levels of performance excellence —many of which are highlighted in this introduction.

Traditionally, success in business has involved the pursuit of functional excellence in fields such as sales (IBM), marketing (Coca-Cola), manufacturing (Ford), and capital formation (Morgan Stanley). As important as functional supremacy is today, it is not enough. It is how all the elements of an organization come together and provide value in the market-place—to customers and other stakeholders—that is the key ingredient to success. Success at the top level requires balancing many things at once. It involves understanding how the system works together. What system is used to run the most successful businesses? Can all the executives in the business articulate what that system is? Can each one draw a picture of that system on a single sheet of paper and explain it to 10-year-old children? I once had the CEO of one of the largest transportation companies in North America ask his 35 direct reports to draw a picture of the system they used to run the business on one sheet of paper. He waited five minutes and collected the draw-ings. As he thumbed through the papers he kept shaking his head in disbelief. No two pieces of paper portrayed the same picture. Think of the message that sends. Here are the 35 senior people in a multibillion-dollar business and they do not have a uniform view of how the business is run or what is most important. This may account, in part, for their poor performance. These executives do not know whether or how they will be able to keep the promises they make to their customers, employees, stockholders, and the communities in which they work and live. Think of the powerful message that could be sent if they all focused on the same themes, pursued the same vision and objectives, and had confidence that the things they were asked to be done were indeed the right things for the business to succeed.

Like it or not, to be successful, organizations must identify and serve customers—although they may choose to call them many other names, such as clients, students, patients, families, constituents, communities, voters, rate-payers, passengers, or shoppers, to name a few. The nomenclature changes depending upon the language of the business; but at the end of the day it's the *customers* who make decisions about whether they are going to do business with us. If we can keep our customers loyal and attract new loyal customers, the organization is going to thrive. Clearly, without loyal customers, organizations cannot survive.

Strange as it may seem, there are organizations that have not put *delighting customers* at the top of their priority list (or anywhere on the list). Delighted customers are five times more likely to buy from you or recommend you to others than those who are simply satisfied. On the other hand, 80 percent of dissatisfied customers are likely to walk away and not even tell you they were dissatisfied. Moreover, dissatisfied customers are likely to tell at least 20 of their friends, while only five will hear of the startling news associated with *delight*. Worst of all, it costs 10 times as much to regain a lost customer as it does to retain a current one. With the large number of Internet-based consumer buying sites in place today, dissatisfied customers can easily tell thousands about their bad experiences. The 21st century has evolved a more demanding customer-driven economy.

If organizations intend to thrive, employees and leaders must understand the requirements and expectations of their customers. More than ever before, they need to personalize the customer relationship and build loyalty. Horst Schulze, the former CEO of Ritz-Carlton, a hotel chain that significantly altered the nature of customer service, points this out when he says, "Customers need a reason to be loyal; give them a reason." While CEO, Schulze took the time to be personally involved in a two-day orientation with all of the staff at the opening of each new Ritz-Carlton hotel. Here was the chief executive making sure that everyone in the business understood the objectives and keys to success. His penetrating but simple questions to staff members up and down the line would focus on who are your customers; what is important to these customers; and how do we make these four or five things that are important to our customers better than anywhere else. To illustrate a typical Ritz-Carlton experience, if a guest has a preference for a hard pillow, a note is entered into the customer database and wherever the guest goes in the Ritz-Carlton chain a hard pillow will be on the bed. In another instance, while cleaning the room in the morning, a housekeeper found a small teddy bear on the floor among the child's dirty clothes. Upon return, the child found the teddy bear sitting at a small table with the Ritz Lion having tea. Now, what do you think went through the minds of the parents and the child?!

To deliver that level of performance consistently, the Ritz-Carlton—or any organization—must put in place a set of processes that focus on customer delight and are capable of delivering consistent results. Again, let's look at the Ritz-Carlton work processes. The person who is recognized as the best at doing a task is the one who documents the process. For three weeks, a new employee follows in the footsteps of an experienced, high-performing employee who volunteers to be a teacher-mentor. At the end of the training period the new person is tested. Passing means the employee begins to work independently; failing means more training and testing. On the job, specific,

quantifiable performance goals are set. Goals and timing for *improvement* are then established and progress is reported quarterly. Processes are aimed at things that customers consider important; employees are focused on delivering them at high levels of achievement; and they are constantly engaged to do it better. This creates an environment of true *continuous improvement*. The environment of customer-focused continuous improvement keeps customers coming back and bragging about their delightful experience to their friends. Horst Schulze has figured out that the friends and acquaintances of current customers are the very people the Ritz is trying to attract.

When key work processes are capable of producing desired results consistently, the outcomes are predictable. That is why a *process* orientation is important. Too many people in nonmanufacturing disciplines, such as sales, education, or healthcare, believe that using process discipline to carry out work is an outdated idea and does not apply in their fast-paced, *professional-driven* world. The recent winners of the Baldrige Award demonstrate clearly that a customer-focused process orientation is critical for success in manufacturing as well as nonmanufacturing (such as healthcare and public school systems) and large and small businesses. Based on discussions with hundreds of leaders who are concerned with the level of performance in their organizations, it appears that the fear of discipline and accountability, which a process orientation brings to the workplace, may be one of the real obstacles to change.

Unfortunately, even when organizations begin to execute processes well, their leaders quickly find that excellence and optimum performance continue to elude them. Organizations can fail to satisfy customers even when key work processes function as designed—if the design was not tied to customer requirements. *Internally focused* processes have often been driven by the desire to do things more efficiently and effectively from the company's point of view—without regard for customer concerns. The resulting organizational arrogance—the belief that we know better than the customer—is almost certain to bring about customer dissatisfaction and ultimately revolt, causing customers to demand change or leave. To be successful, organizations must consistently understand and precisely execute those processes that deliver the four or five characteristics that are critical to customer delight—the vital few. The winners in the highly competitive environment in which we live are the organizations that understand these drivers of customer delight and then design and execute work processes aimed at delivering them better than anyone else.

Many business leaders find it difficult to determine what customers want, fend off the competition, and satisfy workers, all within a budget. That is where the development and execution of *strategy* come into play. Strategy development demands a thorough understanding of the direction in which customers are moving, the direction in which the competition is moving, the direction in which the market is moving; coupling that information with the capabilities and desired direction of the business; and then identifying the few things that are critical to the future success of the business.

Knowing how well all of these factors are working involves having a *dashboard for the business.* No one would think of driving a car on a trip or getting on an airplane if the instrument panel were missing. Yet business leaders often make critical decisions with either one-dimensional instruments (financial) or instruments that provide insufficient information about the state of the business (factors measured because they are available but not necessarily important). Relying only on financial instruments is comparable to driving the car by only looking in the rear-view mirror. The good news is the picture is pretty clear. The bad news is that you will crash sooner or later since you cannot make adjustments in anticipation of problems. Of course, leaders in every organization must be aware of the organization's financial health. That information, however, comes too late to lead the organization effectively through difficult and challenging times. The organization's leaders must be aware of *leading* indicators and know what is important to customers, how well it is delivering on those things that are important, the reaction of its customers, the direction in which their expectations are moving, and the capability and capacity of its work processes and delivery systems. With this *advance* knowledge, leaders are in a much improved position to make better decisions about the actions needed to be successful, bring value to the market-

place, and respond to changing circumstances and new opportunities.

While customer focus, strategic planning, and data to support effective decision making are critical components of the successful organization, these factors combined are still not sufficient to ensure success. Every organization must acquire good people, train them, motivate them, and retain them. Today, to be successful, organizations must attract and develop employees who understand that the customers are *the* most import aspect of the business. Employees must have the competencies to use facts and information to make good decisions, and to continue learning and contribute to their own growth and development. In a world where product and service superiority lasts only a short time, it is the capabilities of the people that will be the source of ongoing excellence and differentiation. No longer are companies simply looking for employees with the right skills. Today, businesses need employees who are data-driven, customer-focused, and process-oriented—empowered people willing and able to make the decisions that can move a business forward.

The ability to make this system come together and work harmoniously is the responsibility of leadership. Basically, leadership has two functions:

1. To set the direction very clearly, based on a strategy that brings value to the marketplace; and
2. To establish the environment in which that direction is carried out consistently.

Some leaders find it difficult to establish and articulate a clear vision and role model a set of values. Without a clear direction, the people in an organization are forced to substitute their own ideas about the *right direction.* When many do this, the organization finds itself pulled in different directions. Leaders cannot expect people to know what to do if they have not established and continuously reinforced the norms of desired behavior. Leadership is very much about setting and leading by example—role modeling what the company stands for and living the change expected of all.

The best organizations in every sector have demonstrated that all parts of the system must be effectively integrated to optimize performance. It is not possible to achieve excellence by only doing the things that are easy and ignoring the rest. The concept of smoothly integrating all the facets of a business into a system is easy to understand but very difficult to execute.

With his best-selling series and his personal involvement, Dr. Blazey has been helping leaders and organizations of all types and in all sectors achieve success and develop enviable performance levels. He has helped them develop practical approaches for continuous improvement that serve as the cornerstone for leadership and organizational success. Blazey's personal insight and clear explanations help make complex Baldrige concepts much simpler. That is what makes this book a best-seller. *Insights to Performance Excellence* is a book for beginners as well as experts in the field of organizational development and operational excellence. The book delivers the lessons, provides the insights, and sets the framework for a successful journey to performance excellence.

John Lawrence
Retired Vice President of Quality
Xerox Business Services
1997 Baldrige Winner

Preface

A substantial portion of my professional life has been spent helping people understand the power and benefits of this integrated management system and become examiners for many performance excellence awards. These people come from all types of organizations and from all levels within those organizations. Participants include CEOs, corporate quality directors, state organization chiefs, small-business owners, heads of hospitals, teachers, professors, medical doctors, and school superintendents, to name a few.

This book was originally developed for them. It was used as a teaching text to guide their decisions and deliberations as they provided feedback to organizations that documented their continuous improvement efforts using Baldrige Award-type management systems. Many examiners who used this text, especially Tom Kubiak, asked me to publish it in a stand-alone format. They wanted to use it to help their own organizations, customers, and suppliers guide and assess their continuous improvement efforts.

These two groups of readers—examiners of quality systems and leaders of organizations seeking high levels of performance—can gain a competitive edge by understanding not only the parts of a high-performance management system, but also how these parts connect and align. My goal for this book is that readers will understand fully what each area of the quality system means for organizations and find the synergy within the six major process-oriented parts of the system—leadership; strategic planning; customer and market focus; measurement, analysis, and knowledge management; human resource focus; and process management that lead to excellent business results.

Leaders have reported that this book has been valuable as a step-by-step approach to help identify and put in place properly focused continuous improvement systems. As progress is made, improvement efforts in one area will lead to improvements in other areas. This process is similar to experiences we have all encountered as we carry out home improvement: improve one area, and many other areas needing improvement become apparent. This book will help identify areas that need immediate improvement as well as areas that are less urgent but, nevertheless, vitally linked to organizational and operational excellence.

I am continually looking for feedback about this book and suggestions about how it can be improved. Please contact me via e-mail at authors@asq.org.

Acknowledgments

Harry Hertz, Curt Reimann, and the dedicated staff of the Malcolm Baldrige National Quality Award office have provided long-standing support and guidance in promoting quality excellence. Karen Davison, John Lawrence, and Paul Grizzell provided substantial editorial and analytical assistance. In addition, John and Paul, respectively, contributed to analyses comparing Baldrige with ISO 9001 and JCAHO requirements.

Many others have helped shape my thinking about performance excellence and refine this book, including Joe Sener, Olga Striltschuk, April Corniea, Rosye Faulk, Jeff Calhoun, Rob Ecklin, Rob Marchelonis, Harry Zechman, Mary Gamble, Angie Germain, Orland Pitts, Ed Hare, April Umluf, Debra Danziger-Barron, Jim Shipley, Tom Kubiak, Rich Harris, Ginger Baker-Betz, Patricia Billings, Wendy Brennan, Gerald Brown, Beverly Centini, Sheryl Billups, Joe Kilbride, Linda Vincent, Jim Percy, Elizabeth Hale, Joan Wills, Steve Hoisington, Liz Menzer, John Gustafson, Brian Lassiter, Jean Bronk, Gary Floss, Mike Reagan, Jack Evans, Arnie Weimerskirch, Don Cates, Marty Mariner, Jerry Holt, Bill MacLachlan, Doug Green, Paul Kuchuris, Bob Ewy, Jo-Ann Kratz, Sandra Cokley-Pederson, Gary Jones, Bill Smith, Mike Smith, Janice Weinman, Peggy Siegel, Paul Schindler, Steve Uebbing, Lynn Erdle, Brian Dunster, Robert Frisina, James Miller, Jack Smith, Fred Smith, Dennis Nystrom, Rich Rose, Kathy Malcolm, Harold Stafford, Roberta Early, Judd Prozeller, Dan Thorpe, Ed Bergin, Linda Watson, Mickey Mayland, Diane Rivers, Michael Chapman, Linda Janczak, Judith Cherrington, Laurie Emerson, Patricia Stevens, Charlie Blass, Kelly Gilhooly, Pat Webb, Annemieke Hytinen, and George Raemore. I would like to thank Jessica Norris for typing, background research, and proofreading. I also greatly appreciate the work of Scott Blazey of Enterprise Design and Publishing for working with me every step of the way to prepare this book for publication. Without his efforts, this book would not exist.

The chapter on site visits including the Expected Results Matrix, the Criteria model and integrated management systems analysis, the management and performance excellence surveys, the performance standard for leadership, the sections concerning the potential adverse consequences of not doing what the Criteria require, the application preparation files, and the Scoring Calibration Guide are used with permission of Quantum Performance Group. I would also like to recognize and thank members of the Minnesota Council for Quality including Brian Lassiter, April Corneia, Jean Bronk, Mike Reagan, Lois Mackin, and Katherine Mackin for helping to expand the Expected Results Matrix into its current form.

The analysis of Six Sigma, Lean and Balanced Scorecard, and JCAHO is used with permission of Paul Grizzell of Performance Leadership Group. The Core Values, Criteria, selected glossary terms, award winners, and background information in this book are drawn from information in the public domain supplied by the Malcolm Baldrige National Quality Award program. Kevin Hendricks and Vinod Singhal provided research results that were used in this book from their extensive study of financial performance. Data from the Economic Evaluation of the Baldrige National Quality Program by Albert Link and John Scott, prepared for NIST in October 2001, and data from Foundation for the Malcolm Baldrige National Quality Award regarding the perception of chief executive officers from more than 300 U.S. organizations are also included in this book.

Mark Blazey

Introduction

The Malcolm Baldrige National Quality Award (MBNQA) 2006 Criteria for Performance Excellence and scoring guidelines are powerful assessment instruments that help leaders identify organizational strengths and key opportunities for improvement. The primary task of leaders is then to use the information to improve work processes and achieve higher levels of performance.

Building an effective management system capable of driving performance improvement is an ongoing challenge because of the intricate web of complex relationships among management, labor, customers, stakeholders, partners, and suppliers. The best organizations have put in place a management system that improves its work processes continually. They measure every key facet of business activity and closely monitor organizational performance. Leaders of these organizations set high expectations, value employees and their input, communicate clear directions, and align the work of everyone to optimize performance and achieve organizational goals.

Unfortunately, because of the complexity of modern management systems, the criteria used to examine them are also complex and sometimes difficult to understand. *Insights to Performance Excellence 2006* helps performance-excellence examiners and organization-improvement practitioners to understand the 2006 Baldrige performance excellence criteria and the linkages and relationships among the items.

Six types of information are provided in this book for each of the items in Categories 1 through 6:

1. The actual language of each item, including notes (presented in the shadow box). [Author's note: The information in these shadow boxes presents the official Baldrige Criteria and serves as the only basis for the examination. The other five types of information presented in this book for each Item (elements 2 through 6) provide the author's interpretation of the official Criteria requirements and should not be used as a basis for establishing additional requirements during an examination or performance review.]

2. A plain-English explanation of the requirements of each Item with some suggestions about the rationale for the Item and ways to meet key requirements.

3. A summary of the requirements of each Item in flowchart form. The flowcharts capture the essence of each item and isolate the requirements of each item to help organizations focus on the key points the item is assessing. Note that most boxes in the flowcharts contain an item reference in brackets [ ]. This indicates that the criteria require the action. If there is no item reference in brackets, it means the action is suggested but not required. Occasionally a reference to *[scoring guidelines]* is included in a box. This means that the authority for the requirement comes from the scoring guidelines.

4. The key linkages between each item and the other items. The major or primary linkages are designated using a solid arrow (———). The secondary linkages are designated using a dashed arrow (-- --).

5. An explanation of some potential adverse consequences that an organization might face if it fails to implement processes required by each Item. (Examiners may find this analysis useful as they prepare relevant feedback concerning opportunities for improvement. However, these generic statements should be customized—based on key factors, core values, or specific circumstances facing the organization being reviewed—before using them to develop feedback comments supporting opportunities for improvements in Categories 1 through 6.)

6. Examples of effective practices that some organizations have developed and followed consistent with the requirements of the Item. These samples

present some ideas about how to meet requirements. (Remember, examiners should not convert these sample effective practices into new requirements for organizations they are examining.)

Changes to this 2006 edition include:

- New information from the Baldrige 2006 Criteria for Performance Excellence to help leaders focus on priority opportunities for improvement and better understand the role they must play in refining their management systems and processes.

- The CD-ROM included with this book has been modified to bring templates and related analyses up to date with the changes in the Criteria.

- New 2006 version of *Insights to Performance Excellence in Health Care* is included on the CD-ROM.

- New 2006 version of *Insights to Performance Excellence in Education* is included on the CD-ROM.

Reading *Insights to Performance Excellence 2006* will strengthen your understanding of the Criteria and provide insight on analyzing your organization, improving performance, and applying for the award.

Insights to Performance Excellence

This section provides information for leaders who seek to transform their organizations to achieve performance excellence. This section:

- Presents a business case for using the Baldrige Criteria to improve organizational performance

- Describes the core values that drive organizational change to high levels of performance and underlie the Baldrige Criteria

- Provides practical insights and lessons learned—ideas on transition strategies to put high-performance systems in place and promote organizational learning

This section emphasizes themes driven by the 2006 Criteria and Core Values. It also includes suggestions about how to start down the path to systematic organizational improvement, as well as lessons learned from those who chose paths that led nowhere or proved futile despite their best intentions.

BALDRIGE BEGINNINGS AND ONGOING REFINEMENT

During the 1980s, many U.S. businesses suffered losses in the marketplace due to stronger international competition. We found that for nearly 30 years, Japanese business leaders were able to improve the performance of their organizations by following the teachings of W. Edwards Deming and striving to meet the requirements of the Deming Prize Criteria. The story of the Japanese recovery from the devastation of World War II to a dominant global economic power was documented in the CBS documentary *If Japan Can, Why Can't We?*

The documentary explained the strong, positive impact the prize had on the desire and ability of Japanese business leaders to improve organizational performance. Moreover, it served as a catalyst for the creation of a national quality award for the United States. It was hoped that a similar award would help U.S. business leaders focus on the systems and processes that would lead them to recovery much as the Deming Prize Criteria helped the Japanese.

After nearly five years of work, in 1987, the U.S. Congress created the national quality award named in honor of the secretary of the Department of Commerce, Malcolm Baldrige, who had died a short time earlier in a rodeo accident. The MBNQA or *Baldrige Award* had one key purpose: to help U.S. businesses improve their competitiveness in the global marketplace.

After much debate and discussion, the creators of the award criteria—led by Dr. Curt Reimann of the U.S. Department of Commerce—agreed that the award criteria should not be based on theories of how organizations ought to conduct business in order to win. They had seen too many instances where organizations followed the many piecemeal theories of the management gurus that led nowhere.

On the other hand, some argued that the United States should simply adopt the Deming Prize Criteria, which had been in place for 35 years. After monitoring the performance of earlier Deming Prize winners, however, it became apparent that the practices that enabled many of them to achieve high performance in the past were no longer sufficient to ensure high performance in the present and future. Changes in the marketplace, customer requirements, competition, worker skills and availability, and technology (to name a few) have forced organizations to change the way they manage their business in order to continue to succeed and win.

The designers of the U.S. national award wanted to avoid problems inherent in both approaches. Accordingly, the principle was adopted that the Criteria must be continually refreshed and be based on the verified management practices of the world's best-performing companies that enabled them to achieve such high levels of performance, productivity, customer satisfaction, and market dominance.

To ensure that the Baldrige Criteria for Performance Excellence continue to be relevant, the U.S. Department of Commerce, National Institute of Standards and Technology (NIST) reviews the drivers of high performance each year. Based on these analyses, the Criteria for the Malcolm Baldrige National Quality Award are validated and refined.

In spite of this ongoing renewal, some critics of the Baldrige Criteria argue that the Baldrige standards are *outdated* and *passé*. These critics often ask, "If the Baldrige Criteria are updated each year, why don't they reflect the newest management techniques?" Early critics, pointing to the rising success of e-commerce and the dot-coms, seemed to prefer to employ unproven theories of what is needed to be successful in the global market. None of these critics, however, were able to offer any performance-based evidence to support their opinions. In fact, the collapse of thousands of badly managed dot-coms and other organizations seems to indicate that unproven theories and management fads do no more to build solid performance today than they did in prior decades.

The main reason why the Baldrige Criteria do not require the use of the latest management fads is because a management practice must be a proven driver of high performance before the practice is included as a requirement. Such *proofs* require strong evidence of widespread practice and related performance outcomes.

A new management practice might work well for one organization but not for another. Fact-based evidence must demonstrate that the practice leads to high performance in many types of organizations, including small and large, manufacturing and service, union and nonunion, and public and private.

Because it usually takes two or more years for a *promising practice* to prove its value, the Baldrige Criteria will lag behind the newest, unproven fads. However, the rigor of the Baldrige review is part of the value the Baldrige Criteria add to business excellence. The Criteria help leaders sort out the fads from the proven techniques. *The Baldrige Criteria reflect leading-edge, validated management practices essential to achieving optimum performance.*

Finally, it is important to mention that the Baldrige Criteria were never intended to limit improvement, innovation, and creativity—in fact, the Criteria require those traits in all process Areas. Specifically, the Criteria require leaders to improve their own effectiveness [1.2a(2)] and promote innovation throughout the organization [1.1a(3)], in both work and jobs [5.1a(1)]. The Criteria require, in many areas, that the organization keep certain work processes current with changing business needs, including:

- Listening to customers [3.1a(3)]
- Building relationships with customers [3.2a(4)]
- Determining customer satisfaction [3.2b(4)]
- Performance-measurement system [4.1a(3)]
- Data and information availability [4.2a(3)]
- Software and hardware systems [4.2a(3)]
- Value-creation processes [6.1a(6)
- Support processes [6.2a(6)]

The best leaders use the principles described by the Baldrige Criteria as the fundamental way they manage the organization, and then search for methods to refine and enhance their work systems to provide even more competitive advantage. They experiment with new techniques and are not content to simply follow a management cookbook. However, they install a solid management system first, then experiment and improve—not the other way around.

Many of these top leaders use the Baldrige principles and management systems to achieve high performance without any public announcements or fanfare. They have never applied for the award and do not intend to do so. They are content to achieve excellence and win in the business world, rather than compete for a prize.

Nearly all business leaders and managers who reject the value of the Criteria out of hand do not understand the principles they contain, even those who claim to have "tried Baldrige." The system that effectively drives top performance in organizations is complex. After all, if it was easy to achieve excellence, everyone would do it. The landscape is littered with organizations that never understood or failed to continue using the validated, leading-edge management practices defined by the Baldrige Criteria. This book is for those leaders who are willing and able to commit to becoming effective leaders, optimizing performance, and sustaining the excellence they have helped to achieve.

THE BUSINESS CASE FOR USING THE BALDRIGE PERFORMANCE EXCELLENCE CRITERIA

All leaders know that change is not easy. They will be asked and perhaps tempted to turn back many times. They may not even be aware of these temptations or of the backsliding that occurs when their peers and subordinates sense their commitment is wavering. Leaders who are dedicated to achieving high performance appreciate examples of success from organizations that are ahead of them on the journey. These excellent leaders have held the course despite nagging doubts, organizational turbulence, and attempts at sabotage.

The following section of the book:

- Summarizes perceptions and predictions about business trends and the value of the MBNQA, based on survey responses of chief executive officers from 308 major U.S. organizations. (This survey was conducted by the Foundation for the Malcolm Baldrige National Quality Award, April 1998.)

- Summarizes research on financial performance of approximately 400 firms that were recognized by local, state, or national awards for quality management practices. (Research results are reported with permission of Dr. Vinod R. Singhal. Research was conducted by Kevin B. Hendricks and Vinod R. Singhal.)

- Describes public- and private-sector organizations that have gained ground and made rapid strides forward on their journeys, having

achieved recognition as winners of the MBNQA. It then identifies the core values that have guided these organizations to achieve high levels of performance excellence.

VALUE OF BALDRIGE CRITERIA AND AWARDS

In a report entitled "The Nation's CEOs Look to the Future," 308 CEOs from large, small, and several noncorporate organizations described what they believe lies ahead for business in the United States and the value of the Baldrige Criteria and Award. These trends relate in many ways to the 2006 Criteria and are considered as the Criteria are revised to reflect the current business environment and the most effective management practices for that environment.

The vast majority (67 percent to 79 percent) of the CEOs believe that the Baldrige Criteria and Awards are very or extremely valuable in stimulating improvements in quality and competitiveness in U.S. businesses. Given the trends and business environment they describe in the survey, and how they see U.S. businesses keeping pace, the Criteria provide a valuable competitive advantage.

MAJOR TRENDS

More than 70 percent of the CEOs reported the following trends as major directions that will be likely to affect the business environment significantly in the coming years:

- *Globalization.* This trend, identified as critical by 94 percent of respondents, has implications for all categories, but particularly Strategic Planning, where global competition and alliances must be included in planning, and for Customer and Market Focus, where building and maintaining customer relationships is critical.

- *Improving knowledge management.* This trend, identified as critical by 88 percent of respondents, means that knowledge-acquisition management is and will continue to be a significant competitive advantage. How information and data are collected, analyzed, stored, retrieved, disseminated, and used to support decision making will be important to achieving high levels of performance in the future.

- *Cost and cycle-time reduction.* This trend, identified as critical by 79 percent of respondents, is particularly relevant to Process Management. Organizations that effectively manage key product and service design and delivery processes will have a competitive edge in the global marketplace.

- *Improving supply chains globally.* This trend, identified as critical by 78 percent of respondents, is a companion to the trend already described as globalization. As business is increasingly taking place on the global stage, supply chain management needs to improve— either with direct suppliers and partners or beyond to partnerships and alliances. These requirements are particularly important to Process Management.

- *Manufacturing at multiple locations in many countries.* This trend, identified as critical by 76 percent of respondents, again relates to globalization and also to improving supply chain management. To be successful at multiple-country manufacturing, one needs to use a systems approach involving all Categories, from Strategic Planning and Process Management, with a strong focus on Customers and Markets as well as Human Resource activities.

- *Managing the use of more part-time, temporary, and contract workers.* This trend, identified as critical by 71 percent of respondents, reflects the rapidly changing environment within which businesses operate. The *hot* skills and technologies of today become out of date quickly. The product-and-service focus of today is tomorrow's throwaway. Organizations must manage successfully with a more flexible and contingent workforce. Yet managers must still manage that workforce effectively; workers still need the right skills and knowledge, motivation and incentives, and satisfaction from work.

This trend is a major challenge particularly relevant to the Human Resource-Focus Category.

OTHER MAJOR TRENDS

More than 51 percent of the CEOs reported the following trends as major directions that will be likely to affect business in the years ahead. These include (from most cited, 69 percent, to least cited, 52 percent):

- Developing new employee relationships based on performance

- Improving human resources management

- Improving the execution of strategic plans

- Developing more appropriate strategic plans

- Measuring and analyzing organizational processes

- Developing a consistent global corporate culture

- Outsourcing of manufacturing

- Creating a learning organization

These directions, together with those listed previously, present a picture of what CEOs predict will be major business trends in the coming decade. The case for using the Baldrige Criteria as a way to manage effectively is validated and strengthened by the specific trends, their close relationship to the Criteria, and also by the next section, in which the same CEOs rate the competencies that major U.S. industries must possess to take advantage of these trends as a competitive advantage. CEOs report a huge gap between current-state competency and future/desired-state competency for many major trends. For example:

- Almost all of the CEOs report globalization as a major trend, but only 18 percent rate major U.S. organization competency as excellent. Seventy percent rated the competency as only fair.

- Improving knowledge management was cited by 88 percent of CEO respondents as a major trend, but only 23 percent see U.S. organization competency as excellent. Fifty-five percent rate the competency level as only fair.

- Competency in cost and cycle-time reduction was rated as excellent by 31 percent and only fair by 52 percent.

These are a sample of competency gaps cited by CEOs in the survey. They reiterate the need to use proven management practices to close these gaps and ensure that U.S. organizations remain or become leaders in the global marketplace to sustain our quality of life.

CEO Skills Needing Improvement

As part of the survey, CEOs were asked to reflect on their own skills and their peer group's skills and to report on which skills were most in need of improvement. The skills cited in the following list were thought by more than 50 percent to need "a great deal" of improvement. They are key to addressing the major business trends reported earlier in this section. The skills include:

- The ability to think globally and execute strategies successfully

- Flexibility in a changing world

- The ability to develop appropriate strategies and rapidly redefine their business

- The understanding of new technologies

Another 40 to 50 percent of CEOs believe that these skills also need to improve "a great deal." Skills needing improvement include the ability to:

- Work well with different stakeholders

- Create a learning organization

- Make the right bets about the future

- Be a visible, articulate, charismatic leader

- Be a strong enough leader to overcome opposition

Stakeholders and Interests That Are Becoming More Important

The majority of CEOs (75 percent or more) think that international customers, consumers, and employees are becoming more important to business success. More than 60 percent believe that suppliers, outside board directors, and institutional shareholders are also becoming more important. Addressing requirements of the Customer and Market Focus Category and Employee Focus Categories is increasing in importance, according to the CEOs surveyed.

Execution of Strategies Is Critical

When asked which required more improvement—the development or execution of appropriate strategies, CEOs selected *execution* by about a three-to-one margin. This means that alignment of work and realistic action plans need to be improved along with accountability. If the organization is pulling in different directions, it is more difficult to accomplish individual unit or division priorities—energies and resources are being drained, execution is flawed, and results are suboptimized.

Expanding Market Size Is Critical

When asked which is more important—to increase market share or expand market size, CEOs selected *expanding market size* by over a four-to-one margin. This will require improved leadership, strategic planning, and customer and market focus, particularly in the global economy. It will also require a more skilled and diverse workforce and more effective work processes.

The Competition Ahead

CEOs had various ideas about where the most serious competition to their businesses will come from in the next decade. Only a small number (12 percent) thought the toughest competition would come from other Fortune 500 companies. About 33 percent thought it was most likely to come from U.S. companies not yet on the Fortune 500 list. About 30 percent thought their toughest competitors were most likely to be foreign companies. Some saw start-up, entrepreneurial businesses as being the most serious competition. Comparing services and products to the competition and determining what the competition is doing to satisfy its customers are central to Baldrige-based assessments.

It is interesting, though, that most CEOs did not see the most serious competitors as being the major Fortune 500 companies of today. Perhaps this, more than any other CEO opinion, presents a compelling case for using the Baldrige Criteria—the fast and relentless pace of business change whereby companies on top today are not likely to be on top tomorrow without corresponding changes and improvements in their business.

Research Supports the Business Case

Two researchers, interested in quality award winners, wanted to determine the extent (if any) quality management impacted business performance. The research of Dr. Kevin B. Hendricks from the College of William and Mary, School of Business, and Vinod R. Singhal from the Georgia Institute of Technology, Dupree College of Management is the basis for the following evidence that supports the use of the Baldrige Criteria. Their research looked beyond hype and the popular press to the real impact of quality management and examined the facts surrounding performance excellence. The research was based on about 600 recipients of various quality awards and similar recognition. The recognition provided to these organizations was based upon similar core values and concepts. Companies were mostly manufacturing firms (75 percent). All were publicly traded companies. Although Hendricks and Singhal did not find that quality management turned "straw into gold," their research added significantly to the business case for using the Criteria as a tool to enhance performance.

Hendricks and Singhal examined the following efficiency or growth measures:

- Percent change in sales
- Stock price performance
- Percent change in total assets
- Percent change in number of employees
- Percent change in return on sales
- Percent change in return on assets

Implementation Costs Do Not Negatively Impact the Bottom Line

The research examined two five-year periods during the quality management implementation cycle. The first period can be called beginning implementation. This period started six years before and ended one year before the receipt of a first award. During this period, organizations are implementing quality management and incurring associated costs of implementation, such as training, communications, and production and design changes. The researchers found no significant differences in financial measures between these companies (winners) and the control group of companies (nonwinners but similar in other respects) for this period. This is important because of the costs (both direct and indirect) associated with implementing quality management systems. The research suggests that the significant cost savings identified during this period of intensified focus on cycle time, time to market, and other factors pay for the implementation costs.

Improved Financial Results Can Be Expected with Successful Implementation

The study then examined results of companies from one year before winning the award to four years after the award was given. This period can be called mature implementation and it is in this period that one would expect the improved management to bear fruit. This was the case with this research. There were significant differences in financial performance between award winners and controls (nonwinners). For example, the growth in operating income averaged 91 percent for winners contrasted to 43 percent for non-award winners. Award-winning companies reported 69 percent growth in sales compared with 32 percent for the control group. The total assets of the winning companies increased 79 percent compared to 37 percent for the controls. Winners had significantly better results than the control group. The graphs on page 7 represent the study findings. Researchers found that award-winning companies outperformed control firms (non-award-winning companies) at least two-to-one, as Figure 1 indicates.

Hendricks and Singhal also found that there was no significant difference between the companies prior to the period of implementation of these quality principles. Performance of the award-winning firms was significantly better after implementation, suggesting the difference was due to the performance excellence systems that they installed.

In addition, Hendricks and Singhal found that small companies did significantly better than large

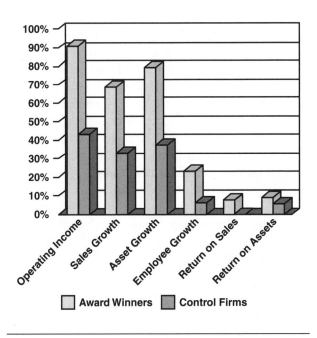

Figure 1 Comparison of award-winning and control firms.

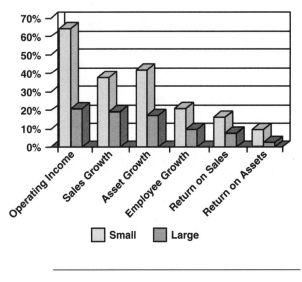

Figure 2 Comparison of large and small award-winning companies.

companies in implementing the quality principles. This is depicted in Figure 2. Although large companies may have more resources with which to implement these systems, small companies may have an easier time deploying these systems fully throughout the organization and achieving maximum benefit.

Although both small (less than $600 million) and large firms benefited, small firms did even better. Small winners outperformed the control counterparts by 63 percent, whereas large firms outperformed their controls by 22 percent. A similar profile existed for low capital- versus high capital-intensive award winners.

Processes Drive Results

One of the key management practices that has been a part of the Baldrige Award criteria for many years is the use of business results to analyze and subsequently improve organizational performance. James R. Evans and Eric P. Jack conducted an extensive correlational study to examine 20 hypothesized linkages between various Baldrige-required management practices and organizational results [Evans, James R. and Eric P. Jack, "Validating Key Results Linkages in the Baldrige Performance Excellence Model." *Quality Management Journal*, 10.2 (April 2003): 7-

24]. The first 10 hypotheses in their study represent linkages among the endogenous (internal system) variables as follows [Note: The strikethrough hypotheses (H3, H4, and H10) were not supported by the data. All other hypotheses were supported.]:

H1: Employee satisfaction has a positive impact on process performance

H2: Work system improvement has a significant impact on productivity

H3: ~~Work system improvement has a significant impact on employee satisfaction~~

H4: ~~Work system improvement has a significant impact on process performance~~

H5: Process performance has a significant impact on productivity

H6: Employee satisfaction has a significant impact on service quality

H7: Employee satisfaction has a significant impact on product quality

H8: Process performance has a significant impact on service quality

H9: Process performance has a significant impact on product quality

~~H10: Supplier performance has a significant impact on product quality~~

The next 10 hypotheses evaluate the direct linkages between the exogenous (external) variables and the exogenous results as follows:

H11: Employee satisfaction has a significant impact on market performance

H12: Service quality has a significant impact on customer satisfaction

H13: Product quality has a significant impact on customer satisfaction

H14: Product quality has a significant impact on financial performance

H15: Supplier performance has a significant impact on financial performance

H16: Process performance has a significant impact on financial performance

H17: Productivity has a significant impact on financial performance

H18: Customer satisfaction has a significant impact on market performance

H19: Market performance has a significant impact on financial performance

H20: Customer satisfaction has a significant impact on financial performance

The study's empirical results support the overall hypothesis that improving internal management practices leads to improvements in external results (Evans and Jack, p 18):

> "Consider the relationships among endogenous variables in the Baldrige results category, such as between employee satisfaction and process performance, and between work system improvement and productivity. Strong correlation among these latent variables suggests the importance of many fundamental management practices that are embedded in the Baldrige requirements, such as a focus on employee well-being and motivation, and attention to the design of work systems and their linkage to other categories, such as process management.

By strengthening the practices that lead to improved levels of internal performance, the analysis indicates that improved performance of production/delivery processes will likewise occur. Second, high levels of the endogenous variables are correlated with exogenous performance results as measured by market share, customer satisfaction, and financial performance. This provides evidence that improving the performance of endogenous variables will positively impact the most important external business performance measures. Thus, this research provides new evidence of the validity of the Baldrige model and its examination/self-assessment process that seeks to validate strong business results as an outcome of high-performance management practices."

The following is a summary of the study findings:

- Employee satisfaction is driven by process performance and product quality. (This is consistent with observations from many Baldrige Award winners that increased employee satisfaction leads to higher performance.)

- Process performance is correlated significantly with employee satisfaction as a dependent variate, and with product quality and market performance as an independent variate.

- Customer satisfaction is driven by product quality, service quality, and work-system improvement. Customer satisfaction is a more significant indicator of satisfaction than customer retention. Customers may indeed be satisfied but still switch allegiance based on other factors. Thus, customer retention is not necessarily a reliable indicator of satisfaction.

- Product quality is driven by employee satisfaction, work-system improvement, and process performance. Product quality drives customer satisfaction and financial performance.

- Service quality is correlated significantly only with customer satisfaction. On-time delivery dominates the relationship.

- Work-system improvement drives product quality, customer satisfaction, and financial performance.

- Financial performance is driven by productivity, market performance, work-system improvement, and product quality. From a practical perspective, this suggests that quality-related initiatives do have a significant impact on financial performance, as many studies have shown (for example, Hendricks and Singhal (1997) and the National Institute of Standards and Technology's continuing study of Baldrige winners). Cost of quality, prevention cost, and warranty cost are the major contributors to productivity and product quality. Return on assets (ROA) and growth in ROA are the major contributors to market performance.

- Productivity is correlated significantly with financial performance. Rework and scrap contribute strongly to the relationship.

- Market performance is correlated significantly with process performance and financial performance.

Quality Management Is a Long-Term Solution

Companies that expect immediate gains from quality management systems are likely to be disappointed. It took years to create the culture you have today; it can take years to change it. Nevertheless, this research, combined with other results, makes a solid business case for using Baldrige-based management Criteria as the way to run the successful business of the future.

High-Performing Organizations

High-performing organizations outrun their competition (or potential competition) by delivering value to stakeholders through an unwavering focus on customers and improved organizational capabilities. Examples of improved capabilities have occurred in all sectors of the economy, not just the private sector. These results range from time and cost savings to customer retention and loyalty.

Many examples of significant improvements from using the Baldrige-based management system are evident. Consider the performance of the six 2005 Baldrige Award recipients: Sunny Fresh Foods, DynMcDermott Petroleum Operations, Park Place

Lexus, Richland College, Jenks Public Schools, and Bronson Methodist Hospital.

Sunny Fresh Foods (SFF), manufacturing winner, headquartered in Monticello, Minnesota, employs 620 stakeholders and manufactures value-added egg-based food products primarily for the food-service industry. SFF produces over 160 products and has more than 2000 customers, including quick-service restaurants, schools, healthcare organizations, and the military. Products are produced under the Sunny Fresh label and under private labels for food service and retail marketers. Products include cholesterol-free and fat-free egg products, precooked frozen and refrigerated entrees, precooked frozen scrambled and diced eggs, refrigerated and frozen liquid pasteurized eggs and scrambled egg mixes, and peeled hard-cooked eggs. SFF received a Baldrige Award in 1999 in the small business category. SFF is a subsidiary of Cargill.

- Since receiving the Baldrige Award in 1999, SFF revenues are up 93 percent.

- In the past four years, SFF's market share has increased, while all other competitors' share has decreased by more than 10 percent.

- SFF evaluates the performance of its senior leaders both formally, through the Performance Management Process (PMP) process and the Stakeholder (employee) Survey, and informally, through the sharing of business performance results.

- SFF's On Time Delivery has improved from 98.1 percent in 2001 to 99.8 percent in 2005. SFF performs above the comparative benchmark levels of other Baldrige Award recipient levels for On Time Delivery performance from 2001 through 2004.

- The length of time to resolve a customer's complaint has declined from 2.8 days in 1997 to 0.8 days in 2005. In 2001, Satisfaction with Technical Services/Resolution was at 92 percent, and from 2002 through 2005 the results have remained at 100 percent levels.

- From 2001 to 2005, sales per employee and profit per employee have increased by 19 percent.

- SFF uses systematic and innovative approaches in addressing its work systems, employee learning and development, and employee well-being and satisfaction. These include a ramp-in schedule that limits the number of on-line hours daily for new production stakeholders to condition muscles and reduce injuries; a three-week program that partners new stakeholders with a high-performing, experienced *buddy*; and a system where production stakeholders rotate stations every 20 minutes.

- Multiple preventative and corrective action steps, numerous in-process checks, and use of statistical process-control methods help SFF achieve better performance, reduce variability, improve products and services, and keep processes current with business needs and directions.

DynMcDermott Petroleum Operations (DM), a service award winner, employs 554 people throughout its Project Management Office in New Orleans, Louisiana, and oil storage, receipt, and delivery locations in Louisiana and Texas. During 2005, DynMcDermott also achieved a 50 percent cost reduction target of $64 million over the period of the present contract ending in 2008, and received the highest performance rating to date from DOE.

- In 2001, DynMcDermott received ISO 9001 registration and since 2001 all four storage sites have achieved Voluntary Protection Program (VPP) certification status from the U.S. Occupational Safety and Health Administration and the Department of Energy. All storage sites exceeded Star status achieving Star Among Stars status. As an example, DM's Lost Workday Case Rate of less than one workday lost (0.83) due to injury per 200,000 worker hours demonstrates industry leadership compared to the Bureau of Labor Statistics average of 5.3, the VPP Star Among Star level of 2.3, and the VPP Super Star level of 1.33.

- Several of DM's sites were directly impacted by the recent hurricanes Katrina and Rita, resulting in the majority of employees being displaced from their homes and worksites. DM was able to restore operations immediately and begin the Oil Exchange Program (providing oil to refiners in order for them to continue operations) in less than five days after Hurricane Katrina. Hurricane Rita forced another evacuation and DM deployed its mobile emergency operations center according to plan. During this period, President Bush declared a drawdown from the SPR, an action that has occurred only twice in 30 years. Even though the Emergency Operation Center had to be relocated over 200 miles, DM made its first drawdown oil delivery three days after Rita.

- Overall customer satisfaction has steadily improved from 67 percent satisfaction in 1999 to 85 percent in 2004, exceeding the DOE target of 75 percent.

- Since 1999, DM's performance scores have ranged from 89 to 95, which is indicative of overall performance and customer satisfaction. These scores exceeded the goal in 10 of 11 semi-annual scoring periods.

- Employee satisfaction increased from 74 percent in 2000 to 83 percent in 2005, which compares favorably to the 43 percent Business Research Lab (BRL) Benchmark. DM employee retention is 97 percent.

- Drawdown systems availability has sustained a 98 percent or better performance level and has exceeded DOE expectations in each year and at each site since 2001. Drawdown readiness shows a steadily improving trend from 95 percent in 1999 to 99 percent or better from 2002 through 2005, exceeding DOE's 95 percent drawdown target. Days to Commence Drawdown, as a measure of performance, has been reduced from 15 in 2002 to 13 in 2005.

- The SPR is the global benchmark in storage efficiency. A 2003 comparison of storage cost per barrel between Japan, Europe, U.S. industry, and DOE SPR shows favorable performance for the DOE SPR. The storage cost per barrel was $3.00 for Japanese Oil Reserves, $2.40 for U.S. industry storage, $1.60 for the European Oil Stockpile and $.20 for the SPR. Operating Cost Per Barrel decreased from $0.1537 in 2001 to $0.1480 in 2005, below DOE's target of $0.1664.

- Security Systems and Computer Network Availability have been maintained at 100 percent since 2001, and system recovery following hurricanes Katrina and Rita, which affected the primary and backup computer centers, was seamless. The SPR Network was reestablished in less than 72 hours after Katrina landfall and infrastructure destruction.

- DM has had no Environmental Notices of Violation from any state or federal environmental protection agencies since 1999. DM has decreased total pounds of hazardous waste from 3802 pounds in 2000 to 515 pounds in 2005, compared to the DOE goal of 539 pounds.

- Data on over 1200 metrics are collected and integrated using a variety of integrated data systems.

- DM ensures a high-performing organization and empowers employees in a number of ways. Employees at the storage sites can stop any practice they deem unsafe and are encouraged and rewarded for identifying improvement ideas. Skill sharing and sharing of best practices between storage sites and within job categories are facilitated through standardization of equipment, procedures, work instructions, and regularly scheduled meetings by job title. Operations and maintenance employees work closely with counterparts at other sites and rotate to meet changing requirements.

- Employee education, training, and development address key organizational needs associated with new-employee orientation, diversity, ethical business practices, safety, the environment, and management and leadership development. For example, new hires attend training to familiarize them with SPR operations, requirements, and responsibilities; videos cover orientation, diversity, and records management; and mandatory training is provided via a special Web page. Annually, each employee must attend workplace diversity and Equal Employment Opportunity training; an ethical business practices course,

and sign an agreement accepting the policy; and numerous courses on workplace and environmental safety.

- DM addresses potential adverse impacts on society and anticipates public concerns with current and future operations through its strategic planning process, its environmental management system, an annual site environmental report, and a voluntary Environmental Advisory Committee (EAC). The EAC is composed of external scientists, technical experts, and community representatives who meet quarterly to help anticipate public concerns, incorporate public involvement in SPR decision making, and provide assessments and advice.

- DM's governance system consists of multiple processes that address accountability for management's actions; fiscal accountability; transparency in operations; independence in internal and external audits; and protection of stakeholder interests. For example, formal reviews of how DM is managed are conducted by DOE, the organization, and/or external entities on a daily, monthly, and annual basis. Accountability for governance is reinforced through the annual contract performance award fee, which is based upon a customer-defined Performance Evaluation and Measurement Plan (PEMP). Since 1993, DM has never been cited for significant findings from internal audits, DOE external audits, or by an independent accounting firm.

Park Place Lexus (PPL) a 2005 small business award recipient, operates two locations in the Dallas, Texas, area, and with a workforce of 420 members, sells new Lexus vehicles and pre-owned luxury vehicles, services Lexus and other vehicles, and sells Lexus parts to the wholesale and retail markets.

- Park Place Lexus Grapevine location had a New Car Client Satisfaction Index (CSI) of 99.8 percent in 2004, making it the highest-rated Lexus dealership in the nation.

- The company's gross profit has increased by 51.3 percent from 2000-2004, exceeding the Lexus Dealer Average.

- The CSI for Clients of new cars approaches 100 percent at both locations, placing them in the top 10 percent of Lexus dealers in the nation. Likewise, Client satisfaction among pre-owned vehicle Clients has increased from 96 percent in 2000 to 98 percent in 2004 (both locations), which is the among the best ratings in the southern region.

- PPL has taken steps to ensure its Clients are just as satisfied after the sale as before. As a result, its CSI for the Service Department at both locations is approaching 98 percent, which is among the best in the southern region. Satisfaction with parts availability has increased from 96 percent in 2000 to 98 percent in 2005, which is among the Lexus best. In addition, 96 percent of service Clients at both locations said their vehicle was ready when promised.

- PPL's continued Client focus has reduced the number of complaints that promises were not met from 130 in 2002 to 3 in 2005, that Clients were misled by staff from 22 in 2002 to 1 in 2005, and about discourteous treatment from 28 in 2002 to 1 in 2005.

- PPL has demonstrated sustained revenue growth from 1995 through 2004. Revenue has increased from about $70 million in 1995 to $350 million in 2004, and the company is on target for $387 million in 2005. This exceeds the Lexus national dealer average.

- A key measure of market performance for PPL is sales volume. Out of 213 Lexus dealers in the nation, the Lexus Retail Sales Report for 2004 ranks Park Place Lexus Plano number 7 with 3242 new car sales in 2004 and Park Place Lexus Grapevine at number 27 with 2339 new car sales in 2004.

- PPL uses Client service rechecks, the percentage of repair work that returns to the dealership because of a problem, as a key measure of quality of service. When calculated as a percentage of the 2800 service orders per month, PPL has maintained a level of less than 1 percent for the past five years.

- PPL uses the Gallup Organization's Q12 Survey to measure general Member satisfaction concerning the work environment and to gauge work-system performance. In fact, all responses but one are well above the 75th percentile reported for national respondents.

- Both the Plano and Grapevine locations have maintained a consistently low Member turnover rate of about 22 percent for the past three years, as compared to the average turnover in the southwest area of 55 percent.

- PPL has committed substantial resources to ensuring that Client relationships, once established, can be maintained in a way that contributes value to both parties. This includes the development and deployment of a Client relationship-management database that tracks all aspects of the PPL-Client interaction and provides the resulting information to Members.

- PPL uses its Client Concern Resolution (CCR) process to address any problems that might occur in any area of the Client experience. CCR empowers the individual Member to resolve Client complaints on the spot by allowing each Member to spend up to $250 to resolve a complaint, or up to $2000 by committee.

- PPL demonstrates its commitment to management by fact through its system of performance measurement and knowledge transfer that provides Members and managers with key operational information needed to make day-to-day decisions. Members are provided with critical information about their own performance and departmental performance for month- and year-to-date in daily PACE reports. Members and managers use this information as they operate daily processes to determine how they are doing against targets, to make adjustments to achieve these targets, and to identify opportunities for improvement and efficiencies in processes.

- All positions at PPL have been analyzed and specific training requirements have been identified. Each Member has a training plan that includes classroom training, on-the-job training, coaching and mentoring, observations, and assessments. Members also plan for their own growth by working with their supervisor to construct a Member achievement plan aimed at helping them reach a specific position over time.

- To create a sustainable organization, PPL focuses on performance improvement through its DRIVE process designed to address specific issues of performance and then focus on improvement. The process includes Defining the problem, Recognizing the cause, Identifying a solution, Verifying actions, and Evaluating the results through an implementation audit conducted by the Organizational Excellence Department within 90 days. This process has resulted in significant improvements in cycle time, productivity, and cost control.

Richland College (RLC) in Dallas, Texas, a 2005 education winner, is one of seven two-year community colleges in the Dallas County Community College District in Dallas, Texas It provides credit and continuing education courses to more than 20,000 students each semester, ranging from adolescents to senior citizens, who speak 90 different first languages. RLC's key student segment is the transfer student, whose primary goal is further education at a four-year university. RLC has 558 full-time faculty, support staff, and administrators; 811 part-time faculty and seasonal staff, and is the first community college to receive a Baldrige Award.

- The number of students who complete the core curriculum in preparation for transfer to four-year institutions has grown from 500 students in 2002 to 1660 in 2005.

- As a result of a reduction in state funding from 70 percent to 30 percent of its total budget, RLC has decreased its operational costs per credit hour, while improving services, adding necessary employees (primarily adjunct faculty), and implementing innovative practices.

- In the five most important student-satisfaction measures (classes scheduled, class-time conve-

nience, quality of instruction, variety of courses, and intellectual growth), RLC increased its levels of satisfaction and surpassed the national norm over the past four years. Overall, RLC was above the Noel Levitz Student Satisfaction Survey norm on 42 of the 79 survey items. (The Noel Levitz Student Satisfaction Survey is a nationally recognized survey of student satisfaction used at community colleges and four-year institutions.)

- RLC has improved its student retention rate, from outperforming only one of its five peer institutions in 1999 to achieving its target and outscoring four of its five peer institutions in 2003. RLC also demonstrated positive trends for retention rates for all credit students, as well as for African-American, Hispanic, and Asian students, and for students in the district's 48-credit-hour core curriculum, transferable to all Texas public colleges and universities.

- RLC's enrollment has increased from about 12,500 credit students in 2000 to about 14,500 in 2005, and has exceeded local competitors in all five years. Enrollment for Rising Star, a donor-funded scholarship program focused on students at risk of not succeeding in school, has grown from about 180 in 2001 to about 450 in 2005, which exceeded the target for enrollment by approximately 48 percent.

- RLC has developed and supports a strong cadre of adjunct faculty, now approximately 60 percent of the total faculty. As a response to budget demands, adjunct instructors are used to respond quickly to changes in the market, to enhance practical application experience, and to help control the cost of instruction. Processes addressing adjuncts' motivation, recognition, and evaluation have been developed to ensure their inclusion within the organization. Adjunct faculty members have a separate support office, are invited to participate in department meetings and RLC's annual meeting for all staff, and are encouraged to attend skill-enhancement training.

- RLC faculty's use of eCampus technology, a tool which provides discussions, assignments, and grades online, has risen steadily from less than 10 percent in 2001 to 37 percent in spring

2005 in credit classes, exceeding best-peer performance in 2005.

- RLC's strategic/operational planning approach is a year-long series of steps designed to monitor internal progress in monthly Key Performance Indicator (KPI)/Quality Enhancement Plan (QEP) reviews. As part of this process, the senior leadership team meets with learning-centered and stakeholder-focused councils, committees, and teams to gather input for the strategic planning cycle. Institutional research staff work with each department and function to help assure alignment among their KPIs and RLC's Strategic Planning Priorities (SPPs) and overall KPIs. With this information, key work groups develop departmental action plans. Senior leaders and work groups monitor progress toward goals, adherence to the budget, and strategic actions throughout the year. When gaps are identified, they are considered for a formal improvement project.

- Faculty teams update their QEPs each semester with three to five learning-based outcomes; support staff update their QEPs with two student-support process outcomes. Department action plans are updated annually as part of the Strategic Planning Process. The Quality Assurance Committee reviews QEPs for completeness, while vice presidents review department action plans to assure that all organizational action plans are addressed.

- The President's Cabinet includes representatives from the faculty and student associations, as well as administrators, deans, directors, and professional support staff.

Jenks Public Schools (JPS) of Jenks, Oklahoma is a 2005 education award recipient. It is a public school district serving both suburban and urban populations. JPS programs and services include an intergenerational program with pre-kindergarten and kindergarten students and the elderly, a *Parents as Teachers Program,* and a student and teacher exchange program with a school in Chengdu, China. The school system has nine schools on five campuses. JPS is the 11th largest school district in Oklahoma, with 9271

students, and has 665 teachers/certified staff and 576 classified (nonteaching) staff.

- Forty-two percent of the teaching staff have master's degrees, 2 percent have doctorates; and 98.5 percent are *highly qualified,* according to No Child Left Behind (NCLB) standards.

- The Academic Performance Index (API) scores for JPS students from 2001 to 2005 exceed the API test scores at the state and national levels. JPS has led the state for K-12 schools of comparable size. The district's Southeast Elementary School was one of four elementary schools in the state to achieve an API perfect score of 1500 points, the target for excellence set by the state to meet the NCLB Act.

- Thirty-seven percent of the district's class of 2004 demonstrated college-level mastery by earning an AP test score of three or better, compared to the national percentage of 13 percent and the highest state percentage of 21.2 percent.

- The *Edline* program enables direct communication with teachers via computer for both parents and students. The Career Action Planning Program (CAPS) facilitates communication between parents, students, and teachers. Parent attendance at high school parent-teacher conferences increased from below 20 percent to 95 percent since the inception of CAPS in 1997.

- JPS has received local, state, and national recognition for its innovative community partnership where prekindergarten and kindergarten classes are held on-site in the Grace Living Center long-term care facility. This intergenerational partnership benefits students, teachers, and elder partners in the JPS community. This program has been recognized by Education Week, CNN News, and People magazine.

- In the past five years, JPS has had 68 National Merit semifinalists and 64 National Merit finalists and two Presidential Scholars. Two classroom teachers were selected as Oklahoma Teachers of the Year; both received the Presidential Award for Excellence in Mathematics and Science Teaching. In 2004, a JPS teacher received the Milken Family

Foundation Educator Award, which honors outstanding educators.

- JPS's graduation rates for 2003 to 2005 exceeded the rates for a former Baldrige Award recipient, with graduation rates at 93 percent in 2003, 94 percent in 2004, and 95 percent in 2005, compared to the former Baldrige Award recipient's rates of 90 percent in 2003, 93 percent in 2004, and 94 percent in 2005.

- JPS fifth-grade students' mathematics proficiency scores were at 89 percent for 2003 and were at 92 percent for 2004, compared to a Baldrige Award recipient's mathematics proficiency scores at 87 percent for 2003 and at 88 percent for 2004. Reading proficiency scores for JPS fifth-grade students were at 88 percent for 2003 and at 86 percent for 2004, compared to a Baldrige Award recipient's scores at 80 percent for 2003 and at 78 percent for 2004. JPS eighth-grade students show reading proficiency scores at 89 percent for 2003 and at 96 percent for 2004, compared to a Baldrige Award recipient's reading proficiency scores at 78 percent for 2003 and at 82 percent for 2004. Mathematics proficiency scores for JPS eighth-grade students were at 88 percent for 2003 and were at 95 percent for 2004, compared to a former Baldrige Award recipient's scores at 78 percent for 2003 and at 79 percent for 2004.

- JPS students consistently outperformed ACT (a college entrance exam) scores at the state and national levels, placing JPS students in the top national quartile for ACT results, and SAT scores for JPS students consistently above state and national levels.

- Drop-out rates have decreased steadily from 6.3 percent in 1999 to 1.2 percent at the close of the 2004 school year, which is less than the 1.6 percent rate of a former Baldrige Award recipient.

- JPS demonstrates improving and positive trends for financial and operational results. The Fund Balance (annual carryover of funds) is on track for meeting and achieving a 6 percent balance, up from 2001, 2002, 2003, and 2004.

- For 2003 and 2004, the JPS turnover rate for certified staff was 11 percent and 6 percent respectively, with the national level at 20 percent for both years.

- JPS has established four pillars—Strong Quality Leadership, Continuous Improvement, Customer Focus, and Systems/Process Focus—that serve as a foundation for the school district. In addition, JPS aligns its goals and action plans to support its strategic objectives, pillars, core values, mission and motto/vision statement, "a tradition of excellence with a vision for tomorrow."

- JPS sets an expectation for performance excellence that supports its Pillar of Continuous Improvement. Continuous improvement is evaluated using four processes: the Performance Appraisal Review Process; the Comprehensive Local Education Plan (CLEP) in which sites include a Plan, Do, Study, Act (PDSA) component; the Performance Measurement System; and surveys and committee evaluations.

- To enhance communications with families, more than 90 percent of elementary teachers prepare monthly newsletters and more than 40 percent have Web pages.

- JPS has a School Emergency Response Team (SERT), composed of administrators, campus police, teachers, a nurse, and staff members. Procedures include management flow charts, media relations, staff responsibilities, and contingencies for a multitude of events such as fire, weather, power loss, mass disturbance, earthquake, bomb threat, suspicious package, and airplane crash into building (one school is close to a busy regional airport). The SERT also coordinates annual full-scale disaster exercises that include collaboration with external agencies, such as emergency management agencies, the FBI, hospitals, fire and police departments, and ambulance services.

- JPS's learning-centered system includes the Curriculum Development Process, the Instructional Process, the Assessment Process, and the School Climate Process. These processes address students' education, well-being, and success by organizing curriculum and decision making around the entire period of a child's education, through the use of research-based instructional strategies and differentiation of instruction, by providing performance data to support instructional decision making and to keep parents informed, and by addressing safety, communication, teamwork, and educational experiences to develop character and citizenship.

- JPS considers service learning by students to be part of preparing all students for productive, responsible citizenship. Students are involved in numerous projects to help the community, including the Community Food Bank, Families in Need, Toys for Tots, Relay for Life, Project Angel Tree, Support for the Troops, Game of Giving, Dynamic Dads Winter Coats Project, La-La Lemonade, Sucker Sales, and Recycling Jeans.

Bronson Methodist Hospital (BMH), a 2005 health care winner, is located in Kalamazoo, Michigan and has a workforce of 3182 employees. With 343 licensed beds and all private rooms, Bronson Methodist Hospital is a tertiary medical center providing inpatient and outpatient care in virtually every specialty—cardiology, orthopedics, surgery, emergency medicine, neurology, oncology—with advanced capabilities in critical care as a Level I Trauma Center; in neurological care as a JCAHO-certified Primary Stroke Center; in cardiac care as the region's only accredited Chest Pain Center; in obstetrics as the leading BirthPlace and only high-risk pregnancy center in southwest Michigan; and in pediatrics as one of only four children's hospitals in the state.

- BMH shows strong performance improvement and results in Medicare Mortality Rate (mortality rates of people over 65 enrolled in Medicare programs), moving from 4.8 percent in 2002 to 3.5 percent for January-July 2005. This performance exceeds both the CareScience Expected Standard, and the CareScience Best Practice. (CareScience provides care management and clinical access solutions and data on outcomes for mortality, morbidity, and length of stay of hospital patients.)

- Patient satisfaction and overall satisfaction of both inpatient and outpatient services at BMH have increased from approximately 95 percent in 2002 to 97 percent in 2004. Since 2001, Arbor Associates annually has presented BMH with its Award for Highest Overall Patient Satisfaction. In 2005, BMH began using the Gallup organization not only to measure overall satisfaction, but also to track increases in the category of patients who are the most satisfied.

- BMH is the sole 2005 recipient of the Michigan Quality Leadership Award—the state equivalent to the Baldrige. Bronson is a two-time honoree, having also received this award in 2001.

- BMH has earned many awards for workplace excellence and work/life balance, including being named among the 100 Best Companies for Working Mothers by *Working Mother Magazine* (2003, 2004, and 2005) and *Fortune Magazine's* 100 Best Companies to Work For (2004 and 2005). Other awards include West Michigan's 101 Best and Brightest Companies to Work for "Best of the Best" Award (2003), "Elite Winner" Award by the Michigan Business and Professional Association (2005), and Voluntary Hospitals of America Leadership Award for Operational Excellence (2005).

- BMH's Strategic Management Model is a systematic approach to align all of BMH's planning, including strategic, workforce, financial, capital, and information technology. Performance is measured through the use of organizational and secondary scorecards.

- A one-page Plan for Excellence captures BMH's vision, culture, and expectations of all staff and leaders. It includes the *3 Cs*—Clinical Excellence, Customer and Service Excellence, and Corporate Excellence. The plan is used extensively during employee, physician, volunteer, and other stakeholder interactions to effectively communicate BMH's direction and focus.

- Using the Gallup national database, BMH results for Loyalty, Likelihood to Return, ranked in the 99th percentile for Inpatients, Outpatient Surgery, and Outpatient Testing. In addition, Likelihood to

Return results show performance in outpatient testing and outpatient surgery in the top 1 percent, with inpatient at the 95th percentile.

- BMH is exceeding best practice levels for key indicators of work-system performance and effectiveness including 2005 annualized employee turnover at 5.6 percent, registered-nurse turnover at 4.7 percent, and job-vacancy rates at 5.3 percent. The rate of vacant positions for registered nurses has been reduced from 6.5 percent in 2002 to 5 percent in 2005, outperforming the 10.6 percent national American Nurse Credentialing Center best practice comparison. In addition, since inception of an employee-referral program in 2002, percent of hires from internal referrals has increased to 38 percent in 2005, up from 10 percent in 2002.

- BMH has received the Environmental Leadership Award presented by Hospitals for a Healthy Environment (H2E) for three years in a row, and is one of only eight hospitals to receive this premier national recognition for pioneering efforts to reduce waste and pollution. Twenty-four percent of the total waste stream has been recycled in 2005 (year-to-date); the amount of medical waste going to landfills has been decreased by 85 percent, and using micro-fiber mops has eliminated 500,000 gallons of water use and 13,000 gallons of chemicals use annually.

- The Staff Performance Management System supports organization-wide expectations of high performance by staff and is the primary mechanism for the achievement of action plans. Leaders' goals are aligned with strategic objectives and the scorecard/organizational performance measures. Reward and recognition are directly related to results achieved. Regular review and coaching are part of the process.

- At BMH, personal learning is valued at all levels, supported by a number of aligned approaches including the annual Education Plan, the Workforce Development Plan, and three formal leadership-training programs—the Leadership Initiative, Physician Leadership Academy, and a new Management Mentor program. Leaders, preceptors, and education instructors foster an environment in which learning is encouraged and the use of knowledge and skills on the job is reinforced.

- Using a Picture Archiving Communications System (PACS), physicians can easily access a patient's medical records and diagnostic images via computer to facilitate effective decision making related to patient care. In addition, the system allows appropriate physicians and other medical organizations outside of BMH to access patient information through a secure Internet connection.

- BMH has developed a four-phase Emergency Management Plan to ensure continuity of operations in the event of an emergency. The plan includes redundant offsite computer systems to secure data and the use of satellite phones.

- The Board of Directors, including physicians and independent community representatives, governs and oversees the operations of BMH, creating accountability and protecting stakeholder interests by empowering the executive team to carry out organizational strategies as defined in the strategic planning process. Each quarter, the strategic oversight teams (SOTs) responsible for the Three C's report to a committee of the board. The entire board reviews organizational performance relative to the strategic plan, including the budget, financial performance, satisfaction and clinical outcomes, and executive compensation and hears reports on accreditation, legal and regulatory compliance, ethics, and governance issues.

- The Board of Directors' annual governance evaluation includes a self-evaluation of the board as well as monthly meeting evaluations, a comprehensive new-member orientation, and ongoing education. In addition, employees provide input relative to leadership effectiveness of the executive team through the annual employee opinion survey. Results are tied directly to executive compensation to support the organizational strategy of corporate effectiveness.

The performance and work processes of earlier winners is just as strong.

The Bama Companies, a 2004 manufacturing winner, is a family-owned business that manufactures frozen ready-to-use food products for the quick-service and casual-dining restaurant business and family-dining chains. Annual revenues are over $200 million and its workforce includes 1043 employees. While the overall frozen baked-goods industry has remained relatively flat since 1999, Bama's sales increased 47 percent. Sales of new and innovative products as a percent of sales have grown from less than 0.5 percent in 2000 to almost 25 percent in 2004. Sales of branded retail products increased from 9 million in 2002 to 25 million in 2004. Bama has become the nation's largest producer of hand-held fruit pies as well as the largest producer of ready-to-bake biscuits. Since 2001, Bama has achieved 98 percent on-time delivery of product to customers, with 99 percent of orders completely filled in the initial shipment. New-product ideas at Bama are *implemented* at a rate nearly 10 times the industry average. Bama's focus on productivity improvements through the use of Six Sigma methodology has saved the company $17.3 million since 2002. Overall customer satisfaction for the company's national accounts has increased from 75 percent in 2001 to nearly 100 percent in 2004, considerably higher than the food-manufacturing benchmark of 85 percent. Bama emphasizes team-based approaches to work design, problem solving, and process improvements. Bama's performance management ensures employees are provided with the assistance and resources to be successful.

Texas Nameplate Company (TNC), a 2004 small business winner, is a small, privately held family business that produces nameplates, identification tags, and labels for a wide variety of products, including high-pressure valves, oil field equipment, and computers. TNC is the smallest business to receive a Baldrige Award and the only small business to have received a Baldrige Award twice. TNC has annual revenues of $3.1 million and employs 39 people. TNC achieved tremendous results in order to receive the Baldrige Award in 1998. TNC increased its profitability from 36 percent in 1998 to above 40 percent in 2003, when its profit level exceeded that of companies in its comparison groups. Third-party customer surveys show that overall customer satisfaction improved from 81 percent in 2000 to approximately 86 percent in 2003. TNC has cross-trained more than 80 percent of its workforce to perform multiple jobs across departments. The company's nonconformance as a percentage of sales shows overall improvement from approximately 1.4 percent in 1998 to about 0.5 percent in 2004, significantly lower than the Industry Week Median (2 percent). Effective use of innovative, systematic processes and new technology has helped TNC achieve its desire to be *better not bigger*. TNC developed several intranet-based programs to collect and aggregate data for decision making; make data and information readily available (with computer screens automatically refreshing every 30 seconds) to employees, customers, and suppliers; and collect information from and share it with these groups. TNC has created a culture of empowerment and continuous learning for its employees. All employees participate in monthly group meetings, and all managers and supervisors participate in weekly or biweekly meetings to review organizational performance against targets and provide feedback on opportunities for improvement. Each employee develops and maintains a personal Web page, a mechanism that reinforces training on computer skills and employee recognition. TNC's Gainshare and Just Earning Time and Saving Resources programs link compensation and paid time off (identified by employees as a strong incentive) to organizational and employee performance in key business and customer-focused performance areas.

The *Kenneth W. Monfort College of Business* (MCB), a 2004 education winner, focuses on delivery of an undergraduate-only business education. MCB is funded by a state budget of $4.5 million and various private donations highlighted by a 15-year commitment from the Monfort Family Foundation, ranging from $500,000 to $925,000 annually. MCB educates approximately 1200 students annually with 32 full-time faculty, nine administrative staff, and 15 part-time adjunct faculty. MCB is one of five undergraduate-only business schools in the nation accredited in both business and accounting by the Association to Advance Collegiate Schools of Business. From 1994 to 2004, student learning performance on Educational Testing Service (ETS) business tests increased 34 percent, reaching the top 10 percent nationally and in Summer and Fall 2004 exceeding the 95th percentile. On 9 of 16 student satisfaction factors measured on the 2004 Business Exit Survey by Educational Benchmarking (EBI), MCB ranks in the top 10 percent nationally among 171 institutions. In 2003 and 2004, MCB scored in the top 1 percent for overall student satisfaction with the program. For the past six years in an EBI student exit survey of 171 schools nationwide, MCB has achieved best-in-class status and has been above the 90th percentile nationally for academic rigor. Key Performance Indicators (KPIs) and Supporting Performance Indicators (SPIs) are linked to MCB's strategic challenges and contribute to continuous improvement activities.

Robert Wood Johnson University Hospital Hamilton (RWJ Hamilton), a 2004 health care winner, is a private, not-for-profit acute-care community hospital, providing healthcare services to more than 350,000 residents in its service area. Primary services include medical, surgical, obstetric, cardiology, orthopedic, and intensive care for both adults and critically ill infants and children. Outpatient services include diagnostic and therapeutic care, ambulatory surgery, medical and radiation oncology, and emergency services, including emergent angioplasty. Community services include health education, health screenings, and disease-prevention programs. It generates annual revenue of $160 million and maintains a workforce of 1734 employees, plus an additional medical staff of more than 650. The hospital improved emergency department patient satisfaction from 85 percent in 2001 to 90 percent in 2004. From 1999 to 2003 its market share percentage in cardiology grew from 20 to nearly 30; in surgery, from about 17 percent to 30 percent; and in oncology from 13 percent to over 30. On average, free health screening is provided to more than 900 community residents per month. The 2002 Gallup Community Survey of customer loyalty ranked RWJ Hamilton first among local competitors in all positive attributes, including most improved; most personal care to patients; advanced, state-of-the-art technology and equipment; best doctors; and best nurses. Between 2001 and 2004, safeguards to prevent patients from receiving wrong medications were successful in 93 percent of cases, far exceeding the national median of approximately 64 percent. Care plans are evaluated

daily and patients are included in the assessment and planning process. Registered nurse-retention (an issue throughout the healthcare sector) improved from 94 percent in 2001 to 99 percent in 2003 and retention of other employees went from 80 percent to 98 percent. RWJ Hamilton's Organizational Performance Measurement System tracks daily performance and operations. Key performance indicators are reviewed weekly by senior leaders, monthly by managers, and quarterly by all employees.

Medrad, a 2003 manufacturing winner, develops, manufactures, markets, and services medical devices that enable and enhance imaging of the human body. Medrad's products are sold to hospitals and medical imaging centers worldwide. Medrad's 1194 employees are located in Pennsylvania and 14 other sites around the world. Revenue growth exceeded the average growth trend of comparable companies, increasing from $35 million in 1988 to $254 million in 2002, an average annual revenue growth rate of 15 percent. Operating income as a percent of revenue increased from 16 percent in 1999 to 20 percent in 2002. Since 1999, overall employee satisfaction exceeded the industry best-in-class benchmark. To develop new products or improve existing ones, Medrad used its Integrated Product Development Process to collect ideas from employees, identify customer requirements, prioritize initiatives, and translate initiatives into specifications. Medrad ensured management and fiscal accountability through external audits and monitoring of performance on its five corporate scorecard goals.

Boeing Aerospace Support (AS), 2003 service winner, provides aircraft maintenance, modification, and repair; training for aircrews and maintenance staff; and spare parts, primarily to the Department of Defense. Annual sales were in excess of $4 billion. Boeing AS has 12,303 employees at nine major sites (eight in the United States, one in Australia) and more than 129 secondary and smaller sites. For the past four years, Boeing AS earnings grew at an average cumulative growth rate of 17 percent per year. New orders improved each year since 1999, exceeding the previous four years, and were significantly higher than competitors' cumulative growth. Annual revenue more than doubled from 1999 to 2003, during a flat market. On-time delivery of maintenance and modification products and services has been at or near 95 percent since 1999. The overall depot quality for the maintenance of C-17s has been at or near 100 percent since 1998, compared to AS's competitor at about 70 percent in 2002 and 90 percent in 2003. AS has provided turnaround times that were steady at three days since 1998, ten times better than the competitor. On-time delivery of significant hardware, aircraft, and kits has been about 99 percent since 2001. Contracting Cycle Time consistently improved from 100 days in 1998 to the 2003 performance level of 23 days. Voluntary terminations by employees decreased from 3.5 percent in 2000 to 2.3 percent in 2003, better than the best-in-class level of 5 percent and the industry-average level of 8 percent.

Caterpillar Financial Services Corporation U.S. (CFSC), a 2003 service winner located in Nashville, Tennessee, employs 750 people. FCSC is the financial services business unit within Caterpillar, a manufacturer of construction and mining equipment, engines, and industrial turbines. CFSC is the second-largest captive-equipment lender in the United States. Since 1998, CFSC increased assets 34 percent and profit 54 percent while industry performance declined 21 percent and 35 percent respectively. The Non-Interest Expense as a Percent of Assets, a key measure of organizational efficiency, remained below 3 percent from 1998 to present, while the industry average increased from 5.46 percent to 8.73 percent. CFSC exceeded customers' expectations 34 percent of the time in 2000 and 2001 and 48 percent in 2002, nearly twice that of its competitors. Employee satisfaction with their involvement in the business improved 15 points to 79 percent since 2001, with the current level of performance significantly better than the industry norm at 51 percent and best-practice benchmark at 68 percent. Managed Assets per Employee improved by more than 10 percent since 1997, with 2003 performance nearly 35 percent better than the average of the financial industry's Top 100. Seventy-nine percent of all Cat users reported that CFSC influenced their decision to buy Cat equipment. The Caterpillar Board of Directors was rated by the Institutional Shareholders Services in the top 11 percent nationwide for overall corporate governance, and in the top 7 percent within the capital goods industry.

Stoner Solutions, 2003 small business winner, is a small, privately-owned manufacturer of more than 300 specialized car-care and auto-detailing products, mold-release agents, and specialty cleaners for electronics and other critical components. Located in Quarryville, Pennsylvania with 45 full-time and five part-time employees, it is one of the smallest business to ever receive a Baldrige Award. Stoner's sales increased 400 percent since 1990. Retail sales increased from zero in 1996 to 20 percent of company sales in 2003. Internet sales increased 1000 percent from 1999 to 2003. Stoner's 39 percent return on assets exceeded the industry average by 29 percent and its best competitor by 14 percent. Manufacturing productivity increased 150 percent since 1991 and weekly average output of aerosol-can products increased 33 percent from 1998 to 2003. Stoner's overall employee morale index increased from 64.6 percent in 2002 to 74.5 percent in 2003, exceeding the 60.5 percent benchmark. Stoner's overall favorable percentage of satisfied employees increased from 72.8 percent in 2002 to 79.5 percent in 2003, exceeding the benchmark of 64.8 percent. Since 2000, Stoner has won three times as many customers as it lost and, over five years, retained more than 98 percent of its top customers. In a national industry survey, Stoner ranked first in satisfaction on four of the five factors most important to its customers—quality, delivery, service, and value. It was in the top quartile for the fifth factor—price. Since 2000, Stoner reduced the amount of toxic chemicals used by 31 percent to achieve greater environmental compatibility, and increased the use of more environmentally friendly water-based formulations by 74 percent. To reduce cost and increase customer satisfaction, Stoner implemented an Enterprise Resource Planning system. As a result, 100 percent of orders were shipped on the same day they were received and the number of shipping errors was reduced to less than 0.05 percent.

Community Consolidated School District 15, 2003 education winner, is a kindergarten-through-eighth-grade school system with 1898 faculty and staff serving 12,390 students in all or part of seven municipalities in and around Palatine, Illinois (a western suburb of Chicago). Its student population includes 37.5 percent minority and 32.5 percent low-income.

Approximately 32 percent come from non-English-speaking backgrounds; 72 different languages are spoken in the homes of its students. The school system has 14 kindergarten-through-sixth-grade schools, three junior high schools, and one alternative school. District 15 operates its own transportation, maintenance, technology, and food services departments. Through intensive reading-intervention programs, in the 2003–04 school year, 92 percent of second-grade students were reading at or above grade level, more than 35 percentage points above the national average. The rate at which special education students met goals showed steady improvement since 1998–99, reaching approximately 14 percent in 2002–03, significantly higher than both national and state averages. The district equaled or outperformed its comparison district at all levels and in all subjects. The number of its teachers achieving National Board Certification went from two in 1994–95 to 48 in 2002–03, the second-highest number in the state. Turnover rate for certified staff was 11.7 percent for 2002–03, compared to a national average of 20 percent. Parent satisfaction with school safety and security was at the 93 percent level in 2002–03. District 15 developed innovative means of assessing performance important to key stakeholders where traditional educational measures were not sufficient. The district received the highest ratings on external audits conducted to ensure its fiscal accountability. The district received several awards for financial practices.

Baptist Hospital (BHI), a 2003 health care winner, is a subsidiary of Baptist Health Care. BHI employs 2252 in two hospitals (Baptist Hospital (BH) of Pensacola, a 492-bed tertiary care and referral hospital and Gulf Breeze Hospital (GBH), a 60-bed medical and surgical hospital), and Baptist Medical Park, an ambulatory care complex that delivers an array of outpatient and diagnostic services. Inpatient and outpatient overall satisfaction was near the 99th percentile of the Press Ganey survey. Ambulatory surgery overall satisfaction for GBH was near the 99th percentile each quarter since the second quarter of 2000 and for BH was above the 95th percentile since the first quarter of 1997. The Emergency Room for GBH was in the 99th percentile as was LifeFlight. Patient surveys of staff sensitivity, attitude, and concern, and overall cheerfulness of hospital staff all have been near the 99th percentile. The employee turnover rate at BH improved from 27 percent in 1997 to 13.9 percent in 2003 and GBH improved from 31 percent to 14 percent. Diverse thinking was captured through the Bright Ideas program, FOCUS-PDCA (a performance-improvement process) teams, around-the-clock employee forums, and peer interviewing using behavior-based questions. The number of ideas *implemented* increased from 370 in 1998 to 5000 in 2003. Health screenings and physicals provided by BHI to the community increased. Heart-risk screenings increased from 1100 in 2000 to more than 2400 in 2003. BHI established a program to improve awareness of heart disease among women, provide education on healthy lifestyles, and provide women with easy access to cardiac testing and treatment. BHI provided 6.7 percent of its total revenue to indigent patients compared to 5.2 percent and 4 percent for its competitors.

Saint Luke's Hospital of Kansas City, a 2003 health care winner, is the largest hospital in the Kansas City, Missouri metropolitan area, with 3186 employees and 500 physicians. SLH is a not-for-profit comprehensive teaching and referral healthcare organization that provides 24-hour coverage in every healthcare discipline. Its facilities include the Mid America Heart Institute, the Mid America Brain and Stroke Institute, an ambulatory surgery center, an outpatient care center, and a nursing college. In 2002, a consumer education organization ranked SLH 35th in the nation out of 4500 hospitals evaluated. The patient rating for SLH physicians was 86 percent compared to a national average of 33 percent. In 2002, the percent rate of Returns Following Ambulatory Procedures was significantly better for SLH compared to similar-size national teaching hospitals. A National Research Corporation study showed that since 1997, patients believed that SLH delivered the best quality healthcare, had the best doctors and nurses, and delivered the best cardiac, neurology, and orthopedic care of the 21 facilities in the market area. SLH's financial performance improvements were exceptional, outperforming the Council of Teaching Hospitals top quartile and ranking in the top 5 percent of hospitals nationwide in total margin. Sustained financial improvements resulted in SLH achieving an A1 Standard and Poor's rating and an A+ bond rating from Moody's. SLH won numerous local, state, and national awards for clinical excellence, patient and employee satisfaction, and overall quality. It also won high marks for its community education programs

Recipients prior to 2003 include the following:

Motorola Commercial, Government, and Industrial Solutions Sector, 2002 manufacturing

Branch-Smith Printing Division, 2002 small business

Sisters of Saint Mary Health Care, 2002 health care

Clarke American Checks, 2001 manufacturing

Chugach School District, 2001 education

The Pearl River School District, 2001 education

The University of Wisconsin-Stout Campus, 2001 education

Pal's Sudden Service, 2001 small business

Dana Corporation—Spicer Driveshaft Division, 2000 manufacturing

KARLEE Company, 2000 manufacturing

Los Alamos National Bank, 2000 small business

Operations Management International, 2000 service

BI, 1999 service (a training organization)

STMicroelectronics, 1999 manufacturing

The Ritz-Carlton Hotel Company (now part of Marriott International), a service winner in 1999 and 1992

Sunny Fresh Foods, a 1999 small business and first food manufacturer to receive the Baldrige Award

Boeing Airlift and Tanker, 1998 manufacturing

Texas Nameplate Company, 1998 small business

Solar Turbines, 1998 manufacturing

3M Dental Products Division, 1997 manufacturing

Merrill Lynch Credit Corporation, 1997 service

Solectron Corporation, 1997 and 1991 manufacturing

Xerox Business Services, 1997 service

ADAC Laboratories of California, 1996 manufacturing

Custom Research, 1996 small business

Dana Commercial Credit Corporation, 1996 service

Trident Precision Manufacturing, 1996 small business

Armstrong World Industries, Building Products Operations, 1995 manufacturing

Corning, Telecommunications Products Division, 1995 manufacturing

AT&T Consumer Communications Services (now Consumer Markets Division), 1994 service

Verizon Information Services (formerly GTE Directories Corporation), 1994 service

Wainwright Industries, 1994 manufacturing

Ames Rubber, 1993 small business

Eastman Chemical Company, 1993 manufacturing

AT&T Network Systems Group, Transmissions System Business Unit, 1992 manufacturing

AT&T Universal Card Services (now part of Citigroup), 1992 service

Granite Rock Company, 1992 small business

Texas Instruments, Defense Systems and Electronics Group, 1992 manufacturing

Marlow Industries, 1991 small business

Zytec Corporation (now part of Artesyn Technologies), 1991 manufacturing

Cadillac Motor Car Company, 1990 manufacturing

Federal Express Corporation, 1990 service

IBM Rochester, 1990 manufacturing

Wallace Company, 1990 small business

Milliken and Company, 1989 manufacturing

Xerox Corporation, Business Products and Systems, 1989 manufacturing

Globe Metallurgical, 1988 small business

Motorola, 1988 manufacturing

Westinghouse Electric Corporation, Commercial Nuclear Fuel Division, 1988 manufacturing

Through 2005, 68 Award recipients have been selected across five categories: 26 manufacturing companies, 14 service companies, 16 small businesses, 7 education organizations, and 5 healthcare organizations.

Economic Impact of the Baldrige National Quality Program

In October 2001, Albert N. Link, Department of Economics, University of North Carolina at Greensboro, and John T. Scott, Department of Economics at Dartmouth College reported on a study they completed that examined the economic impact of the Baldrige National Quality Program. Specifically, their study examined the net private benefits associated with the Baldrige National Quality Program to the U.S. private and public sector and the relationship between economy-wide net benefits and the social costs associated with operating the program.

Based on information collected from a mail survey of the U.S. organizational members of the American Society for Quality (ASQ), the conservative estimate of the value (in constant 2000 dollars) of the net private benefits associated with the Baldrige National Quality Program was $2.17 billion. Conservatively, Link and Scott estimated the value (in con-stant 2000 dollars) of social benefits associated with the Baldrige National Quality Program to be $24.65 billion. Based on information provided by the Baldrige National Quality Program, the value (in constant 2000 dollars) of social costs associated with the program to date was $119 million. Therefore, from an evaluative perspective for the economy as a whole, the benefit-to-cost ratio characterizing the Baldrige National Quality Program was conservatively 207 to 1.

The Worldwide Use of the Baldrige Criteria

As indicated, the performance of U.S. companies using the Baldrige principles has steadily increased since the launch of the Baldrige Award in 1987. U.S. companies began to recapture market share lost to international competition. When the reason for the increased success of U.S. companies became apparent, other countries throughout the world began to create their own national quality awards based on the Baldrige Criteria. Although the U.S. Congress may not have intended the Criteria to benefit companies throughout the world, that is precisely what has happened. After all, the Criteria are not secret. Millions of copies of the Criteria are distributed freely through the World Wide Web.

According to the U.S. Department of Commerce, more than 50 countries throughout the world have adopted the Criteria as a basis for their own quality awards in an effort to improve the competitiveness of businesses in their own countries.

THE INTEGRATED MANAGEMENT SYSTEM

Ingredients to Optimum Performance

Clearly, in today's highly competitive economy, past success means nothing. Desire, without disciplined and appropriate action, also means nothing. However, it is just as clear that implementing a disciplined approach to performance excellence based on the Baldrige Criteria produces winning levels of performance. The key to the success of the Baldrige Criteria has been the identification of the key drivers of high performance. The National Quality Award Office within the National Institute of Standards and Technology (NIST) ensures that each element of the Baldrige Criteria is necessary, and that together they are sufficient to achieve the highest levels of performance. Many management practices of the past have proven to be necessary ingredients of high performance. However, taken piecemeal, these practices by themselves have not been sufficient to achieve optimum performance.

Achieving winning levels of performance requires that each component of the organization's management system be optimized. In many ways, optimizing the performance of an organization's management system is like making an award-winning cake. Too much or too little of any key ingredient suboptimizes the system. For example, a cake may require eggs, flour, sugar, butter, and cocoa. A cake also requires a specific level of heat for a certain time in an oven. Too little or too much of any ingredient, including oven temperature, and the system (in this case the cake) fails to achieve desired results. The same principle applies in an organization. A successful organization requires a strong customer focus, skilled workers, efficient work processes, fact-based decision making, clear direction, and continuous improvement. Organizations that do not focus on all of these elements find that their performance suffers. Focusing on only a few of the required ingredients, such as reengineering to improve work processes or training to improve worker skills, is necessary but not sufficient by itself to drive high levels of performance.

The following figures depict the elements necessary and sufficient to achieve high levels of performance in any organization or part of an organization. The elements apply to any managed enterprise, regardless of size, sector, product, or service.

Get Results, Produce Value. (Figure 3) In the first place, in order for an organization, team, or individual to stay in business (or keep a job) for any length of time, it must produce desired results. The work results must be valued. History has demonstrated that people, organizations, or even governments that failed to deliver value eventually went away or were overturned. Value can be measured in a variety of ways, including fitness for use, return on assets, profitability, reliability, and durability, to name a few.

Customers. (Figure 4) Understand and meet their requirements. In addition, we have learned that it makes no difference if the producer of the goods or services believes they are valuable if the customer or user of the goods or services believes they are not. The customer is the only entity that can legitimately judge the value of the goods or services its suppliers produce. It is the customers who finally must decide whether the organization, team, or government continues to stay in business. Imagine that you go to a restaurant, order seafood, and find that it tastes awful. Upon complaining about the bad-tasting meal, you are not impressed with the chef's claim that "only the finest ingredients were used." It also does not help if the chef claims that he likes the taste of the fish. It still tastes bad to you, and unless the chef is willing to make an adjustment, you are not going to be satisfied and are unlikely to return. If enough customers find the food or service offensive and do not return, the restaurant goes out of business.

Integrated Management System

Figure 3 Get results, produce value.

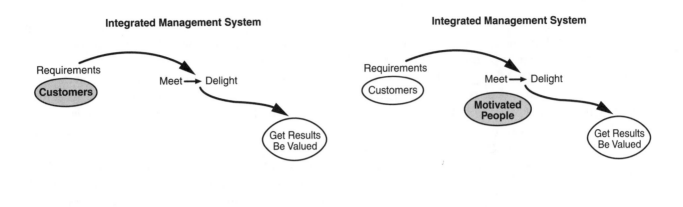

Figure 4 Customer requirements.

Figure 5 Motivated people.

Accordingly, it is very important for the organization to clearly understand the requirements of its customers and obtain feedback from the customers after they have had an opportunity to experience its products or services. The failure to understand the requirements of the customers may cause the organization to deliver the wrong thing, creating customer dissatisfaction, delay, or lower value. Every time our organizations fail to understand and meet customer requirements, value suffers. In order to consistently produce value, therefore, organizations must accurately determine the requirements of their customers and consistently meet or exceed those requirements. This creates the initial value chain that provides the competitive advantage for any organization or part of an organization.

To ensure that the customer is satisfied and likely to return (or recommend a service or product to others), it is important to determine if the customer received appropriate value. If the customer is dissatisfied, you have an opportunity to correct the problem and still maintain customer loyalty. In any case, it is important to remember that it is the customer and not the marketing, engineering, or manufacturing departments or the service provider that ultimately judges value received and determines satisfaction.

Motivated People. (Figure 5) Motivated people are key to the next part of the management system to ensure optimum performance and value. In any organization or part of an organization, people do the

work that produces customer value. As described previously, if the work is not focused on customer requirements, customers may be dissatisfied. In order to satisfy customers, work may have to be redone, adding cost and suboptimizing value. In order to optimize output and value, people doing the work must have the willingness and desire to work. Disgruntled, disaffected, unwilling workers hurt productivity.

However, *motivated people* means more than simply possessing the willingness to work. People must also possess the knowledge and skills to carry out their jobs effectively. In leading-edge technologies such as microelectronics engineering, the half-life of useful knowledge is 11 months. That means that one-half of the relevant knowledge of a microelectronics engineer becomes obsolete within 11 months. In 1989 the half-life was 18 months, approximately 50 percent greater. As new knowledge is created at an accelerating rate, it is more critical than ever to have effective training systems in place to ensure workers stay current and can effectively apply the new knowledge.

In addition, in order to optimize output, people must be free from bureaucratic barriers and arbitrary restrictions that inhibit work. Every minute that work is delayed while waiting for an unnecessary approval adds cost but not value. Every minute that work has to be redone because of sloppy performance of a coworker adds cost but not value. Every minute that work has to be redone because of inadequate knowledge or ability adds cost but not value.

Remember that one person cannot produce optimum levels of performance. However, one person can prevent optimum levels of performance, and may not be aware that he or she is doing so. The question that should concern management is, "In your organization, how many people are disgruntled, discouraged, underskilled, or prevented from working effectively so that they suboptimize the organization's performance?"

Efficient Processes. (Figure 6) Even the most highly skilled, knowledgeable, and willing workers will fail to optimize value if asked to do stupid things. Over time, even the most efficient processes can become suboptimal and inefficient. Business process reengineering has been seen by some as a panacea for organizational optimization. Business process reengineering allows organizations to redesign and quickly eliminate much of the bureaucratic silliness and inefficiency that grow up over time. However, how long does it take for the newly reengineered process to lose efficiency? Even new processes must be evaluated periodically and improved or they eventually become suboptimal and obsolete. Ensuring that processes are optimal requires ongoing evaluation and refinement.

Every process in the organization has the potential for increasing or decreasing the value provided to customers. Obviously, core business processes are perhaps the most important. However, frequently the core processes of an organization are disrupted because of failed support processes. For example, production can come to a halt if key materiel from the procurement office is not available on time.

Production can also be disrupted if key workers that were supposed to be provided by the personnel office are not available.

Any time an organization engages in rework, value for the customer is suboptimized. To make matters worse, if the need to engage in rework is not discovered until the product or service is complete, the cost of correction is higher, driving value lower. It is important, therefore, to uncover potential problems as early as possible, rather than wait for the end result to determine if the product or service is satisfactory. In order to uncover potential problems early we must be able to predict the outcomes of our work processes. This requires *in-process* measures. Through the use of these measures, organizations can determine if the product or service is likely to meet expectations. Consider the two examples that follow:

- Example one: A customer comes to the "Wait-And-See" coffee shop and orders a cup of coffee. The coffee is poured and delivered to the customer. The customer promptly takes a sip and informs the server that the coffee is too cold, too bitter, too weak, and has a harsh aroma. Furthermore, the customer complains that it took too long for the coffee to be served. The server, in an effort to satisfy the customer, discards the original coffee, brews a fresh pot, and delivers a new cup of coffee to the customer at no additional charge. This problem happens frequently. The "Wait-And-See" coffee shop has been forced to raise the price of coffee in order to stay in business and has noticed that fewer customers are willing to pay the higher price. Many customers have stopped coming to this coffee shop entirely. The customers that continue to buy coffee from this shop are subsidizing the sloppy performance and poor quality.

- Example two: In order to increase the likelihood that its customers will like the coffee it serves, the "In-Process-Measure" coffee shop has asked its customers key questions about the quality of coffee and service that they expect. The "In-Process-Measure" coffee shop has determined through testing and surveys that its customers like coffee served hot (between 76° and 82° Celsius); not too bitter or acidic (pH > 7.4);

Integrated Management System

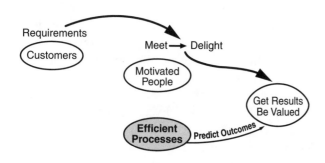

Figure 6 Efficient processes.

strong, but not too strong (75 grams of superfine grind per liter of filtered water); with a fresh aroma (is served within five minutes of brewing). By checking these measures, this coffee shop knows that nearly all customers will be satisfied with the quality and service it delivers. Since its customers like the coffee within the limits described previously, no rework is required, no coffee is discarded, the price is lower, the value is higher, the store is profitable, and it is taking customers from the "Wait-And-See" coffee shop down the street.

Data and Dashboard to Monitor Progress. (Figure 7) Data and information help the organization and its employees make better decisions about their work. This enables them to spot problems more quickly and take actions to improve performance and correct or minimize non-value-added costs. Without appropriate measures, organizations and their employees must rely on intuition. They must wait for customers to respond or guess at their likely satisfaction/dissatisfaction.

One of the problems in basing decisions on intuition or best guess is that it produces highly variable outcomes. The guess of one employee is not likely to be consistent with the guess of another. Appropriate data, therefore, are critical to increase decision-making consistency and accuracy. In order for data to be used correctly to support decision making, organizations must develop a system to manage, collect, analyze, and display the results.

If the data that drive decision making are not accurate or reliable, effective decision making suffers. More mistakes are made, costs increase, and value is suboptimized. Furthermore, in the absence of relevant data and supporting analyses, leaders are generally unwilling to allow subordinates to substitute their intuition for that of the leader. As a result, decisions tend to get pulled to higher and higher levels in an organization, further suboptimizing the contribution of employees who are generally closest to and know the most about the work they do. Failure to fully utilize the talents of workers, as discussed previously, further reduces efficiency and morale and suboptimizes value production.

The system described in Figure 7, which includes customers, motivated people, efficient processes, and a dashboard to monitor progress leading to desired results and value, applies to any managed enterprise. It applies to whole corporations as well as departments, divisions, teams, and individual work.

The system applies to schools, classrooms, government agencies, and healthcare organizations. In each case, in order to produce optimal value, the requirements of customers must be understood and met. People must be motivated, possess the skill and knowledge needed to do their work, and be free from distractions in order to optimize their performance. The organization must develop efficient work processes and monitor effectiveness of work to make adjustments in an effort to maximize value.

Leadership. (Figure 8) What makes an organization unique is the direction that top leaders set for it. Leaders must understand the requirements of customers and the marketplace in deciding what direction is necessary

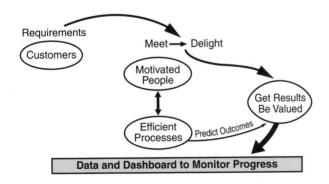

Figure 7 Information and data dashboard.

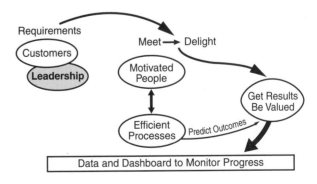

Figure 8 Leadership.

to achieve success. However, it is not enough simply to understand customer requirements. Leaders must also understand organizational capabilities and the needs and capabilities of employees, partners, and suppliers of critical goods and services.

Strategy. (Figure 9) Effective leaders use the process of strategy development to determine the most appropriate direction for the organization and identify level of performance in outcome-oriented terms the organization must actually achieve to be successful in the future. Leaders use this strategy to identify the people and the processes that must be put in place to produce desired results and be valued by customers.

If leaders are not clear about the strategy and direction that must be taken to be successful, they force subordinates to substitute their own ideas about the proper direction and actions. This creates inefficiency within an organization. People come to work and want to be successful. Without direction from the top, they will still work hard but often at cross-purposes. Unless everyone is pulling in the same direction, processes, products, and services will not be optimized and value will be reduced.

Leaders cannot eliminate a single part of this management system and still expect to produce optimum value. Each part is necessary. Furthermore, studies repeatedly demonstrate that when these processes are integrated and used to run the business, they are sufficient to achieve high levels of performance. Imagine what might happen if one or more of the pieces of the integrated management system described previously were missing. The following table provides some suggestions.

Integrated Management System

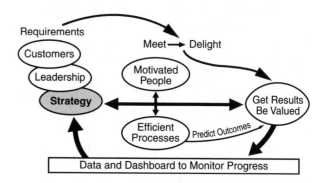

Figure 9 Strategy development and execution.

MISSING ELEMENT	ADVERSE CONSEQUENCE LEADING TO SUBOPTIMUM PERFORMANCE
Systems to understand customer requirements.	Designing, building, and delivering an unsatisfactory product or service. Adds delay. Increases cost due to rework.
Poor employee skills, minimal initiative or self-direction.	Limited expansion opportunities. Unable to keep up with changing technology. Requires close monitoring. Difficulty in finding better ways to carry out work. Ultimately reduces morale, motivation, and performance.
Data about customer satisfaction, key-process performance, and overall organizational performance do not exist or are incomplete.	Makes it difficult to engage employees in decision making about their work. Forces decisions to be made at higher levels on the basis of intuition or guesswork. Reduces decision accuracy and increases incorrect decisions. Makes it difficult to allocate resources appropriately or determine the best use of limited resources.
Leaders do not clearly set direction, performance expectations, vision, or values.	Causes subordinates to invent their own ideas and substitute them for a common set of performance expectations, vision, and values. Creates significant inefficiencies as people throughout the organization begin to work at cross-purposes, suboptimizing organizational performance.
Plans do not contain measurable outcome-oriented objectives and a time line for accomplishing each objective.	Leaders, managers, and employees do not know what level of performance is expected at any given time, making it difficult or impossible to effectively monitor progress. Accountability is weak or not present.
Leaders do not make it clear that customers are the key to success.	If managers and employees do not focus on customers, they become internally focused. Managers, engineers, or marketers drive the business, not customers. Customers and their requirements lose importance.
Top leaders do not encourage employees to develop and use their full potential.	Employee empowerment and well-being become optional. Some managers encourage employee participation, innovation, and creativity; most do not. The organization risks losing its best employees to competitors.
Customer comments and complaints are not encouraged. If a complaint is received it is not resolved promptly. The root cause of complaints is not identified.	Failure to capture customer comments and complaints, identify the root causes of the complaint, and work to prevent the problem from happening again makes it difficult to learn about problems quickly and dooms the organization to repeat its failures. Failure to resolve complaints promptly increases customer dissatisfaction and reduces loyalty.
Poor two-way communication exists between leaders and employees.	Unclear top-down communication makes it difficult to ensure alignment and focus throughout the organization, reducing teamwork and increasing bureaucratic stagnation. Poor upward communication maintains organizational fragmentation and prevents problems and barriers to effective work from being discussed and resolved.

THE CORE VALUES TO ACHIEVE PERFORMANCE EXCELLENCE

The Criteria are built upon a set of interrelated Core Values and Concepts, which are embedded beliefs and behaviors found in high-performing organizations. They are the foundation for integrating key business requirements within a results-oriented framework that create a basis for action and feedback.

The 2006 Core Values and Concepts follow. The text in the box presents the exact wording of the Baldrige core values and concepts.

Visionary Leadership

Every system, strategy, and method for achieving excellence must be guided by visionary leadership.

- Effective leaders convey a strong sense of urgency to counter the natural resistance to change that can prevent the organization from taking the steps that these Core Values for success demand.

- Such leaders serve as enthusiastic role models, reinforcing and communicating the Core Values by their words and actions.

- Words alone are not enough. The actions of great leaders match their words.

Visionary Leadership

Your organization's senior leaders should set directions and create a customer focus, clear and visible values, and high expectations. The directions, values, and expectations should balance the needs of all your stakeholders. Your leaders should ensure the creation of strategies, systems, and methods for achieving performance excellence, stimulating innovation, building knowledge and capabilities, and ensuring organizational sustainability. The values and strategies should help guide all of your organization's activities and decisions. Senior leaders should inspire and motivate your entire workforce and should encourage all employees, including any volunteers, to contribute, to develop

---

and learn, to be innovative, and to be creative. Senior leaders should be responsible to your organization's governance body for their actions and performance. The governance body should be responsible ultimately to all your stakeholders for the ethics, actions, and performance of your organization and its senior leaders.

Senior leaders should serve as role models through their ethical behavior and their personal involvement in planning, communications, coaching, development of future leaders, review of organizational performance, and employee recognition. As role models, they can reinforce ethics, values, and expectations while building leadership, commitment, and initiative throughout your organization.

Customer-Driven Excellence

This value demonstrates a passion for making the organization customer-driven. Without loyal customers, little else matters. Customers are the final judges of how well the organization did its job, and what they say counts. It is their perception of the service and product that will determine whether they remain loyal or constantly seek better providers.

- The organization must focus on systematically listening to customers and acting quickly on what they say.

- The organization must build positive relationships with its customers through focusing on accessibility and management of complaints.

- Dissatisfied customers must be heeded most closely, for they often deliver the most valuable information.

- If only satisfied and loyal customers (those who continue to do business with us no matter what) are paid attention, the organization will be led astray. The most successful organizations keep an eye on customers who are not satisfied and work to understand their preferences and meet their demands.

Customer-Driven Excellence

Quality and performance are judged by an organization's customers. Thus, your organization must take into account all product and service features and characteristics and all modes of customer access that contribute value to your customers. Such behavior leads to customer acquisition, satisfaction, preference, referral, retention and loyalty, and to business expansion. Customer-driven excellence has both current and future components: understanding today's customer desires and anticipating future customer desires and marketplace potential.

Value and satisfaction may be influenced by many factors throughout your customers' overall experience with your organization. These factors include your organization's customer relationships, which help to build trust, confidence, and loyalty.

Customer-driven excellence means much more than reducing defects and errors, merely meeting specifications, or reducing complaints. Nevertheless, these factors contribute to your customers' view of your organization and thus also are important parts of customer-driven excellence. In addition, your organization's success in recovering from defects, service errors, and mistakes is crucial to retaining customers and building customer relationships.

Customer-driven organizations address not only the product and service characteristics that meet basic customer requirements but also those features and characteristics that differentiate products and services from competing offerings. Such differentiation may be based on new or modified offerings, combinations of product and service offerings, customization of offerings, multiple access mechanisms, rapid response, or special relationships.

Customer-driven excellence is thus a strategic concept. It is directed toward customer retention and loyalty, market share gain, and growth. It demands constant sensitivity to changing and emerging customer and market requirements and to the factors that drive customer satisfaction and loyalty. It demands listening to your customers. It demands anticipating changes in the marketplace. Therefore, customer-driven excellence demands awareness of developments in technology and competitors' offerings, as well as rapid and flexible responses to customer, environmental, and market changes.

Organizational and Personal Learning

The most potent value is organizational and personal learning. High-performing organizations are learning organizations—they evaluate and improve everything they do. They strive to get better at getting better.

- A culture of continuous improvement is essential to maintaining and sustaining true competitive advantage.

- Without systematic improvement and ongoing learning, organizations will ultimately face extinction.

- With systematic, continuous, organizational improvement, time becomes a powerful ally. As time passes, the organization grows stronger and smarter.

- Leaders embed this value by linking rewards, recognition, and incentives for employees, supervisors, and managers at all levels to innovation, improvement, and learning. Otherwise, people do not think continuous change is important.

- Personal learning that is shared widely becomes organizational learning. Individuals can improve processes they own, but maximum organizational benefit does not occur unless these learnings (improvements) are shared/adopted throughout the organization.

Organizational and Personal Learning

Achieving the highest levels of organizational performance requires a well-executed approach to organizational and personal learning. Organizational learning includes both continuous improvement of existing approaches and significant change, leading to new goals and approaches. Learning needs to be embedded in the way your organization operates. This means that learning (1) is a regular part of daily work;

Continued

Continued

(2) is practiced at personal, work unit, and organizational levels; (3) results in solving problems at their source ("root cause"); (4) is focused on building and sharing knowledge throughout your organization; and (5) is driven by opportunities to effect significant, meaningful change. Sources for learning include employees' and volunteers' ideas, research and development (R&D), customers' input, best practice sharing, and benchmarking.

Organizational learning can result in (1) enhancing value to customers through new and improved products and services; (2) developing new business opportunities; (3) reducing errors, defects, waste, and related costs; (4) improving responsiveness and cycle time performance; (5) increasing productivity and effectiveness in the use of all your resources; and (6) enhancing your organization's performance in fulfilling its societal responsibilities and its service to your community.

Employees' success depends increasingly on having opportunities for personal learning and on practicing new skills. In organizations that rely on volunteers, the volunteers' personal learning also is important, and their learning and skill development should be considered with employees. Organizations invest in employees' personal learning through education, training, and other opportunities for continuing growth and development. Such opportunities might include job rotation and increased pay for demonstrated knowledge and skills. On-the-job training offers a cost-effective way to train and to better link training to your organizational needs and priorities. Education and training programs may benefit from advanced technologies, such as computer- and Internet-based learning and satellite broadcasts.

Personal learning can result in (1) more satisfied and versatile employees who stay with your organization, (2) organizational cross-functional learning, (3) the building of your organization's knowledge assets, and (4) an improved environment for innovation.

Thus, learning is directed not only toward better products and services but also toward being more responsive, adaptive, innovative, and efficient—giving your organization marketplace sustainability and performance advantages and giving your employees satisfaction and motivation to excel.

Valuing Employees and Partners

Organizations must invest in their people to ensure they have the skills for today and to do what is necessary to succeed in the future. This core value has broadened from employee participation and development to valuing employees and partners. In high-performing organizations, the people who do the work of the organization should make most of the decisions about how the work is done. A significant barrier exists, however, that limits employee decision making—access to data and poor data-based decision-making skills.

Organizations cannot effectively push decision making down to the level where most of the work is done unless those doing the work have access to the necessary data and are skilled at making fact-based decisions. As mentioned previously, leaders are unwilling to let subordinates make decisions based on intuition—they reserve that type of decision for themselves. Therefore, access to data and developing skills to manage by fact are prerequisites for optimizing employee contributions to the organization's success.

Valuing Employees and Partners

An organization's success depends increasingly on the diverse backgrounds, knowledge, skills, creativity, and motivation of all its employees and partners, including both paid employees and volunteers, as appropriate.

Valuing employees means committing to their satisfaction, development, and well-being. Increasingly, this involves more flexible, high-performance work practices tailored to employees with varying workplace and home life needs. Major challenges in the area of valuing employees include (1) demonstrating your leaders' commitment to your employees' success, (2) providing recognition that goes beyond the regular compensation system, (3) offering development and progression within your organization, (4) sharing your organization's knowledge so your employees can better serve your customers and contribute to achieving your strategic objectives, (5) creating an environment that encourages risk taking and innovation, and (6) creating a supportive environment for a diverse workforce.

Organizations need to build internal and external partnerships to better accomplish overall goals. Internal partnerships might include labor-management cooperation. Partnerships with employees might entail employee development, cross-training, or new work organizations, such as high-performance work teams. Internal partnerships also might involve creating network relationships among your work units to improve flexibility, responsiveness, and knowledge sharing.

External partnerships might be with customers, suppliers, and nonprofit or education organizations. Strategic partnerships or alliances are increasingly important kinds of external partnerships. Such partnerships might offer entry into new markets or a basis for new products or services. Also, partnerships might permit the blending of your organization's core competencies or leadership capabilities with the complementary strengths and capabilities of partners to address common issues.

Successful internal and external partnerships develop longer-term objectives, thereby creating a basis for mutual investments and respect. Partners should address the key requirements for success, means for regular communication, approaches to evaluating progress, and means for adapting to changing conditions. In some cases, joint education and training could offer a cost-effective method for employee development.

Agility

Agility is a value usually driven by customer requirements and the desire to improve operating efficiency and lower costs.

- Except for a few pleasurable experiences, everyone wants things faster.

- Organizations that develop the capacity to respond faster by eliminating activities and tasks that do not add value find that productivity increases, costs go down, and customers are more loyal.

- Analyzing and improving work processes enables organizations to perform better, faster, and cheaper.

- To improve work processes, organizations must focus on improving design quality and preventing problems. The cost of preventing problems and building quality into products and services is significantly less than the cost of taking corrective action later.

- It is critical to capture learning from other design projects.

- Use information concerning customer preference, competitors' products, cost and pricing, marketplace profiles, and research and development (R&D) to optimize the process from the start, and avoid delay and rework.

- Public-responsibility issues and factors, including environmental demands, must be included at the design stage.

Agility

Success in today's ever-changing, globally competitive environment demands agility—a capacity for rapid change and flexibility. E-business requires and enables more rapid, flexible, and customized responses. Organizations face ever-shorter cycles for the introduction of new/improved products and services, and nonprofit and governmental organizations are increasingly being asked to respond rapidly to new or emerging social issues. Major improvements in response times often require simplification of work units and processes or the ability for rapid changeover from one process to another. Cross-trained and empowered employees are vital assets in such a demanding environment.

A major success factor in meeting competitive challenges is the design-to-introduction (product or service initiation) or innovation cycle time. To meet the demands of rapidly changing markets, organizations need to carry out stage-to-stage integration (such as concurrent engineering) of activities from research or concept to commercialization or implementation.

All aspects of time performance now are more critical, and cycle time has become a key process measure. Other important benefits can be derived from this focus on time; time improvements often drive simultaneous improvements in organization, quality, cost, and productivity.

Focus on the Future

To remain competitive, every organization must be guided by a common set of measurable outcome-oriented goals and a focus on the future.

- These outcome-oriented goals, which emerge from the strategic planning process, help to align the work of everyone in the organization and serve as a basis for factual monitoring of progress.

- Measurable goals allow everyone to know where they are going and when they deviate from their path.

- Without measurable goals, everyone still works hard, but they tend to focus on the things they believe are important, not the direction set by top leaders. As a result, they can easily go in different directions—suboptimizing the success of the organization.

- Focusing on the future requires the organization's leaders to consider new, even revolutionary, ideas. Strategic objectives should reflect this future focus.

Focus on the Future

In today's competitive environment, creating a sustainable organization requires understanding the short- and longer-term factors that affect your organization and marketplace. Pursuit of sustainable growth and market leadership requires a strong future orientation and a willingness to make long-term commitments to key stakeholders—your customers, employees, suppliers, partners, stockholders, the public, and your community.

Your organization's planning should anticipate many factors, such as customers' expectations, new business and partnering opportunities, employee development and hiring needs, the increasingly global marketplace, technological developments, the evolving e-business environment, changes in customer and market segments, evolving regulatory requirements, changes in community and societal expectations and needs, and strategic moves by competitors. Strategic objectives and resource allocations need to accommodate

---

these influences. A focus on the future includes developing employees and suppliers, accomplishing effective succession planning, creating opportunities for innovation, and anticipating public responsibilities and concerns.

Managing for Innovation

The accelerating rate of change today demands ever-increasing innovation. Such innovation cannot be random. It must be focused on factors that are essential to organizational success. To be focused, innovation must be managed. Innovation should focus on changing products, services, and processes to create more value for the organization's stakeholders, employees, and customers. The winners in the highly competitive race to innovate will be the organizations that uncover new paradigms of breakthrough performance. To begin to optimize this breakthrough capacity, everyone in the organization needs to be involved. The more brain power, the better. *Requirements for innovation should be a part of every employee and managerial performance plan and appraisal.* Just like continuous improvement, innovation must be embedded in the culture and fabric of daily work. The best organizations are not satisfied to just *improve* or *innovate*. The best organizations work hard at increasing the speed at which they improve and innovate. Anything less allows competitors to overtake them. Anything less allows customer expectations to exceed the speed of change, causing the customers to look elsewhere.

Managing for Innovation

Innovation means making meaningful change to improve an organization's products, services, programs, processes, and operations and to create new value for the organization's stakeholders. Innovation should lead your organization to new dimensions of performance. Innovation is no longer strictly the purview of research and development departments; innovation is important for all aspects of your operations and all processes. Organizations should be led and managed so that innovation becomes part of the learning culture. Innovation should be integrated into daily work and should be supported by your performance improvement system.

Innovation builds on the accumulated knowledge of your organization and its employees. Therefore, the ability to rapidly disseminate and capitalize on this knowledge is critical to driving organizational innovation.

Management by Fact

Management by fact is the cornerstone value for effective planning, operational decision making at all levels, employee involvement and empowerment, and leadership.

- People make decisions every day. However, without data, the basis for decision making is usually intuition—gut feel. Although intuition can be valuable at times, it introduces too much variation into the decision-making process. Intuition is not consistent person-to-person or time-to-time. It is also difficult to explain the rationale for decisions based on intuition. That makes communication more difficult within the organization. Finally, if the decision must be made on the basis of intuition, it is usually the boss' intuition that drives the decision. Because of this phenomenon, issues are pulled to ever-higher levels for resolution. As a result, excessive reliance on intuition minimizes employee empowerment.

- Most drivers decide when to fill their fuel tanks based on data from the fuel gage and get very uncomfortable if the gage is broken. Yet people routinely make decisions of enormous consequence about customers, strategies, goals, and employees with little or no data. This is a recipe for disaster, not one designed to ensure optimization.

Management by Fact

Organizations depend on the measurement and analysis of performance. Such measurements should derive from business needs and strategy, and they should provide critical data and information about key processes, outputs, and results. Many types of data and information are needed for performance management. Performance measurement should include customer, product, and service performance; comparisons of operational, market, and competitive performance; supplier, employee, cost, and financial performance; and governance and compliance. Data should be segmented by, for example, markets, product lines, and employee groups to facilitate analysis.and corporate governance and compliance. Data should be segmented by, for example, markets, product lines, and employee groups to facilitate analysis.

Analysis refers to extracting larger meaning from data and information to support evaluation, decision making, and improvement. Analysis entails using data to determine trends, projections, and cause and effect that might not otherwise be evident. Analysis supports a variety of purposes, such as planning, reviewing your overall performance, improving operations, accomplishing change management, and comparing your performance with competitors' or with *best practices* benchmarks.

A major consideration in performance improvement and change management involves the selection and use of performance measures or indicators. The measures or indicators you select should best represent the factors that lead to improved customer, operational, financial, and ethical performance. A comprehensive set of measures or indicators tied to customer and organizational performance requirements represents a clear basis for aligning all processes with your organization's goals. Through the analysis of data from your tracking processes, your measures or indicators themselves may be evaluated and changed to better support your goals.

Social Responsibility

Every high-performing organization practices good public responsibility and citizenship.

- Organizations must determine and anticipate any adverse effects to the public of their products, services, and operations. Failure to do so can undermine public trust and distract workers, and also adversely affect the bottom line. This is true of both private and public organizations.

- During the last few years we have seen several examples of companies that have been seriously hurt by failing to practice good citizenship or protect the interests of the public from risks they created. Enron and Arthur-Anderson are well-known examples. Even when unintended, failure to protect stakeholder interests can cripple companies. Consider Dow-Corning and the silicone breast implants, banks sued because they failed to provide adequate security for automatic teller machines (cash machines), or Exxon for the massive oil spill in the Pacific.

- Safety and legal requirements need to be met beyond mere compliance. The best organizations stay ahead of minimum requirements and actually lead efforts to raise the bar. In this manner, when regulatory agencies increase requirements, the best organizations are not caught off guard and may even be able to place their competitors at a disadvantage.

Social Responsibility

An organization's leaders should stress responsibilities to the public, ethical behavior, and the need to practice good citizenship. Leaders should be role models for your organization in focusing on ethics and protection of public health, safety, and the environment. Protection of health, safety, and the environment includes your organization's operations, as well as the life cycles of your products and services. Also, organizations should emphasize resource conservation and waste reduction at the source. Planning should anticipate adverse impacts from production, distribution, transportation, use, and disposal of your products. Effective planning should prevent problems, provide for a forthright response if problems occur, and make available information and support needed to maintain public awareness, safety, and confidence.

For many organizations, the product or service design stage is critical from the point of view of public responsibility. Design decisions impact your production processes and often the content of municipal and industrial waste. Effective design strategies should anticipate growing environmental concerns and responsibilities.

Organizations should not only meet all local, state, and federal laws and regulatory requirements, but they should treat these and related requirements as opportunities for improvement *beyond mere compliance*. Organizations should stress ethical behavior in all stakeholder transactions and interactions. Highly ethical conduct should be a requirement of and should be monitored by the organization's governance body.

Practicing good citizenship refers to leadership and support—within the limits of an organization's resources—of publicly important purposes. Such purposes might include improving education and healthcare in your community, pursuing environmental excellence, practicing resource conservation, performing community service, improving industry and business practices, and sharing nonproprietary information. Leadership as a corporate citizen also entails influencing other organizations, private and public, to partner for these purposes.

Managing social responsibility requires the use of appropriate measures and leadership responsibility for those measures.

Focus on Results and Creating Value

A results focus and an emphasis on creating value helps organizations communicate requirements, monitor actual performance, make appropriate adjustments in priorities, and reallocate resources effectively. Without a results focus, organizations can become fixated on internal, self-directed processes and lose sight of the important factors for success—such as customers and their requirements.

Strategic objectives should be results- or outcome-oriented, not activity-oriented. When the focus shifts from achieving outcomes to competing activities, accountability erodes. Many times managers and workers carry out assigned tasks but the required outcome or benefit has not occurred.

Focus on Results and Creating Value

An organization's performance measurements need to focus on key results. Results should be used to create and balance value for your key stakeholders—customers, employees, stockholders, suppliers, partners, the public, and the community. By creating value for your key stakeholders, your organization builds loyalty, contributes to growing the economy, and contributes to society. To meet the sometimes conflicting and changing aims that balancing value implies, organizational strategy explicitly should include key stakeholder requirements. This will help ensure that plans and actions meet differing stakeholder needs and avoid adverse impacts on any stakeholders. The use of a balanced composite of leading and lagging performance measures offers an effective means to communicate short- and longer-term priorities, monitor actual performance, and provide a clear basis for improving results.

Systems Perspective

Taken together, the Baldrige Criteria promote a systems perspective and define the processes required to achieve optimal organizational performance. As with any system, no part can be ignored and the whole still be expected to perform at peak levels. When part of a well-functioning system begins to underperform or work in a manner that is inconsistent with system requirements, the performance of the whole system suffers.

The same is true of a management system. If leaders are ambiguous, if plans are not clear, if work processes are not consistent, if people are not able to do the work they are asked to do, and if it is difficult to keep track of progress and make appropriate adjustments, it will be impossible for the organization to achieve maximum levels of performance. For most of the 20th century, a long list of management gurus has suggested a variety of quick and simple remedies to enhance organizational performance. By itself, each quick fix has failed. Hopefully we have learned that no single solution is sufficient to optimize performance in a complex system. Leaders who approach management from a systems perspective are more likely to optimize organizational performance than leaders who continue to take a piecemeal approach to organizational management. There is no magic potion for excellent management to achieve high performance.

There are always better ways to do things. The challenge is to find them, but we are not likely to find them alone. We must create an environment—a work climate where better ways will be sought out, recognized, and put in place by everyone.

Systems Perspective

The Baldrige Criteria provide a systems perspective for managing your organization and its key processes to achieve results—performance excellence. The seven Baldrige Categories and the Core Values form the building blocks and the integrating mechanism for the system. However, successful

Continued

Continued

management of overall performance requires organization-specific synthesis, alignment, and integration. Synthesis means looking at your organization as a whole and builds on key business requirements, including your strategic objectives and action plans. Alignment means using the key linkages among requirements given in the Baldrige Categories to ensure consistency of plans, processes, measures, and actions. Integration builds on alignment, so that the individual components of your performance management system operate in a fully interconnected manner.

These concepts are depicted in the Baldrige framework. A systems perspective includes your senior leaders' focus on strategic directions and on your customers. It means that your senior leaders monitor, respond to, and manage performance based on your results. A systems perspective also includes using your measures, indicators, and organizational knowledge to build your key strategies. It means linking these strategies with your key processes and aligning your resources to improve overall performance and satisfy customers and stakeholders.

Thus, a systems perspective means managing your whole organization, as well as its components, to achieve success.

PRACTICAL INSIGHTS

Connections and Linkages

A popular children's activity, connect the dots, helps them understand that, when properly joined, apparently random dots create a meaningful picture. In many ways, the seven Categories, 19 Items, 33 Areas to Address, and 84 subparts in the Baldrige Criteria are like the dots that must be connected to reveal a meaningful picture. With no tools to connect the dots, human resource activities are not related to strategic planning; measurement, analysis, and knowledge management are isolated from process management; and overall improvement efforts are disjointed, fragmented, and do not yield robust results. This book describes the linkages among and between each item. The exciting part about having them identified is that you can look for these linkages in your own organization and, if they don't exist, start building them.

Transition Strategies

Putting high-performance management systems in place is a major commitment that will not happen quickly or easily. At the beginning, you will need a transition strategy to get you across the bridge from management by opinion or intuition to more data-driven management. The next part of this section describes one approach that has worked for many organizations in various sectors: creating a performance improvement council.

Performance Improvement Council

Identify a top-level executive leadership group of six to eight members. Each additional member beyond this number will seem to double the complexity of issues and render decision making much more cumbersome. The executive leadership group could send a message to the entire organization by naming the group *the performance improvement council*—reinforcing the importance of continuous performance improvement to the future success of the organization.

The performance improvement council should be the primary policy-making body for the organization. It should spawn other performance improvement councils at lower levels to share practices and policies with every employee in the organization as well as to involve customers and suppliers. The structure permeates the organization as members of the performance improvement council become area leaders for major improvement efforts and sponsors for several process or continuous improvement task teams throughout the organization. The council structure, networked and cascaded fully, can effectively align the work and optimize performance at all levels and across all functions.

Council Membership

Selecting members for the performance improvement council should be done carefully. Each member should be essential for the success of the operation, and together they must generate a synergy sufficient for success. The most important member is the senior leader of the organization or unit. This person must participate actively, demonstrating the kind of leadership that all should emulate. Of particular importance is a commitment to consensus building as the modus operandi for the council. This tool, a core of performance improvement programs, is often overlooked by leadership. Other council members selected should have leadership responsibility for broad areas of the organization such as human resources, operations planning, customers, and data systems.

Performance Improvement Council Learning and Planning

The performance improvement council should be extremely knowledgeable about high-performance management systems. If not, as is often the case, performance improvement council members should be among the first in the organization to learn about continuous improvement tools and processes.

To be effective, every member of the council (and every member in the organization) must understand the Baldrige Criteria, because the Criteria describe the components of the entire management system. Participation in examiner training has proved to be a great way to understand the complexities of the system needed to achieve performance excellence. Any additional training beyond this should be carried out in the context of planning—that is, learn tools and use them to plan the performance improvement implementation, practices, and policies.

The performance improvement council should:

- Develop a business plan that integrates continuous improvement and strategic performance improvement.

- Create the web (communication plan and infrastructure) to transmit performance improvement policies, practices, and priorities throughout the organization.

- Define the roles of employees, including new recognition and reward structures, to cause needed behavioral changes.

- Develop a master training and development plan. Involve team representatives in planning so they can learn skills close to when they are needed. Define what is provided to whom, and when and how learning and abilities will be measured.

- Launch improvement projects that will produce both short- and long-term successes. Improvement projects should be clearly defined by the performance improvement council and driven by the strategic plan. Typical improvement projects include important human resource processes such as career development, performance measurement, and diversity, as well as improving operational products and services in the line areas.

- Develop a plan to communicate the progress and successes throughout the organization. Through this approach, the need for performance improvement processes is consistently communicated to all employees. Barriers to optimum performance are weakened and eliminated.

- Create champions to promote performance excellence through the Categories of the Baldrige Criteria.

Category Champions

This section describes the responsibilities of category champions. The people in the administrative or leadership cabinet should each be the champion of a category and have appropriate staff support.

Organizational Leadership Champion

The **organizational leadership champion** is a senior executive who, in addition to other executive duties, works to coordinate and enhance leadership effectiveness and alignment throughout the organization. It is both a strategic and an operational activity.

From the strategic side, the champion should focus on ensuring that all senior leaders:

- Understand what is expected of them as leaders of organizational change.

- Ensure that effective governance systems are in place to protect the interests of all stakeholder groups and maintain organizational integrity and ethical behavior.

- Consistently speak with one voice as a senior leadership team.

- Serve as role models of performance excellence for managers and employees at all levels of the organization.

- Set clear strategy and directions to enhance future opportunities for the organization.

- Develop future leaders (succession planning) throughout the organization.

- Create measurable outcome-oriented performance expectations and monitor performance to achieve the key improvements and strategic objectives of the organization. This means that necessary data and analyses must be coordinated to ensure appropriate information is available for the champion and the entire senior leadership team.

From the operational side, the champion should work to identify and eliminate both individual and system deficiencies, territorial conflicts, and knowledge shortfalls that limit leaders' ability to meet expectations and goals consistently.

The champion should be the focal point in the organization to ensure all parts of the organization have systematic processes in place so they fully understand leadership and management requirements.

A process should exist to monitor ongoing initiatives to ensure leaders effectively set and communicate organizational values to employees:

- They must demonstrate that they focus on delivering value to customers and other stakeholders.

- They must aggressively reinforce an environment that promotes empowerment and innovation throughout the workforce. This may involve reviewing policies, systems, work processes, and the use of resources—ensuring sufficient data are available to assist in manager and employee decision making.

- They should review (conduct independent audits) ethical and legal behavior of all leaders and managers and hold them accountable for their actions.

The champion should coordinate the activities involving the review of organizational performance and capabilities:

- Define key performance outcome and in-process measures.

- Install systems to review organizational success, performance, and progress relative to outcome-oriented goals.

- Use performance-review findings to identify priorities for improvement. Communicate those priorities to all units that have responsibilities for making the improvements, including suppliers and partners.

- Systematically use performance-review findings, together with employee feedback, to assess and improve senior leadership (including the chief executive) effectiveness and the effectiveness of managers throughout the leadership system.

The champion must work as part of the senior leadership team to help coordinate all facets of the management system to drive high performance. This involves teaching the team about the requirements of effective and consistent leadership at all levels and its impact on organizational performance. The senior leader of the organization usually serves as the organizational leadership champion and leads this council.

Finally, the senior leader champion must ensure that everyone in a leadership position supports the values and activities critical to achieving performance excellence. Implement policies of zero tolerance for managers who do not support these efforts fully. To be successful, implementing the system cannot be seen as optional. This is essential to ensure the systems and processes required to achieve optimum performance are launched and sustained.

Strategic-Planning Champion

The *strategic-planning champion* is a senior executive who, in addition to other executive duties, works to coordinate and enhance strategic planning and action-plan alignment throughout the organization. It is both a strategic and an operational activity.

From the strategic side, the champion should ensure that the focus of strategy development is on sustained competitive leadership, which usually depends on achieving revenue growth, as well as consistently improving operational effectiveness. The strategic-planning champion should help the senior leadership team acquire a view of the future and provide clear strategic guidance to the organization through goals, objectives, action plans, and measures.

From the operational side, the champion should work to ensure sufficient data are available regarding:

- The organization's operational and human resource strengths and weaknesses

- External risks and threats that may arise from competitors, supplier weaknesses, regulatory changes, economic conditions, and financial, ethical, and societal risks

- The competitive environment and other challenges that might affect future direction

The champion should be the focal point in the organization to ensure all parts of the organization have systematic processes in place so they fully understand the implications of strategy on their daily work.

The champion should ensure that strategy is customer- and market-focused and is actually used to guide ongoing decision making and resource allocation at all levels of the organization:

- All strategic objectives or goals should define, in measurable terms, the outcomes the organization must actually achieve to be successful in the future. *Activities* are not strategic objectives.

- A process should exist at each level of the organization to convert measurable, outcome-oriented strategic objectives into actions, which are

aligned to achieve goals necessary for business success. These actions may define the activities believed to be critical to achieving desired outcomes, but may not substitute for the outcomes.

- Every employee should understand his or her role in carrying out actions to achieve the organization's goals.

The champion should coordinate the work of strategy development and deployment to:

- Acquire and use various types of forecasts, projections, scenarios, or other techniques to understand the plausible range of future options.

- Determine how the projected performance of competitors is likely to compare with the projected performance of the organization in the same time frame in order to set goals to ensure competitive advantage.

- Define the expected path along which growth and performance are likely to take for each strategic objective. Time lines (the schedule) of projected future performance should match the frequency of organizational performance reviews.

- Determine what changes in services or products might be needed as a part of strategic positioning and direction. Strategy should define what the organization must achieve to be successful in the future, not simply justify a continuation of current activities.

- Ensure a system is in place to develop action plans and activities that address strategic goals and objectives. Ensure those action plans and activities are understood throughout the organization, as appropriate.

- Determine what capabilities must be developed within the organization to achieve strategic goals and coordinate with other members of the senior leadership team and category champions to ensure those capabilities are in place. Ensure a system is in place to identify the human resource requirements necessary to achieve strategic goals and objectives. This may include training, support services for employees, reorganization, and new recruitment, to name a few.

- Ensure a system is in place to allocate resources throughout the organization sufficient to accomplish the action plans.

- Coordinate with the leadership system during performance reviews to help ensure that priorities for improvement and innovation at different levels throughout the organization are aligned with strategy and action plans.

- Ensure the process for strategic planning, plan deployment, the development of action plans, and the alignment of resources to support actions is systematically evaluated and improved each cycle. Also evaluate and improve the accuracy of determining the projected performance of competitors for use in goal setting.

Finally, the champion must work as contributing member of the senior leadership team to help coordinate all facets of the management system to drive high performance. This involves teaching the team about the requirements of strategic planning and its impact on organizational performance.

Customer-Value Champion

The *customer-value champion* is a senior executive who, in addition to other executive duties, coordinates and enhances customer satisfaction, relations, and loyalty throughout the organization. It is both a strategic and an operational activity.

From the strategic side, the champion should focus on ensuring that the drivers of customer satisfaction, customer retention, and related market share (which are key factors in competitiveness, profitability, and business sustainability) are considered fully in the strategic planning process. This means that necessary data and analyses must be coordinated to ensure appropriate information is available for the executive planning councils.

From the operational side, the champion should work to identify and eliminate system deficiencies, territorial conflicts, and knowledge shortfalls that limit the organization's ability to meet customer satisfaction, retention, and loyalty goals consistently.

The champion should be the focal point in the organization to ensure all parts of the organization have systematic processes in place so they fully understand key customer, market, and operational

requirements as input to customer satisfaction and market goals.

A process should exist to monitor ongoing initiatives to ensure they are aligned with the customer aspects of the strategic direction. This may involve:

- Reviewing policies, systems, work processes, the use of resources, and the availability of employees who are knowledgeable and focus on customer relations and loyalty.

- Ensuring sufficient data are available to assist in decision making about customer issues.

- Ensuring that strategies and actions relating to customer issues are aligned at all levels of reorganization from the executives to the work unit or individual job level.

The champion should coordinate the activities involving understanding customer requirements as well as managing the interaction with customers, including how the organization determines customer satisfaction and satisfaction relative to competitors. (Satisfaction relative to competitors and the factors that lead to customer preference are of increasing importance to managing in a competitive environment.)

- The champion should also examine the means by which customers have access to seek information, assistance, or comment and complain.

- The champion should coordinate the definition of customer-contact requirements (sometimes called customer-service standards) and the deployment of those requirements to all points and people in the organization that have contact with customers.

- The champion should ensure that systems exist to respond quickly and resolve complaints promptly to recover customer confidence that might be otherwise lost.

- The champion should ensure that employees responsible for the design and delivery of products and services receive information about customer complaints so they may eliminate the causes of these complaints.

- The champion should work with appropriate line managers to help set priorities for improvement projects based on the potential impact of the cost of complaints and the impact of customer dissatisfaction and attrition on the organization.

- The champion should be charged with coordinating activities to build loyalty and positive referral, as well as evaluating and improving customer relationship-building processes throughout the organization.

Finally, the champion must work as contributing member of the senior leadership team to help coordinate all facets of the management system to drive high performance. This involves teaching the team about the requirements of customer and market focus and its impact on organizational performance.

Measurement, Analysis, and Knowledge-Management Champion

The **measurement, analysis, and knowledge-management champion** is an executive-level person who, in addition to other executive duties, coordinates and enhances information, analysis, and knowledge-management systems throughout the organization to ensure they meet the decision-making needs of managers, employees, customers, and suppliers. It is both a strategic and an operational activity.

From the strategic side, information and analyses and the resulting knowledge can provide a competitive advantage. The champion should focus on ensuring, to the extent possible, that timely and accurate information and analyses are available to enhance knowledge acquisition and the development and delivery of new and existing products and services to meet ongoing and emerging customer needs.

From the operational side, the champion should work to ensure that information and analyses are available throughout the organization to aid in decision making at all levels. This means coordinating with all other champions to ensure data are available for day-to-day review and decision making at all levels for their areas of responsibility.

The measurement, analysis, and knowledge-management champion has responsibility for the information infrastructure as well as ensuring the appropriate use of data for decision making. The champion should coordinate activities through-

out the organization involving data collection, accuracy, analysis, retrieval, and use for decision making. The champion should ensure:

- Complete data are available and aligned to strategic goals, objectives, and action plans to ensure performance against these goals, objectives, and action plans can be effectively monitored.

- Systems are in place to collect and use comparative data and information to support strategy development, goal setting, and performance improvement.

- Data and information throughout the organization are accurate and reliable to enhance fact-based decision making.

- Data and information are used to support a better understanding of the cost and financial impacts of various improvement options.

- Appropriate correlations and performance projections are available to support strategic planning.

- The performance-measurement system is evaluated and improved to ensure it meets business needs.

- Data analysis supports the senior executives' organizational performance review and organizational planning.

- Data analysis addresses the overall health of the organization.

- Information, data, and supporting analyses are available to workgroup and functional-level operations to support decision making at those levels.

- Data analysis supports daily decisions regarding operations throughout the organization to ensure actions align with plans.

- Information management systems, including hardware and software, are easy to use, reliable, and regularly updated to keep them current with changing decision-making needs. Data in these systems are correct (accurate), consistent (reliable), complete (integrity), free from tampering or inappropriate disclosure (secure and confidential), and available when needed (timely).

Finally, the champion must work as part of an organization-wide council to help coordinate all facets of the management system to drive high performance.

Human Resource-Focus Champion

The *human resource-focus champion* is an executive-level person who, in addition to other executive duties, coordinates and enhances systems to enable employees to develop and utilize their full potential, consistent with the organization's strategic objectives. This includes building and maintaining a work environment conducive to full employee participation and growth. It is both a strategic and an operational activity.

From the strategic side, the human resource constraints of the organization must be considered in the development of strategy, and subsequently eliminated to ensure the workforce is capable of achieving the strategies necessary for business success.

From the operational side, the champion should ensure that the work climate enhances employee satisfaction and well-being and that work is organized and jobs are designed to enable employees to achieve higher levels of performance.

The human resource-focus champion has responsibility for ensuring that employees' (including managers and supervisors at all levels, permanent, temporary, and part-time personnel, and contract employees and volunteers supervised by the organization) needs are met to enable them to contribute fully to the organization's goals and objectives. The champion should ensure:

- Work and jobs are structured to promote cooperation, collaboration, individual initiative, innovation, and flexibility.

- An effective system exists to provide accurate feedback about employee performance and to enhance their performance that is aligned with strategic objectives. This includes systems to identify skill gaps and recruit or reassign employees to close those gaps, as well as to ensure that fair work practices are followed within the organization. This may also include evaluating managers and enhancing their ability to provide accurate feedback and effective coaching to improve employee performance.

- Compensation, recognition, and rewards are aligned to support high-performance and customer-focused objectives of the organization (contained in strategic plans and action plans and reported in the balanced scorecard or business results report card).

- Support business objectives and building employee knowledge, skills, and capabilities to enhance employee career progression and performance. This includes ensuring employees understand tools and techniques of performance measurement, performance improvement, quality control methods, and benchmarking. This also includes ensuring that managers and supervisors reinforce knowledge and skills on the job.

- The work environment is safe, with measurable performance measures and targets for each key factor affecting employee safety.

- Factors that affect employee well-being, satisfaction, and motivation are routinely measured and actions are taken promptly to improve conditions that adversely affect morale, motivation, productivity, and other related business results.

Finally, the champion must work as part of an organization-wide council to help coordinate all facets of the management system to drive high performance.

Process-Management Champion

The *process-management champion* is an executive-level person who, in addition to other executive duties, coordinates and enhances all aspects of the organization's systems to manage and improve work processes to meet the organization's strategic objectives. This includes activities and processes to create value for customers and other stakeholders and involves customer-focused design, product and service delivery, and internal support services. It is both a strategic and operational activity.

From the strategic side, rapid and accurate design, development, and delivery of products and services create a competitive advantage in the marketplace.

From the operational side, the champion should work to ensure all key work processes are examined and optimized to achieve higher levels of performance, reduce cycle time and costs, and subsequently add to organizational profitability.

The process-management champion has responsibility for creating a process-management orientation within the organization. Since all work is a process, the process-management champion must ensure that the process owners (including other champions) systematically examine, improve, and execute their processes consistently. The champion should ensure:

- Systematic continuous improvement activities are embedded in all processes, which lead to ongoing refinements.

- Initial and ongoing customer requirements are incorporated into all product and service designs, production and delivery systems, and processes. This includes core production processes as well as key business (such as research and development, asset management, technology acquisition, and supply chain management) and internal support processes (such as finance and accounting, facilities management, administration, procurement, and personnel).

- Design, production, and delivery processes are structured and analyzed to reduce cycle time; increase the use of learning from past projects or other parts of the organization; reduce costs; increase the use of new technology and other effectiveness or efficiency factors; and ensure all products and services meet performance requirements.

Finally, the champion must work as part of an organization-wide council to help coordinate all facets of the management system to drive high performance.

Results Champion

The *results champion* is an executive-level person who, in addition to other executive duties, coordinates the display of the organization's business results. This champion has substantially different work than the champions for Categories 1 through 6. No actions leading to or resulting from the performance-outcome data are championed by the results champion. Those actions are driven by the Category 1 through 6 champions because they have responsibility for taking action to implement and deploy procedures necessary to produce the business results.

For example, the measurement, analysis and knowledge management champion (Category 4) is responsible for collecting data that reflect all areas of strategic importance leading to business results. The measurement, analysis and knowledge-management champion is also responsible for ensuring data accuracy and reliability.

The results champion is responsible, however, for ensuring that the organization is able to display all business results required by Category 7 to provide evidence of the organization's performance improvement in key business areas and facilitate monitoring by leaders. These include product and service performance, customer satisfaction, financial and marketplace performance, human resource results, operational performance, and leadership and social responsibility.

Results must be displayed by appropriate segment and group, such as different customer groups, market segments, employee groups, or supplier groups. Appropriate comparison data must be included in the business-results display to judge the relative *goodness* or *strength* of the results achieved. These results are used by senior leaders to monitor organizational performance.

Finally, the results champion must work as part of an organization-wide council to help coordinate all facets of the management system to drive high performance. For example, if the organization is not collecting data necessary for inclusion in the business results report card, the results champion coordinates work with the other champions on the council to ensure those data are available, used for decision making, and included in appropriate reports.

The Critical Skills

A uniform message, set of skills or core competencies, and constancy of purpose are critical to success. Core training should provide all employees the knowledge and skills on which to build a learning organization that continually gets better. Such training typically includes team building, leadership skills, consensus building, communications, and effective meeting management. These are necessary for effective teams to become involved in solving critical problems.

Another important core skill involves using a common process to define customer requirements accurately, determine the ability to meet those requirements, measure success, and determine the extent to which customers—internal and external—are satisfied. When a problem arises, employees must be able to define the problem correctly, isolate the root causes, generate and select the best solution to eliminate the root causes, and implement the best solution.

It is also important to be able to understand data and make decisions based on facts, not merely intuition or feelings. Therefore, familiarity with tools to analyze work processes and performance data is important. With these tools, work processes can be analyzed and vastly improved. Reducing unnecessary steps in work processes, increasing process consistency, reducing variability, and reducing cycle time are powerful ways to improve quality and reduce cost simultaneously.

Courses in techniques to acquire comparison and benchmarking data, work-process improvement and reengineering, supplier partnerships and certification, role modeling for leaders, strategic planning, team building, and customer satisfaction and loyalty will help managers and employees increase their effectiveness.

LESSONS LEARNED

General Lessons

Twenty years ago the fierce global competition that inspired the quality movement in the United States was felt primarily by major manufacturers. Today, all sectors are under intense pressure to "be the best or be history." The demand for performance excellence reaches all corners of the economy, from manufacturing and service industries to professional services, education, healthcare, public utilities, and government. All of these segments have contributed valuable lessons to the quality movement and have played an important part in our recovery from the economic slump of the 1970s caused by poor service and products. Relying on the Baldrige model, I will share some of the insights and lessons learned from leaders of high-performing organizations.

Desire and History Are Not Enough

It is important to point out a fact that is perhaps obvious to most: *In order to optimize organizational performance, organizations must actually use the principles contained in the Baldrige Criteria.* It is not enough to think about them. It is not enough to have used them in the past and no longer continue to do so. It is not enough to use a part but not all of the Criteria. To leave out any part suboptimizes the performance of the organization.

The experience of Xerox provides a useful example. Xerox won the Baldrige Award in 1989. They demonstrated significant performance improvement through the 1980s and continued to grow substantially through the 1990s. They used the Baldrige Criteria as the way they ran their business, not just a list of additional activities they would do if they felt like it. They were absolutely customer-focused. They made decisions based on data, and fully engaged and involved their entire workforce. They continuously evaluated and improved their effectiveness in every aspect of their work. In fact, one business unit, Xerox Business Services (XBS), which makes copies of and manages documents, won the Baldrige Award again in 1997. The performance of XBS was similar to Xerox as a whole. In 1989, XBS, with a few hundred employees, generated approximately $300 million in annual revenue. They worked so efficiently and satisfied customers so well that their market grew from $300 million in 1989 to approximately $2 billion in 1997 and to approximately $6 billion in 2000.

However, the new Xerox CEO, Richard Thoman (a transplant from IBM who replaced Paul Allaire), did not use the Baldrige Criteria to provide the leadership needed to maintain the customer focus and bring the company into the emerging digital market. Within a year and a half Xerox performance plummeted. So did its stock price, losing approximately 80 percent of its value. The Xerox board of directors, after firing Thoman and rehiring the previous CEO and other senior leaders, has been struggling to rebuild the processes and systems that led Xerox to high levels of performance excellence in the past. However, it will take the company years to recover.

The Xerox story points out an important lesson. While using the Baldrige Criteria can help an organization reach high levels of performance, organizations cannot expect to *sustain* those levels of performance without continuing to use the Criteria as the way they run the business. High-performing athletes of all types know this lesson well. To continue to win, they cannot rest on the success of the past. To continue to win, world-class athletes must continue to follow the discipline of training, diet, and effective coaching, and take advantage of technological advances in equipment. The same is true in any competitive environment.

A Tale of Two Leaders

It was a time of turbulence; it was a time of peace. It was a time of growth and streamlining. It was the happiest of times; it was also the most painful of times. Most of all it was a time that demanded change—although it was more comfortable to consider it a time for the status quo.

The following tales are of two leaders. One is consistent and persistent in communicating the direction and message that will bring about excellent results and high performance. Another is uncertain and vague. He does not wish to push his people into anything, let alone the significant commitment required to use the Baldrige Criteria as the way to run the business. After all, the business is still profitable and healthy. Why rock the boat? You may know these

people or someone who reminds you of them. If so, you will understand the reason for this section.

There is no lonelier, more challenging, yet critical and rewarding job than that of the leader. I work with many, many leaders who listen to advice carefully. They really want to know the best approaches to optimize their organizations. Yet what they do with the advice and counsel is always interesting and unpredictable. This section is intended to help those leaders go resolutely down the right path.

Neither leader exists in real life, but both leader profiles are based on actual events and observations of different people in leadership positions.

Tale One

John was the CEO of a *Fortune 500* manufacturing company that was slowly but surely losing market share. Shareholders and employees were happy because profits and growth, although slower, were still hearty. However, their business that once enjoyed a near monopoly position was rapidly facing more and more competition. Customers who had to beg and plead for limited products and service over the years were happily turning to competitors that were trying in earnest to meet their needs and even delight them. In such an environment, aggressive, customer-focused companies were winning the hearts, minds, and pocketbooks of John's customers. After working with a consulting firm or two and studying the work of W. Edwards Deming, John decided that performance excellence was urgently needed to keep the company in business more than five years.

The First Message to the Leadership Team
John called an urgent meeting of his senior team. Many members of this team had been there since the company began its 20-year growth spurt and had been good soldiers in times of runaway growth and profit. John was wondering how many members of the senior staff would welcome the message he was about to send. The meeting was scheduled the next week for five days at the corporate headquarters. Short of an emergency illness, attendance was required.

During the next few days, John received 20 phone calls from secretaries who informed John their bosses could not attend because of other priority commitments. Priorities were quickly realigned when they were informed that attendance was not optional.

The week-long meeting began with training—the kind of training in which the group was required to participate, listen, and discuss the content. The training was presented by an outside firm with frequent discussions of company-wide application and emphasis presented by John. At the end of three days, John took over the meeting and asked for input on how best to apply these principles to the organization at all levels. The leadership group voiced resistance to change, some more than others. They basically voiced concern that "this performance excellence stuff with all of its requirements for empowerment and data" would get in the way of their doing business and was not needed.

John clarified the objectives of the group by walking to the white board and writing: "This new program, performance excellence, is in the way of doing business effectively." The senior staff pretty much agreed.

John responded by placing a large *X* through the word *in*. The statement now read, "Performance excellence is the way of doing business effectively." John notified the attendees, "I will negotiate an exit package with anyone who does not understand the implications of this message, and who does not want to be part of this new way of doing business." John learned that day that to institute meaningful change, it may be necessary to fire someone he liked. He also realized that to ignore the challenges and lack of commitment would be seen by everyone as tacit approval and send the message that the new way of doing business was *optional*.

The Next Steps

John focused on two next steps: 1) making sure his top team role-modeled behavior that would facilitate the needed changes; and 2) planning and implementing a company-wide training requirement to communicate the new skills and performance expectations. John started to change his behavior and the behavior of his top staff, feeling that *walking the talk* would signal the importance of new behaviors more than any speech or videotaped presentation. The next top staff meeting was called within a week to plan the design and rollout of training corporate-wide, including all foreign and domestic sites. The top staff had very little interest in training, feeling largely that this was a human resource function and should be dele-

gated to that department. Based on the advice of external advisors, John informed the staff that it was now their job to plan, design, and execute this training. A *core design team* was formed with senior leaders and expert-content and course-design specialists to design the training within one month and present it to the senior corporate leaders.

In spite of prior agreements to manage their meetings effectively, to be on time, not interrupt, and follow the agenda, most continued to ignore the rules. Behaviors of the top leadership group at this meeting included the usual set of interruptions, "I told you so's," and everyone talking at the same time. John, whose goal was to create a listening and learning environment, challenged the group to "ante up." He asked that all top leaders bring 50 $20 bills to the meeting. John introduced new meeting ground rules. They were simple. Interruptions, put downs, blocking behaviors, and talking over someone else were violations of meeting ground rules. On the other hand, building on ideas, clarifying ideas, supporting, and disagreeing respectfully were good meeting behaviors. Every violation was worth a $20 bill. Good meeting behaviors were rewarded, although they did not materialize until several meetings had been completed.

At first, it seemed that the pot would win big time—no one took John seriously. After about the third meeting, with penalties piling up, leadership group participants' behavior actually changed. Other meeting-management skills were slowly introduced, such as time-frame limits and action planning. Then John was confident his team could role-model this behavior to others. He ordered that, "This is the way we treat each other at all meetings, including staff meetings, communication forums, and all company business meetings." A core value and new behavior of courtesy and professionalism became deployed company-wide through the senior management team.

Training and the Change Process

Each five-day, high-performance management course was identical, ensuring that a uniform message and set of skills were communicated. Each course was eventually taught by two instructors, a shop supervisor and a manager, so that management and the workforce would both be involved. John personally taught the top leadership team the entire five-day course, assisted by a member of the design team, and this tale spread across the organization like wildfire. It became the thing to be invited to take part in this instruction because their leader had done it. The core skills became part of the fabric of the organization—the way to conduct business. They included fact-based decisions, a focus on customers, and using and improving processes. Also included was a way to solve problems continually with a well-defined process at the level the problem was occurring.

The focus had shifted from status quo to a thirst for improvement. Improvement began to bring rewards whereas the status quo was disdained. A comprehensive business evaluation was conducted and improvement targets were identified. Clear assignments with reasonable but aggressive goals were cascaded to all levels of the organization. Performance planning, goals, compensation, and recognition were aligned to support the overall business strategy, especially the need to focus better on satisfying internal and external customers. Managers who did not work to meet these new goals, who did not role-model the behaviors necessary to achieve high performance, were reassigned to jobs that did not require their management skills. New role models emerged to lead the organization at all levels. Within three years the company regained market share, improved profitability, expanded its employee base, and became, once again, one of the world's most admired companies.

Tale Two

Victor was the CEO of a West Coast manufacturing company that also was a proud member of the *Fortune 500.* Company performance had been uneven over the past few years. Profits were low this year relative to previous years, but the company still met financial targets. Product demands were high and the outlook was fairly good for the next quarter. The industry as a whole was fairly evenly matched as far as management problems. Trends for return on investment were also uneven, and other indicators such as sales volume and net profit were up and down. Investors were not happy, especially when other companies consistently outperformed theirs. Victor thought it was time to do something different. Victor consulted several valuable and trusted advisors and then decided that high-performance excellence might be worth considering.

The First Message to the Leadership Team

Victor scheduled a series of weekly dinner meetings over the next month (January) and engaged several top consultants to talk to the group about the business case for using high-performance management. He invited 50 top-level managers from across the country to attend. Most top leaders attended the meetings, enjoyed the dinners, and Victor attended most but not all of them. The sessions were interesting—the top leaders found the meetings were a great forum for politicking, posturing, wining and dining, and trying to sharpshoot the consultant. Victor asked his top leaders to come together for a half day in the spring to discuss the content and direction of the high-performance initiative, being convinced intellectually by the dinner discussions that this was the right direction for the company. At the half-day meeting, it was obvious that about half of the group agreed with the CEO and about half were uncertain or downright resistant, particularly one very senior vice president. Victor left the team with this message, "Let me take your comments under advisement and think about them as we go forward." Later, at the consultant's suggestion, he conducted an organizational assessment to identify problems that might be contributory to the uneven, up-and-down performance. The assessment uncovered several serious problems that required change, yet the senior leaders continued to resist.

The Next Steps

Victor finally hired one of the external advisors who had withstood the test of several dinner meetings and the challenges of his threatened senior management team. Victor asked the advisor to speak to the top leaders of the entire company about what a great group they were and how important the performance excellence initiative was going to be for the company. The advisor closed by telling them that only the best go after high performance; if they did not, their competitors would. During the following discussion sessions, Victor's chief operating officer (COO) announced to the group that he was far from convinced and stated he was not going to change the way he did business. That comment went unchallenged by Victor or anyone else in the company. Frustration continued to build.

In an effort to regain momentum, Victor wanted to create a change team. He asked each division to send a person to *facilitate* the initiative and receive appropriate training in managing change. The people selected were far from the best each division could offer since no selection criteria had been provided and many thought this was a waste of time and talent. The division leaders supplied people who were expendable. The people who formed the facilitator group, for their part, were very enthusiastic but not particularly respected or credible. They were given absolutely no relief from any regular duties so they were stretched very thin. Also, the division heads were not supportive in any way of their participation, so they were almost punished for participating on this team. As the facilitators worked to please the demands of the CEO, there was no clear charter or mission as to what they were actually supposed to accomplish—no way to assess their performance or keep track of progress.

The power struggle intensified between the COO (who thought this was not the way to go and would have none of it) and the CEO. The CEO and the top management team arranged to travel to a leadership conference where they could hear presentations from high-performance organizations that had used the performance excellence techniques successfully. The CEO made it a priority to plan only morning presentations so everyone could play tennis or golf together each afternoon. Tennis and golf, not the need for better management systems, was the main topic of discussion at the evening dinners. A good time was had by all, but no consensus around change developed or was even discussed.

Training and the Change Process

Still, Victor wanted the facilitators to continue their work to assist change. The internal facilitators were placed in charge of conducting training for the entire organization. After the initial training was designed, a date was set to present a half-day version to the senior staff. Although the training designed for employees and lower-level managers was a four-day course, the senior staff did not feel they needed the same intense training or skills as the workforce. However, Victor made it a high priority for his direct reports to attend. At the last minute, Victor had to attend a function related to the board of directors and did not attend the training.

The training was, to put it mildly, a disaster. The executives, prompted by the snide comments of the COO, never gave it a chance. They concluded that the training was not effective and should not be rolled out to the employees. In the face of compelling opposition, Victor quietly diverted his attention elsewhere.

Leadership Style Summary

It is probably obvious what is the current state of John's high-performance *way to run the business* versus the high-performance *initiative* at Victor's company. Perhaps you could spot some of the problems each type of leader addressed and solutions they supported.

Using symbols and language to manage the change to high performance is tricky and usually demands that some external person be involved who can provide good sound advice, based on experience and expertise, to the CEO. Using power constructively is absolutely critical, since failure of the top leader to use all forms of power and influence available will intensify conflict and power struggles that act as a *de facto* barrier to change.

Motivating people to act constructively, and not feel threatened, is another challenge. Providing a clear focus on the future state while rewarding behavior that facilitates the transition will work to ensure the change actually happens. Victor's vision was unclear. He did not act as a leader. He ensured his facilitators would never succeed by never championing their work in any way. The next time Victor gets a new idea, these people (if they are still employees) will take a nosedive rather than be at the forefront of the initiative.

John never lost his vision or influence as CEO. He ensured his management team was supportive by first defining and clarifying organizational values, direction, and expectations; encouraging them to climb on board; and ensuring they acquired the skills and support to spread the approaches throughout the company.

Leadership Lessons

Based on the CEO research cited earlier, coupled with the relentless pace of change in all sectors and increasingly global competition, there are several strong messages leaders need to understand. Then they must be willing to take the necessary steps to change. This will require an assessment of current management systems and a willingness to drive the necessary adjustment. Once the assessment is complete and priorities are agreed upon, line up plans and resources and support the change wholeheartedly. Focus on the marketplace for your cues to change. Ask, for example:

- Is your competition growing weaker?

- Is the economy more stable and secure?

- Are the demands of your customers declining?

- Do you have all of the resources you need to meet your current and future goals?

- Do you believe your employees will be willing or able to continue working at the pace you have set for them? Will they do more?

If the answer is no to any of these questions, read on. Assess management systems and launch improvements. This will require your organization to assess its management systems against the Baldrige Criteria. After the assessment is complete, identify the vital few next steps, assign responsibility, make improvements, and reevaluate.

Great Leaders Are Great Communicators Who Lead by Example

One characteristic of a high-performance organization is outstanding performance results. How does an organization achieve such results? How does it become world-class? We have found unanimous agreement on the critical and fundamental role of leadership. There is not one example of an organization or unit within an organization that achieves superior levels of performance without the personal and active involvement of its top leadership. Similarly, in all cases where an organization has not been able to achieve or sustain high performance, the cause can be traced to leadership failures.

Top leaders in high-performing organizations create a powerful vision that focuses and energizes the workforce. They drive change and innovation. Everyone is pulling together toward the same goals. An inspired vision, combined with appropriately aligned recognition and reward, is the catalyst that

builds trust and launches initiatives to overcome the organizational *status quo.*

Great leaders also communicate clear objectives. They assign accountability, ensure that employees have the tools and skills required, and create a work climate where individual initiative and the transfer of learning thrive. They reward teamwork and data-driven improvement. Practicing what they preach, they serve as role models for continuous improvement, consensus building, and fact-based decision making. They push authority and accountability to the lowest possible levels.

One lesson from great leaders is to refrain from the use of the word *quality*. Unfortunately, the use of the word quality can create an unintended barrier of mistrust and negativism that leaders must overcome before even starting on the road to performance excellence. Too often, when skilled, hard-working, dedicated employees are told by leaders, "We must improve quality," they conclude that their leaders believe their work is poor. They frequently retort with, "We already do quality work!" Registered professionals (engineers, chemists, psychologists, physicians, teachers, to name a few) often exacerbate the communication problem by arguing that they, not customers, are the best ones in a position to know and define quality. These messages confuse the workforce.

Instead, we advise leaders to create a work climate that enables employees to develop and use their full potential, to improve continually the way they work—to seek higher performance levels and reduce activities that do not add value or optimize performance.

Most employees readily agree that there is always room for improvement—all have seen work that does not add value.

The use of the word *quality* can also open leadership to challenges as to what definition of quality the organization should use. This leads to our second lesson learned. Leaders will have to overcome two organizational tendencies—to reject any management model or approach *not invented here* and to think that there are many equally valid models. Quality differs from a decision tree or problem-solving model where there are many acceptable alternatives. The Baldrige model—and the many national, state, and organization assessment systems based on it—is accepted as *the* standard for defining performance excellence in organizations worldwide. Its criteria define validated, leading-edge practices for managing an organization to achieve peak performance.

Sixteen years of extraordinary business results shown by Baldrige Award recipients and numerous state-level, Baldrige-based Award recipients have helped convince those willing to learn and listen.

To be effective, leaders must understand the Baldrige model of performance excellence and communicate to the workforce and leadership system their decision to use that model for assessment and improvement. Without clear, unwavering leadership commitment to achieving the requirements of the comprehensive Baldrige model, resources may be wasted chasing fads, special projects, and isolated strategies. Although programs such as activity-based costing, management by objective, reengineering, project management, quality circles, balanced score-cards, Six Sigma, Lean thinking, and ISO 9000 certification, to name a few, have produced some good results, unless leaders focus on the entire system, performance is not optimized.

Without clear leadership there will be many *hikers* walking around but no marked trails for them to follow. Unless leaders understand the entire system and take their responsibility for transforming the workplace, performance optimization is not attainable. This brings us to our third leadership lesson learned.

A significant portion of senior leaders' time—as much as 60 to 80 percent—should be spent in visible Baldrige-related leadership activities such as goal setting, planning, reviewing performance, recognizing and rewarding high performance, and spending time understanding and communicating with customers and suppliers, not micromanaging subordinates' work. In setting goals, planning, and reviewing performance, senior leaders must look at the inside from the outside. Looking at the organization through the critical eyes of external customers, suppliers, and other stakeholders is a vital perspective.

A key role of the effective senior leader is to focus the organization on satisfying customers through an effective leadership system. Leaders must champion change. They must role-model the tools of performance excellence and ensure the organization focuses on its vision, mission, and strategic direction to keep customers loyal.

Listen

Successful leaders know the power in listening to their people—those they rely on to achieve their goals. One vital link to the pulse of the organization is employee feedback. To determine whether what you have said has been understood, ask for feedback and then listen carefully. To know whether what you have outlined as a plan makes sense or has gaping faults, ask for feedback and then listen. Your leadership system cannot improve without your listening and acting on employee feedback, and your goals and action plans cannot be improved without it. In fact, the 2006 Baldrige Criteria [Item 1.2a(2), Note 3] suggests that leaders use employee feedback in assessing and improving their effectiveness and the effectiveness of managers at all levels.

Manage and Drive Change

Business leaders can count on relentless, rapid change being part of the business world. The rate of change confronting business today is far greater than ever before. Skills born out of the Industrial Revolution carried our parents through a 40-year work life. Human knowledge now doubles every five years, instead of the 40 years it took in the mid- to late-twentieth century. Today, our children are told to expect five career (not job) changes during their work life.

There are several lessons for leaders today. Change may not occur on the schedule they set for it. It is often too fast or too uneven to predict at all. Also, change driven by leaders is often resisted by their most successful followers—they have difficulty seeing the need to change. Take, for example, a school district that scheduled a Baldrige-based improvement workshop for its middle school faculty. The day before the training, the district leadership received a letter protesting the workshop on the grounds it was not needed. The letter was signed by the 20 best teachers in the school. To the credit of the school district leadership, they held the workshop anyway, and the truly outstanding teachers saw the value in continuous improvement once they began to listen.

Leaders who share the values of high performance will need to drive change to make the necessary improvements. Change will not happen naturally. It is rarely driven by those at the bottom (except for revolutionaries). Embracing the concepts of organizational (not just individual) learning will facilitate change in the organization. Leaders will need to develop a system that drives new knowledge throughout the organization.

Strategic Planning Lessons

Deploy through People Not Paper

Strategic planning helps leaders examine the factors that will affect an organization's future. The resulting strategic plan must define the things the organization must accomplish or achieve to be successful in the future. The planning process should begin by ensuring that all contributors agree on terminology. Otherwise the strategic plan may be incomplete—a marketing plan, a budget plan, or a financial business plan, depending on who is leading the team. The resulting goals or strategic objectives *must* be defined in measurable, outcome-oriented terms.

Developing separate plans for each aspect of business success is counterproductive. This approach almost guarantees a nonintegrated and short-lived systematic performance-improvement effort. Therefore, leaders should concentrate on the few critical improvement goals in the strategic plan necessary for organizational success, such as improving customer loyalty and reducing waste, errors, or cycle time. The well-developed strategic plan also:

- Documents the financial and market impact of achieving these objectives.

- Details actions to support the objectives.

- Discusses the competitive environment.

- Specifies, in measurable terms, the expected performance milestones that must be met to achieve the goals. The milestones (or time lines) match the leaders' cycle for reviewing progress (that is, if leaders review progress quarterly, then the plan should predict quarterly outcome-oriented milestones).

The most critical lesson learned when it comes to strategic plans is that there can be no rest until everyone in the organization understands their role in the plan and how their contribution will be measured. The goals, actions, measures, and milestones need not be complex. For every unit, they can be presented as a one-page electronic scorecard, to which senior leaders refer each month during performance reviews. Everyone at all levels should be able to use their own one-page scorecard to deploy the plan, define actions needed, and monitor actual progress against expected progress.

Customer and Market Focus Lessons

Customers Expect Solutions to Problems They Don't Know They Have

The high-performing organization systematically determines its customers' short- and long-term service and product requirements. It does this based on information from former as well as current and potential customers. It builds relationships with customers and continuously obtains information, using the data to improve its service and products and better understand customer preferences. The smart organization prioritizes the drivers of satisfaction and loyalty of its customers, compares itself to its competitors (or organizations providing similar products or services), and continuously strives to improve customer satisfaction and loyalty.

As the organization becomes more systematic and effective in determining customer needs, it learns that there is high variation in customer needs. The more sophisticated the measurement system, the more variation will become apparent. It is particularly important that organizations focus on this vital process and make it a top priority that their customers have access to people to make known their requirements and their preferences. How else can modern organizations ensure they are building relationships with their customers? After all, few of us have storefront windows on Main Street where our customers come and chat regularly.

One specific lesson learned comes from voice mail—a big step forward in convenience and efficiency can be a big step backward in customer relationship building if used poorly. For example, a major international financial institution put its highest priority customers on a new voice-mail system. Customers were never informed about the system and one day called their special line to find rock music and a multi-tiered voice-menu system instead of their personal financial account manager. These preferred customers were furious even though the phone was answered on the first ring. This is a good example of a step in the wrong direction—customers were never asked about their requirements and preferences, and the organization lost accounts and created many frustrated customers.

Another important first lesson is to segment customers according to their needs and preferences and do what is necessary to build strong, positive relationships with them. More and more customers are looking for service providers to help define their unique needs and respond to those unique needs. In short, customers are expecting solutions to problems that they, the customers, have not yet realized.

Organizations that make it easy for customers to complain are in a good position to hear about problems early so they can fix them and plan ahead to prevent them. If organizations handle customer complaints effectively at the first point of contact, customer loyalty and satisfaction will increase. When organizations do not make it easy for customers to complain, when finally given the chance to provide feedback customers may not bother to complain, but simply no longer do business with these organizations.

The next lesson has to do with educating the organization's leadership in the fundamentals of customer loyalty and customer-satisfaction research models before beginning to collect customer-satisfaction data. Failure to do this may affect the usefulness of the data as a strategic tool. At the very least, it will make the development of data-collection instruments a long, misunderstood effort, creating rework and unnecessary cost.

Do not expect everyone in your organization to welcome customer feedback—many fear accountability. Time and time again, the organizations most resistant to surveying customers, conducting focus groups, and making it easy for customers to complain are the same organizations that do not have everyday contact-handling systems, response-time standards, or trained and empowered front-line employees to serve customers and resolve their concerns promptly. Front-line employees who do not have sufficient decision-making authority and are not ready to acknowledge customer concerns are not capable of assuming responsibility to solve customer problems.

No single customer-feedback tool is sufficient by itself. A mail-based survey does not take the place of personal interviews. Focus groups do not replace surveys. The high-performance organization uses multiple listening posts and trains front-line employees to collect customer feedback and improve those listening posts. In the high-performance organization, for example, even an accounts-receivable system is viewed as a listening post.

Do not lose sight of the fact that the best customer-feedback method, whether it be a survey, focus group, or one-on-one interview, is only a tool:

- Make sure the data gathered are actionable

- Aggregate the data from all sources to permit complete analyses

- Use the data to improve work processes and strategic planning

Finally, be aware that customers are not interested in your problems. They merely want products or services delivered as promised. They become loyal when consistent value is provided that sets you above all others. Merely meeting their basic expectations brands you as marginal. To be valued you must consistently delight and exceed the customers' expectations.

Measurement, Analysis, and Knowledge-Management Lessons

Data-Driven Management and Avoiding Contephobia

The high-performance organization collects, manages, and analyzes data and information to drive excellence and improve its overall performance. Said another way, information is used to drive actions and build accountability. Using data and information as strategic weapons, effective leaders constantly compare their organization to competitors, similar service providers, and world-class organizations. They identify shortfalls in their own organization as a result, and take action to close the gaps.

While people tend to think of data and measurement as objective and hard, there is often a softer by-product of measurement. That by-product is the basic human emotion of fear. This perspective on data and measurement leads to the first lesson learned about measurement, analysis, and knowledge management. Human fear must be recognized and managed in order to practice data-driven management.

This fear can be found in two types of people. The first are those who have a simple fear of numbers—those who hated mathematics in school and probably stretch their quantitative capabilities to balance their checkbook. These individuals are lost in numerical-data discussions. When asked to measure or when presented with data, they can become fearful, resistant, or even angry. These reactions can undermine improvement efforts.

The second type of individual, who may be comfortable with numbers, realizes that numbers can impose higher levels of accountability. The fear of accountability, *contephobia* (from 14th-century Latin *to count,* modified by the French *to account*), is based on the fear of real performance failure that numbers might reveal or, more often, an overall fear of the unknown that will drive important decisions. Power structures can and do shift when decisions are data driven.

Fearful individuals can undermine effective data-driven management systems. In managing this fear, leaders must demonstrate that system and process improvement is the goal, not punishing individuals.

A mature, high-performance organization will collect data on competitors and similar providers and benchmark itself against world-class leaders. Some individuals may not be capable of seeing the benefit of using this process-performance information. The process of collecting these types of data is known as benchmarking. The focus is on identifying, learning from, and adopting best practices or methods from similar processes, regardless of industry or product similarity. Adopting the best practices of other organizations has driven breakthrough improvements and provided great opportunities for gaining a competitive advantage.

Lesson number two, therefore, is that an organization that has difficulty comparing itself with dissimilar organizations is not ready to benchmark and is not likely to be able to optimize or even improve its own performance as a result.

The third lesson in this area relates to not being a DRIP. This refers to a tendency to collect so much data (which contributes to contephobia) that the organization becomes d̲ata r̲ich and i̲nformation p̲oor. This is wrong. Avoid wasting capital resources by asking this question: "Will these data help us make better decisions?" If the answer is no, do not waste time collecting, analyzing, or trying to use the data. Ideally, data should not be collected unless it supports decision making.

Human Resource Lessons

Human Resources (Broad Concept, Not the Internal Department)

Personnel departments have been renamed in many organizations to *human resources.* This name change is intended to draw attention to the fact that people are valuable resources of the organization, not just dispensable commodities to be hired, commanded, and fired. Now, however, the leap made by successful organizations is that human resources need to be part of every strategic and operational decision of the organization. This focus goes far beyond the department of human resources. In high-performing organizations, employees are treated like any valuable asset—and investment and development are critical to optimize the asset.

One of the valuable lessons learned in this regard is not to let an out-of-date or territorial personnel or human resources department use archaic rules to stop your performance-improvement program. Although many human resources professionals are among the brave pioneers in high-performance organizations, others have tried to keep compensation and promotions tied to length of service, seniority, or tenure rather than performance. This outdated approach will definitely stop progress in its tracks or slow it significantly.

The Big Challenge Is Trust

The high-performing organization values its employees and demonstrates this by enabling them to develop and realize their full potential while providing them incentives to do so. The organization that is focused on human resource excellence maintains a climate that builds trust. Trust is essential for employee participation, engagement, personal and professional growth, and high organizational performance.

The first human resource lesson is perhaps the most critical one. That is, revise—overhaul, if necessary—recognition, compensation, promotion, and feedback systems to align with and support high-performance work systems, a customer focus, and strategic objectives. If leaders personally demonstrate all the correct leadership behaviors, yet continue to recognize and reward *fire-fighting* performance, offer pay and bonuses tied only to traditional bottom-line results, and promote individuals who do not represent high-performance role models—their organization-wide improvement effort will be short lived.

Promotion, compensation, recognition, and reward must be tied to the achievement of key high-performance outcomes, such as customer satisfaction, innovation, performance improvement, and other business results. The promotion/compensation/recognition tool is a powerful lever to assist in aligning, or misaligning, the work of the organization.

Developing and Maintaining Skills

A second human resource lesson learned relates to training and development. Training is not a panacea or a goal in itself. The organization's direction and goals must support training, and training must support organization priorities as set forth in strategic objectives and related action plans. Training must be part of an overall business strategy. If not, money and resources are probably better spent on a memorable holiday party.

Timing is critical. Broad-based workforce skill training should not come first. Many organizations rush out and train their entire workforce only to find themselves having to retrain months or years later. Key participants should be involved in developing training plans and schedules to ensure workers develop important skills just in time to use them in their assignments.

Continuous skill development requires management support to reinforce the use of new skills on the job. Training must be offered when an application exists to use and reinforce the skill. Otherwise, most of what is learned will be forgotten. The effectiveness of training must be assessed based on the extent of learning and impact on the job, not merely the likability of the instructor or the clarity of course materials.

Leadership development at all levels of the organization needs to be built into employee development.

New technology has increased training flexibility so that all knowledge does not have to be transferred in a classroom setting. Consider many options when planning how best to update skills.

Employee Satisfaction

Empowered, satisfied employees enhance organizational productivity, customer satisfaction, and financial success.

Employee surveys are often used to measure and identify weaknesses in employee satisfaction that may disrupt employee productivity. Surveys are especially useful to identify key issues that should be discussed in open employee forums. Such forums are truly useful if they clarify perceptions, provide more in-depth understanding of employee concerns, and open the communication channels with leaders. Organizations have success in improving employee satisfaction by conducting routine employee-satisfaction surveys, promptly meeting with employees to plan improvements, and tying improvements in satisfaction ratings to managers' compensation/recognition.

Two final human resource excellence lessons have to do with engaging and involving employees in decisions about their work. Involving employees in decision making without the right skills or a sense of direction produces chaos, not high performance.

- First, leaders who empower employees before communicating and testing that a sense of direction has been fully understood and that the necessary skills are in place will find that they are managing chaos—employees moving in different directions, working at cross-purposes.

- Second, not everyone wants to be empowered, and to do so may represent a barrier to high performance. While there may be individuals who truly seek to avoid responsibility for making improvements, claiming "that's management's job," these individuals do not last long in a high-performing organization. They begin to stick out like a lone bird during a cold and snowy winter. Team members who want the organization to thrive do not permit such people to influence (or even remain on) their team.

The bigger reason for individuals failing to *take empowerment and run with it* is management's mixed messages. In short, management must convince employees that they (managers) really believe that employees know their own processes and, with proper training and support, are best suited to make decisions about their work. Consistent leadership is required to help employees overcome legitimate, long-standing fear of traditional management practices used so often in the past to control and punish.

Remember, aligning compensation and reward systems to reinforce performance plans and core values is one of the most critical means to enhance organizational performance; however, getting employees to believe their leaders really trust them to make decisions and improve their own processes is difficult.

Process Management Lessons

Listen to Process Owners and Keep Them Involved

Process management involves the continuous improvement of processes required to meet customer requirements and deliver quality products and services. Virtually every high-performance organization identifies its key value-creation processes and manages them to ensure that customer requirements are met consistently and performance is improved continuously.

The first lesson learned has to do with the visibility of processes. Many processes are highly visible, such as serving a meal or purchasing. However, when processes are hard to observe as so many are in the service sector (for example, service design or customer response), they are hard to improve. The simple exercise of drawing a process-flow diagram with people involved in a process can be a struggle, but also a valuable source of information that can help identify process shortfalls and improvement opportunities. With no vantage point from which to see work as a process, many people never think of themselves as engaged in a process. Some even deny it. The fact that all work—visible and invisible—is part of a process should be understood before employees can begin to execute and improve key processes consistently.

Once this is understood, a second process management lesson comes to light. Process owners are the best ones, but not the only ones, to improve their

processes. They should be part of process-improvement teams, but outsiders should be involved as well. Effective process-improvement teams are often made up of carefully selected cross-discipline, cross-functional, multilevel people who bring detailed inner knowledge and fresh insight to the examination of a process. Do not lose sight of the process owner—the person with expert knowledge of the process who should be accountable for long-term improvement to it. In a misguided effort to ensure that all of its process-improvement teams were cross-functional and multilevel, one organization enlisted volunteers to join process-improvement teams. Using this democratic process, one marketing process-improvement team ended up with no credible marketing expertise among its members. Instead, a group of frustrated support and technical staff members, who knew nothing about marketing, wasted time and money mapping and redesigning a process doomed to fail.

The third process management lesson learned involves an issue mentioned earlier. When focusing too closely on internal process data, there is a tendency to lose sight of external requirements. Organizations often succeed at making their processes better, faster, and (maybe) cheaper for them, but not necessarily to the benefit of their customers. When analyzing work processes, someone must stubbornly play the role of advocate for the customers' perspective. Ensure that process changes will help make improvements for customers, key financials, employees, or top result areas. Avoid wasting resources on process improvements that do not appropriately benefit customers, employees, or the key performance objectives of your organization.

A fourth lesson involves design processes, an important but often neglected part of process management. The best organizations have learned that improvements made early in the process, beginning with design, save more time and resources than those made farther *downstream*. To identify how design processes can be improved it is necessary to include ongoing evaluation and improvement cycles. Create a series of in-process measures to help spot and fix process failures early. Remember the lesson taught by one of the founding fathers of the United States, Benjamin Franklin, "A stitch in time saves nine." To save resources, find the hole and fix it quickly.

Results Lessons

The Right Activities Lead to Desired Results

Results fall into six equally important categories:

1. Product and service performance

2. Customer-focused, such as customer satisfaction and customer-perceived value product and service quality

3. Financial and market performance

4. Human resource performance

5. Organizational effectiveness such as key design, production, delivery, and support performance

6. Leadership effectiveness, such as the extent to which strategic objectives were achieved; regulatory and legal compliance, ethics, and fiscal accountability

Product and service quality results provide critical information on key measures of the product or service itself. This information allows an organization to predict whether customers are likely to be satisfied—without asking them. For example, one of the nation's most successful and fastest-growing coffee shops knows from its customers that a good cup of coffee is hot, has a good taste, is not too bitter, and has a rich aroma. The measures for these product characteristics are temperature, pH (acidity), and the time lapsed between brewing and serving. With these measures, they can predict whether their customers are likely to be satisfied with the coffee before they serve it. One important lesson in this area is to select measures that correlate with, and predict, customer preference, satisfaction, and loyalty.

Some organizations have found it beneficial to have their customers analyze some of their business results with the idea of learning from them as well as building and strengthening relationships. This may or may not be appropriate for your organization, but many successful ones have shared results with key customer groups at a level appropriate for their specific organization.

Systems must exist to make sure that results data are used at all levels to plan and make improvements. Customer-satisfaction data are particularly impor-

tant. Remember that when customers are asked their opinion, an expectation is created in their minds that the information will be used to make improvements that benefit them.

Financial and market performance is a key to survival. Organizations that make improvements that do not ultimately improve financial performance are wasting resources and growing weaker financially. This is true for for-profit and not-for-profit, education, healthcare, and government organizations. It is important to avoid overreliance on financial results. Financial results are the lagging indicators of organization performance. Leaders who focus primarily on lagging financial indicators often overlook problems or are not alerted in time to be able to respond to changing business needs. Focusing on finances to run the business—to the exclusion of leading indicators such as operational performance and employee satisfaction—is like driving your car by looking only in the rear-view mirror. You cannot avoid potholes and turns in the road.

Human resource performance results provide earlier alerts to problems that may threaten success. Absenteeism, turnover, accidents, low morale, grievances, poor skills, or ineffective training suboptimize organizational effectiveness. By monitoring performance in these areas, leaders can adjust more quickly and prevent minor problems from overwhelming the organization.

Organizational effectiveness and operational and service results pertain to measures of internal effectiveness that may not be of immediate interest to customers, such as cycle time (how long it takes to brew a pot of coffee), waste (how many pots you have to pour out because the coffee sat too long), and payroll accuracy (which may upset the affected workers). Ultimately, improving internal work-process efficiency can result in reduced cost, rework, waste, scrap, and other factors that affect the bottom line, whether profit-driven or budget-driven. In either case, customers are indirectly affected. To stay in business, to remain competitive, or to meet increased performance demands with fewer resources, the organization will be required to improve processes that enhance operational and support service results.

Regulatory and legal compliance, and citizenship, including behaving ethically as an organization and as individuals, has proven critical to long-term organizational survival. Just think of Enron and the problems that poor ethics and inadequate governance have caused the entire U.S. economy.

No single process leads to winning levels of performance. No single result can alert you to areas that need attention. The most important lesson is that every element of the entire Baldrige management system is required to achieve and sustain peak performance.

LEADERSHIP SUMMARY: SEVEN MUST-DO PRACTICES

Keys to Optimizing Performance

There is no evidence of an organization optimizing performance and achieving Baldrige recognition without enhancing the entire management system, from leadership and planning to customers, people, and processes. Although all of these factors are critical in the long term, it is the responsibility of top leaders to set the direction, values, and expectations that drive change and create a sense of urgency. Leader actions absolutely determine the speed and success of the effort to optimize organizational performance. If leaders fail to take the following actions, the transformation to a high-performing organization will be seriously delayed and most likely not take place at all.

1. *Role-model effective leadership practices.* Like it or not, leader example drives the actions of others far better than words. Rhetoric without appropriate action is virtually worthless and may be counter-productive. Do not expect anyone else to do the things you will not. The concept of "do as I say, not as I do" has never worked to guide or change behavior.

- If you do not aggressively drive performance excellence in word and deed, others will think it is optional. When change is perceived as optional it does not occur.

- If you do not have time to innovate, no one else will think innovation is important.

- If you do not empower the employees with whom you work, other managers will follow your lead (and fail to empower and engage their employees).

- If you do not seek improvement ideas from your subordinates, they will not demand in turn and people will stop thinking of ways to improve.

- If you do not hold managers accountable for empowering their subordinates, they will believe empowerment is optional. (See the first bullet.)

- If you do not learn new things, you may not keep up with important changes affecting your business and others will not see the value in learning.

Develop a list of attributes you want to role-model in addition to those listed. Check how you are perceived on these leadership attributes from peer, subordinate, and employee feedback. Change where you are role-modeling the wrong things.

2. ***Favor actions based on fact rather than intuition.*** The lack of facts and data forces leaders to default to intuition as the basis for decision making. Many great leaders have relied on intuition when facts were unavailable. However, no great leader relied only on intuition, or even mostly on intuition in the face of valid facts. The best leaders make consistently good decisions, which require reliable, accurate, valid and timely facts and data.

We rarely have access to all of the information we want prior to making decisions. However, we will surely not have enough fact-based information unless we prepare in advance. To make consistently better decisions, the best leaders drive fact-based diagnoses of organizational performance that focus on closing the gaps in areas critical to success. This information must be available when needed and easy to understand.

3. ***Learn constantly.*** Great leaders recognize that current knowledge limits their capabilities and success. You may think you have all of the knowledge and skills you need, but how do you know what you do not know? Do not expect your subordinates to learn for you because they suffer from the same limits. Considering the pace of change and the speed with which human knowledge is doubling, unless you aggressively pursue new knowledge, you will most certainly become obsolete or less effective faster.

Identify and list the things you must learn to become a better leader. Ask your subordinates to give you feedback to help you complete the list. Set learning goals and time lines to monitor the pace of new learning. Make adjustments to stay on track.

4. ***Share knowledge.*** Enhance the impact of your new knowledge by sharing it with others. By teaching others and answering their questions, your understanding becomes stronger and you can apply new knowledge faster and better. It is also a good way to

role-model the value of learning. Set a schedule to teach others about performance excellence systems and processes at least two to four times each year, and stick to it.

5. ***Require other leaders in the organization to do the same.*** The performance of individuals drives the performance of the organization. If your performance is suboptimal because you lack certain knowledge, skills, and abilities, the same is certainly true for your subordinates and their employees. After they see the value you place in role-modeling effective practices, learning, and coaching, make it clear you expect them to do the same. It is critical to clearly set this expectation for learning, as well as set clear, measurable expectations for work after they complete the training.

Discuss your concerns and expectations, and answer their questions. You will have to do this very often at first. Be consistent. Those who resist change look for loopholes and ways to avoid change. Do not create loopholes for them. Permit no excuses for those who refuse to learn. Champion the requirements leading to optimum organizational performance. Be prepared to remove leaders who do not support continuous improvement and performance excellence systems.

6. ***Align expectations, measures, rewards, and recognition.*** The system you have put in place is perfectly suited to produce the results you are currently getting. If you want to change the outcomes you must change the people and processes that produce them. Training is only a part of the change process.

- Express new expectations for both individual and group performance in measurable, outcome-oriented terms.

- Measure progress regularly and give prompt feedback.

- Visibly reward and recognize the desired behavior.

- Find other work for those who cannot or will not do the things needed for driving high performance. By rewarding those who achieve desired results and removing those who do not, you make it clear that performance excellence is crucial to success—it will not be perceived as optional. If you keep a manager in place who has not taken the necessary steps to improve, you must realize that the subordinates of that manager will conclude that such performance must be acceptable in your eyes. Your failure to act sends the wrong message.

To enhance desired business results, ensure that goals, strategic objectives, actions, measures, analysis, training, reward, and recognition are completely aligned. Remember, *what gets measured gets done. What gets rewarded gets done first.* If achieving strategic objectives is truly critical to your future success, be sure to assign actions, make sure your people have the skills they need to do the work, measure and monitor progress, and reward desired behavior and outcomes.

7. *Use training as a tool to develop skills and inform—not as a substitute for personal leadership direction.* Employees desire and expect important information to come from their leaders. Do not simply tell employees to do something new and different and expect it will be done. You must check understanding, measure and monitor progress, and provide appropriate incentives to actually get the desired behavior.

- Sending subordinate managers and employees to training and expecting the trainer to give the new management directions will rarely produce the desired results. It usually produces high skepticism and hostility, and reinforces the idea that leaders are not serious and committed to the new program or change—otherwise they would intro-

duce it themselves. It also makes the trainer and the curriculum the target of criticism and blame:

- "This class is a waste of time."

- "The trainer should tell us what to do when we get back to the office."

- "I do not know why I am here."

- "Just how serious is management about these changes/programs? Have they taken this training?"

- "What resources is management going to commit to this effort?"

Before anyone is sent to training, participants need to understand and *be able to describe* why they are there and what they are expected to get out of the training. These expectations should be set by the leaders who send the participants, not the trainers. Leaders could ask trainers to pretest the class to determine the extent to which participants understand why they are there. Those who are not prepared should be sent back. It should be the job of the sending managers to provide the proper foundation and preparation for their subordinate employees prior to training.

If you do not do the seven listed activities, you are by your actions telling your employees and subordinate managers that performance excellence is optional—something to do if they feel like it. In that event, you and your organization will most certainly fail to achieve the desired change and improvement.

LEADING THE CHANGE TO HIGH PERFORMANCE

Changing organizational culture is not easy and requires dedicated and unwavering consistency in support of the *new way* or *desired way* of behaving and believing. The following actions are usually critical to change culture in an organization:

- *Establish clear goals and a clear direction.* Explain clearly what will be required and how the new requirements are different from the old. If you do not know what new behaviors are required, find out. Talk to leaders who have successfully engineered this kind of improvement in the past. Leaders who are not clear invite confusion and inaction.

- *Show unwavering commitment.* Leaders are pivotal to the success of the enterprise—employees watch them closely. Don't blink in the face of setbacks—quitting is easy and doing so will make employees more cynical and demoralized. When leadership commitment and support are seen as tentative, employees and other subordinates will perceive the changes as optional, take-or-leave suggestions. Considering the profound ability most people have to resist change, this creates more support for doing nothing.

- *Prove you will change.* If leaders do not *walk the talk* and demonstrate their eagerness to operate differently, others once again conclude that the leaders are not serious and the new requirements are optional.

- *Keep the energy level high and focused on both process improvements and better performance outcomes*. Select improvements that are easy as well as difficult. Small successes are needed to keep the energy and support for performance excellence high. Larger improvement projects take longer to carry out but usually bring greater benefit. Celebrate process improvements as well as better performance outcomes.

- *Encourage people to challenge the status quo when doing so is consistent with enhancing customer value and achieving organizational goals.* Do not tolerate system craziness—break

old bureaucratic rules and policies that prevent or inhibit high-performance work toward goals. Free your people from bureaucratic silliness and you will find great energy and support from employees.

- *Change rewards to make them consistent with goals and objectives.* Make following the new culture and achieving goals worthwhile by rewarding desired behaviors and making the continued use of the old ones unpleasant. All employees must understand that the rewards are issued for behaving in a certain way and for achieving desired results. Rewards, including compensation and incentives, should not be considered an entitlement of employment. It is important to test the effectiveness of rewards and recognition. Remember, just because you value a reward does not mean that employees will do the same.

- *Measure progress against desired outcomes.* When leaders use measurements to track progress, people think they are serious about the outcome. If you do not bother measuring, employee productivity is usually lower. In addition, measurements help identify those who should be rewarded and those who should not. Finally, keep measurements simple and efficient. Do not allow the process of measurement to divert energy and focus. Stop collecting data that no longer supports effective decision making.

- *Communicate, communicate, communicate.* Communication cannot replace an inspiring vision and sound goals, but poor communication can scuttle them. People perform better when they understand the logic and rationale behind the vision and goals. Leaders must tell them what's coming, how they will be affected, and what's expected of them. Remember to take every opportunity to communicate your desires—once is not enough. The opponents of change will work nonstop to undermine the new goal, vision, and culture; communicate consistently to overcome this resistance. Also remember that even motivated and supportive people forget; remind them often of the vision and new expectations. Leaders who do not communicate effectively invite the rumor mill to fill in the blank spaces by default. Bad news, bad rumors, and outright lies frequently fill the communication gap leaders might inadvertently leave.

- *Involve everyone.* Remember, this is not *optional* activity. People who do not actively support change oppose it, perhaps reflexively. Insist on full involvement and define a role for everyone. Find ways to make everyone accountable for transforming the culture and improving performance. If a manager fails to support the changes needed to improve performance, it is probably a good idea to encourage that person to find other work—preferably with a competitor.

- *Start fast, then go faster.* Slow progress, which the opponents of change like to see, creates a self-fulfilling prophecy—that the proposed changes will not be effective. However, speed creates a sense of urgency that helps overcome organizational inertia, achieve stunning results, and defeat the gloom and pessimism of naysayers.

Remain steadfast in support, walk the talk, involve everyone, communicate, achieve quick results, measure, and reward progress.

Improve Performance, Efficiency, and Timeliness

What Does It Mean?

- Includes but is not limited to process identification, analysis, and ongoing improvement. We must define and measure process cycle time and defects and reduce them consistently.

What Is the Leader's Responsibility?

- Set an example—ask for data/measurements on cycle time and defects

- Make time available

- Make training available

- Ensure that records discipline exists

- Charter teams

- Set high goals, get high performance

- If you do not tell employees what you expect, do not be surprised if they do not get where you want them to go

Create a Participative, Cooperative Workplace

What Does It Mean?

- Includes but is not limited to setting boundary conditions and relevant goals, then moving decisions to the lowest possible level, using work teams for planning and process improvement, and creating a *family-friendly* work environment. Leaders motivate people, provide training for managers and employees, encourage the development of self-directed work teams, delegate authority and decision making downward, empower people to focus on achieving mission and vision, value diversity, provide open communication in all directions, and measure and improve employee well-being, motivation, and satisfaction.

What Is the Leader's Responsibility?

- Coach and counsel, rather than control

- Encourage participation with the goal of achieving better decision quality and better performance—make better use of human resources

- Create and build a highly motivated and satisfied workforce

Taking Action

- All leaders have a responsibility for communicating the mission, vision, strategic objectives, and enabling activities to all employees.

- It is very important that leaders and employees understand and agree fully with the planned objectives. It is even more important that they carry out the actions needed to actually achieve the objectives. The plan-deployment process cascades from top management to all locations and levels of the organization. Top managers do not micromanage the process. This means that the top leaders determine the objective or target and an action officer determines the means. This then sets the target for the next level to determine means. Figure 10 provides one example of this effect.

Personal Management Effectiveness —The Use of Upward Evaluations

Formal upward evaluations have been used for more than 50 years to help assess job performance of leaders. As organizations become committed to improving labor relations and manager effectiveness, upward evaluation has become a widely used tool that more and more leaders value.

Three reasons why upward feedback is beneficial include:

1. *Validity*. Subordinates interact regularly with their managers and have a unique vantage from which to assess manager style.

2. *Reliability*. Confidential feedback from numerous subordinates provides the best chance for accurate data. Employees who are hurt by poor management hope their feedback brings change.

3. *Involvement and morale.* Asking people to comment on the effectiveness and style of their managers boosts morale and sends a clear message that the organization is serious about increasing employee involvement—but only if the manager takes action to improve; otherwise, morale and motivation can get worse.

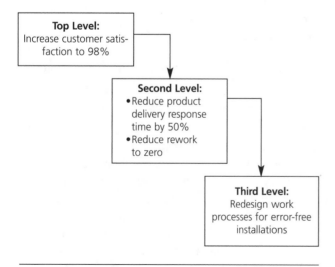

Top Level:
Increase customer satisfaction to 98%

Second Level:
• Reduce product delivery response time by 50%
• Reduce rework to zero

Third Level:
Redesign work processes for error-free installations

Figure 10   Deploying strategic objectives.

Before managers take action to change the way they manage, they should gather facts about their current style. They need to know what aspects of their style are considered strong and should not be changed. The starting point for improving management style, therefore, is an honest assessment of each manager's current behavior by subordinates, peers, and supervisors. This is also called a 360-degree evaluation.

The Feedback Process

1. Leaders solicit feedback on how they perform against specific behaviors that are characteristic of an effective manager. The Baldrige Criteria provide examples.

2. They use this information to plan personal improvement strategies.

3. They share the results of the survey with their employees and discuss possible improvement actions, then refine their plan.

4. They make improvements as planned and start the process again no more than one year later.

Figure 11 maps the process.

This process enables employees to help their manager understand how he or she is perceived, as well as identify areas of strength on which the manager can build. However, some important procedures should be in place to prevent improper use of the tool:

• Feedback should always be used and interpreted in the spirit of continuous personal improvement. Personally identifiable results should go only to the manager who was rated and should not be used as a basis for performance ratings, promotion, assignments, or pay adjustments (unless, of course, the manager refuses to work to improve).

• Anonymity for those completing questionnaires should be carefully protected. No one other than the employee should see the actual completed questionnaire. To further protect anonymity, questionnaires should be summarized and reported to the manager in cases where fewer than five employees completed the questionnaire.

• Personally identifiable results should be provided only to the manager named on the questionnaire. When the managers receive the

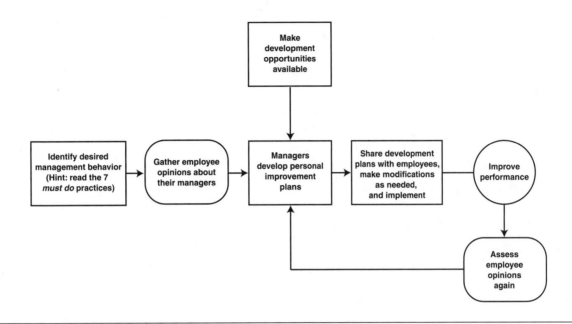

Figure 11 Improving leadership effectiveness.

results, they review their own ratings to determine their strengths and opportunities for improvement. Then they take steps to improve.

Aggregate data should be reported to top leadership to monitor as part of an organization-wide improvement priority. If the average scores do not improve appropriately, then the leaders may elect to see personally identifiable data of low-performing managers to encourage them to do more.

The Management Effectiveness Survey (Figures 12 and 13) can provide information that might help leaders and managers at all levels determine areas to address to strengthen their personal effectiveness. It represents one set of questions to examine leadership communication, openness, and effectiveness. Certainly other questions may be asked as circumstances change. In fact, in order to determine if any survey is asking the correct questions, the survey itself should be evaluated. This can be done by using open-ended questions and asking the employees to identify other issues that are of concern to them and should be included in the survey. Also, ask if some of the questions are not relevant or important and should be eliminated; then adjust the survey accordingly.

In addition to aggregating scores from employees, it is also useful to compare the perceptions of managers with the perception of the leader or manager who is the target of the assessment. Many times, employees identify a specific weakness that the leader believes is much stronger. These differences, together with key areas where both parties agree that a weakness exists, could be targeted for specific improvement. By aggregating the assessment data for all managers and making the overall results available to individuals, they can determine how their stage of development compares with other managers in the office.

MANAGEMENT EFFECTIVENESS SURVEY

The following questionnaire lists some key indicators to help you assess your manager's style in several key areas. Enter 1 for strongly disagree, 2 for disagree, 3 for agree, and 4 for strongly agree. If you cannot answer a question leave it blank.

General

1. My manager keeps me well informed about what's going on in the office.   1 2 3 4
2. My manager clearly and accurately explains the reasons for decisions that affect my work.   1 2 3 4
3. I am satisfied with my involvement in decisions that affect my work.   1 2 3 4
4. My manager delegates the right amount of responsibility to me and does not micromanage.   1 2 3 4
5. My manager gives me honest feedback on my performance.   1 2 3 4
6. I have confidence in my manager's decisions.   1 2 3 4
7. My manager has the knowledge he/she needs to be effective.   1 2 3 4
8. I can depend on my manager to honor the commitments he/she makes to me.   1 2 3 4
9. My manager treats people fairly and with dignity and respect.   1 2 3 4
10. My manager is straightforward and honest with me.   1 2 3 4
11. My manager is committed to resolving the concerns that may be identified in this survey and has made improvements based on past surveys (if applicable).   1 2 3 4
12. My manager strongly supports doing the right thing for the customer and all other stakeholders.   1 2 3 4
13. The communication process in my unit is effective. I always understand what is being communicated. (Unit refers to the level in the office your manager heads.)   1 2 3 4
14. In my unit, there is an environment of openness and trust.   1 2 3 4
15. I feel free to speak up when I disagree with a decision.   1 2 3 4
16. I feel I can elevate issues to higher-level managers without fear of reprisal.   1 2 3 4
17. The people I work with cooperate to get the job done.   1 2 3 4
18. In my unit, we are simplifying the way we do our work.   1 2 3 4
19. We have an effective process for preparing people to fill open positions.   1 2 3 4
20. All employees have fair advancement opportunities based on skills and abilities. Diversity of ideas is valued.   1 2 3 4

Effective Management Practices

My manager frequently…

21. provides me with honest feedback on my performance.   1 2 3 4
22. encourages me to monitor my own efforts.   1 2 3 4
23. encourages me to make suggestions to improve work processes.   1 2 3 4
24. ensures I have the knowledge, information, facts, and analysis I need to make decisions about my job.   1 2 3 4
25. defines his/her requirements of me in clear, measurable terms.   1 2 3 4
26. acts as a positive role model for performance excellence.   1 2 3 4
27. ensures that organizational goals/strategic objectives and related actions are understood at all levels.   1 2 3 4
28. favors facts before making decisions affecting our customers, employees, partners, and organization.   1 2 3 4
29. identifies and removes barriers to getting work done.   1 2 3 4
30. encourages people in our unit to work as a team.   1 2 3 4
31. informs us regularly about the state of the business/unit.   1 2 3 4
32. encourages me to ask questions and creates an environment of openness and trust.   1 2 3 4
33. behaves in ways that demonstrate respect for others.   1 2 3 4
34. ensures regularly scheduled reviews of progress toward goals using accurate performance-outcome measures.   1 2 3 4
35. monitors my progress and compares it against goals using accurate performance-outcome measures   1 2 3 4
36. ensures that rewards and recognition are fairly applied and closely tied to strategic goals, objectives, and required action plans.   1 2 3 4
37. sets work plans based on strategic objectives and customer requirements.   1 2 3 4
38. runs effective meetings.   1 2 3 4
39. uses a disciplined, fact-based process to make business and operational decisions and solve problems.   1 2 3 4
40. treats performance excellence as a basic operating principle.   1 2 3 4

Please list on the back of this form additional questions that the survey should ask about your manager. Also tell us which questions already on the survey are not very important and should be removed. In this way we can improve the effectiveness of the survey and better identify areas most needing improvement.

Figure 12 Sample Management Effectiveness Survey.

SAMPLE SCORED SURVEY – 10 employees completed the instrument

General

	#	1	2	3	4	Mean

1. My manager keeps me well informed about w... | 10 | 3 | 5 | 1 | (1) | 2.0
2. My manager clearly and accurately explains th... my work. | 10 | | 2 | 5 | 3 | 3.1
3. I am satisfied with my involvement in decisions that affect my work. | 10 | | 5 | 5 | | 2.5
4. My manager delegates the right amount of responsibility to me and does not micromanage. | 10 | 2 | 3 | 3 | 2 | 2.5
5. My manager gives me honest feedback on my performance. | 10 | 4 | 2 | 3 | 1 | 2.1
6. I have confidence in my manager's decisions. | 10 | | 5 | 5 | | 2.5
7. My manager has the knowledge he/she needs to b... | 10 | | 5 | 5 | | 2.5
8. I can depend on my manager to honor the commit... e makes to me. | 10 | | | 2 | 8 | 3.8
9. My manager treats people fairly and with dignity and respect. | 10 | | | 3 | 3 | 4 | 3.1
10. My manager is straightforward and honest with me. | 10 | 2 | 7 | 1 | | 1.9
11. My manager is committed to resolving the concerns that ... fied in this survey and has made improvements based on past surveys (if applicable). | 10 | 3 | 4 | 2 | 1 | 1.9
12. My manager strongly supports doing the right thing for the customer and all other stakeholders. | 10 | | | 6 | 4 | 3.4
13. The communication process in my unit is effective. I always understand what is being communicated. (Unit refers to the level in the office your manager heads.) | | | | | | 0
14. In my unit, there is an environment of openness and trust. | | | | | | 0
15. I feel free to speak up when I disagree with a decision. | | | | | | 0
16. I feel I can elevate issues to higher-level managers without fear of reprisal. | | | | | | 0
17. The people I work with cooperate to get the job done. | | | | | | 0
18. In my unit, we are simplifying the way we do our work. | | | | | | 0
19. We have an effective process for preparing people to fill open positions. | | | | | | 0
20. All employees have fair advancement opportunities based on skills and abilities. Diversity of ideas is valued. | | | | | | 0

Callout boxes (pointing into the table):
- The manager's self score (circle) is different than the employee's. Possible failure to recognize a problem.
- Relatively strong
- Relatively weak

Effective Management Practices

My manager frequently . . .

21. provides me with honest feedback on my performance. | 0
22. encourages me to monitor my own efforts. | 0
23. encourages me to make suggestions to improve work processes. | 0
24. ensures I have the knowledge, information, facts, and analysis I need to make decisions about my job | 0
25. defines his/her requirements of me in clear, measurable terms. | 0
26. acts as a positive role model for performance excellence. | 0
27. ensures that organizational goals/strategic objectives and related actions are understood at all levels | 0
28. favors facts before making decisions affecting our customers, employees, partners, and organization. | 0
29. identifies and removes barriers to getting work-done. | 0
30. encourages people in our unit to work as a team. | 0
31. informs us regularly about the state of the business/unit. | 0
32. encourages me to ask questions and creates an environment of openness and trust. | 0
33. behaves in ways that demonstrate respect for others. | 0
34. ensures regularly scheduled reviews of progress toward goals using accurate performance-outcome measures. | 0
35. monitors my progress and compares it against goals using accurate performance-. outcome measures | 0
36. ensures that rewards and recognition are fairly applied and closely tied to strategic goals, objectives, and required action plans. | 0
37. sets work plans based on strategic objectives and customer requirements. | 0
38. runs effective meetings. | 0
39. uses a disciplined, fact-based process to make business and operational decisions and solve problems. | 0
40. treats performance excellence as a basic operating principle. | 0

Figure 13 Sample Management Effectiveness Survey partially scored.

Create Performance Excellence Standards for Managers—A Key Job Element

Virtually every organization has the ability to determine what performance requirements are critical for the success of employees and managers. These critical performance requirements are usually included as a key element in performance plans and appraisals. By declaring that performance excellence is critical to the success of the organization, a specific key performance requirement can be included in the performance plan (sometimes these are called personal commitment plans, personal improvement plans, personal management objectives, or individual development plans, to name a few) and evaluation of managers and leaders. Using this approach, every manager and supervisor begins to take performance excellence more seriously.

- Using the following performance standards as an example, in order for a manager to receive a rating at a particular level, that manager must have accomplished all of the activities described for that rating level. If all are not met, the rating goes to the lowest level at which all are met.

- The writer of the performance appraisal must cite measurable examples in the performance appraisal for actions listed under the rating level.

- Supervising reviewers must verify that these actions have indeed been taken. Under this system, managers are strongly encouraged to keep accurate records of activities that might exemplify compliance with these standards.

Overall Performance Standard for Leadership

The individual visibly demonstrates adherence to the high personal standards and characteristics of leaders in a high-performing organization. The individual:

- Understands the business processes of the unit.

- Is customer-focused and customer-driven.

- Demonstrates a firm commitment to the principles of customer satisfaction. Understands customer requirements and consistently works to meet and exceed them.

- Understands and personally uses performance excellence principles and tools for decision making and planning:

  - Favors the use of data and facts to drive decisions and ensures that employees and subordinate managers do the same.

  - Ensures that organizational goals/strategic objectives are converted to appropriate actions to align work within the organizational unit.

  - Measures and monitors progress toward achieving the goals/strategic objectives within the organizational unit.

- Demonstrates a firm commitment to the principles of employee empowerment, well-being, and satisfaction:

  - Promotes flexibility, individual initiative, and innovation.

  - Encourages and supports the personal and professional development of self and employees.

  - Supports effective training aligned to support action plans and reinforces the use of new skills on the job.

  - Ensures compensation is aligned to support high-performance business objectives and a customer focus.

  - Rewards and recognizes employees who achieve objectives and incorporate the principles of performance excellence in their day-to-day work.

  - Fosters an atmosphere of open, honest communication and knowledge sharing among employees and business units throughout the organization.

- Rigorously drives the systematic, continuous improvement of all work processes, including personal self-improvement as an effective leader.

- Achieves consistently improving performance outcomes in customer satisfaction, employee well-being, motivation, and satisfaction, operational excellence, and financial (cost/budget) performance.

Rating No. 1: Performance is unsatisfactory. The individual frequently fails to meet the performance standard for leadership.

- Does not fully understand the business processes of the unit.

- Consistently disregards the needs of customers.

- Does not understand and has not taken steps to implement performance excellence (may even work against the changes needed).

  – Intuition, not data or facts, tends to dominate decision making.

  – Organizational goals and actions are not aligned to actions within the unit.

  – May measure and monitor some performance outcomes (such as budget tracking), but most measures are not aligned to organizational goals.

- Does not effectively promote employee well-being, motivation, and morale.

  – Tends to micromanage—does not delegate decision-making authority to the lower levels except as directly instructed to do so.

  – Rarely listens to employees or cares what they think.

  – Does not consistently promote flexibility and individual initiative.

  – Does not consistently encourage and support the personal and professional development of self and employees.

  – May send employees to training but does not consistently reinforce the use of new skills on the job.

  – Has not taken effective steps to ensure that compensation and other rewards or recognition are aligned to support business strategies and actions.

  – Reward and recognition are not aligned to support organizational goals or the principles of performance excellence or customer satisfaction.

- Does not communicate effectively or foster an atmosphere of knowledge sharing among employees and business units.

- Does not regularly assess or improve work processes, including their personal effectiveness as a leader.

- Does not achieve consistently improving performance outcomes in customer satisfaction, employee well-being, motivation, and satisfaction, operational excellence, and financial (cost/budget) performance.

Rating No. 2: Performance is minimally acceptable. Individual occasionally fails to meet the performance standard for leadership. Performs higher than indicated by level one but does not meet all level-three requirements.

Rating No. 3: Performance is acceptable. Individual basically meets the performance standard for leadership.

- Is considered to be a capable leader.

- Understands the key business processes of the unit.

- Is customer-driven and promotes customer-focused values throughout the unit.

  – Demonstrates a commitment to the principles of customer satisfaction.

  – Develops systems to understand customer requirements, strengthen customer relationships, resolve customer problems and prevent them from happening again, and obtain information about customer satisfaction and dissatisfaction.

- Personally uses many performance excellence principles and tools for decision making and planning.

- Visibly supports performance excellence within the organization. Usually uses data and facts to drive decisions and ensures that many employees and subordinate managers do the same.

- Ensures that key organizational goals are converted to appropriate actions to align most work within the organizational unit. Most goals and actions have defined measures of progress and time lines for achieving desired results.

- Demonstrates some commitment to the principles of employee empowerment, well-being, and satisfaction. Is well-regarded by employees for:

  - Involving the workforce in identifying improvement opportunities and developing improvement plans.

  - Valuing employee input on work-related matters.

  - Promoting flexibility and individual initiative and ensuring that many subordinate managers do the same.

  - Encouraging and supporting the personal and professional development of self and employees.

  - Supporting effective training and reinforcing the use of new skills on the job.

  - Ensuring compensation is aligned to support business strategies and actions.

  - Rewarding and recognizing employees who incorporate the principles of performance excellence in their day-to-day work.

- Fosters an atmosphere of open, honest communication and knowledge sharing among employees and business units throughout the organization.

- Visibly drives continuous improvement of many work processes, including personal effectiveness as a leader.

- Achieves consistently improving performance outcomes in customer satisfaction, employee well-being, motivation, and satisfaction, operational excellence, and financial (cost/budget) performance.

- The levels of performance outcomes are better than average when compared with organizations providing similar programs, products, or services.

Rating No. 4: Performance is very good. Individual occasionally exceeds the performance standard for leadership. Performs higher than indicated by level three but does not meet all requirements of level five.

Rating No. 5: Performance is superior. Individual consistently exceeds the performance standard for leadership. *Is considered a role model for leadership.*

- Understands the business processes of the unit in great detail.

- Is customer-driven and actively promotes customer-focused values throughout the unit.

  - Demonstrates a firm commitment to the principles of customer satisfaction.

  - Develops effective systems to understand customer requirements, strengthen loyalty and customer relationships, resolve customer problems immediately and prevent them from happening again, and obtain timely information about customer satisfaction and dissatisfaction.

  - Advocates the needs of customers through the collection and use of information on customer satisfaction, dissatisfaction, and product performance.

- Personally uses performance excellence principles and tools for decision making and planning.

  - Serves as a performance excellence champion within the organization and as a resource within the work unit, providing guidance, counsel, and instruction in performance excellence tools, processes, and principles.

  - Is a role model for using data and facts to drive decisions and ensures that employees and subordinate managers do the same.

  - Ensures that all organizational goals are converted to appropriate actions to align work within the organizational unit.

  - Each goal and action has defined measures of progress and time lines for achieving desired results.

- Demonstrates a firm commitment to the principles of employee empowerment, well-being, and satisfaction. Is highly regarded by employees for:

  – Involving the workforce in setting standards of performance, identifying improvement opportunities, and developing improvement plans.

  – Seeking and valuing employee input on work-related matters.

  – Promoting flexibility and individual initiative and ensuring that subordinate managers do the same.

  – Encouraging and supporting the personal and professional development of self and employees.

  – Supporting effective training and reinforcing the use of new skills on the job.

  – Ensuring compensation is aligned to support business strategies and actions.

  – Rewarding and recognizing employees who incorporate the principles of performance excellence in their day-to-day work.

- Fosters an atmosphere of open, honest communication and knowledge sharing among employees and business units throughout the organization.

  – Checks the effectiveness of nearly all communication and makes changes to improve.

- Rigorously drives the systematic, continuous improvement of all work processes, including personal self-improvement as an effective leader.

  – Develops personal action plan and always incorporates results of 360-degree feedback to continuously improve personal leadership effectiveness and ensures subordinate managers do the same.

- Achieves consistently improving performance outcomes in customer satisfaction; employee well-being, motivation, and satisfaction; operational excellence; and financial (cost/budget) performance.

  – The levels of performance outcomes are among the highest in the organization and are also high when compared with organizations providing similar programs, products, or services.

The following tables display the performance excellence ratings side by side to make it easier to see the progression from poor (1) to excellent (5).

Performance Excellence Standards Table

Level 1	Level 2	Level 3	Level 4	Level 5
Performance is unsatisfactory: Individual frequently fails to meet the performance standard for leadership. Is considered a poor leader.	**Better than level 1 and some of level 3.**	**Performance is acceptable: Individual meets the performance standard for leadership. Is considered to be a capable leader.**	**All of level 3 and some of level 5.**	**Performance is superior: Individual consistently exceeds the performance standard for leadership. Is considered a role model for leadership.**
• Does not fully understand the key business processes of the unit		• Understands the key business processes of the unit		• Understands the business processes of the unit in great detail
• Consistently disregards the needs of customers		• Is customer-driven and promotes customer-focused values throughout the unit – Demonstrates a commitment to the principles of customer satisfaction – Develops systems to understand customer requirements, strengthen customer relationships, resolve customer problems and prevent them from happening again, and obtain information about customer satisfaction and dissatisfaction		• Is customer-driven and actively promotes customer-focused values throughout the unit – Demonstrates a firm commitment to the principles of customer satisfaction – Develops effective systems to understand customer requirements, strengthen loyalty and customer relationships, resolve customer problems immediately and prevent them from happening again, and obtain timely information about customer satisfaction and dissatisfaction – Advocates the needs of customers through the collection and use of information on customer satisfaction, dissatisfaction, and product performance

Performance Excellence Standards Table

Level 1	Level 2	Level 3	Level 4	Level 5
Performance is unsatisfactory: Individual frequently fails to meet the performance standard for leadership. Is considered a poor leader.	**Better than level 1 and some of level 3.**	**Performance is acceptable: Individual meets the performance standard for leadership. Is considered to be a capable leader.**	**All of level 3 and some of level 5.**	**Performance is superior: Individual consistently exceeds the performance standard for leadership. Is considered a role model for leadership.**
• Does not understand and has not taken steps to implement performance excellence (may even work against the changes needed) – Intuition, not data or facts, tends to dominate decision making – Organizational goals and actions are not aligned to actions within the unit – May measure and monitor some performance outcomes (such as budget tracking) but most measures are not aligned to organizational goals		• Personally uses many performance excellence principles and tools for decision making and planning – Visibly supports performance excellence within the organization – Usually uses data and facts to drive decisions and ensures that many employees and subordinate managers do the same – Ensures that key organizational goals are converted to appropriate action to align most work within the organizational unit – Most goals and actions have defined, outcome-oriented measures of progress and time lines for achieving desired results		• Personally uses nearly all performance excellence principles and tools for decision making and planning – Serves as a performance excellence champion within the organization and as a resource within the work unit, providing guidance, counsel, and instruction in performance excellence tools, processes, and principles – Is a role model for using data and facts to drive decisions and ensures that employees and subordinate managers do the same – Ensures that all organizational goals are converted to appropriate actions to align nearly all work within the organizational unit – Each goal and action has defined, outcome-oriented measures of progress and time lines for achieving desired results

Performance Excellence Standards Table

Level 1	Level 2	Level 3	Level 4	Level 5
Performance is unsatisfactory: Individual frequently fails to meet the performance standard for leadership. Is considered a poor leader.	**Better than level 1 and some of level 3.**	**Performance is acceptable: Individual meets the performance standard for leadership. Is considered to be a capable leader.**	**All of level 3 and some of level 5.**	**Performance is superior: Individual consistently exceeds the performance standard for leadership. Is considered a role model for leadership.**
• Does not effectively promote employee well-being, motivation, and morale – Tends to micromanage; does not delegate decision-making authority to the lower levels except as directly instructed to do so – Rarely listens to employees or cares what they think – Does not consistently promote flexibility and individual initiative – Does not consistently encourage and support the personal and professional development of self and employees – May send employees to training but does not consistently reinforce the use of new skills on the job – Has not taken effective steps to ensure compensation and other rewards or recognition are aligned to support business strategies and actions – Reward and recognition are not aligned to support organizational goals or the principles of performance excellence or customer satisfaction		• Demonstrates some commitment to the principles of employee empowerment, well-being, and satisfaction Is well-regarded by employees for – Involving the workforce in identifying improvement opportunities and developing improvement plans – Valuing employee input on work-related matters – Promoting flexibility and individual initiative and ensuring that many subordinate managers do the same – Encouraging and supporting the personal and professional development of self and employees – Supporting effective training and reinforcing the use of new skills on the job – Ensuring compensation is aligned to support business strategies and actions – Rewarding and recognizing employees who incorporate the principles of performance excellence in their day-to-day work		• Demonstrates a firm commitment to the principles of employee empowerment, well-being, and satisfaction Is highly regarded by employees for: – Involving the workforce in setting standards of performance, identifying improvement opportunities, and developing improvement plans – Seeking and valuing employee input on work-related matters – Promoting flexibility and individual initiative and ensuring that nearly all subordinate managers do the same – Encouraging and supporting the personal and professional development of self and employees – Supporting effective training and reinforcing the use of new skills on the job – Ensuring compensation is aligned to support business strategies and actions – Rewarding and recognizing employees who incorporate the principles of performance excellence in their day-to-day work

Performance Excellence Standards Table

Level 1	Level 2	Level 3	Level 4	Level 5
Performance is unsatisfactory: Individual frequently fails to meet the performance standard for leadership. Is considered a poor leader.	**Better than level 1 and some of level 3.**	**Performance is acceptable: Individual meets the performance standard for leadership. Is considered to be a capable leader.**	**All of level 3 and some of level 5.**	**Performance is superior: Individual consistently exceeds the performance standard for leadership. Is considered a role model for leadership.**
• Does not communicate effectively or foster an atmosphere of knowledge-sharing among employees and business units		• Fosters an atmosphere of open, honest communication and knowledge sharing among employees and business units throughout the organization		• Fosters an atmosphere of open, honest communication and knowledge sharing among employees and business units throughout the organization – Checks the effectiveness of nearly all communication and makes changes to improve
• Does not regularly assess or improve work processes, including his or her personal effectiveness as a leader		• Visibly drives continuous improvement of many work processes, including his or her personal effectiveness as a leader		• Rigorously drives the systematic, continuous improvement of all work processes, including his or her personal effectiveness as a leader – Develops personal action plan and always incorporates results of 360-degree feedback to continuously improve his/her leadership effectiveness and ensures subordinate managers do the same
• Does not achieve consistently improving performance outcomes in customer satisfaction, employee well-being, motivation, and satisfaction, operational excellence, and financial (cost/budget) performance		• Achieves consistently improving performance outcomes in customer satisfaction, employee well-being, motivation, and satisfaction, operational excellence, and financial (cost/budget) performance – The levels of performance outcomes are better than average when compared with organizations providing similar programs, products, or services		• Achieves consistently improving performance outcomes in customer satisfaction, employee well-being, motivation, and satisfaction, operational excellence, and financial (cost/budget) performance – The levels of performance outcomes are among the highest in the organization and are also high when compared with organizations providing similar programs, products, or services

Lessons Learned Conclusions

Successful leaders will create a customer focus and a context for action at all levels of the organization. Effective leaders will distribute authority and decision making to all levels of the organization. Nearly instantaneous, two-way communication will permit clear strategies, measurable outcome-oriented objectives, and priorities to be identified and deployed organizationwide. Problems will be identified and resolved with similar speed. Success in this environment will demand different skills of employees and managers. Unless all managers and employees understand where the organization is going and what must be done to beat the competition, it will be difficult for them to make effective decisions consistent with overall direction and strategy. If employees at all levels are not involved in decision making, organizational effectiveness is reduced—making it more difficult to win in a highly competitive arena.

In closing this section, I would like to suggest that the scenario previously described is already happening today among the world's best-performing organizations.

- These organizations have effective leadership at all levels, with a clear strategy focused on maximizing customer value. Middle-level managers support, rather than block, the values and direction of the top leaders.

- They have developed ways to challenge themselves and improve their own processes when doing so promotes customer value and improves operating effectiveness.

- They engage workers fully and promote organizational and personal learning at all levels. They ensure that knowledge is shared within the organization to avoid duplication of effort.

- They have created effective data systems to enhance decision making at all levels.

- They have developed and aligned reward, recognition, compensation, and incentives to support the desired customer-focused behavior among all leaders, managers, and employees.

- They have found ways to design effective work processes and ensure that those processes are executed consistently and improved continuously.

- They closely monitor their performance and the performance of their principal competitors. They use this information to adjust their goals/objectives and their work and they continue to improve faster than ever.

These organizations are among the best in the world at what they do and they will continue to win, as long as they continue to apply the current principles of performance excellence.

AWARD CRITERIA FRAMEWORK

Organizations must position themselves to respond well to the environment within which they compete. They must understand and manage threats and vulnerabilities as well as capitalize on their strengths and opportunities, including the vulnerabilities of competitors. These factors guide strategy development, support operational decisions, and align measures and actions—all of which must be done well for the organization to succeed. Consistent with this overarching purpose, the Award Criteria contain the following basic elements: Driver Triad, Work Core, Brain Center, and Results/Outcomes (Figure 14).

The Driver Triad

The Driver Triad (Figure 15) consists of the categories of Leadership, Strategic Planning, and Customer and Market Focus. Leaders use these processes to set direction and goals, monitor progress, make resource decisions, and take corrective action when progress is not achieved according to plan. The processes that make up the Driver Triad require leaders to set direction and expectations for the organization to meet customer and market requirements and fully empower employees (Category 1), provide the vehicle for determining the short- and long-term strategies for success as well as communicating and

aligning the organization's work (Category 2), and produce information about critical customer requirements and levels of satisfaction and strengthen customer relations and loyalty (Category 3).

The Work Core

The Work Core (Figure 16) describes the processes through which the primary work of the organization takes place and consists of Human Resource-Focus (Category 5) and Process Management (Category 6). These Categories recognize that the people of an organization are responsible for doing the work. To achieve peak performance, these people must possess the right skills and must be allowed to work in an environment that promotes initiative and self-direction. The work processes provide the structure for continuous learning and improvement to optimize performance.

Results/Outcomes

The processes defined by the Driver Triad, Work Core, and Brain Center produce the Results (Category

Figure 15 Driver Triad.

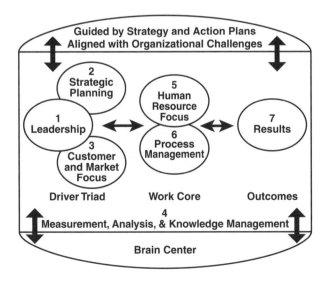

Figure 14 Performance excellence framework.

Figure 16 Work Core.

7). Results (Figure 17) reflect the organization's actual performance and serve as the basis for leaders to monitor progress against goals and make adjustments to increase performance. These Results include customer focus, financial and market performance, human resource performance, and internal operating effectiveness.

Brain Center

The foundation for the entire management system is Measurement, Analysis, and Knowledge Management (Category 4). These processes (Figure 18) capture, store, analyze, and retrieve information and data critical to the effective management of the organization and to a fact-based system for improving organization performance and competitiveness. Rapid access to reliable data and information systems is especially critical to enhance effective decision making in an increasingly complex, fast-paced, global competitive environment.

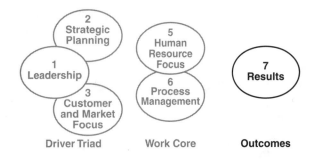

Figure 17 Outcomes.

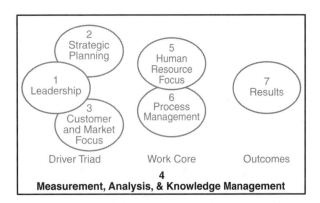

Figure 18 Measurement, Analysis, and Knowledge Management.

Measurement, Analysis, and Knowledge Management are also called the Brain Center of an effective management system (Figure 19).

Organizations develop effective strategic plans to help set the direction necessary to achieve future success. Unfortunately, these plans are not always communicated and used to drive actions. The planning process and the resulting strategy are virtually worthless if the organization does not use the plan and strategy to guide decision making at all levels of the organization (Figure 20).

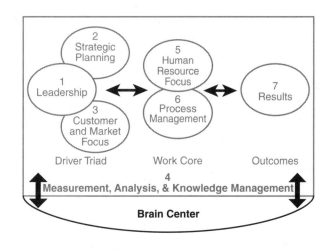

Figure 19 Brain Center.

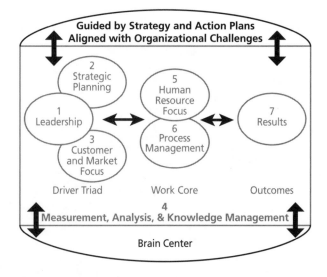

Figure 20 Guide decision making.

When decisions are not guided by strategy, managers and other employees tend to substitute their own ideas for the correct direction. This frequently causes teams, individuals, and whole business units to work at cross-purposes, suboptimizing performance and making it more difficult for the organization to achieve desired results.

Taken together, these processes define the essential ingredients of a complex, integrated management system designed to promote and deliver performance excellence. If any part of the system is missing, the performance results suffer. If fully implemented, these processes are sufficient to enable organizations to achieve winning performance.

Award Criteria Organization

Categories

The seven Criteria Categories are subdivided into Items and Areas to Address. Figure 21 demonstrates the organization of Category 1.

Items

There are 19 Items, each focusing on a major requirement.

Areas to Address

Items consist of one or more Areas to Address (Areas). Information is submitted by applicants in response to the specific requirements of these Areas. There are 33 Areas to Address.

Subparts

There are 84 subparts in the 2006 Criteria, not counting the Organizational Profile. Areas consist of one or more subparts, where numbers are shown in parentheses. A response should be made to each subpart.

Notes

If a note indicates the process *should* include something, examiners will interpret it as a requirement. If a note indicates that the process *might* include something, examiners will not treat the list as a requirement—only as an example. There are 74 notes, not counting the Organizational Profile. A number of Items have notes that provide additional guidance specifically for nonprofit organizations. These nonprofit-specific notes appear at the end of the Item in *italics*.

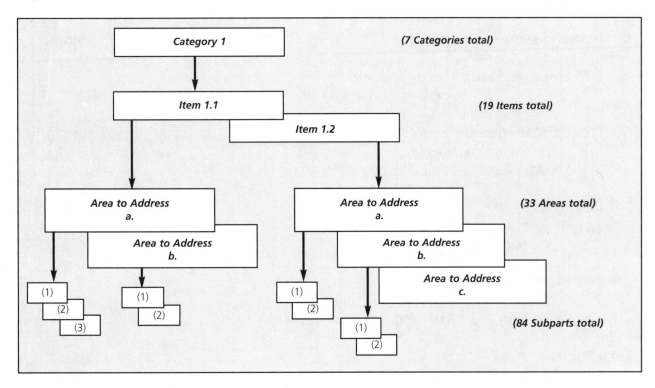

Figure 21   Organization of Category 1.

BALDRIGE AWARD CATEGORIES AND POINT VALUES

Examination Categories/Items	Maximum Points
Preface Organizational Profile	**(0 points)**
P.1 Organizational Description	0
P.2 Organizational Challenges	0
1 Leadership	**(120 points)**
1.1 Senior Leadership	70
1.2 Governance and Social Responsibilities	50
2 Strategic Planning	**(85 points)**
2.1 Strategy Development	40
2.2 Strategy Deployment	45
3 Customer and Market Focus	**(85 points)**
3.1 Customer and Market Knowledge	40
3.2 Customer Relationships and Satisfaction	45
4 Measurement, Analysis, and Knowledge Management	**(90 points)**
4.1 Measurement, Analysis, and Review of Organizational Performance	45
4.2 Information and Knowledge Management	45
5 Human Resource Focus	**(85 points)**
5.1 Work Systems	35
5.2 Employee Learning and Motivation	25
5.3 Employee Well-Being and Satisfaction	25
6 Process Management	**(85 points)**
6.1 Value Creation Processes	45
6.2 Support Processes and Operational Planning	40
7 Results	**(450 points)**
7.1 Product and Service Outcomes	100
7.2 Customer-Focused Outcomes	70
7.3 Financial and Market Outcomes	70
7.4 Human Resource Outcomes	70
7.5 Organizational Effectiveness Outcomes	70
7.6 Leadership and Social Responsibility Outcomes	70
Total Points	**1000**

KEY CHARACTERISTICS—2006 PERFORMANCE EXCELLENCE CRITERIA

The Criteria focus on organizational-performance results and the processes required to achieve them. Results are a composite of the following organizational performance areas:

- Product and service outcomes

- Customer-focused outcomes

- Financial and market outcomes

- Human resource outcomes

- Organizational effectiveness outcomes, including key internal operational performance measures

- Leadership and social responsibility outcomes

The use of this composite of indicators is intended to ensure that strategies are balanced—that they do not inappropriately trade off among important stakeholders, objectives, or short- and longer-term goals.

These results areas cover overall organization performance, including financial performance. The results areas also recognize the importance of suppliers and of community and national well-being.

The Criteria *do not* prescribe that the organization should or should not have any particular functions, such as departments for quality, planning, or personnel. The Criteria do not prescribe how the organization should be structured or how different units in the organization should be managed. These factors differ among organizations, and they are likely to change within an organization over time as needs and strategies evolve. The Criteria are nonprescriptive for the following reasons:

- The focus is on results, not on procedures, tools, or organizational structure. Organizations are encouraged to develop and demonstrate creative, adaptive, and flexible approaches for meeting requirements. Nonprescriptive requirements are intended to foster incremental and major ("breakthrough") improvements, as well as basic change through innovation.

- The selection of tools, techniques, systems, and organizational structure usually depends on

factors such as business type and size, organizational relationships, the organization's stage of development, and employee capabilities and responsibilities.

- A focus on common requirements, rather than on common procedures, fosters better understanding, communication, sharing, alignment, and integration, while supporting innovation and diversity in approaches.

The Criteria support a systems approach to maintaining organization-wide goal alignment. The systems approach to goal alignment is embedded in the integrated structure of the Core Values and Concepts, the Organizational Profile, the Criteria, the Scoring Guidelines, and the results-oriented, cause-effect linkages among the Criteria parts.

Alignment in the Criteria is built around connecting and reinforcing measures derived from the organization's processes and strategy. The measures in the Criteria tie directly to customer value and to overall performance that relate to key internal and external requirements of the organization. Measures serve both as a communications tool and a basis for deploying consistent performance requirements. Such alignment ensures consistency of purpose while at the same time supports speed, innovation, and decentralized decision making.

Learning Cycles and Continuous Improvement

In high-performing organizations, action-oriented learning takes place through feedback between processes and results facilitated by learning or continuous improvement cycles. The learning cycles have four clearly defined and well-established stages (Figure 22).

1. Plan—planning, including design of processes, selection of measures, and deployment of requirements

2. Do—execute plans

3. Study/Check—assess progress, taking into account internal and external results

4. Act—revise plans based on assessment findings, learning, new inputs, new requirements, and opportunities for innovation

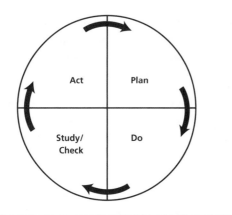

Figure 22 Continuous improvement cycle.

Goal-Based Diagnosis

The Criteria and the Scoring Guidelines are the two elements that combine to make the diagnostic tool, which is part of a developmental assessment. A developmental assessment, unlike a compliance review, seeks to determine how advanced an organization is and then identify the vital few processes that need to be developed to move to the next higher level. The basic systems must be in place before they can be refined and enhanced. In a compliance review, on the other hand, all conditions or requirements must be met or the organization is *out of compliance* and may not be certified or registered. By design, compliance reviews audit against a set of minimum standards. A developmental review, such as that provided through the Baldrige Criteria, identifies continuous improvement opportunities to help the organization achieve best-in-class performance—to excel and win.

This diagnostic assessment is a useful management tool that goes beyond most performance reviews and is applicable to a wide range of strategies and management systems.

Changes from the 2005 Criteria

The Criteria for Performance Excellence have evolved significantly over time to help businesses address a dynamic environment, focus on strategy-driven performance, and, most recently, address concerns about governance, ethics, and organizational sustainability. The Criteria have continually progressed toward a comprehensive, integrated systems perspective of overall organizational performance management.

Each year, the decision whether to revise the Criteria balances two important considerations. On one hand, the Criteria must reflect the leading edge of validated management practice to help users address the increasingly complex challenges they face; on the other hand, the Criteria must be stable enough to allow users continuity in their performance assessments. In 2005, the Baldrige Criteria were significantly revised to address the focused demands on senior leaders, the need for long-term (as well as short-term) organizational sustainability, the great challenges of innovating organizations (not just technology), the difficulty of executing new processes and strategic plans, and the benefits of improved alignment of all aspects of the management system with results measurements. Recognizing the challenges for organizations to address these opportunities, the decision was made to make no substantive revisions to the Criteria for 2006.

The most significant changes in the Criteria booklet for 2006 are:

- In anticipation of a Baldrige nonprofit category that will include government agencies and all other nonprofit organizations, the language throughout the Criteria booklet has been adjusted to better address nonprofit organizations, as well as for-profit businesses.

- The number of Item Notes increased from 65 to 74 and some Item Notes were modified. Item Notes were added that specifically address nonprofit organizations. Information in the Notes that address concepts of importance to nonprofit organizations is presented in *italics*. Notes that address only nonprofit organizations are at the end of the Notes for that Item.

- Each Criteria Item title now includes a simple question that addresses the basic requirement of the item and identifies the fundamental theme or central concept of the Item.

- *Employee* has been added to the Glossary of Key Terms to help users understand all the people who may be considered employees for the purposes of a Baldrige assessment. Other terms in the Glossary have been changed to align better with the new language in the Criteria that addresses nonprofit organizations.

Organizational Profile

*The **Organizational Profile** is a snapshot of your organization, the key influences on how you operate, and the key challenges you face.*

IMPORTANCE OF THE ORGANIZATIONAL PROFILE

The Organizational Profile is critically important because:

- It is the most appropriate starting point for self-assessment and for writing an application.

- It helps you identify potential gaps in key information and focus on key performance requirements and business results.

- It is used by the examiners and judges in all stages of application review, including the site visit, to understand your organization and what you consider important. It sets the context for the assessment.

- It may be used by itself for an initial self-assessment. If you identify topics for which conflicting, little, or no information is available, it is possible that your assessment need go no further and you can use these topics for action planning.

Page Limit

For Baldrige Award applicants, the Organizational Profile is limited to five pages. These are not counted in the overall 50-page limit for the application. Typing and format instructions for the Organizational Profile are the same as for the application. These instructions are given in the Baldrige Award Application Forms booklet, a copy of which appears on the compact disk enclosed with this book.

P.1 ORGANIZATIONAL DESCRIPTION: What are your key organizational characteristics?
Describe your organization's operating environment and your key relationships with customers, suppliers, partners, and stakeholders.

Within your response, include answers to the following questions:

a. Organizational Environment

(1) What are your organization's main products and services? What are the delivery mechanisms used to provide your products and services to your customers?

(2) What is your organizational culture? What are your stated purpose, vision, mission, and values?

(3) What is your employee profile? What are your categories and types of employees? What are their educational levels? What are your organization's workforce and job diversity, organized bargaining units, use of contract employees, and special health and safety requirements?

(4) What are your major technologies, equipment, and facilities?

(5) What is the regulatory environment under which your organization operates? What are the applicable occupational health and safety regulations; accreditation, certification, or registration requirements; relevant industry standards; and environmental, financial, and product regulations?

b. Organizational Relationships

(1) What are your organizational structure and governance system? What are the reporting relationships among your governance board, senior leaders, and parent organization, as appropriate?

(2) What are your key customer and stakeholder groups and market segments, as appropriate? What are their key requirements and expectations for your products, services, and operations? What are the differences in these requirements and expectations among customer and stakeholder groups and market segments?

(3) What role do suppliers, partners, and distributors play in your value creation and key support processes? What role, if any, do they play in your organizational innovation processes? What are your most important types of suppliers, partners, and distributors? What are your most important supply chain requirements?

(4) What are your key supplier and customer partnering relationships and communication mechanisms?

Notes:

N1 Product and service delivery mechanisms to your customers (P.1a[1]) might be direct or through dealers, distributors, collaborators, or channel partners.

N2 Market segments (P.1b[2]) might be based on product or service lines or features, geography, distribution channels, business volume, or other factors that are important to your organization to define related market characteristics.

N3 Customer and stakeholder group and market segment requirements (P.1b[2]) might include on-time delivery, low defect levels, ongoing price reductions, electronic communication, rapid response, and aftersales service. *For some nonprofit organizations, requirements also might include administrative cost reductions, at-home services, rapid response to emergencies, and multilingual services.*

N4 Communication mechanisms (P.1b[4]) should be two-way and might be in person, via regular mail or e-mail, Web-based, or by telephone. For many organizations, these mechanisms may change as marketplace, customer, or stakeholder requirements change.

Continued

Notes: *Continued*

N5 *While some nonprofit organizations offer products and services (P.1a[1]), many might appropriately interpret this phrase as programs or projects and services.*

N6 *Customers (P.1a[1]) are the users and potential users of your products, programs, and services. In some nonprofit organizations, customers might include members, taxpayers, citizens, recipients, clients, and beneficiaries. Market segments might be referred to as constituencies.*

N7 *Many nonprofit organizations rely heavily on volunteers to supplement the work of their employees. These organizations should interpret employees (P.1a[3]) to mean employees and volunteers.*

N8 *For nonprofit organizations, relevant industry standards (P.1a[5]) might include "industry-wide" codes of conduct and policy guidance.*

N9 *For some nonprofit organizations, governance and reporting relationships (P.1b[1]) might include relationships with major agency or foundation funding sources.*

N10 *For some nonprofit organizations, key suppliers and distributors (P.1b[3,4]) might include collaborators and collaborating organizations.*

P.1 Organizational Description Item Linkages

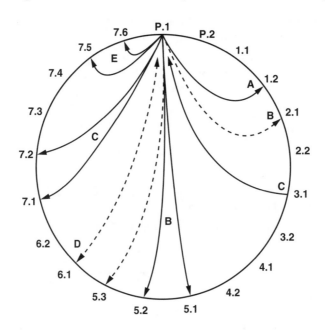

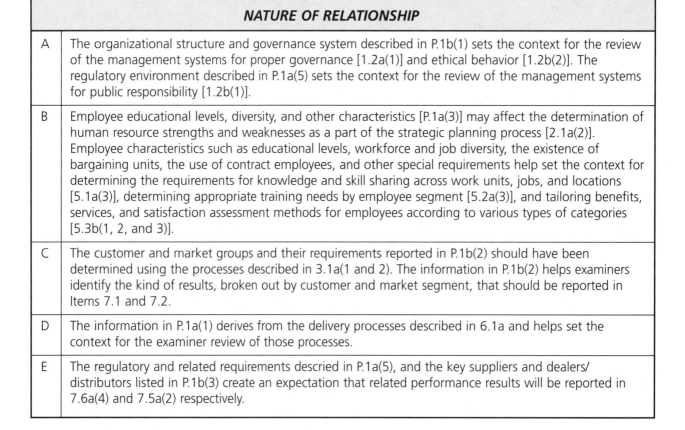

	NATURE OF RELATIONSHIP
A	The organizational structure and governance system described in P.1b(1) sets the context for the review of the management systems for proper governance [1.2a(1)] and ethical behavior [1.2b(2)]. The regulatory environment described in P.1a(5) sets the context for the review of the management systems for public responsibility [1.2b(1)].
B	Employee educational levels, diversity, and other characteristics [P.1a(3)] may affect the determination of human resource strengths and weaknesses as a part of the strategic planning process [2.1a(2)]. Employee characteristics such as educational levels, workforce and job diversity, the existence of bargaining units, the use of contract employees, and other special requirements help set the context for determining the requirements for knowledge and skill sharing across work units, jobs, and locations [5.1a(3)], determining appropriate training needs by employee segment [5.2a(3)], and tailoring benefits, services, and satisfaction assessment methods for employees according to various types of categories [5.3b(1, 2, and 3)].
C	The customer and market groups and their requirements reported in P.1b(2) should have been determined using the processes described in 3.1a(1 and 2). The information in P.1b(2) helps examiners identify the kind of results, broken out by customer and market segment, that should be reported in Items 7.1 and 7.2.
D	The information in P.1a(1) derives from the delivery processes described in 6.1a and helps set the context for the examiner review of those processes.
E	The regulatory and related requirements descried in P.1a(5), and the key suppliers and dealers/distributors listed in P.1b(3) create an expectation that related performance results will be reported in 7.6a(4) and 7.5a(2) respectively.

P.2 ORGANIZATIONAL CHALLENGES: What are your key organizational challenges?

Describe your organization's competitive environment, your key strategic challenges, and your system for performance improvement.

Within your response, include answers to the following questions:

a. Competitive Environment

(1) What is your competitive position? What is your relative size and growth in your industry or markets served? What are the numbers and types of competitors and key collaborators for your organization?

(2) What are the principal factors that determine your success relative to your competitors? What are any key changes taking place that affect your competitive situation, including opportunities for collaboration, as appropriate?

(3) What are your key available sources of comparative and competitive data from within your industry? What are your key available sources of comparative data for analogous processes outside your industry? What limitations, if any, are there in your ability to obtain these data?

b. Strategic Challenges

What are your key business, operational, and human resource strategic challenges? What are your key strategic challenges associated with organizational sustainability?

c. Performance Improvement System

How do you maintain an overall organizational focus on performance improvement, including organizational learning? How do you achieve systematic evaluation and improvement of key processes?

Notes:

N1 Principal factors (P.2a[2]) might include differentiators such as price leadership, design services, e-services, geographic proximity, accessibility, and warranty and product options. *For some nonprofit organizations, differentiators also might include relative influence with decision makers, ratio of administrative costs to programmatic contributions, past reputation for program or service delivery, and wait times for service.*

N2 Strategic challenges (P.2b) might include rapid technological change, disruptive technologies that rapidly revolutionize or make obsolete existing processes or products, reduced cycle times for product or service introduction, industry volatility, declining market share, the changing marketplace, mergers and acquisitions, global marketing and competition, customer retention, changing or emerging customer or regulatory requirements, employee retention, an aging workforce, competition from new nonprofit or for-profit organizations, and value chain integration.

N3 Performance improvement (P.2c) is an assessment dimension used in the Scoring System to evaluate the maturity of organizational approaches and deployment. This question is intended to help you and the Baldrige Examiners set an overall context for your approach to performance improvement.

N4 Overall approaches to process improvement (P.2c) might include implementing a Lean Enterprise System, applying Six Sigma methodology, using ISO 9000:2000 standards, or employing other process improvement tools.

N5 *Nonprofit organizations frequently believe they are not in a competitive environment; however, they often must compete with other organizations and with alternative sources for similar services to secure financial and volunteer resources, membership, visibility in appropriate communities, and media attention.*

N6 *The term "industry" (P.2a[1]) is used throughout the Criteria to refer to the sector in which you operate. For nonprofit organizations, this sector might be charitable organizations, professional associations, or government or sub-sectors of one of these.*

N7 *For nonprofit organizations, the term "business" (P.2b) is used throughout the Criteria to refer to factors related to your main mission area or enterprise activity.*

P.2 Organizational Challenges Item Linkages

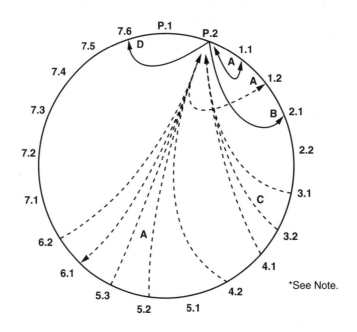

	NATURE OF RELATIONSHIP
A	Leaders [1.1a(3)] are responsible for creating an environment that drives organizational learning, which in turn contributes to the overall focus on performance improvement [P.2c(1)]. The overall approaches to systematic evaluation and improvement, organizational learning, and knowledge sharing identified in P.2c should be consistent with overall requirements for improvement specifically required in Items 1.2a(2) leadership effectiveness; 3.1a(3) improving customer requirements definition; 3.2a(4) improving customer relationships and customer access; 3.2b(4) improving processes to determine customer satisfaction; 4.1a supporting innovation and keeping up with rapid or unexpected organizational or external changes; 4.2a(4) keeping data availability (including software and hardware) current, especially in a volatile work environment; 5.2a(6) improving training and education effectiveness; 5.3a(1) improving workforce health, safety, and well-being; 6.1a(6) improving the value creation processes; and 6.2a(6) improving support services.
B	The competitive environment defined in P.2a should be examined as part of the strategy development process [2.1a(2)]. In addition, the strategic challenges identified in P.2b should be addressed by the strategic objectives in 2.1b(2).
C	Information about competitors or comparable organizations, which is needed to create the description for P.2a, uses processes discussed in Items 3.1a(1), 3.2b(3), and 4.1a(2).
D	Progress in achieving strategic challenges, as described in P.2b, should be reported in Item 7.6a(1).

*Note: To make the circle diagrams less cluttered, all of the links described in paragraph A will not be repeated on the other diagrams.

1 Leadership—120 Points

*The **Leadership** Category examines how your organization's senior leaders guide and sustain your organization. Also examined are your organization's governance and how your organization addresses its ethical, legal, and community responsibilities.*

The leadership system must promote organizational core values, set performance expectations, and promote an organization-wide focus on stakeholders, customers, employee empowerment, learning, and innovation. The Leadership Category looks at how senior leaders guide and sustain the organization in setting directions and organizational vision, developing future leaders, seeking future opportunities, and developing an environment that supports ethical behavior and high performance. Senior leaders must communicate clear values and performance expectations that address the needs of all stakeholders. The Category also looks at the how the organization practices effective governance, meets its legal and ethical responsibilities to the public, and practices good citizenship.

The Category contains two Items:

Senior Leadership

- Communicating and reinforcing clear values, performance expectations, and a focus on creating value for customers and other stakeholders

- Reinforcing an environment for empowerment and innovation and employee and organizational learning

- Providing effective governance that holds management accountable for the organization's actions, provides for fiscal accountability, and protects stockholder and stakeholder interests

- Reviewing organizational performance and capabilities, competitiveness, and progress relative to goals, and setting priorities for improvement

- Evaluating and improving the effectiveness of senior leadership and management throughout the organization, including employee input in the process

Governance and Social Responsibilities

- To ensure accountability for management's actions, transparency in operations and protecting stakeholder interests

- To evaluate the performance of senior leaders, the CEO, and the Board

- To address any adverse impacts on society caused by the organization's products, services, and operations

- To ensure ethical business practices in all transactions

- To strengthen and support key communities

1.1 SENIOR LEADERSHIP: How do your senior leaders lead? (70 Pts.) PROCESS

Describe how senior leaders guide and sustain your organization. Describe how senior leaders communicate with employees and encourage high performance.

Within your response, include answers to the following questions:

a. Vision and Values

(1) How do senior leaders set organizational vision and values? How do senior leaders deploy your organization's vision and values through your leadership system, to all employees, to key suppliers and partners, and to customers and other stakeholders, as appropriate? How do their personal actions reflect a commitment to the organization's values?

(2) How do senior leaders promote an environment that fosters and requires legal and ethical behavior?

(3) How do senior leaders create a sustainable organization? How do senior leaders create an environment for performance improvement, accomplishment of your mission and strategic objectives, innovation, and organizational agility? How do they create an environment for organizational and employee learning? How do they personally participate in succession planning and the development of future organizational leaders?

b. Communication and Organizational Performance

(1) How do senior leaders communicate with, empower, and motivate all employees throughout the organization? How do senior leaders encourage frank, two-way communication throughout the organization? How do senior leaders take an active role in employee reward and recognition to reinforce high performance and a customer and business focus?

(2) How do senior leaders create a focus on action to accomplish the organization's objectives, improve performance, and attain your vision? How do senior leaders include a focus on creating and balancing value for customers and other stakeholders in their organizational performance expectations?

Notes:

N1 Organizational vision [1.1a(1)] should set the context for strategic objectives and action plans, which are described in Items 2.1 and 2.2.

N2 A sustainable organization [1.1a(3)] is capable of addressing current business needs and possesses the agility and strategic management to prepare successfully for its future business and market environment. In this context, the concept of innovation includes both technological and organizational innovation to succeed in the future.

N3 A focus on action [1.1b(2)] considers both the people and the hard assets of the organization. It includes ongoing improvements in productivity that may be achieved through eliminating waste or reducing cycle time, and it might use techniques such as Six Sigma and Lean Production. It also includes the actions to accomplish the organization's strategic objectives.

N4 Your organizational performance results should be reported in Items 7.1–7.6.

N5. *For nonprofit organizations that rely on volunteers to supplement the work of their employees, responses to 1.1b(1) also should discuss your efforts to communicate with, empower, and motivate the volunteer workforce.*

Item 1.1 examines the key aspects of senior leaders' responsibilities to set and communicate the organization's vision and values, and focuses on the need to create and sustain a high-performance organization.

Top leaders must consistently promote high performance, set clear values and directions, and communicate them effectively to make sure all stakeholders understand their responsibilities. The most successful leaders present a strong future orientation and a commitment to improvement, innovation, and the disciplined change that is needed to carry it out. This requires creating an environment for empowerment, learning, innovation, and organizational agility, as well as the means for rapid and effective application of knowledge. This environment cannot be seen by employees as optional. Leaders must have zero tolerance for managers and employees who are not committed to work consistent with these principles.

To be successful and sustain that success, senior leaders must commit to developing the organization's future leaders and to the reward and recognition of employee performance consistent with the principles listed above. They personally participate in development of future leaders, and integrate that development into the organization's succession planning. Senior leaders should personally mentor and teach some leadership development courses. Senior leaders in high-performing organizations are personally involved in employee recognition opportunities and events to demonstrate their own unwavering commitment to excellence.

Effective communication is the main theme of Item 1.1. Through their outward focus, senior leaders push values, create expectations, and align the work of the organization. In promoting high performance, senior leaders set and deploy values, short- and longer-term directions, and performance expectations and balance the expectations of customers and other stakeholders. Leaders develop and implement systems to ensure values are understood and consistently followed. An organization's failure to achieve high levels of performance can almost always be traced to a failure in leadership.

Leaders must ensure that organizational values actually guide the behavior of managers and employees throughout the organization or the values are meaningless. To enhance performance excellence the *right* values must be adopted. These values must include a focus on customers and other stakeholders. Since various customer and stakeholder groups often have conflicting interests, leaders must strike a balance that optimizes the interests of all groups. The failure to ensure a customer focus usually causes the organization and its employees to focus internally. The lack of a customer focus forces workers to default to their own ideas of what customers really *need.* This increases the risk of becoming arrogant and not caring about the requirements of customers. It also increases the potential for creating and delivering products and services that customers do not want or value. That, in turn, increases rework, scrap, waste, and added cost/lower value.

Senior leaders must ensure two-way communication with subordinate leaders and other employees, key suppliers, and partners regarding organizational values, directions, and expectations. This two-way communication also provides an opportunity for senior leaders to receive feedback from others about their effectiveness as leaders. Two-way communication should help foster feedback from employees about leadership effectiveness. Accordingly, it is recommended that part of the communication with employees involve formal and informal employee and peer feedback of leader effectiveness, such as using a 360-degree feedback survey or an upward evaluation. This information could be structured to help evaluate the effectiveness of leaders at all levels, including the board of directors, as required in Item 1.2a(2).

Leaders must create an environment for empowerment and agility, as well as the means for rapid and effective application of knowledge. Empowerment relates to giving employees more authority over decisions about their work. Employees need adequate data and the skills to interpret the data correctly, in order to make consistently good decisions. Agility generally relates to eliminating barriers and unnecessary control gates that bureaucracies and insecure leaders put in place. Unnecessary levels of review and approval make agility impossible.

1.1 Senior Leadership

How senior leaders guide the organization in setting direction and developing and sustaining an effective leadership system throughout the organization

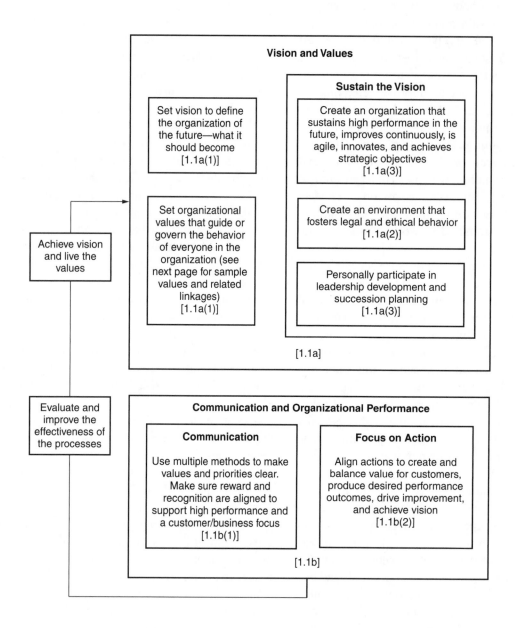

Vision and Values Linkages

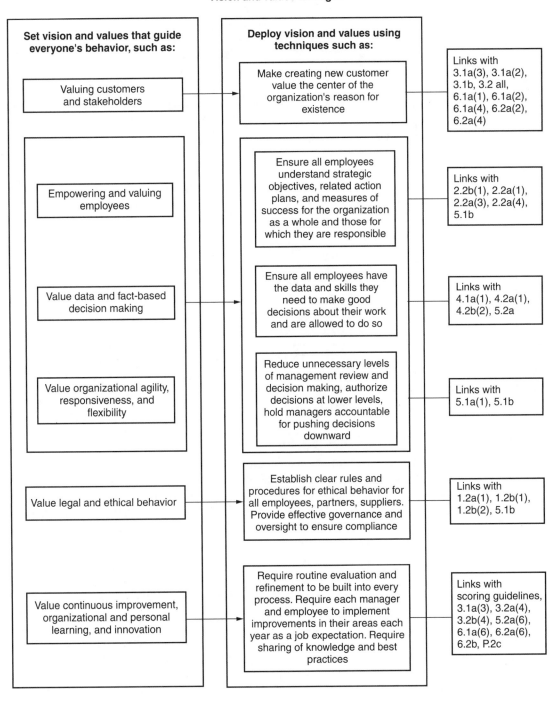

1.1 Senior Leadership Item Linkages

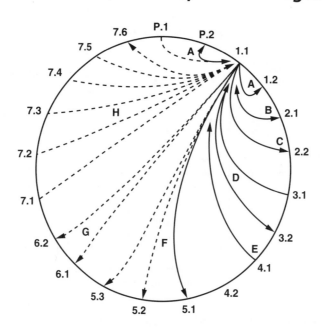

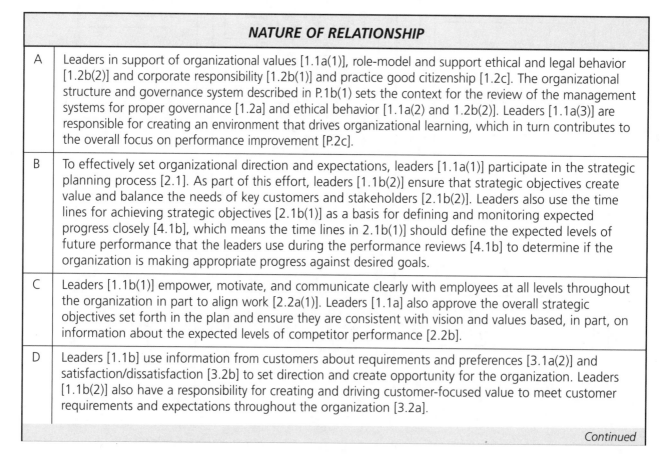

	NATURE OF RELATIONSHIP
A	Leaders in support of organizational values [1.1a(1)], role-model and support ethical and legal behavior [1.2b(2)] and corporate responsibility [1.2b(1)] and practice good citizenship [1.2c]. The organizational structure and governance system described in P.1b(1) sets the context for the review of the management systems for proper governance [1.2a] and ethical behavior [1.1a(2) and 1.2b(2)]. Leaders [1.1a(3)] are responsible for creating an environment that drives organizational learning, which in turn contributes to the overall focus on performance improvement [P.2c].
B	To effectively set organizational direction and expectations, leaders [1.1a(1)] participate in the strategic planning process [2.1]. As part of this effort, leaders [1.1b(2)] ensure that strategic objectives create value and balance the needs of key customers and stakeholders [2.1b(2)]. Leaders also use the time lines for achieving strategic objectives [2.1b(1)] as a basis for defining and monitoring expected progress closely [4.1b], which means the time lines in 2.1b(1)] should define the expected levels of future performance that the leaders use during the performance reviews [4.1b] to determine if the organization is making appropriate progress against desired goals.
C	Leaders [1.1b(1)] empower, motivate, and communicate clearly with employees at all levels throughout the organization in part to align work [2.2a(1)]. Leaders [1.1a] also approve the overall strategic objectives set forth in the plan and ensure they are consistent with vision and values based, in part, on information about the expected levels of competitor performance [2.2b].
D	Leaders [1.1b] use information from customers about requirements and preferences [3.1a(2)] and satisfaction/dissatisfaction [3.2b] to set direction and create opportunity for the organization. Leaders [1.1b(2)] also have a responsibility for creating and driving customer-focused value to meet customer requirements and expectations throughout the organization [3.2a].

Continued

	NATURE OF RELATIONSHIP *Continued*
E	Leaders [1.1] use analyses of data [4.1b(1, 2)] to monitor organizational performance and understand relationships among performance, employee satisfaction, customers, markets, and financial success. These analyses are also used for decision making at all levels to set priorities for action and allocate resources for maximum advantage [4.1b(2)]. They are also responsible for using comparative data [from 4.1a(2)] to set meaningful goals to achieve organizational success.
F	Leaders [1.1a(3)] create an environment for employee empowerment, innovation, and learning throughout the entire organization through the design of work and jobs [5.1a(1)]. They ensure that the compensation and recognition system [5.1b] encourages employees at all levels to achieve performance excellence in areas most critical to the organization and they personally participate in reward and recognition to reinforce the importance of high performance and a customer focus [1.1b(2)]. Leaders [1.1a(3)] are also responsible for creating an environment that supports appropriate skill development of all employees through training and development systems and reinforcing learning on the job [5.2a], as well as creating effective systems to enhance employee satisfaction, well-being, and motivation [5.3b].
G	Leaders [1.1a(3) and 1.1b(2)] are responsible for creating an environment that supports high performance and continuous improvement, including monitoring processes for value creation [6.1] and support services [6.2]. Leaders must ensure that design, production/delivery, support, and supplier performance processes are aligned and consistently evaluated and refined.
H	To reinforce values, vision, and sustain business success, senior leaders [1.1] use performance results data [from Category 7] for many activities, including monitoring organizational performance [4.1b(1)]; deploying priority improvement areas to focus work and ensure alignment [4.1b(2)]; strategic planning [2.1a]; setting goals and priorities [2.1b(1)]; reinforcing or rewarding employee performance [5.1b]; and for improving their effectiveness and the effectiveness of leaders at all levels [1.2a(2)]. In addition, key results of leadership performance, such as results related to ethical behavior [1.2b(2)] and fiscal accountability [1.2a(1)], and meeting strategic objectives [2.1b(2)] are reported in Leadership and Social Responsibility Results [7.6a(1, 2, and 3)].

IF YOU DON'T DO WHAT THE CRITERIA REQUIRE . . .	
Item Reference	**Possible Adverse Consequences**
1.1a(1)	If senior leaders fail to make vision, values, and performance expectations clear (especially defining them in measurable terms), it may create uncertainty among managers and employees throughout the organization about what they must accomplish, and the direction they must follow. This may cause managers to substitute their own ideas, objectives, and directions, which may not be in alignment with those of top leadership. The lack of alignment may also contribute to redundancy and wasted resources. As a consequence, some parts of the organization may work at cross-purposes with other parts of the organization.
1.1a(2)	If senior leaders do not create an environment that requires legal and ethical behavior in all interactions, those who operate without regard to law and ethics will create problems for the organization that could threaten its existence (consider Enron).
1.1a(3)	Failing to put systems in place to sustain high performance has caused some organizations to decline and fail...even past Baldrige Award recipients. Creating a sustainable organization requires leaders to embed values of empowering employees, continuous improvement, fact-based decision making, and a passion for satisfying customers. To help sustain these practices, rewards and recognition systems must demand these behaviors, reinforce the use of these tools, and discipline those who fail to use them.
1.1b(1)	If senior leaders do not create an environment that promotes employee empowerment, they risk not leveraging the high power of a formidable asset—their people. As a consequence, leaders may be effectively sending a message that employees do not have the skills or ability to make decisions on their own—that micromanagement is the preferred approach within the organization. This kind of environment tends to migrate decision making to higher and higher levels in the organization, creating excessive delay and working against organizational agility. Unnecessary levels of review and approval may also tend to minimize innovation and creativity throughout the organization. Taken together, these problems are likely to add cost but not value—making it increasingly difficult to be successful in a highly competitive industry.
1.1b(2)	If senior leaders do not create an environment that focuses on creating value for customers and other stakeholders, employees and managers within the organization may become internally focused and risk negatively impacting the customer value on which the organization was built. An internal focus may contribute to a climate where employees are not primarily interested in listening to customer requirements or concerns. This may produce a high level of organizational arrogance where employees believe they know what the customers want better than the customer. This type of behavior can antagonize customers and produce high levels of customer dissatisfaction.

In a related area, if senior leaders do not create an environment that focuses on balancing value for customers and other stakeholders—especially when different customer groups have competing interests—it may erode customer confidence in one group and eventually cause a loss of customers. For example, end users of a product want inexpensive, reliable products, while stockholders want profits and stock price to increase. Excessive focus on one group over the other makes it difficult to maximize value and keep both end users and stockholders loyal. |

1.1 SENIOR LEADERSHIP—SAMPLE EFFECTIVE PRACTICES

Perhaps most critical is that senior leaders demonstrate absolute, unwavering commitment to performance excellence—including aligning reward and recognition to provide incentives and disincentives. The best senior leaders do not tolerate a lack of aggressive commitment and urgent action from subordinate managers throughout the organization. They send a clear message to employees that the effort is serious.

A. Vision and Values

- All senior leaders are personally involved in performance improvement.

- Senior leaders spend a significant portion of their time on performance improvement activities.

- Senior leaders carry out many visible activities (for example, goal-setting, planning, and recognition and reward of performance and process improvement).

- Senior leaders regularly communicate performance excellence values to managers and ensure that managers demonstrate those values in their work.

- Senior leaders participate on performance improvement teams and use quality tools and practices.

- Senior leaders mentor managers and ensure that promotion criteria reflect organizational values, especially customer satisfaction.

- Senior leaders study and learn about the improvement practices of other organizations.

- Senior leaders clearly and consistently articulate values (customer focus, customer satisfaction, role model leadership, continuous improvement, workforce involvement, and performance optimization) throughout the organization.

- Senior leaders ensure that organizational values are used to provide direction to all employees in the organization to help achieve the mission, vision, and performance goals.

- Senior leaders use effective and innovative approaches to reach out to all employees to spread the organization's values and align its work to support organizational goals.

- Senior leaders effectively surface problems and encourage employee risk taking.

- Roles and responsibilities of managers are clearly defined, understood by them, and used to evaluate and improve their performance.

- Managers serve as role models (walk the talk) in leading quality and systematic performance improvement.

- Job definitions with quality indices are clearly delineated for each level of the organization, objectively measured, and presented in a logical and organized structure.

- Leader behavior (not merely words) clearly defines what is expected of the organization and its employees.

- Systems and procedures are deployed that encourage cooperation and a cross-functional approach to management, team activities, and problem solving.

- Leaders monitor employee acceptance and adoption of vision and values using annual surveys, employee focus groups, and e-mail questions.

- A systematic process is in place for evaluating and improving the integration or alignment of quality values throughout the organization.

B. Communication and Organizational Performance

- Many different techniques are used to reinforce quality values. Leaders at all levels make two-way communication easy through personal methods such as voice mail, e-mail, town hall meetings, and face-to-face meetings.

- Actions are taken to assist units that are not meeting goals or performing to plan.

- Leaders at all levels determine how well they carried out their activities (what went right or wrong and how they could be done better).

- There is evidence of adopting changes to improve leader effectiveness.

- Senior leaders require all key processes to have defined the customers (internal and external) and other stakeholders that might have competing interests, for their specific requirements, in measurable terms, a process to monitor their satisfaction, and a process to correct problems quickly.

1.2 GOVERNANCE AND SOCIAL RESPONSIBILITIES: How do you govern and address your social responsibilities? (50 Pts.)   PROCESS

Describe your organization's governance system. Describe how your organization addresses its responsibilities to the public, ensures ethical behavior, and practices good citizenship.

Within your response, include answers to the following questions:

a. Organizational Governance

(1) How does your organization address the following key factors in your governance system:

- Accountability for management's actions

- Fiscal accountability

- Transparency in operations and selection and disclosure policies for governance board members, as appropriate

- Independence in internal and external audits

- Protection of stakeholder and stockholder interests, as appropriate

(2) How do you evaluate the performance of your senior leaders, including the chief executive? How do you evaluate the performance of members of the governance board, as appropriate? How do senior leaders and the governance board use these performance reviews to improve both their personal leadership effectiveness and that of your board and leadership system, as appropriate?

b. Legal and Ethical Behavior

(1) How do you address any adverse impacts on society of your products, services, and operations? How do you anticipate public concerns with current and future products, services, and operations? How do you prepare for these concerns in a proactive manner, including using resource-sustaining processes, as appropriate? What are your key compliance processes, measures, and goals for achieving and surpassing regulatory and legal requirements, as appropriate? What are your key processes, measures, and goals for addressing risks associated with your products, services, and operations?

(2) How does your organization promote and ensure ethical behavior in all your interactions? What are your key processes and measures or indicators for enabling and monitoring ethical behavior in your governance structure, throughout your organization, and in interactions with customers, partners, and other stakeholders? How do you monitor and respond to breaches of ethical behavior?

c. Support of Key Communities

How does your organization actively support and strengthen your key communities? How do you identify key communities and determine areas of emphasis for organizational involvement and support? What are your key communities? How do your senior leaders and your employees contribute to improving these communities?

Notes:

N1   Societal responsibilities in areas critical to your organization's ongoing success also should be addressed in Strategy Development (Item 2.1) and in Process Management (Category 6). Key results, such as results of regulatory and legal compliance (including the results of mandated financial audits) or environmental improvements through use of "green" technology or other means, should be reported as Leadership and Social Responsibility Results (Item 7.6).

Continued

Notes:

Continued

N2 Transparency in operations [1.2a(1)] should include your internal controls on governance processes. *For those nonprofit organizations that serve as stewards of public funds, stewardship of those funds and transparency in operations are areas of emphasis.*

N3 Leadership performance evaluation [1.2a(2)] might be supported by peer reviews, formal performance management reviews [5.1b], and formal or informal employee and other stakeholder feedback and surveys. *For some businesses and governmental organizations, external advisory boards might evaluate the performance of senior leaders and the governance board.*

N4 Measures or indicators of ethical behavior [1.2b[2]) might include the percentage of independent board members, measures of relationships with stockholder and non-stockholder constituencies, instances of ethical conduct breaches and responses, survey results on employee perceptions of organizational ethics, ethics hotline use, and results of ethics reviews and audits. They also might include evidence that policies, staff training, and monitoring systems are in place with respect to conflicts of interest and proper use of funds.

N5 Areas of community support appropriate for inclusion in 1.2c might include your efforts to strengthen local community services, education, and health; the environment; and practices of trade, business, or professional associations.

N6 The health and safety of employees are not addressed in Item 1.2; you should address these employee factors in Item 5.3.

N7 *Nonprofit organizations should report in 1.2b(1), as appropriate, how they address the legal and regulatory requirements and standards that govern fundraising and lobbying activities.*

This Item [1.2] looks at the organization's governance systems; how it fulfills its public responsibilities, how the senior leaders ensure ethical and legal behavior, and how senior leaders and employees encourage, support, and practice good citizenship.

The first part of this Item [1.2a] looks at how the organization addresses the need for a responsible, informed, and accountable governance or advisory body that can protect the interests of key stakeholders, such as stockholders (if they exist). It should have independence in review and audit functions. It also should have a performance-evaluation function that monitors organizational and CEO performance.

Senior leaders must review organizational performance in a disciplined, fact-based manner, and use review findings to drive improvement and innovation. This organizational review should cover all areas of performance, and provide a complete and accurate picture of the *state of health* of the organization. This includes not only how well the organization is currently performing but also how well it is moving to secure future success [4.1b(1)].

Key performance measures should focus on and reflect the key drivers of success leaders regularly review. These measures should relate to the strategic objectives necessary for success.

Leaders should use these reviews to drive improvement and change. These reviews should provide a reliable means to guide the improvement and change needed to achieve the organization's key objectives, success factors, and measures.

Leaders must create a consistent process to translate the review findings into an action agenda, sufficiently specific for deployment throughout the organization and to suppliers/partners—people who need to take action to improve [4.1b(2)].

The organization must evaluate the effectiveness of senior leaders, board members, and the entire leadership system. To ensure the evaluation is accurate, employees should provide feedback to the leaders and managers at all levels, which may be accomplished, in part, by the two-way communication required in Item 1.1a(1) and using tools such as 360-degree reviews and upward evaluations.

Leaders and managers at all levels should take action, based on the feedback, to improve their effectiveness. It is critical that leaders, managers, and supervisors at all levels and in all parts of the organization effectively drive and reinforce the principles of performance excellence through words and actions. Remember, nearly every failure to achieve and sustain excellence can be traced to a failure on the part of leaders and managers. Jack Welch, former CEO of General Electric, in his last letter to stockholders emphasized the importance of rewarding and nurturing the top 20 percent of employees, and getting rid of the bottom 10 percent. The same is true of managers who do not or will not aggressively and effectively lead the effort to enhance performance excellence.

The second part of this Item [1.2b] looks at how the organization addresses current and future impacts on society in a proactive manner, and how the organization, its senior leaders, and its employees ensure ethical business practices are followed in all stakeholder transactions and interactions. The impacts and practices are expected to cover all relevant and important areas—products, services, and operations.

An integral part of performance management and improvement is proactively addressing the need for ethical behavior, legal and regulatory requirements, and risk factors. Addressing these areas requires establishing appropriate measures and/or indicators that senior leaders track in their overall performance review. The organization should be sensitive to issues of public concern, whether or not these issues are currently embodied in law. Role-model organizations look for opportunities to exceed requirements and to excel in areas of legal and ethical behavior. The failure to address these areas can expose the organization to future problems when it least expects them. Problems can range from a sudden decline in consumer confidence to extensive and costly litigation. In this regard, it is important to anticipate potential problems the public may have with both current and future products. Sometimes a well-intended product or service could create adverse public consequences.

For example, consider the use of automatic teller machines (ATMs) or cash machines as they are called today. When these machines were first introduced, many in the industry believed that the public would never accept the machines as a surrogate for a human being. For the most part, these machines were considered an eyesore and were installed in out-of-the-way places, usually at the back of the bank building. The extraordinary success of these devices, however, resulted in hundreds of millions of people conducting cash transactions outside the relative safety of the bank building. This gave rise to more robberies, abductions, and even murder. By failing to consider the potential adverse consequence of these cash machines located in out-of-the-way places, banks were exposed to increased litigation and costs associated with relocating or providing appropriate security enclosures for the machines in an effort to reduce public risk.

The organization must also address the use of resource-sustaining processes. These processes might include *green* technologies, replacement of hazardous chemicals with water-based chemicals, energy conservation, use of cleaner energy sources, or the recycling of by-products or wastes. Good social responsibility implies going beyond minimum compliance with laws and regulations. Top-performing organizations frequently serve as role models of responsibility and provide leadership in areas key to business success. For example, a manufacturing company might go beyond the requirements of the environmental protection regulations and develop innovative and award-winning systems to protect the environment and reduce pollution. This has a double benefit. Not only do they develop good relations with regulators (and occasionally receive the benefit of the doubt), but when regulators increase requirements, the high-performing organizations are already in compliance, usually way ahead of competitors who only met minimum requirements.

Standards of ethical behavior should be defined (preferably in measurable terms) and everyone in the organization should understand and follow the standards. The organization must systematically monitor ethical behavior throughout the organization and with key suppliers, partners, and within the governance structure. Failing to follow the standards of ethical behavior should have prompt and serious consequences for every governing board member, leader, manager, employee, supplier, and partner.

Ensuring ethical business practices are followed by all employees lessens the organization's risk of adverse public reaction as well as criminal prosecution. Programs to ensure ethical business practices typically seek to prevent activities that might be perceived as criminal or near criminal. Examples of unethical business practices might include falsifying expense reports or quality-control data, accepting lavish gifts from a contractor, or seeking kickbacks.

The third part of this Item [1.2c] looks at how the organization, its senior leaders, and its employees identify, support, and strengthen key communities as part of good citizenship practices:

Good citizenship practices typically vary according to the size, complexity, and location of the organization. Larger organizations are generally expected to have a more comprehensive approach to citizenship than small organizations. Good citizenship opportunities are available to organizations of all sizes. These opportunities include encouraging and supporting employees' community service.

Examples of organizational community involvement include: influencing the adoption of higher standards in education by communicating employability requirements to schools and school boards; partnering with other businesses and healthcare providers to improve health in the local community by providing education and volunteer services to address public-health issues; and partnering to influence trade and business associations to engage in beneficial, cooperative activities, such as sharing best practices to improve overall U.S. global competitiveness and the environment.

In addition to activities directly carried out by the organization, opportunities to practice good citizenship include employee community service that is encouraged and supported by the organization. Frequently, the organization's leaders actively participate on community boards and actively support their work. Usually, organizations—like people—support causes and issues they value. Top-performing organizations are not content to simply donate money, people, and products/services to these causes without examining the impact of this support. Just as senior leaders examine the other parts of their business, they also evaluate and refine the effectiveness of community support, consistent with business strategies and objectives.

1.2 Governance and Social Responsibilities

How the organization addresses governance and public responsibilities, ensures legal and ethical behavior, and practices good citizenship

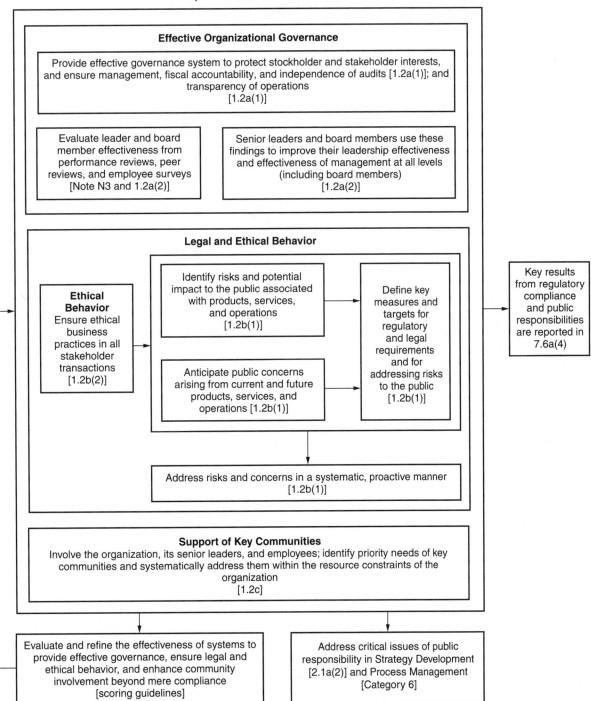

Responsibilities to the Public

Effective Organizational Governance

Provide effective governance system to protect stockholder and stakeholder interests, and ensure management, fiscal accountability, and independence of audits [1.2a(1)]; and transparency of operations [1.2a(1)]

Evaluate leader and board member effectiveness from performance reviews, peer reviews, and employee surveys [Note N3 and 1.2a(2)]

Senior leaders and board members use these findings to improve their leadership effectiveness and effectiveness of management at all levels (including board members) [1.2a(2)]

Legal and Ethical Behavior

Ethical Behavior
Ensure ethical business practices in all stakeholder transactions [1.2b(2)]

Identify risks and potential impact to the public associated with products, services, and operations [1.2b(1)]

Anticipate public concerns arising from current and future products, services, and operations [1.2b(1)]

Define key measures and targets for regulatory and legal requirements and for addressing risks to the public [1.2b(1)]

Key results from regulatory compliance and public responsibilities are reported in 7.6a(4)

Address risks and concerns in a systematic, proactive manner [1.2b(1)]

Support of Key Communities
Involve the organization, its senior leaders, and employees; identify priority needs of key communities and systematically address them within the resource constraints of the organization [1.2c]

Evaluate and refine the effectiveness of systems to provide effective governance, ensure legal and ethical behavior, and enhance community involvement beyond mere compliance [scoring guidelines]

Address critical issues of public responsibility in Strategy Development [2.1a(2)] and Process Management [Category 6]

1.2 Governance and Social Responsibilities Item Linkages

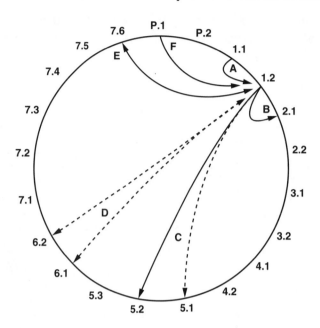

NATURE OF RELATIONSHIP	
A	Leaders, in support of organizational values [1.1a(1)], have a responsibility for setting policies and ensuring that practices and products of the organization and its employees do not adversely impact society or violate ethical standards, regulations, or law [1.2b]. They are also responsible to be personally involved and to ensure that the organization and its employees strengthen key communities in areas such as local community services, education, health, the environment, and business, professional, and trade associations, [1.2c].
B	Public health and safety concerns, environmental protection, and waste management issues [1.2b] are important factors to consider in strategy development [2.1a(2)].
C	Training [5.2] is provided to ensure all employees understand the organization's ethical business practices [1.2b] as well as the importance of strengthening key communities [1.2c]. In addition, recruitment and hiring and the design of work systems should capitalize on the ideas, culture, and thinking of key communities and their impact on the organization [5.1c(2)].
D	Governance, ethical, and legal rules [1.2a and b] guide the development and execution of value creation [6.1] and support processes [6.2]. Managers at all levels have responsibility for ensuring that work practices of the organization [6.1 and 6.2] are consistent with the organization's standards of ethics and public responsibility [1.2b].
E	Key results, such as results of regulatory and legal compliance [1.2b], anticipating public concerns [1.2b(1)], ethical behavior [1.2b(2)], and support to key communities [1.2c], are reported in Leadership and Social Responsibilities Results [7.6a(2,4,5)]. In addition, these results are monitored to determine if process changes are needed. (Results in areas of employee safety and well-being are reported in 7.4, based on processes described in Item 5.3, Employee Well-Being and Satisfaction, and are not a part of the requirements in 1.2.)
F	The regulatory environment described in P.1a(5) sets the context for the review of the management systems for governance [1.2a] and legal/ethical behavior [1.2b].

	IF YOU DON'T DO WHAT THE CRITERIA REQUIRE . . .
Item Reference	**Possible Adverse Consequences**
1.2a(1)	The adverse consequences of corrupt or incompetent organizational governance can be sudden and spectacular. One need only consider the impact of poor governance on Enron and similar companies whose businesses failed suddenly, hurting thousands of stakeholders, and tearing the economic fabric of the national and world economy. With increased stakeholder scrutiny and decreased trust, organizations that do not have visible and effective processes in place to ensure fiscal and management accountability and protect stockholder and employee interests may not be able to overcome the climate of distrust that permeates the corporate sector today. Their stock prices and consumer confidence may remain flat. Intrusive government oversight may increase, which diverts leadership attention and company resources away from value-adding outcomes needed to beat competitors and satisfy customers and other stakeholders.
1.2a(2)	Even a new employee can tell the difference between an effective leader and an incompetent one. Unfortunately, an incompetent leader is frequently blind to this fact. (Where do you think Scott Adams gets his material for the *Dilbert* cartoon?) The combination of organizational performance outcomes and employee (subordinate) feedback can provide critical information to help leaders throughout the leadership system identify personal strengths and opportunities for improvement. Without this information, leaders may not be able to focus effectively on areas where improvement would be essential not only to personal growth and development but also to better organizational results. Leaders who do not receive accurate feedback about their strengths and weaknesses may not be able to keep pace with changing business needs and directions, as they are challenged to work smarter by customers, competitors, and the demands of stockholders and other stakeholders. They may not be able to lead their organization to winning levels of performance excellence.
1.2b(1)	Organizations that fail to consider the impact on the public of their products, services, and operations may be seriously impaired in the future if it is determined that these products or services cause harm. (The problem may be so serious that it could cause the organization to go out of business relatively quickly, as in the case of Dow-Corning and the silicone breast implants.) In the short term, organizations that fail to comply with regulatory and legal requirements may find themselves facing costly sanctions or be inhibited from conducting business. The failure to consider risks associated with products, services, and operations may contribute to costly corrective action or litigation. For example, banks throughout the world have been forced to pay damages to users of automatic teller machines (ATMs) because of the failure to provide adequate security, which resulted in abductions, robbery, and murders. Organizations that fail to anticipate and consider potential concerns that the public may have with current and future products, services, and operations may be faced with costly redesign or redirection. When an organization appears to treat the public and the community within which it works with impunity and disregards their concerns, it becomes extremely difficult to recover trust and confidence. When the organization finds it needs public support to carry out its work or expand its operations, it may find it difficult to secure that support from the public.

Continued

	IF YOU DON'T DO WHAT THE CRITERIA REQUIRE . . . Continued
Item Reference	**Possible Adverse Consequences**
1.2b(2)	Organizations that do not ensure ethical business practices in all transactions and interactions with stakeholders (public, customers, stockholders, employees, suppliers, and so on) run the risk of violating the public trust. Accordingly, these organizations may face serious adverse consequences when their misdeeds are discovered. (One only need consider the difference between Enron and Tylenol. Both companies faced disasters that threatened their existence. Tylenol responded ethically and is still thriving.) Moreover, if the unethical practices of leaders are considered an acceptable business standard in the organization and repeated by others, they can contribute to numerous unpredictable problems that divert human and financial resources to correct.
1.2c	Organizations that fail to act as good corporate citizens and support the local community may find it difficult to get support in return, especially for projects or initiatives that require local approval. For example, local communities typically provide the bulk of support for services as well as new workers. Organizations that fail to support local education or trade and professional associations may find themselves faced with a shortage of skilled workers in key areas and important services they need to conduct business.

1.2 GOVERNANCE AND SOCIAL RESPONSIBILITIES—SAMPLE EFFECTIVE PRACTICES

A. Organizational Governance

- Independence of the board of directors is ensured by requiring that a substantial percentage of directors come from outside the organization.

- Fiscal accountability is assured by a variety of processes including independent audits and separation of consultants from auditing functions. Audit and consulting services are not provided by the same or affiliated companies.

- Stockholders approve the election slates for the board of directors and even place names on the slate.

- Board term limits enable rotating membership to ensure fresh and objective voices are present on the board.

- Board audit committees contain at least one financial expert who is independent of the company.

- The full board of directors reviews financial statements quarterly after the CEO and CFO certify accuracy.

- Directors with competing interests, such as key suppliers or interlocking directors, are eliminated or minimized.

- Dissent, debate, and open criticism are encouraged among board members.

- CEOs promote candor and meaningful discussion at board meetings by sharing relevant information with directors before meetings to permit careful analysis before deliberations begin.

- Board members formally assess their peers in writing and ask poorly performing members to resign.

- A climate of trust and candor exists among board members. No secret group wields power to make back-room decisions.

- Demonstrated proficiency in the use of the Baldrige Criteria is a prerequisite to promotion to leadership positions.

B. Legal and Ethical Behavior

- The organization's principal business activities include systems to analyze, anticipate, and minimize public hazards or risk.

- Indicators for risk areas are identified and monitored.

- Improvement strategies are used consistently, target performance levels are set, and progress is reviewed regularly and tied to recognition and reward.

- The organization considers the impact that its operations, products, and services might have on society and considers those impacts in planning.

- The effectiveness of systems to meet or exceed regulatory or legal requirements is systematically evaluated and improved.

- A formal system is in place to train all employees about ethical business requirements.

- A process is in place to test the understanding of ethical principles for all people who must follow the principles. This may include employees, governing board members, suppliers, and partners.

- An audit process is in place to communicate and ensure ethical requirements, and practices are deployed to all levels of the organization and to key partners, suppliers, and members of the board of directors (governance group).

- The effective capability of systems to meet or exceed ethical requirements is systematically evaluated and improved.

- Senior leaders systematically and routinely check the effectiveness of their leadership activities (for example, seeking feedback at least annually from employees and peers using an upward or 360-degree evaluation), and take steps to improve.

C. Support of Key Communities

- Senior leaders and employees at various levels in the organization are involved in professional organizations, committees, task forces, or other community activities.

- Organizational resources are allocated to support involvement in community activities outside the organization. The effectiveness of these allocations is examined to determine if expectations are met and resources are used wisely.

- Employees participate in local, state, or national quality award programs and receive recognition from the organization.

- Employees participate in a variety of professional quality- and business-improvement associations.

- The effectiveness of processes to support and strengthen key communities is systematically measured, evaluated, and improved.

2 Strategic Planning—85 Points

*The **Strategic Planning** Category examines how your organization develops strategic objectives and action plans. Also examined are how your chosen strategic objectives and action plans are deployed and changed if circumstances require, and how progress is measured.*

The Strategic Planning Category looks at the organization's process for strategic and action planning, and deployment of plans to make sure everyone is working to achieve those plans. This Category examines how plans are changed if change is required, and how accomplishments are measured and sustained. Customer-driven quality, long-term sustainability, and operational performance excellence are key strategic issues that need to be integral parts of the organization's overall planning.

- Customer-driven quality is a strategic view of quality. The focus is on the drivers of customer satisfaction, customer retention, new markets, and market share—key factors in competitiveness, profitability, and business success.

- Operational performance improvement contributes to short- and longer-term productivity growth and cost/price competitiveness. Building operational capability—including speed, responsiveness, and flexibility—represents an investment in strengthening the organization's competitive position now and into the future.

- Organizational and personal learning are necessary strategic considerations in today's intense environment. The Criteria emphasize that improvement and learning must be embedded in work processes. The special role of strategic planning is to align work processes and learning initiatives with the organization's strategic directions, thereby ensuring that improvement and learning prepare organization personnel and reinforce organizational priorities.

Over the years, much debate and discussion have taken place around planning. Professors in our colleges and universities spend a great deal of time trying to differentiate strategic planning, long-term planning, short-term planning, tactical planning, operational planning, quality planning, business planning, and human resource planning, to name a few. A much simpler view, however, might serve us better. For our purposes, the following captures the essence of planning:

- Strategic planning is simply an effort to identify in outcome-oriented, measurable terms, the things we must actually achieve to be successful in the future.

- Once we have determined what we must actually achieve to be successful in the future (the plan), we must take steps to execute that plan (the actions).

In addition, strategic planning helps provide a basis for aligning the organization's work processes with its strategic directions, thereby ensuring people and processes in different parts of the organization are not working at cross-purposes. To the extent that alignment does not occur, the organization's effectiveness and competitiveness are reduced.

The Strategic Planning Category looks at how the organization:

- Determines its strengths, weaknesses, opportunities, threats, and its ability to execute its strategy.

- Understands the key customer, market, and operational requirements as input to setting strategic directions. This helps to ensure that ongoing process improvements are aligned with the organization's strategic directions.

- Optimizes the use of resources, ensures the availability of trained employees, and bridges short-

and longer-term requirements that may involve capital expenditures, supplier development, new human resource recruitment strategies, reengineering key processes, technology development, and other factors affecting organizational success.

- Ensures that deployment will be effective—that there are mechanisms to transmit requirements and achieve alignment on three basic levels: 1) the organization and executive level; 2) the key-process level; and 3) the work-unit and individual-job level.

The requirements for the Strategic Planning Category are intended to encourage strategic thinking and acting—to develop a basis for achieving and maintaining a competitive position. These requirements do not demand formalized plans, planning systems, departments, or specific planning cycles. They also do not imply that all improvements could or should be planned in advance. They do, however, require plans and the alignment of actions to achieve those plans at all levels of the organization.

An effective improvement system combines improvements of many types and degrees of involvement. An effective system to improve performance and competitive advantage requires fact-based strategic guidance, particularly when improvement alternatives compete for limited resources. In most cases, priority setting depends heavily upon a cost rationale. However, an organization might also have to deal with critical requirements, such as public responsibilities, that are not driven by cost considerations alone.

Strategic planning consists of the planning process, the identification of goals (measurable outcome-oriented strategic objectives) and actions (activities with measures to monitor progress and completion) necessary to achieve success, and the deployment of those actions to align the work of the organization.

Strategy Development

Sample elements considered during strategic planning include the following:
- Customers: market requirements and evolving expectations and opportunities

- Competitive environment and capabilities relative to competitors: industry and market

- Technologies and other innovations that might affect products and services and future business operations

- Internal strengths and weaknesses, including human resource capabilities and needs, resource availability, and operational capabilities and needs

- Financial, societal, ethical, regulatory, and other potential risks that may affect business success

- Opportunities to redirect resources to higher-priority products, services, or business areas

- Changes in economic conditions (local, national, or global) that might affect the business

- Unique organizational factors such as supplier and supply chain, capabilities, and needs

- Clear strategic objectives with timetables that help leaders determine where the organization should be at given points in time so they can effectively monitor progress

Strategy Deployment

Sample elements considered during strategic deployment include the following:

- Translate strategy into action plans and related human resource plans

- Align and deploy action-plan requirements, performance measures, and resources throughout the organization to ensure changes or improvements are sustained

- Define measures for tracking progress on action plans and ensure actions are aligned throughout the organization

- Project expected performance results, including assumptions of competitor performance increases

2.1 STRATEGY DEVELOPMENT: How do you develop your strategy? (40 Pts.) PROCESS

Describe how your organization establishes its strategy and strategic objectives, including how you address your strategic challenges. Summarize your organization's key strategic objectives and their related goals.

Within your response, include answers to the following questions:

a. Strategy Development Process

(1) How does your organization conduct its strategic planning? What are the key process steps? Who are the key participants? How does your process identify potential blind spots? What are your short- and longer-term planning time horizons? How are these time horizons set? How does your strategic planning process address these time horizons?

(2) How do you ensure that strategic planning addresses the key factors listed below? How do you collect and analyze relevant data and information pertaining to these factors as part of your strategic planning process:

- Your organization's strengths, weaknesses, opportunities, and threats

- Early indications of major shifts in technology, markets, competition, or the regulatory environment

- Long-term organizational sustainability and business continuity in emergencies

- Your ability to execute the strategic plan

b. Strategic Objectives

(1) What are your key strategic objectives and your timetable for accomplishing them? What are your most important goals for these strategic objectives?

(2) How do your strategic objectives address the challenges identified in response to P.2 in your Organizational Profile? How do you ensure that your strategic objectives balance short- and longer-term challenges and opportunities? How do you ensure that your strategic objectives balance the needs of all key stakeholders?

Notes:

N1 "Strategy development" refers to your organization's approach (formal or informal) to preparing for the future. Strategy development might utilize various types of forecasts, projections, options, scenarios, or other approaches to envisioning the future for purposes of decision making and resource allocation. Strategy development might involve key suppliers, distributors, partners, and customers. *For some nonprofit organizations, strategy development might involve organizations providing similar services or drawing from the same donor population or volunteer workforce.*

N2 "Strategy" should be interpreted broadly. Strategy might be built around or lead to any or all of the following: new products, services, and markets; revenue growth via various approaches, including acquisitions, grants, and endowments; divestitures; new partnerships and alliances; and new employee or volunteer relationships. Strategy might be directed toward becoming a preferred supplier, a local supplier in each of your major customers' or partners' markets, a low-cost producer, a market innovator, or a high-end or customized product or service provider.

N3 Your organization's strengths, weaknesses, opportunities, and threats (2.1a[2]) should address all factors that are key to your organization's future success, including the following, as appropriate: your customer and market needs, expectations, and opportunities; your competitive environment and your capabilities relative to competitors and comparable organizations; your product life cycle; technological and other key innovations or changes that might affect your products and services and how you operate, as well as the rate of that innovation; your

Continued

Notes: *Continued*

human and other resource needs; your opportunities to redirect resources to higher priority products, services, or areas; financial, societal, ethical, regulatory, technological, and other potential risks; changes in the national or global economy; partner and supply chain needs, strengths, and weaknesses; and other factors unique to your organization.

N4 Your ability to execute the strategic plan (2.1a[2]) also should address your organizational agility based on contingency plans or if circumstances require a shift in plans and rapid execution of new or changed plans.

N5 Strategic objectives that address key challenges (2.1b[2]) might include rapid response, customization, co-location with major customers or partners, specific joint ventures, virtual manufacturing, rapid innovation, ISO 9000:2000 or ISO 14000 registration, Web-based supplier and customer relationship management, and product and service quality enhancements. Responses to Item 2.1 should focus on your specific challenges—those most important to your ongoing success and to strengthening your organization's overall performance.

N6 Item 2.1 addresses your overall organizational strategy, which might include changes in services, products, and product lines. However, the Item does not address product and service design; you should address these factors in Item 6.1, as appropriate.

This Item [2.1] looks at how the organization develops measurable, outcome-oriented strategic objectives, with the aim of strengthening overall performance and competitiveness.

The first part of this Item [2.1a(1)] asks the organization to describe its strategic planning process and identify the key participants, key steps, and planning-time horizons. This helps examiners understand the steps and data used in the planning process. It is usually a good idea to provide a flowchart of the planning process. This helps examiners understand how the planning process works without wasting valuable space in the application.

The organization must consider the key factors that affect its future success. These factors cover external and internal influences on the organization. Each factor must be addressed and should show how relevant data and information are gathered and analyzed. Although the organization is not limited to the number of factors it considers important in planning, the factors identified in Item 2.1a(2) must be addressed unless a valid rationale can be offered as to why the factor is not appropriate. (Note: If a strategic challenge listed in P.2b is not really a challenge that must be addressed, it may be a good idea to delete it from the P.2b list to prevent confusion within the examiner team.) Together, these factors will cover the

most important variables for any organization's future success.

The planning process should examine all the key influences, risks, challenges, and other factors that might affect the organization's future opportunities and directions—taking as long-term a view as possible. This approach is intended to provide a thorough and realistic context for the development of a customer- and market-focused strategy to guide ongoing decision making, resource allocation, and overall management.

This planning process should cover all types of businesses, competitive situations, strategic issues, planning approaches, and plans. The strategic plan produces a future- and results-oriented basis for action but does not require any specific type of formalized planning, planning departments, planning cycles, or a specified way of visualizing the future. Even if the organization is seeking to create an entirely new business situation, effective planning still requires setting outcome-oriented objectives to define and guide future actions and monitor performance to ensure appropriate progress is being made.

Strategic planning helps identify the factors and actions the organization must take to achieve and sustain a leadership position in a competitive market. This usually requires ongoing revenue growth and improvements in operational effectiveness. Achieving and sustaining a leadership position in a competitive market requires a view of the future that includes not only the markets or segments in which the organization competes, but also how it competes. How it competes presents many options and requires understanding of the organization's and competitors' strengths and weaknesses.

No specific time horizon for planning is required by the Criteria; the thrust of this Item is finding ways to create and ensure sustained competitive leadership.

To maintain competitive leadership, an increasingly important part of strategic planning requires processes to project the competitive environment accurately. Such projections help detect and reduce competitive threats, shorten reaction time, and identify opportunities. Depending on the size and type of business, maturity of markets, pace of change, and competitive parameters (such as price or innovation rate), organizations might use a variety of modeling, scenario, or other techniques and judgments to project the competitive environment.

The second part of this Item [2.1b] asks for a summary of the organization's key strategic objectives and the timetable for accomplishing them. It also asks how these objectives address the challenges outlined in the Organizational Profile. Strategic plan execution is a significant challenge, especially given market demands for agility and preparation for unexpected change. Therefore, this Item and Item 2.2 highlight the need to focus not only on developing plans but also on the capability to execute them.

The purpose of the timetable required by Item 2.1b(1) is to provide a basis for projecting the path that improvement is likely to take. This allows the leaders who monitor progress to determine when performance is deviating from plan and when adjustments should be made to get back on track. Consider Figure 23. The performance goal four years into the future is to achieve a level of performance of 100. Currently the organization is at 20. At the end of year one, the organization achieved a performance level of 40, represented by the circle symbol. It appears that that level of performance is on track toward the goal of 100. However, the path from the current state to the future state is rarely a straight line. Unless the expected trajectory is known (or at least estimated), it is not possible to evaluate the progress accurately to ensure strategic objectives are integrated with other requirements of senior leader review [4.1b(1)] and priority setting [4.1b(2)]. Without timetables or trajectories, leaders are forced to default to best guess or intuition as a basis for comparing actual, measurable progress against expected progress.

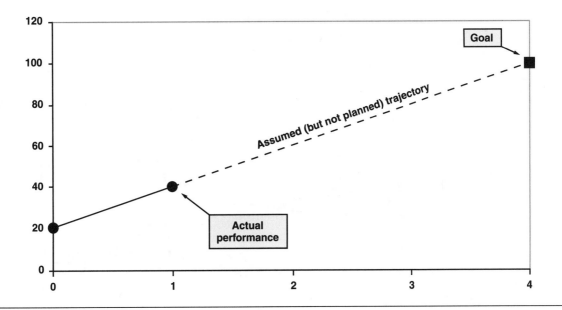

Figure 23 Assumed trajectory.

In Figure 24, the planned trajectory is represented by the triangle symbols. When compared with the current level of performance (circle symbol), it is clear that there is a performance shortfall of approximately 30.

In Figure 25, the planned trajectory is represented by the square symbols. When compared with the current level of performance (the circle symbol), it is clear that the performance is ahead of schedule.

There are several possible decisions that leaders could make based on this information. It might mean that the original estimates/goals were low and should be reset. It might also mean that the process did not need all of the resources it had available. These

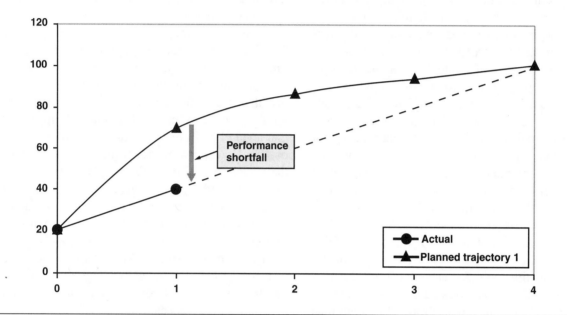

Figure 24 Planned trajectory 1—performance shortfall.

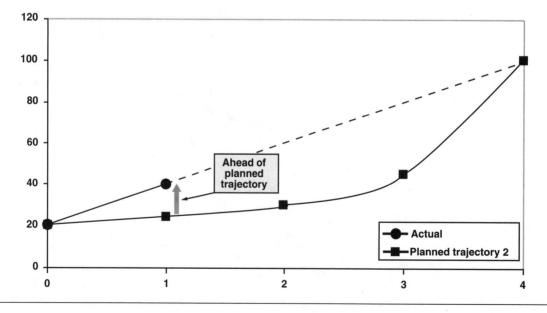

Figure 25 Planned trajectory 2—ahead of plan.

resources may be better used in areas where performance is not ahead of schedule.

In any case, without knowing the expected path toward a goal, leaders are forced to guess whether the level of progress is appropriate.

Finally, the last part of this Item requires the organization to evaluate the options it considered in the strategic planning process to ensure it responded fully to the factors identified in Item 2.1a(2) that were most important to business success. This last step helps the organization *close the loop* to make sure the factors influencing organization success were adequately analyzed and support key strategic objectives.

2.1 Strategy Development

How the organization establishes strategic objectives, including how it enhances its competitive position, overall performance, and future success

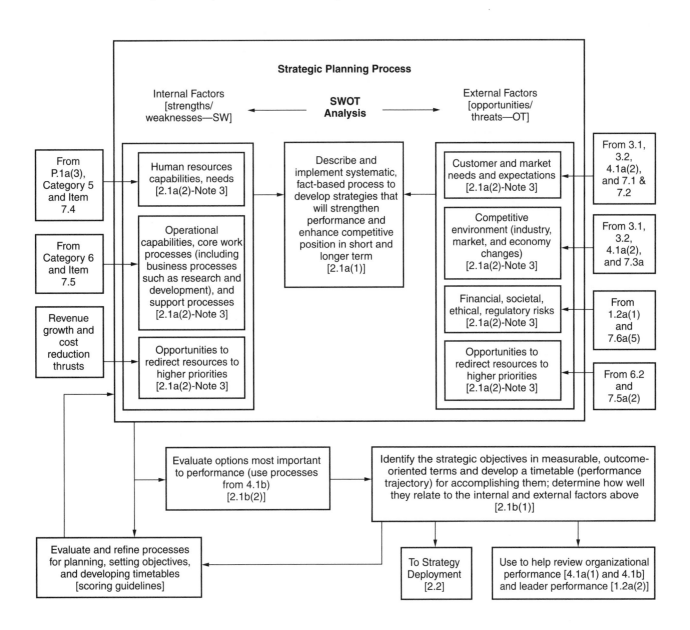

2.1 Strategy Development Item Linkages

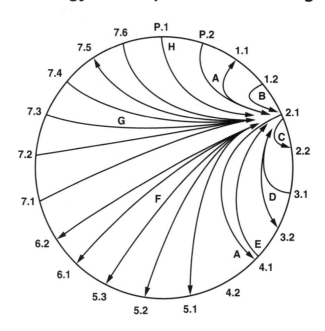

	NATURE OF RELATIONSHIP
A	The planning process [2.1] includes senior leaders—as part of their responsibilities for creating an organizational vision that sets the context for strategic objectives and for creating a sustainable organization [1.1]. In addition, the time lines or expected performance trajectories [2.1b(1)] provide a basis for leaders to determine if progress is on track when they monitor progress [4.1b(1)]. The competitive environment [partly defined in P.2a] is also examined as part of the strategy development process [2.1a(2)]. In addition, before the planning cycle is complete, leaders must ensure that the strategic objectives [2.1b(2)] address the challenges identified in the Organizational Profile [P.2b].
B	Public health, environmental, waste management, and related concerns [1.2b(1)] as well as the need to promote ethical behavior in all transactions [1.2b(2)], are considered, as appropriate, in the strategy development process [2.1a(2)].
C	The planning process [2.1a] produces a set of strategic objectives [2.1b(1)] that must be converted into action plans that are deployed to the workforce [2.2a].
D	The planning process [2.1] includes information on current and potential customer requirements and preferences and the projected competitive environment [3.1], as well as intelligence obtained from customer-contact people (complaints and comments) [3.2a] and customer satisfaction data [3.2b].
E	Key organizational and competitive comparison data [4.1a(2)] and analytical data, including various forecasts and projections [4.1b], are used for planning [2.1a(2)] and setting objectives [2.1b].

Continued

	NATURE OF RELATIONSHIP *Continued*
F	Information on human resource capabilities [Category 5] and work process capabilities [Category 6] is considered in the strategic planning process as part of the determination of internal strengths and weaknesses and to help determine if resources should be redirected to higher priority products, services, or areas [2.1a(2)]. *To avoid cluttering diagrams in Categories 5 and 6, these linkage arrows will not be repeated in other diagrams.*
G	Product and service quality [7.1], customer-focused [7.2], financial and market [7.3], human resource [7.4], organization effectiveness [7.5], and leadership and social responsibility [7.6] outcomes are used in the planning process [2.1a(2)] to set strategic objectives [2.1b(1)]. In addition, results in 7.6a(1) must specifically report on progress toward achieving the strategic objectives and are used in subsequent planning.
H	Employee educational levels, diversity, and other characteristics [P.1a(3)] relate to human resource strengths and weaknesses and are considered during the strategic planning process [2.1a(2)].

	IF YOU DON'T DO WHAT THE CRITERIA REQUIRE . . .
Item Reference	**Possible Adverse Consequences**
2.1a(1)	Without clearly defined short- and longer-term planning horizons, it may be difficult to properly align the analysis and collection of market and industry forecast data to support effective planning. The shorter the planning horizon, the easier it is to be accurate in forecasting. However, the planning horizon must be at least as long as the time it takes the organization to design, develop, and deliver new products and services required by customers and markets. For example, if the design–delivery cycle is seven years (as it was in the U.S. automobile industry), then to be effective an organization must be able to forecast or anticipate customer and market requirements seven years out—which is difficult to do accurately. Alternatively, if the organization reduced its design–delivery cycle time to less than 24 months (as did the Japanese automobile industry), it was able to reduce the required planning horizon, and more accurately anticipate customer and market requirements.
2.1a(2)	The failure to address key factors in the planning process(the organization's strengths, weaknesses, opportunities, and threats; major shifts in technology, markets, competition, or regulatory environment; organizational sustainability and business continuity in emergencies; or the ability to execute the strategic plan) usually results in a flawed strategic plan—a plan that has overlooked an element critical to future success. For example, an organization may fail to achieve strategic objectives if it assumed (incorrectly) that a key supplier would be able to deliver critical components at a certain time. Likewise, a strategic plan that does not adequately account for the arrival of competitive offerings or new technologies in the marketplace can be faced with major hurdles (consider the impact of the quartz watch on the traditional Swiss watch industry). Failing to consider or correctly forecast the impact of these elements may result in a strategic plan that cannot be achieved.

Continued

	IF YOU DON'T DO WHAT THE CRITERIA REQUIRE . . . *Continued*
Item Reference	**Possible Adverse Consequences**
2.1b(1)	Knowing whether the strategy is unfolding as expected is critical to the successful performance of the organization and the leadership. The failure to develop a timetable with clearly defined targets for accomplishing strategic objectives that are integrated (consistent) with the performance review frequency makes it extremely difficult for leaders to monitor organizational performance effectively [as required by Item 4.1b(1)]. Without defined milestones, leaders may be forced to guess whether the rate of progress is appropriate or not. Without clear time lines or trajectories for growth, leaders frequently assume the path between current state and desired state (goals) is linear. Data indicate that the actual path is almost never linear; so the assumptions of linearity that leaders make in the absence of clear time lines and trajectories are usually incorrect.
2.1b(2)	Strategy development is an ongoing, dynamic process. It is often a difficult process that takes a considerable amount of time to complete initially and then requires continual attention to address rapidly changing threats and opportunities. However, if leaders fail to ensure that planning fully addresses organizational changes it faces and ensures that the strategic objectives effectively balance the needs of all key stakeholders, the plan may be ineffective and the time it took to develop the plan may be wasted. Worse yet, these blind spots, if not addressed, may threaten the organization's existence.

2.1 STRATEGY DEVELOPMENT— SAMPLE EFFECTIVE PRACTICES

A. Strategy Development Process

- Business goals, strategies, and issues are addressed and reported in measurable terms. Strategic objectives consider future requirements needed to achieve organizational leadership after considering the performance levels that other organizations are likely to achieve in the same planning time frame.

- Web-based or e-commerce initiatives are considered as part of developing new business or new markets.

- The planning and objective-setting process encourages input (but not necessarily decision making) from a variety of people at all levels throughout the organization.

- Data on customer requirements, key markets, benchmarks, supplier and partner, human resource, and organizational capabilities (internal and external factors) are used to develop business plans.

- Plans and the planning process itself are evaluated each cycle for accuracy and completeness—more often if needed to keep pace with changing business requirements.

- Opportunities for improvement in the planning process are identified systematically and carried out in each planning cycle.

- Refinements in the process of planning, plan deployment, and receiving input from work units have been made. Improvements in plan cycle time, plan resources, and planning accuracy are documented.

B. Strategic Objectives

- Strategic objectives are presented as measurable, outcome-oriented results the organization must achieve to be successful in the future. Strategic objectives are then converted into actions— which may be expressed as a series of activities.

- Strategic objectives are identified and a timetable (or planned growth trajectory) for accomplishing the objectives is set. The time lines match the senior leaders' review cycle. For example, if leaders review progress against goals quarterly, the time lines identify the expected level of performance by quarters.

- Options to obtain best performance for the strategic objectives are systematically evaluated against the internal and external factors used in the strategy development process.

- The process of setting time lines or trajectories and the accuracy of the projections are analyzed and refined.

- Best practices from other providers, competitors, or outside benchmarks are identified and used to provide better estimates of trajectories.

2.2 STRATEGY DEPLOYMENT: How do you deploy your strategy? (45 Pts.)   PROCESS

Describe how your organization converts its strategic objectives into action plans. Summarize your organization's action plans and related key performance measures or indicators. Project your organization's future performance on these key performance measures or indicators.

Within your response, include answers to the following questions:

a. Action Plan Development and Deployment

(1) How do you develop and deploy action plans to achieve your key strategic objectives? How do you allocate resources to ensure accomplishment of your action plans? How do you ensure that the key changes resulting from your action plans can be sustained?

(2) How do you establish and deploy modified action plans if circumstances require a shift in plans and rapid execution of new plans?

(3) What are your key short- and longer-term action plans? What are the key changes, if any, in your products and services and your customers and markets, and how you will operate?

(4) What are your key human resource plans that derive from your short- and longer-term strategic objectives and action plans?

(5) What are your key performance measures or indicators for tracking progress on your action plans? How do you ensure that your overall action plan measurement system reinforces organizational alignment? How do you ensure that the measurement system covers all key deployment areas and stakeholders?

b. Performance Projection

For the key performance measures or indicators identified in 2.2a(5), what are your performance projections for both your short- and longer-term planning time horizons? How does your projected performance compare with the projected performance of your competitors or comparable organizations? How does it compare with key benchmarks, goals, and past performance, as appropriate? If there are current or projected gaps in performance against your competitors or comparable organizations, how will you address them?

Notes:

N1   Strategy and action plan development and deployment are closely linked to other Items in the Criteria. The following are examples of key linkages:

- Item 1.1 for how your senior leaders set and communicate directions

- Category 3 for gathering customer and market knowledge as input to your strategy and action plans and for deploying action plans

- Category 4 for measurement, analysis, and knowledge management to support your key information needs, to support your development of strategy, to provide an effective basis for your performance measurements, and to track progress relative to your strategic objectives and action plans

- Category 5 for your work system needs and employee education, training, and development needs, and for implementing human resource-related changes resulting from action plans

- Category 6 for process requirements resulting from your action plans

- Item 7.6 for specific accomplishments relative to your organizational strategy and action plans

N2   Deployment of action plans (2.2a[1]) might include key partners, collaborators, and suppliers.

Continued

Notes: *Continued*

N3   Measures and indicators of projected performance (2.2b) might include changes resulting from new ventures; organizational acquisitions or mergers; new value creation; market entry and shifts; new legislative mandates, legal requirements, or industry standards; and significant anticipated innovations in products, services, and technology.

The first part of this Item [2.2a] looks at how the organization translates its measurable, outcome-oriented strategic objectives (which were identified in item 2.1b) into action plans to accomplish the objectives and to enable assessment of progress relative to action plans. Overall, the intent of this item is to ensure that strategies are converted to actions and deployed at all levels throughout the organization to align work for goal achievement.

Item [2.2a] calls for information on how action plans are developed and deployed. This includes spelling out key performance requirements and measures, as well as allocating resources and aligning work throughout the organization. Leaders must develop action plans that address the key strategic objectives (which were developed using the processes in Item 2.1). Organizations must summarize key short- and longer-term action plans. Particular attention is given to products/services, customers/markets, how the organization operates, and key human resource plans that will enable accomplishment of strategic objectives and action plans.

The organization should provide the key measures/indicators used in tracking progress relative to the action plans. The organization should also use these measures or indicators to achieve organizational alignment and coverage of all key work units

and stakeholders. Consistently accomplishing action plans and making necessary course corrections or adjustments require resources and performance measures, as well as the alignment of work unit and supplier/partner plans. Alignment and consistency are intended to provide a basis for setting and communicating priorities for ongoing improvement activities—part of the daily work of all units. Action plans should include human resource plans that support the overall strategy.

Without effective alignment, routine work and acts of improvement can be random and serve to suboptimize organizational performance. In Figure 26, the arrows represent the well-intended work carried out by employees of organizations who lack a clear set of expectations and direction. People, managers, and work units strive diligently to achieve goals they believe are important. Each is pulling hard—but not necessarily in ways that ensure performance excellence. The lack of clear, overarching strategic objectives and action plans encourages the creation of *fiefdoms* or *silos* within organizations.

With a clear, well-communicated strategic objective and related actions, it is easier to know when daily work is out of alignment and not integrated throughout the organization. The large arrow in Figure 27 represents the strategic plan pointing the

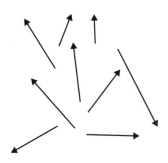

Figure 26   Nonaligned work.

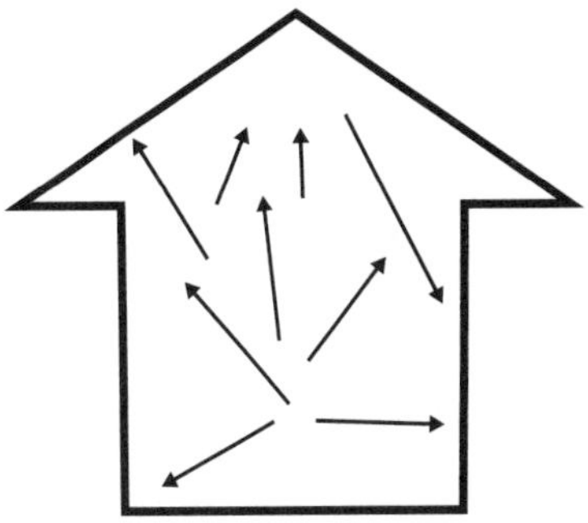

Figure 27   Strategic direction.

direction the organization must take to be successful and achieve its mission and vision. The strategic plan and accompanying measures make it possible to analyze work and business practices to know when they are not aligned and to help employees, including leaders, to know when adjustments are required.

A well-deployed and understood strategic plan helps everyone in the organization distinguish between random acts of improvement and aligned improvement. Random acts of improvement give a false sense of accomplishment and rarely produce optimum benefits for the organization. For example, a decision to improve a business process that is not aligned with the strategic plan (as the small bold arrow in Figure 28 represents) usually results in a wasteful expenditure of time, money, and human resources—improvement without benefiting customers or enhancing operating effectiveness.

On the other hand, by working systematically to strengthen processes that are aligned with the strate-

gic plan, the organization moves closer to achieving success, as Figure 29 indicates.

Ultimately, all processes and procedures of an organization should be aligned to maximize the achievement of strategic plans, as Figure 30 demonstrates.

Critical action-plan resource requirements include human resource plans that support the overall strategy. Examples of possible human resource plan elements are:

- Redesign of work organization and/or jobs to increase employee empowerment and decision making

- Initiatives to promote greater labor-management cooperation, such as union partnerships

- Initiatives to foster knowledge sharing and organizational learning

- Modification of compensation and recognition systems to recognize team, organizational, stock market, customer, or other performance attributes

- Education and training initiatives, such as developmental programs for future leaders, partnerships with universities to help ensure the availability of future employees, and/or establishment of technology-based training capabilities

The second part of this Item [2.2b] asks the organization to provide a projection of key performance measures and/or indicators, including key performance targets and/or goals for both short- and longer-term planning time horizons. This projected performance is the basis for comparing past performance and perfor-

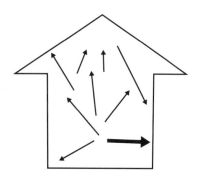

Figure 28 Random improvement.

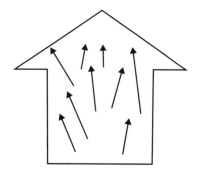

Figure 29 Moving toward alignment.

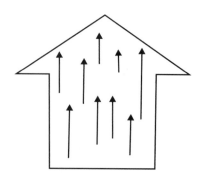

Figure 30 Systematic alignment.

mance relative to competitors and benchmarks, as appropriate.

Projections and comparisons in this Area are intended to help the organization's leaders improve their ability to understand and track dynamic, competitive performance factors. Through this tracking process, they should be better prepared to take into account rate of improvement and change relative to competitors and relative to their own targets or stretch goals. Such tracking serves as a key diagnostic management tool.

In addition to improvement relative to past performance and to competitors, projected performance also might include changes resulting from new business ventures, entry into new markets, e-commerce initiatives, product/service innovations, or other strategic thrusts. Without this comparison information, it is possible to set goals that, even if attained, may not result in competitive advantage. More than one high-performing company has been surprised by a competitor that set and achieved more aggressive goals. Consider the example represented by Figure 31. Imagine that you are ahead of your competition and committed to a 10 percent increase in profit over your base year. After eight years you are twice as profitable. To your surprise, you find that your competitor has increased 20 percent each year. You have achieved your goal, but your competitor has beaten you, making slightly more. After 10 years, the competitor has a significant lead. It is not good enough to achieve your goals unless your goals place you in a competitive position.

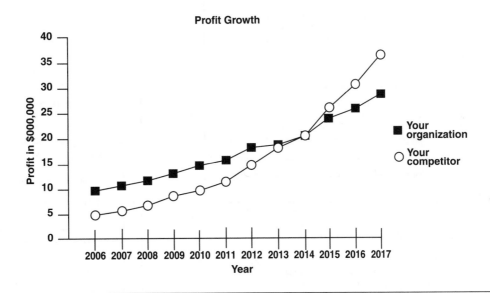

Figure 31   Projecting competitor's future performance.

2.2 Strategy Deployment

Summary of strategy, action plans, and related key performance measures and indicators and performance projections; how they are developed, communicated, and deployed

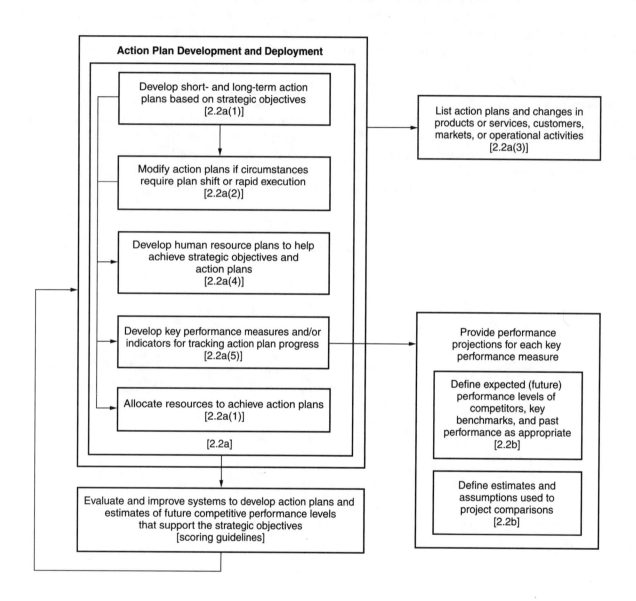

Action Plan Development and Deployment

Develop short- and long-term action plans based on strategic objectives [2.2a(1)]

Modify action plans if circumstances require plan shift or rapid execution [2.2a(2)]

Develop human resource plans to help achieve strategic objectives and action plans [2.2a(4)]

Develop key performance measures and/or indicators for tracking action plan progress [2.2a(5)]

Allocate resources to achieve action plans [2.2a(1)]

[2.2a]

List action plans and changes in products or services, customers, markets, or operational activities [2.2a(3)]

Provide performance projections for each key performance measure

Define expected (future) performance levels of competitors, key benchmarks, and past performance as appropriate [2.2b]

Define estimates and assumptions used to project comparisons [2.2b]

Evaluate and improve systems to develop action plans and estimates of future competitive performance levels that support the strategic objectives [scoring guidelines]

2.2 Strategy Deployment Item Linkages

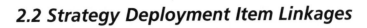

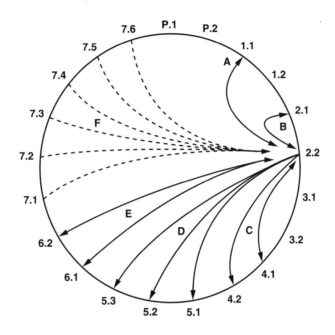

	NATURE OF RELATIONSHIP
A	To ensure vision is accomplished, the leadership team [1.1a] ensures that action plans are aligned throughout the organization with strategic objectives, and that resources are allocated to ensure the actions are accomplished [2.2a(1)].
B	The planning process [2.1a] develops the strategic objectives [2.1b(1)] that are converted into action plans to support these objectives [2.2a(1)].
C	The action plans [2.2a(1)] and related performance measures [2.2a(5)] define part of the data that need to be collected to monitor alignment [4.1a] and analyzed to support decision making [4.1b], and help define requirements for data availability and hardware and software reliability [4.2b]. Benchmarking comparison data [4.1a(2)] are used to project future performance of competitors [2.2b].
D	Measures, action plans, and human resource plans [2.2a] are used to align and develop human resources [5.1, 5.2, 5.3]. It is particularly important that action plans and measures [2.2a] are aligned with and supported by employee feedback and related recognition and reward [5.1b].
E	Measures and action plans [2.2a] are used to drive and align actions to achieve improved performance [6.1, 6.2].
F	Results data [Category 7] are used to help determine performance projections for short- and longer-term goal setting [2.2b]. *To avoid clutter and make the diagrams more readable, these relationships will not be repeated on all of the Category 7 linkage diagrams.*

	IF YOU DON'T DO WHAT THE CRITERIA REQUIRE . . .
Item Reference	**Possible Adverse Consequences**
2.2a(1)	The failure to develop action plans to carry out strategic objectives and employ them at all levels of the organization usually means that work may not be aligned to achieve the strategy. Instead, there is a tendency for managers and other employees to focus their work on things they believe are important. This can result in significant resources being spent on activities that do not contribute to the objectives the organization's leaders have determined are critical for its future success. In addition, the failure to allocate resources appropriately to accomplish action plans frequently means that some plans are not accomplished because of insufficient resources, while other plans are accomplished inefficiently because of too many resources. In both cases, the value to the customer and the organization is suboptimized.
2.2a(2)	In a fast-paced, highly competitive market, the failure to adjust plans quickly and execute them rapidly places the organization at a competitive disadvantage. It may cause significant market erosion from which recovery is difficult. For example, in the late 1990s Motorola was slow to change plans and deliver digital cellular phones to the market. They went from being the market leader to third place, and they have not yet recovered.
2.2a(3)	The inability to articulate and communicate key short- and longer-term action plans usually means those plans do not exist, or they are expressed as vague generalities. Unclear plans make it more difficult to help employees at all levels of the organization understand what work they must do to help the organization achieve future success. Again, without clear direction from the top, employees will still work hard, but their work may be unfocused as they follow their own ideas for appropriate action—everyone is not pulling in the same direction.
2.2a(4)	By definition, *plans* describe activities or actions that have not yet taken place. Many times, in order to execute plans, employees must possess skills, knowledge, or abilities that they do not currently possess. Without appropriate plans to develop, acquire, or motivate the human resources necessary to carry out desired actions, the organization may not be able to achieve its strategic objectives. Its employees may not have the knowledge, skills, or abilities to carry out the actions required for success in the future.
2.2a(5)	Without appropriate measures or indicators it is difficult for leaders, managers, and employees throughout the organization to determine if they are making appropriate progress. It is also more difficult for leaders to communicate expectations accurately. Unclear expectations increase the likelihood that employees will not understand what they are required to do to achieve strategic objectives. Consider the adage, *what gets measured gets done*. Without appropriate measures it is difficult to focus everyone on doing the right things.
2.2b	In the best-performing organizations, strategic goals are designed to enable the organization to win in highly competitive situations. If an organization desires to achieve a leadership position, it must understand where the competition is likely to be in the future before it sets its goals. Unless the organization's leaders understand the likely future performance levels of key competitors (in the same planning horizon), they may set an aggressive goal, achieve that goal, and still lose—finding themselves behind the competition.

2.2 STRATEGY DEPLOYMENT— SAMPLE EFFECTIVE PRACTICES

A. Action Plan Development and Deployment

- Plans are in place to optimize operational performance and improve customer focus using tools such as reengineering, streamlining work processes, and reducing cycle time.

- Actions have been defined in measurable terms, which align with strategic objectives and enable the organization to sustain leadership positions for major products and services for key customers or markets.

- Actions to achieve key organizational results (operational performance requirements) are defined and tracked at all levels of the organization.

- Planned performance and productivity levels are defined in measurable terms for key features of products and services.

- Planned actions are challenging, realistic, achievable, and understood by employees throughout the organization.

- Resources are available and committed to achieve the plans (no unfunded mandates). Capital projects are funded according to business improvement plans and priorities.

- Plans are absolutely used to guide operational performance improvements. Plans drive budget and action, not the other way around.

- Incremental (short-term) tactics to achieve long-term plans are defined in measurable terms and time lines are in place to help monitor progress.

- Business plans, short- and long-term goals, and performance measures are understood and used to drive actions throughout the organization.

- Every individual in the organization, at all levels, understands how their work contributes to achieving organizational goals and plans.

- Plans are followed to ensure that resources are deployed and redeployed as needed to support goals.

- Human resource plans support strategic plans and goals. Plans show how the workforce will be developed to enable the organization to achieve its strategic goals.

- Key issues of training and development, hiring, retention, employee participation, involvement, empowerment, and recognition and reward are addressed as a part of the human resource plan. Appropriate measures and targets for each are defined.

- Innovative human resource plans may involve one or more of the following:

  - Redesigning work to increase employee responsibility.

  - Improving labor–management relations. (That is, prior to contract negotiations, train both sides in effective negotiation skills so people focus on the merits of issues, not on positions. A goal, for example, is to improve relations and shorten negotiation time by 50 percent.)

  - Forming partnerships with education institutions to develop employees and ensure a supply of well-prepared future employees.

  - Developing gain-sharing or equity-building compensation systems for all employees to increase motivation and productivity.

  - Broadening employee responsibilities; creating self-directed or high-performance work teams.

- Key performance measures (for example, employee satisfaction or work-climate surveys) have been identified to gather data to manage progress. (Note: Improvement results associated with these measures should be reported in 7.4.)

- The effectiveness of human resource planning and alignment with strategic plans is evaluated systematically.

- The process to develop action plans to support strategic objectives is systematically evaluated.

B. Performance Projection

- Projections of two- to five-year changes in performance levels are developed and used to collect data (measure) and track progress.

- Data from competitors, key benchmarks, and/or past performance form a valid basis for comparison. The organization has valid strategies and goals in place to meet or exceed the planned levels of performance for these competitors and benchmarks.

- Plans include expected future levels of competitor or comparison performance and are used to set and validate the organization's own plans and goals.

- Future plans and projections of performance consider new acquisition, optimum but secure growth, reducing costs through operational-excellence processes, and anticipated research and development of innovations internally or among competitors. The accuracy of these projections is mapped and analyzed. Techniques to improve accuracy are developed and implemented.

3 Customer and Market Focus—85 Points

*The **Customer and Market Focus** Category examines how your organization determines the requirements, needs, expectations, and preferences of customers and markets. Also examined is how your organization builds relationships with customers and determines the key factors that lead to customer acquisition, satisfaction, loyalty, and retention, and to business expansion and sustainability.*

This Category addresses how the organization seeks to understand the voices of customers and of the marketplace, with emphasis on determining customers' expectations, requirements, and preferences, and building customer loyalty. The Category stresses relationships as an important part of an overall listening, learning, and performance excellence strategy. Customer satisfaction and dissatisfaction results provide vital information for understanding customers and the marketplace. Such results and trends often provide the most meaningful information, not only on customers' views but also on marketplace behaviors—repeat business and positive referrals—and how these views and behaviors may contribute to the organization's sustainability in the marketplace.

Customer and Market Focus contains two Items that focus on understanding customer and market requirements, and building relationships and determining satisfaction.

Customer and Market Knowledge

- Determining market or customer segments to pursue for both current and future business

- Determining customer requirements for important product or service features

- Using complaint information and data from potential and former customers for planning, process improvements, and business development

Customer Relationships and Satisfaction

- Making customer contact and feedback easy and useful

- Handling complaints effectively and responsively

- Ensuring complaint data are used to eliminate causes of complaints

- Building customer relationships and loyalty

- Systematically determining customer satisfaction and the satisfaction of competitor's customers

3.1 CUSTOMER AND MARKET KNOWLEDGE: How do you use customer and market knowledge? (40 Pts.)   PROCESS

Describe how your organization determines requirements, needs, expectations, and preferences of customers and markets to ensure the continuing relevance of your products and services and to develop new opportunities.

Within your response, include answers to the following questions:

a. Customer and Market Knowledge

(1) How do you identify customers, customer groups, and market segments? How do you determine which customers, customer groups, and market segments to pursue for current and future products and services? How do you include customers of competitors and other potential customers and markets in this determination?

(2) How do you listen and learn to determine key customer requirements, needs, and changing expectations (including product and service features) and their relative importance to customers' purchasing decisions? How do your determination methods vary for different customers or customer groups? How do you use relevant information and feedback from current and former customers, including marketing and sales information, customer loyalty and retention data, win/loss analysis, and complaint data for purposes of planning products and services, marketing, making process improvements, and developing new business opportunities? How do you use this information and feedback to become more customer-focused and to better satisfy customer needs and desires?

(3) How do you keep your listening and learning methods current with business needs and directions, including changes in your marketplace?

Notes:

N1   Your responses to this Item should include the customer groups and market segments identified in P.1b(2).

N2   If your products and services are sold or delivered to end-use customers via other businesses (for example, those businesses that are part of your "value chain" such as retail stores, dealers or local distributors), customer groups (3.1a[1]) should include both the end users and these intermediate organizations.

N3   "Product and service features" (3.1a[2]) refers to all the important characteristics of products and services and to their performance throughout their full life cycle and the full "consumption chain." This includes all customers' purchase and interaction experiences with your organization that influence purchase and relationship decisions. The focus should be on features that affect customer preference and loyalty—for example, those features that differentiate your products and services from competing offerings or other organizations' services. Those features might include price, reliability, value, delivery, timeliness, ease of use, requirements for hazardous materials use and disposal, customer or technical support, and the sales relationship. Key product and service features and purchasing decisions (3.1a[2]) might take into account how transactions occur and factors such as confidentiality and security.

N4   Listening and learning (3.1a[2]) might include gathering and integrating survey data, focus group findings, Web-based data, and other data and information that affect customers' purchasing and relationship decisions. Keeping your listening and learning methods current with business needs and directions (3.1a[3]) also might include use of newer technology, such as Web-based data gathering.

N5   *For additional considerations on products, services, customers, and the business of nonprofit organizations, see Item P.1, Notes 5 and 6, and Item P.2, Note 7.*

This Item [3.1] looks at the organization's key processes for gaining knowledge about its current and future customers and markets, in order to offer relevant products and services, understand emerging customer requirements and expectations, and keep pace with changing market demands. Processes required by Item 3.1 permit the organization to gather intelligence about its customers and competition. It is a critical starting place for determining direction and strategic planning.

This information is intended to support marketing, business development, and planning. In a rapidly changing competitive environment, many factors may affect customer preference and loyalty and the interface with customers in the marketplace, making it necessary to listen and learn on a continuous basis. To be effective, such listening and learning techniques need to have a close connection with the organization's overall business strategy. For example, if the organization customizes its products and services, the listening and learning process needs to identify unique and common requirements to permit accurate predictions about the nature of future customized requests.

The organization must have a process for determining or segmenting key customer groups and markets. To ensure that a complete and accurate picture of customer requirements and concerns is obtained, organizations should consider the requirements of potential customers, including competitors' customers. (Note: A potential customer is a customer the organization wants but is currently being served by another organization or competitor.) The organization should use this information to determine which customers to pursue for current and future business. In addition, the organization should tailor its listening and learning techniques to different customer groups and market segments to be sure the information is accurate. A relationship or listening strategy might work with some customers, but not with others.

Information sought should be sensitive to specific product and service requirements and their relative importance or value to the different customer groups. This determination should be supported by use of information and data, such as complaints and gains and losses of customers. Techniques may include asking customers to rank their requirements in order of performance or group requirements into three categories (most important, important, least important).

Another technique for determining priorities involves paired-choice or forced-choice analyses where customers are asked to state a preference of requirement A or B; A or C; A or D; B or C; B or D, and so on. Regardless of the techniques used, the organization must be able to prioritize key customer requirements and drivers of purchase decisions, which may be different for different customer groups and market segments.

In a rapidly changing competitive environment, many factors may affect customer preference and loyalty and the interface with customers in the marketplace. This makes it necessary to listen and learn on a continuous basis. Effective organizations link listening and learning with the overall business strategy and strategy planning process. E-commerce is changing the competitive arena rapidly. This may significantly affect the relationships with customers and the effectiveness of listening and learning strategies. It may also force the organization to redefine customer groups and market segments.

A variety of listening and learning strategies are commonly used by top-performing organizations. Increasingly, companies interact with customers via multiple modes. Some examples of listening and learning strategies include:

- Close integration with key customers

- Rapid innovation and field trials of products and services to better link research and development (R&D) and design to the market

- Close tracking of technological, competitive, and other factors that may bear upon customer requirements, expectations, preferences, or alternatives

- Defining the customers' value chains and how they are likely to change

- Focus groups with leading-edge customers

- Use of critical incidents, such as complaints, to understand key service attributes from the point of view of customers and customer-contact employees

- Interviewing lost customers to determine the factors they use in their purchase decisions

- Survey/feedback information, including information collected on the Internet

- Win/loss analysis relative to competitors

- Increased use of electronic feedback and e-commerce

As with other elements of the Criteria, the organization must have a system in place to improve its customer-listening and learning strategies to keep current with changing business needs and directions. The organization may need to evaluate and improve its customer-listening and learning strategies more often than annually. The organization should be able to demonstrate that it has made appropriate improvements to ensure its techniques for understanding customer requirements and priorities keep pace with changing business needs.

3.1 Customer and Market Knowledge

How the organization determines requirements, expectations, and preferences of target or potential customers and markets to anticipate their needs and to develop business opportunities

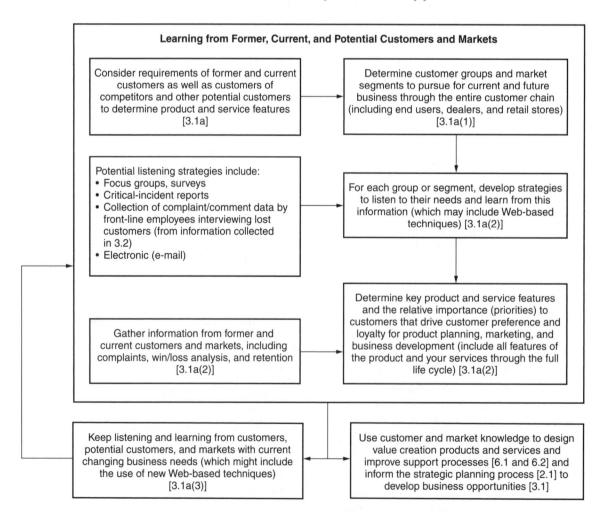

3.1 Customer and Market Knowledge Item Linkages

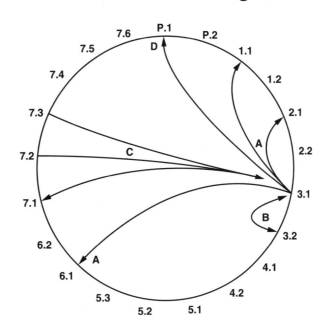

	NATURE OF RELATIONSHIP
A	Customer input and related information about current and future customer and market requirements and preferences [3.1a(2)] are used for strategic planning [2.1a], to design value-creation products and services and revise work processes [6.1a(2, 3, and 4)], and to help leaders set vision and directions for the organization [1.1a(1)].
B	Customer complaints [3.2a(3)] are used to help assess current customer expectations and refine requirements [3.1a(2)]. Information about customer-requirement priorities [3.1a(2)] is used to build instruments and better target questions to assess customer satisfaction [3.2b(1)] and better follow up on recent transactions [3.2b(2)].
C	Customer satisfaction, complaints [7.2a], product and service data and trends [7.1a(2)], and market data [7.3a(2)] are used to help validate customer expectations and refine requirements [3.1a(2)].
D	The products and services reported in P.1b(2) were determined using the processes described in 3.1a(2).

IF YOU DON'T DO WHAT THE CRITERIA REQUIRE . . .	
Item Reference	**Possible Adverse Consequences**
3.1a(1)	The failure to classify or group customers or markets into meaningful segments may make it difficult to identify and differentiate key requirements that may be critical to one group but not another. For example, frequent or high-volume customers may have different expectations than infrequent or low-volume customers. Dealers may have different requirements than end users. Unless these differences are understood, it may be difficult for the organization to customize information collection techniques as well as programs, products, and services according to the needs and expectations of different groups of customers.
3.1a(2)	Different techniques may be needed to understand the requirements of different groups of customers. The failure to listen and learn about the key customer requirements for products and services, especially those features that are most important to customer purchasing decisions, may make it difficult to design and develop those products and services that are most likely to delight (or even satisfy) customers and increase market share. In addition to gathering feedback directly from current and former customers, the organization should collect and analyze complaint and lost customer data to gain additional insights into unmet requirements and opportunities for future work. If an organization does not know why it lost or gained customers, it is more difficult to deliver the right products and services to keep customers.
3.1a(3)	The failure to systematically evaluate the processes used to listen and learn about customer requirements may make it difficult to identify specific areas needing change. For example, it does not do much good to create a survey to identify customer requirements if the questions asked on the survey are not the right questions. Incorrect information generated by this survey may cause the organization to design and deliver the wrong products or services. Furthermore, it does little good to use a written survey tool when face-to-face interviews may be a better way to acquire accurate and actionable information. The failure to evaluate the effectiveness of the approaches used to identify and prioritize customer requirements may make it difficult to keep up with changing customer and market needs and gather critical information necessary for strategic planning [Item 2.1a(2)] as well as the design and development of new value-creation products and services [Item 6.1a(3)].

3.1 CUSTOMER AND MARKET KNOWLEDGE—SAMPLE EFFECTIVE PRACTICES

A. Customer and Market Knowledge

- Various systematic methods are used to gather data and identify current requirements and expectations of customers (for example, surveys, focus groups, and the use of Web-based systems).

- Key product and service features are defined in order of importance to customers. Product and service features refer to all important characteristics and to the performance of products and services that customers experience or perceive throughout their use. Factors that bear on customer preference and loyalty—
for example, those features that enhance or differentiate products and services from competing offerings—are defined in measurable terms.

- Customer requirements are identified or grouped by customer segments. This information is consistently used for planning, data analysis, product and service design, production, and delivery processes, and for reporting and monitoring progress.

- Customer data such as complaints and gains or losses of customers are used to support the identification or validation of key customer requirements.

- Fact-based, systematic methods are used to identify the future requirements and expectations of customers. These are tested for accuracy and estimation techniques are improved.

- Customers of competitors are considered and processes are in place to gather expectation data from potential customers.

- Effective listening and learning strategies include:

  - Close monitoring of technological, competitive, societal, environmental, economic, and demographic factors that may bear on customer requirements, expectations, preferences, or alternatives

  - Focus groups with demanding or leading-edge customers

  - Training of front-line employees in customer listening and using these employees as a source of collection

  - Use of critical incidents in product or service performance or quality to understand key service attributes from the point of view of customers and front-line employees

  - Interviewing lost customers to determine why they left

  - Win/loss analysis relative to competitors

  - Analysis of major factors affecting key customers

- Tools such as forced- or paired-choice analysis are used (where customers select between options A and B, A and C, B and C, and so on). Using this technique, organizations quickly prioritize requirements and focus on delivering those that make the greatest impact on satisfaction, repeat business, and loyalty.

- Methods to listen and learn from customers are evaluated and improved through several cycles. Examples of factors that are evaluated include:

  - The adequacy and timeliness of customer-related information

  - Improvement of survey design

  - Approaches for getting reliable and timely information—surveys, focus groups, customer-contact personnel

  - Improved aggregation and analysis of information

- Best practices for gathering customer requirements and forecasting are identified and used to make improvements.

3.2 CUSTOMER RELATIONSHIPS AND SATISFACTION: How do you build relationships and grow customer satisfaction and loyalty? (45 Pts.)   PROCESS

Describe how your organization builds relationships to acquire, satisfy, and retain customers and to increase customer loyalty. Describe also how your organization determines customer satisfaction.

Within your response, include answers to the following questions:

a. Customer Relationship Building

(1) How do you build relationships to acquire customers, to meet and exceed their expectations, to increase loyalty and repeat business, and to gain positive referrals?

(2) How do your key access mechanisms enable customers to seek information, conduct business, and make complaints? What are your key access mechanisms? How do you determine key customer contact requirements for each mode of customer access? How do you ensure that these contact requirements are deployed to all people and processes involved in the customer response chain?

(3) How do you manage customer complaints? How do you ensure that complaints are resolved effectively and promptly? How do you minimize customer dissatisfaction and, as appropriate, loss of repeat business? How are complaints aggregated and analyzed for use in improvement throughout your organization and by your partners?

(4) How do you keep your approaches to building relationships and providing customer access current with business needs and directions?

b. Customer Satisfaction Determination

(1) How do you determine customer satisfaction, dissatisfaction, and loyalty? How do these determination methods differ among customer groups? How do you ensure that your measurements capture actionable information for use in exceeding your customers' expectations? How do you ensure that your measurements capture actionable information for use in securing your customers' future business and gaining positive referrals, as appropriate? How do you use customer satisfaction and dissatisfaction information for improvement?

(2) How do you follow up with customer on the quality of products, services, and transactions to receive prompt and actionable feedback?

(3) How do you obtain and use information on your customers' satisfaction relative to their satisfaction with your competitors, other organizations providing similar products or services, and/or industry benchmarks?

(4) How do you keep your approaches to determining satisfaction current with business needs and directions?

Notes:

N1   Customer relationship building (3.2a) might include the development of partnerships or alliances with customers.

N2   Determining customer satisfaction and dissatisfaction (3.2b) might include use of any or all of the following: surveys, formal and informal feedback, customer account histories, complaints, win/loss analysis, and transaction completion rates. Information might be gathered on the Internet, through personal contact or a third party, or by mail.

N3   Customer satisfaction measurements (3.2b[1]) might include both a numerical rating scale and descriptors for each unit in the scale. Actionable customer satisfaction measurements provide useful information about specific product and service features, delivery, relationships, and transactions that affect customers' future actions—repeat business and positive referral.

Continued

Notes: *Continued*

N4   Other organizations providing similar product or services (3.2b[3]) might include other organizations with whom
     you don't compete but provide similar products and services in other geographic areas or to different populations
     of people.

N5   Your customer satisfaction and dissatisfaction results should be reported in Item 7.2.

N6   *For some nonprofit organizations (for example, some government agencies or charitable organizations), customers
     ma be assigned or may be required to use your organization and relationships may be short term. For those orga-
     nizations relationship building (3.2a[1]) might be focused on meeting and exceeding expectations during the short-
     term relationship, resulting in positive comments to other people, including key stakeholders of your organization.*

Item 3.2 describes processes that examine the impact of products and services on customer relationships and satisfaction. In particular, this Item looks at the organization's processes for building customer relationships and determining customer satisfaction, with the aim of acquiring new customers, retaining existing customers, and developing new market opportunities. Relationships provide an important means for organizations to understand and manage customer expectations and to develop new business. Also, customer-contact employees may provide vital information to build partnerships and other longer-term relationships with customers.

Overall, Item 3.2 emphasizes the importance of obtaining actionable information, such as feedback and complaints from customers. To be actionable, the information gathered should meet two conditions:

- Customer responses should be tied directly to key product, service, and business processes, so that opportunities for improvement are clear

- Customer responses should be translated into cost/revenue implications to support the setting of improvement and change priorities

The first part of this Item [3.2a(1)] looks at the organization's processes for providing easy access for customers and potential customers to seek information or assistance and/or to comment and complain. This access makes it easy to get timely information from customers about issues that are of real concern to them. Timely information, in turn, is transmitted to the appropriate place in the organization to drive improvements or new levels of product and service.

Gather from customers information that is actionable. To be actionable, information should be tied to key business processes, and used to determine cost/revenue implications for improvement priority setting.

Organizations must also determine key customer-contact requirements and how these vary for different modes of access, and make sure all employees who are involved in responding to customers understand these requirements. The organization should describe key access mechanisms for customers to seek information, conduct business, and make complaints. Also important is how customer-contact requirements are deployed along the entire response chain.

Customer-contact requirements essentially refer to customer expectations for service after contact with the organization has been made. Typically, the organization translates customer-contact requirements into customer-service standards. Customer-contact requirements should be set in measurable terms to permit effective monitoring and performance review.

- A good example of a measurable customer-contact requirement might be the customer expectation that a malfunctioning computer would be back online within 24 hours of the request for service. Another example might be the customer requirement that a knowledgeable and polite human being is available within 10 minutes to resolve a problem with software. In both cases, a clear requirement and a measurable standard were identified.

• A bad example of a customer service standard might be "we get back to the customer as soon as we can." With this example, no standard of performance is defined. Some customer-contact representatives might get back to a customer within a matter of minutes. Others might take hours or days. The failure to precisely define the contact requirement makes it difficult to allocate appropriate resources to meet that requirement consistently. These customer-service standards must be deployed to all employees who are in contact with customers. Such deployment needs to take account of all key points in the response chain—all units or individuals in the organization that make effective interactions possible. These standards then become one source of information to evaluate the organization's performance in meeting customer-contact requirements.

Organizations should capture, aggregate, analyze, and learn from the complaint information and comments they receive. A prompt and effective response and solutions to customer needs and desires help increase satisfaction and loyalty.

Effective complaint management requires the prompt and courteous resolution of complaints. This leads to recovery of customer confidence. Customer loyalty and confidence are enhanced when problems are resolved by the first person the customer contacts. In fact, prompt resolution of problems helps to ensure higher levels of loyalty than if the customer never had a problem in the first place. Even if the organization ultimately resolves a problem, the likelihood of maintaining a loyal customer is reduced by 10 percent each time that customer is referred to another place or person in the organization.

The organization must also have a mechanism for learning from complaints and ensuring that design/production/delivery-process employees receive information needed to eliminate the causes of complaints. Effective elimination of the causes of complaints involves aggregation of complaint information from all sources for evaluation and use in overall organizational improvement—both design and delivery stages (see Items 6.1 and 6.2). Complaint aggregation, analysis, and root-cause determination should lead to effec-

tive elimination of the causes of complaints and to priority setting for process, product, and service improvements. Successful outcomes require effective deployment of information throughout the organization.

For long-term success, organizations should build strong relationships with customers since business development and product/service innovation increasingly depend on maintaining close relationships with customers. Organizations should keep approaches to all aspects of customer relationships current with changing business needs and directions, since approaches to and bases for relationships may change quickly. Organizations should also develop an effective process to determine the levels of satisfaction and dissatisfaction for the different customer groups, including capturing actionable information that reflects customers' future business and/or positive referral intentions. Satisfied customers are a requirement for loyalty, repeat business, and positive referrals.

The second part of this Item [3.2b] looks at how the organization determines customer satisfaction and dissatisfaction. The organization must gather information on customer satisfaction and dissatisfaction, including any important differences in approaches for different customer groups or market segments. This highlights the importance of the measurement scale in determining those factors that best reflect customers' market behaviors—repurchase, new business, and positive referral. The organization must keep its approaches to determining customer satisfaction current with changing business needs and directions. Changing business needs and directions might include new modes of customer access, such as the Internet. In such cases, key contact requirements might include online security for customers and access to personal assistance.

The organization should systematically follow-up with customers regarding products, services, and recent transactions to receive feedback that is prompt and actionable. Prompt feedback enables problems to be identified quickly to help prevent them from recurring. This helps prevent future customer dissatisfaction.

The organization should determine the satisfaction levels of the customers of competitors in order to identify threats and opportunities to improve future performance. Such information might be derived from the organization's own comparative studies or from independent studies. The factors that lead to customer preference are of critical importance in understanding factors that drive markets, potentially affect longer-term competitiveness, and are particularly helpful during strategic planning.

Customers complain when they have a problem. They do not tend to hold their complaint until the organization finds it convenient to ask them. Therefore, data from the complaint processes in Item 3.2a are collected at the customer's convenience. However, data collected by survey or similar means, as required by Item 3.2b, produce information at the convenience of the organization.

Although the complaint-type customer feedback (from Item 3.2a) is timely, it is often difficult to develop reliable trend data since very few customers who have a problem actually complain about it to the organization. The processes in Item 3.2b make it easier to obtain accurate and reliable satisfaction data over time. Both techniques are required to fully understand customer-satisfaction dynamics that build loyalty, retention, and positive referral. To be effective, both techniques should be used to drive improvement actions.

3.2 Customer Relationships and Satisfaction

How customer satisfaction is determined, relationships are strengthened, and current products and services are enhanced to support customer- and market-related planning

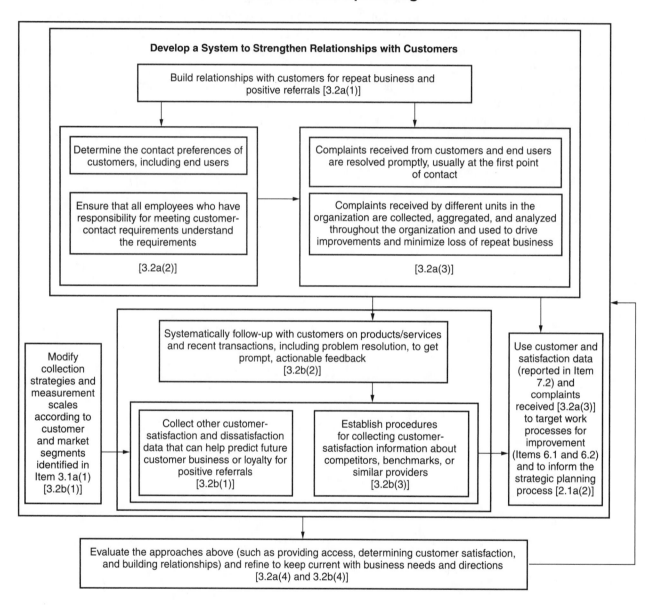

Develop a System to Strengthen Relationships with Customers

Build relationships with customers for repeat business and positive referrals [3.2a(1)]

Determine the contact preferences of customers, including end users

Ensure that all employees who have responsibility for meeting customer-contact requirements understand the requirements

[3.2a(2)]

Complaints received from customers and end users are resolved promptly, usually at the first point of contact

Complaints received by different units in the organization are collected, aggregated, and analyzed throughout the organization and used to drive improvements and minimize loss of repeat business

[3.2a(3)]

Systematically follow-up with customers on products/services and recent transactions, including problem resolution, to get prompt, actionable feedback [3.2b(2)]

Modify collection strategies and measurement scales according to customer and market segments identified in Item 3.1a(1) [3.2b(1)]

Collect other customer-satisfaction and dissatisfaction data that can help predict future customer business or loyalty for positive referrals [3.2b(1)]

Establish procedures for collecting customer-satisfaction information about competitors, benchmarks, or similar providers [3.2b(3)]

Use customer and satisfaction data (reported in Item 7.2) and complaints received [3.2a(3)] to target work processes for improvement (Items 6.1 and 6.2) and to inform the strategic planning process [2.1a(2)]

Evaluate the approaches above (such as providing access, determining customer satisfaction, and building relationships) and refine to keep current with business needs and directions [3.2a(4) and 3.2b(4)]

3.2 Customer Relationships and Satisfaction Item Linkages

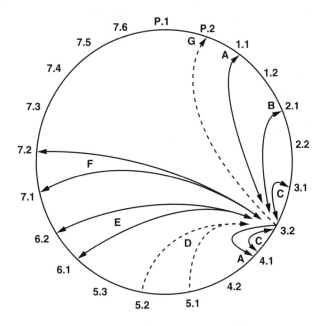

	NATURE OF RELATIONSHIP
A	The climate establishing customer-focused priorities and customer-contact requirements (service standards) for customer service personnel [3.2a(2)] is driven by top leadership [1.1b(2)]. They receive useful information from those customers to improve management decision making. Customer relationships/complaint data [3.2a(3)] and satisfaction data [3.2b(1 and 2)] are typically used by senior leaders to review performance [4.1b(1)] and set priorities for action [4.1b(2)].
B	Information about customer satisfaction [3.2b(1 and 2)] and complaints [3.2a(3)] collected by customer-contact employees is used in the planning process [2.1a(2)]. In addition, strategic objectives [2.1b(1)] influence customer relationship management [3.2a] and customer satisfaction determination processes [3.2b] by identifying key focus areas.
C	Information concerning customer requirements, expectations, and preferences [3.1a(2)] and benchmark data [4.1a(2)] are used to help identify customer contact requirements (service standards) [3.2a(2)]. Customer complaint data [3.2a(3)] are analyzed [4.1b(1)] and used to help leaders ensure conclusions and decisions are valid.
D	Training [5.2] and feedback, reward, and recognition tied to customer satisfaction [5.1b] should enhance the willingness of customer-contact employees [3.2a(2)] to understand requirements and develop the skills to resolve complaints promptly and satisfy customers [3.2a(3)].
E	Information collected through customer relations employees [3.2a(2 and 3)] is used to enhance design of products and services and to improve value creation and support processes [6.1a and 6.2a].
F	Information and complaints from customer relations processes [3.2a(3)] can help in the design of customer satisfaction determination measures [3.2b(1)] and produce data on customer satisfaction outcomes [7.2] and related product and service quality outcomes [7.1]. In addition, customer satisfaction results [7.2] are used to set customer contact requirements (service standards) [3.2a(2)].

Continued

	NATURE OF RELATIONSHIP	*Continued*
	Efforts of improved accessibility and responsiveness in complaint management [3.2a(3 and 4)] should result in improved complaint response time, effective complaint resolution, and a higher percentage of complaints resolved on first contact. These results should be reported in 7.1 and/or 7.2.	
G	Processes in Item 3.2b(3) produce information about the satisfaction of competitors' customers, which is needed to create the description for P.1b(2).	

	IF YOU DON'T DO WHAT THE CRITERIA REQUIRE . . .
Item Reference	**Possible Adverse Consequences**
3.2a(1)	The failure to build lasting relationships and loyalty with customers makes it easier for customers to *jump ship* when problems arise. Loyal customers are twice as likely to use an organization's products and services than those who are simply satisfied. The TARP Studies have found that the cost to win a new customer versus retain a current customer varies from 2:1 to 20:1.* If the organization lacks a disciplined approach for building relationships and cultivating loyalty, the benefits of having loyal customers become hit-or-miss opportunities. For example, in many manufacturing companies today, service is a key differentiator. Products that were once considered specialty items, such as personal computers, are now commodities. Therefore, service can become the factor that differentiates companies and cultivates loyal customers. Furthermore, since it is more costly to acquire a new customer than to keep an existing customer, organizations can avoid unnecessary expenses by building relationships and strengthening the loyalty of current customers. Loyal customers are far more likely to provide positive referrals than a dissatisfied or even minimally satisfied customer. *From J. Goodman. "Basic Facts on Customer Complaint Behavior and the Impact of Service on the Bottom Line." *Competitive Advantage* (June 1999): 1–5. The article can be read at http://www.e-satisfy.com/basic facts.pdf.
3.2a(2)	Customer contact requirements (sometimes called customer service standards) help define the customers' expectations for service after initiating a contact, question, or complaint. For example, a large, direct-order computer company surveyed its customers and determined that they expected to have a technician helping solve their problem within 10 minutes of making the initial contact. By knowing the customer contact requirements and the hour-to-hour call volume, the organization was able to put enough technicians in place to ensure the average response time was nine minutes or less. The failure to understand and meet customer contact requirements and make it easy for customers to contact the organization makes it more difficult to build loyalty and learn quickly about customer problems.
3.2a(3)	Once the organization learns about a customer problem, the speed and efficiency with which it resolves that problem contributes greatly to customer loyalty and willingness to make positive referrals. The failure to resolve a problem to the customer's satisfaction at the first point of contact cuts almost in half the likelihood of maintaining a loyal customer. In addition, the failure to collect, aggregate, analyze, and use complaint data to drive improvements throughout the organization (and as appropriate to key suppliers or partners) increases the

Continued

	IF YOU DON'T DO WHAT THE CRITERIA REQUIRE . . . *Continued*
Item Reference	**Possible Adverse Consequences**
	likelihood that the problem will recur again and again. Failing to prevent the problem from recurring directly adds cost but no value to the products or services delivered to customers. Rework associated with recurring problems is a pure waste of resources and can be a significant source of customer dissatisfaction.
3.2a(4)	The failure to systematically evaluate the processes used to build relationships, resolve complaints, and prevent them from recurring may make it difficult to identify specific areas needing change. Making it easy for customers to complain but not resolving those complaints effectively and promptly may create even higher levels of dissatisfaction. Ignorance about the effectiveness of customer access and complaint resolution processes may blind the organization to a problem of its own creation, especially in a highly competitive arena where customer and market requirements can change quickly. Without an ongoing system to evaluate and improve processes to build relationships and satisfy customers, current processes may not be able to keep up with changing business or market demands.
3.2b(1)	The failure to accurately determine customer satisfaction and dissatisfaction may make it difficult for the organization to make timely adjustments to the products and services it offers. Furthermore, if the data collection processes do not help the organization understand what drives customer behavior, the organization may not know until it is too late (the customer goes elsewhere) that they have a serious problem. The failure to predict customer behavior and the likelihood for positive referral also makes it difficult to forecast product demand, which may create supply chain difficulties, such as excessive inventories or excessive delays in restocking. In addition, the failure to take into account differences in customer or market segments and adjust the techniques for collecting customer satisfaction and dissatisfaction data appropriately may cause the organization to collect inaccurate or unreliable information, which threatens the accuracy of the organization's decision making and planning.
3.2b(2)	The longer an organization waits to gather customer satisfaction data, the more time it takes to identify and correct a problem. Organizations that fail to follow up with customers whenever a transaction occurs and learn about problems promptly increase the likelihood that other customers will experience the same problem because it will not have been identified or corrected. Similarly, organizations that fail to follow up with customers may be unaware of elements that drive dissatisfaction and disloyalty that could be spread to other parts of the organization or to other products and services.
3.2b(3)	By failing to obtain information on the satisfaction of the competitors' customers, the organization may not learn what it must do differently to satisfy and acquire (win over) the customers of its competitors.
3.2b(4)	Organizations that do not evaluate the effectiveness of their techniques to determine customer satisfaction and dissatisfaction run the risk of making bad decisions based on misleading or even useless information. It does little good to gather customer satisfaction data unless the organization asks the right questions. Failing to ask the right questions rarely produces accurate, actionable information to support effective decision making. Moreover, the failure to evaluate the effectiveness of the approaches used to assess customer satisfaction may make it difficult to keep up with changing customer and market needs and gather critical information necessary for strategic planning as well as the development of new or improved products and services.

3.2 CUSTOMER RELATIONSHIPS AND SATISFACTION—SAMPLE EFFECTIVE PRACTICES

A. Customer Relationship Building

- Several methods are used to ensure ease of customer contact, 24 hours a day if necessary (for example, toll-free numbers, pagers for contact personnel, Web sites, e-mail, surveys, interviews, focus groups, electronic bulletin boards).

- Customer-contact employees are empowered to make decisions to address customer concerns.

- Adequate staff members are available to maintain effective customer contact, within the time limits expected by customers.

- Measurable performance expectations are set for employees whose job brings them in regular contact with customers. The performance of employees against these expectations is tracked.

- A system exists to ensure that customer complaints are resolved promptly and effectively by the first point of contact. Customer-contact employees have been trained and given the authority for resolving a broad range of problems.

- Complaint data are tracked, analyzed, and used to initiate prompt corrective action to prevent the problem from recurring.

- Training and development plans and replacement procedures exist for customer-contact employees. These processes have been measured and refined.

- Measurable customer-contact requirements (service standards) have been derived from customer expectations (for example, timeliness, courtesy, efficiency, thoroughness, and completeness).

- Requirements for building relationships are identified and may include factors such as product knowledge, employee responsiveness, and various customer-contact methods.

- A systematic approach is in place to evaluate and improve service levels, customer-focused decision making, and customer relationships.

B. Customer Satisfaction Determination

- Several customer-satisfaction indicators are used (for example, repeat-business measures, praise letters, and direct measures using survey questions and interviews).

- Comprehensive satisfaction and dissatisfaction data are collected and segmented or grouped to enable the organization to predict customer behavior (likelihood of remaining a customer).

- Customer satisfaction and dissatisfaction measurements include both a numerical rating scale and descriptors assigned to each unit in the scale. An effective (actionable) customer satisfaction and dissatisfaction measurement system provides the organization with reliable information about customer ratings of specific product and service features and the relationship between these ratings and the customers' likely market behavior.

- Customer-dissatisfaction indicators include complaints, claims, refunds, recalls, returns, repeat services, litigation, replacements, performance-rating downgrades, repairs, warranty work, warranty costs, misshipments, and incomplete orders.

- Satisfaction data are collected from former customers for each customer/market segment.

- Competitors' customer satisfaction is determined using external or internal studies. This information is used to refine services and product features.

- Procedures are in place and evaluated to ensure that customer contact is initiated to follow-up on recent transactions to build relationships. Data from these contacts are used.

- The process of collecting complete, timely, and accurate customer-satisfaction and dissatisfaction data is regularly evaluated and improved. Customer preferences, by customer segment, are considered when designing procedures to determine satisfaction levels. Some prefer surveys, others focus groups, and others prefer face-to-face interactions. Several improvement cycles are evident.

4 Measurement, Analysis, and Knowledge Management—90 Points

*The **Measurement, Analysis, and Knowledge Management** Category examines how your organization selects, gathers, analyzes, manages, and improves its data, information, and knowledge assets. Also examined is how your organization reviews its performance.*

The Measurement, Analysis, and Knowledge Management Category is the main point within the Criteria for all key information about effectively measuring, analyzing, and reviewing performance and managing organizational knowledge to drive improvement and organizational competitiveness.

This Category is like the *motherboard* on a personal computer. All information flows into and out of it. In the simplest terms, Category 4 is the *brain center* for the alignment of the organization's operations and its strategic objectives. Such use of data and information depends on their quality and availability. Moreover, since information, analysis, and knowledge management might themselves be sources of competitive advantage and productivity growth, the Category also may have strategic value and its capabilities should be considered as part of the strategic planning process.

Measurement, Analysis, and Knowledge Management evaluates the selection, management, and effectiveness of use of information and data to support processes, action plans, and the performance management system. Systems to analyze, review, capture, store, retrieve, and distribute data to support decision making are also evaluated.

Measurement, Analysis, and Review of Organizational Performance

- This Item looks at the processes associated with data collection, information, and measures (including comparative data) for planning, decision making, improving performance, and supporting action plans and operations.

- The Item also looks at the analytical processes used to make sense out of the data to ensure decision makers draw valid conclusions. In addition, it looks at how these analyses are deployed throughout the organization and used to support organization-level review, decision making, and planning.

Information and Knowledge Management

- This Item looks at how the organization ensures that data and information are accessible to employees, suppliers and partners, and customers as needed and appropriate to support decision making. This Item also seeks to ensure that hardware and software are reliable and user-friendly throughout the organization. In many organizations, people with minimal computer skills must be able to access and use data to support decision making.

- The data system must provide for and ensure data integrity, reliability, accuracy, timeliness, security, and confidentiality.

4.1 MEASUREMENT, ANALYSIS, AND REVIEW OF ORGANIZATIONAL PERFORMANCE: How do you measure, analyze, and review organizational performance? (45 Pts.)

PROCESS

Describe how your organization measures, analyzes, aligns, reviews, and improves its performance data and information at all levels and in all parts of your organization.

Within your response, include answers to the following questions:

a. Performance Measurement

(1) How do you select, collect, align, and integrate data and information for tracking daily operations and for tracking overall organizational performance, including progress relative to strategic objectives an action plans? What are your key organizational performance measures? How do you use these data and information to support organizational decision making and innovation?

(2) How do you select and ensure the effective use of key comparative data and information to support operational and strategic decision making and innovation?

(3) How do you keep your performance measurement system current with business needs and directions? How do you ensure that your performance measurement system is sensitive to rapid or unexpected organizational or external changes?

b. Performance Analysis and Review

(1) How do you review organizational performance and capabilities? How do your senior leaders participate in these reviews? What analyses do you perform to support these reviews and to ensure that conclusions ar valid? How do you use these reviews to assess organizational success, competitive performance, and progress relative to strategic objectives and action plans? How do you use these reviews to assess your organization's ability to rapidly respond to changing organizational needs and challenges in your operating environment?

(2) How do you translate organizational performance review findings into priorities for continuous and breakthrough improvement and into opportunities for innovation? How are these priorities and opportunities deployed to work group- and functional-level operations throughout your organization to enable effective support for their decision making? When appropriate, how are the priorities and opportunities deployed to your suppliers, partners, and collaborators to ensure organizational alignment?

Notes:

N1   Performance measurement is used in fact-based decision making for setting and aligning organizational directions and resource use at the work unit, key process, departmental, and whole organization levels.

N2   Comparative data and information (4.1a[2]) are obtained by benchmarking and by seeking competitive comparisons. "Benchmarking" refers to identifying processes and results that represent best practices and performance for similar activities, inside or outside your organization's industry. Competitive comparisons relate your organization's performance to that of competitor and other organizations providing similar products and services.

N3   Organizational performance reviews (4.1b[1]) should be informed by organizational performance measurement and guided by the strategic objectives and action plans described in Items 2.1 and 2.2. The reviews also might be informed by internal or external Baldrige assessments.

N4   Analysis includes examining trends; organizational, industry, and technology projections; and comparisons, cause-effect relationships, and correlations intended to support your performance reviews, help determine root causes, and help set priorities for resource use. Accordingly, analysis draws on all types of data: customer-related, financial and market, operational, and competitive.

Continued

Notes: *Continued*

N5   The results of organizational performance analysis and review should contribute to your organizational strategic planning in Category 2.

N6   Your organizational performance results should be reported in Items 7.1–7.6.

Item 4.1, Measurement, Analysis, and Review of Organizational Performance, looks at the selection, collection, alignment, integration, management, analysis, and use of data and information in support of organizational decision making, planning, and performance improvement. The processes and systems required by this item provide a solid foundation for consistently good decision making. Processes required by this Item serve as a central collection and analysis point in an integrated performance measurement and management system that relies on financial and nonfinancial information to guide the organization's process management toward the achievement of key business results and strategic objectives. This system also enhances the organization's ability to anticipate and respond to rapid or unexpected organizational or external changes.

The first part of this Item, Performance Measurement [4.1a], requires the organization to select and use measures to track daily operations and enhance decision-making accuracy. It should select and integrate measures for monitoring overall organizational performance.

Data alignment and integration are key concepts for successful implementation of the performance measurement system. They are viewed in terms of extent and effectiveness of use to meet performance assessment needs. Alignment and integration include how measures are aligned throughout the organization, how they are integrated to yield organization-wide measures, and how performance measurement requirements are deployed by senior leaders to track work-group and process-level performance on key measures targeted for organization-wide significance and/or improvement.

The organization should show how competitive comparisons and benchmarking data are selected and used to help drive performance improvement. The

major reasons for using competitive and comparative information are: (1) the organization needs to know where it stands relative to competitors and best practices, especially as it works to achieve top levels of performance; (2) comparative and benchmarking information often provides a focus for significant (*breakthrough*) improvement or change; and (3) preparation for comparing performance information frequently leads to a better understanding of the organization's own processes and related performance. Benchmarking information also may support business analyses and decisions relating to core competencies, alliances, and outsourcing.

Effective selection and use of competitive comparisons and benchmarking information require: (1) determination of needs and priorities; (2) criteria for seeking appropriate sources for comparisons—from within and outside the organization's industry and markets; (3) use of data and information to set stretch targets and to promote major or breakthrough improvements in areas most critical to the organization's competitive strategy; and (4) relevant comparison of Category 7 results to demonstrate the strengths or *soundness* of the organization's performance outcomes.

Item 4.1a also looks at how the organization's performance measurement system is kept current with changing business needs. This involves ongoing, fact-based evaluation and subsequent refinements.

The second part of this Item, Performance Analysis [4.1b], looks at how the organization analyzes data to support decision making and how leaders review performance and set priorities.

Raw data do not usually provide an effective basis for setting organizational priorities and effective decision making. Accordingly, close alignment is needed between analysis and organizational performance review and between analysis and organizational planning. This ensures that analysis supports decision making and that decision making is based on relevant data and information.

Effective decision making usually requires leaders to understand cause–effect connections among and between processes and business/performance results. Process actions and their results may have many resource implications. High-performing organizations find it necessary to have support systems that provide an effective analytical basis for decisions because resources for improvement are limited and cause–effect connections are often unclear.

Organizations must have the ability to perform effective analyses to support senior leaders' assessments of all areas of performance and strategic planning. This includes assessment of current performance as well as how well the organization is moving toward the future. Review findings should provide a reliable means to guide both improvement and opportunities for innovation that are tied to the organization's key objectives, success factors, and measures. The results of organizational-level analysis must be effectively communicated by leaders to support decision making throughout the organization and to suppliers, partners, and key customers, and ensure those decisions are aligned with business results, strategic objectives, and action plans.

Accordingly, systematic processes must be in place for analyzing all types of data and to determine overall organizational health, including key organizational results, action plans, and strategic objectives. In addition, organizations must evaluate the effectiveness of their analytical processes and make improvements based on the evaluation.

Facts, rather than intuition, should be used to support most decision making at all levels based on the analyses conducted to make sense out of the data collected. Analyses that organizations typically conduct to gain an understanding of performance and needed actions vary widely depending on the type of organization, size, competitive environment, and other factors. These analyses help the organization's leaders understand the following:

- The extent to which product and service improvement drives customer satisfaction, customer retention, and market share

- The impact of customer-related problems and effective problem resolution on cost/revenue growth, repeat business, and lost customers

- Interpretation of market-share changes in terms of customer gains and losses and changes in customer satisfaction

- The impact of improvements in key operational performance areas such as productivity, cycle time, waste reduction, new-product introduction, and defect levels

- Relationships between employee/organizational learning (improvement processes) and value added per employee, productivity, and organizational growth

- Financial benefits derived from improvements in employee safety, absenteeism, turnover, and well-being and satisfaction

- Benefits and costs associated with education and training of all types

- Benefits and costs associated with improved organizational knowledge management, innovation rates, and sharing of best practices

- The extent to which identifying and meeting employee requirements correlate with employee retention, motivation, and productivity

- Cost/revenue implications of employee-related problems and effective problem resolution

- Individual or aggregate measures of productivity cost trends and and quality relative to competitors

- Relationships among product/service quality, operational-performance indicators, and overall financial-performance trends as reflected in indicators such as operating costs, revenues, asset utilization, and value added per employee

- Allocation of resources among alternative improvement projects based on cost/ benefit implications or environmental/ community impact

- Net earnings derived from quality, operational, and human resource performance improvements

- Comparisons among business units showing how quality and operational performance improvement affect financial performance

- Contributions of improvement activities to cash flow, working capital use, and shareholder value

- Profit impacts of customer retention

- Cost/revenue implications of new market entry, including global market entry or expansion

- Cost/revenue, customer, and productivity implications of engaging in and/or expanding e-commerce/e-business and use of the Internet and intranets

- Market share versus profits

- Trends in economic, market, and shareholder indicators of value and the impact of these trends on organizational sustainability

The availability of electronic data and information of many kinds (for example, financial, operational, customer-related, accreditation/regulatory) and from many sources (for example, internal, third party, and public sources; the Internet; Internet tracking software) permits extensive analysis and correlations. Effectively using and prioritizing this wealth of information are important to the success of top-performing organizations.

Senior leaders must review organizational performance in a disciplined, fact-based manner, and use the review findings to drive improvement and innovation [4.1b]. This organizational review should cover all areas of performance, and provide a complete and accurate picture of the *state of health* of the organization. This includes not only how well the organization is currently performing but also how well it is moving to secure future success.

- Key performance measures should focus on and reflect the key drivers of success leaders regularly review. These measures should relate to the strategic objectives necessary for success.

- Leaders should use these reviews to set priorities to focus on improvement and change activities needed to achieve the organization's key objectives, success factors, and measures.

- Leaders must create a consistent process to translate the review findings into an action agenda, sufficiently specific for deployment throughout the organization and to suppliers and partners—people who need to take action to improve.

4.1 Measurement, Analysis, and Review of Organizational Performance

How the organization measures, aligns, improves, analyzes, and uses information and data to support decision making for key processes and to improve performance at all levels and parts of the organization

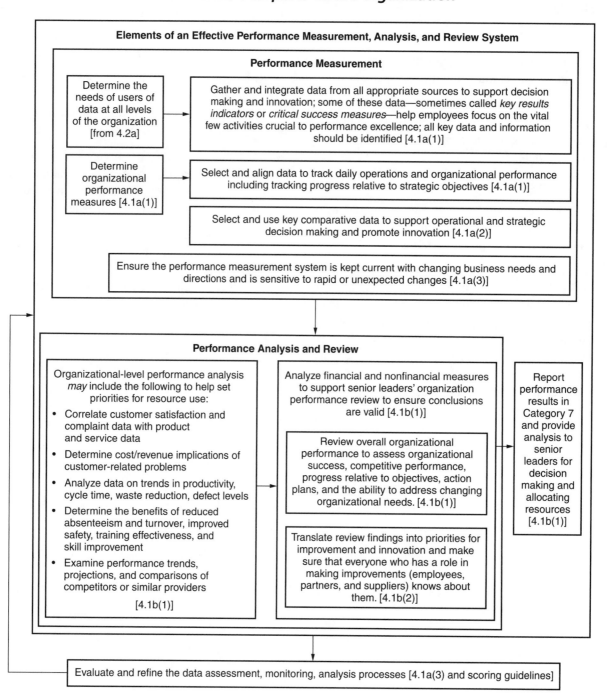

Elements of an Effective Performance Measurement, Analysis, and Review System

Performance Measurement

Determine the needs of users of data at all levels of the organization [from 4.2a]

Gather and integrate data from all appropriate sources to support decision making and innovation; some of these data—sometimes called *key results indicators* or *critical success measures*—help employees focus on the vital few activities crucial to performance excellence; all key data and information should be identified [4.1a(1)]

Determine organizational performance measures [4.1a(1)]

Select and align data to track daily operations and organizational performance including tracking progress relative to strategic objectives [4.1a(1)]

Select and use key comparative data to support operational and strategic decision making and promote innovation [4.1a(2)]

Ensure the performance measurement system is kept current with changing business needs and directions and is sensitive to rapid or unexpected changes [4.1a(3)]

Performance Analysis and Review

Organizational-level performance analysis *may* include the following to help set priorities for resource use:

- Correlate customer satisfaction and complaint data with product and service data

- Determine cost/revenue implications of customer-related problems

- Analyze data on trends in productivity, cycle time, waste reduction, defect levels

- Determine the benefits of reduced absenteeism and turnover, improved safety, training effectiveness, and skill improvement

- Examine performance trends, projections, and comparisons of competitors or similar providers

[4.1b(1)]

Analyze financial and nonfinancial measures to support senior leaders' organization performance review to ensure conclusions are valid [4.1b(1)]

Review overall organizational performance to assess organizational success, competitive performance, progress relative to objectives, action plans, and the ability to address changing organizational needs. [4.1b(1)]

Translate review findings into priorities for improvement and innovation and make sure that everyone who has a role in making improvements (employees, partners, and suppliers) knows about them. [4.1b(2)]

Report performance results in Category 7 and provide analysis to senior leaders for decision making and allocating resources [4.1b(1)]

Evaluate and refine the data assessment, monitoring, analysis processes [4.1a(3) and scoring guidelines]

4.1 Measurement, Analysis, and Review of Organizational Performance Item Linkages

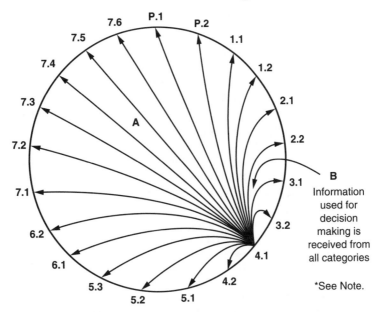

	NATURE OF RELATIONSHIP
A	Data and information are collected and analyzed [4.1] and made available [4.2] for developing the Organizational Profile [P.1 and P.2], planning [2.1a(2)], setting strategic objectives [2.1b(1)], day-to-day leadership decisions [1.1], setting public responsibility standards (regulatory, legal, ethical) for community involvement [1.2], reporting performance results [7.1, 7.2, 7.3, 7.4, 7.5, and 7.6], improving work processes [6.1 and 6.2] and human resource systems [5.1, 5.2, and 5.3], determining customer requirements [3.1], managing customer complaints and building customer relations [3.2a], and determining customer satisfaction [3.2b].
B	Data and information used to support analysis, decision making, and continuous improvement [4.1] are received from all processes. Information from customer satisfaction data [7.1] are analyzed [4.1b] and used to help determine ways to assess customer requirements [3.1a(2)], to determine appropriate standards or required levels of customer service [3.2a(2)], and to design instruments to assess customer satisfaction [3.2b(1)]. Data and information are received from the following areas and analyzed to support decisions: human resources capabilities, including work-system efficiency, initiative, and self-direction [5.1a(1)]; training and development needs [5.2a(2 and 3)] and effectiveness [5.2a(4)]; and safety, retention, absenteeism, organizational effectiveness, and well-being and satisfaction [5.3]. Data are aggregated and analyzed [4.1] to improve value creation [6.1] and support work processes [6.2] that will reduce cycle time, waste, and defect levels. Performance data from all parts of the organization are integrated and analyzed [4.1] to assess performance in key areas such as product and service quality [7.1], customer-related performance [7.2], operational performance [7.5], financial and market performance [7.3], human resource performance [7.4], and regulatory and legal compliance [7.6] relative to competitors or similar providers in all areas. Leaders [4.1b(1, 2)] monitor organizational performance and understand relationships among performance, employee satisfaction, customers, markets, and financial success. Leaders also use this information to support decision making at all levels, to set priorities for action, and allocate resources for maximum advantage [4.1b(2)].

*Note: Because the information collected and used for decision making links with all other Items, all of the linkage arrows will not be repeated on the other Item maps. Only the most relevant will be repeated.

	IF YOU DON'T DO WHAT THE CRITERIA REQUIRE . . .
Item Reference	**Possible Adverse Consequences**
4.1a(1)	The failure to systematically gather appropriate data and information from throughout the organization to support the daily operational, organizational decision making, and tracking progress in achieving strategic objectives and action plans can create an environment where decisions are typically based on intuition, gut feel, or guesswork. Furthermore, information gathered in this way may ignore some of the linkages critical to sustaining high performance in an organization. Decisions based on intuition or guesswork tend to be highly variable, which introduces error. Furthermore, in an environment where decisions are based on intuition it is usually the boss' intuition that drives the decision, which can lead to the disengagement of the people in the organization. Decisions made in this manner erode the organization's efforts to promote employee empowerment and innovation [Item 1.1a(3)]. Finally, the failure to integrate data and information may make it difficult to monitor overall organizational performance. Disjointed, nonintegrated data are difficult to consolidate and report in a manageable, easy-to-understand *dashboard* to support effective decision making.
4.1a(1)	Data and information provide a basis for decision making at all levels of the organization: top leaders use the data to make decisions about the direction of the organization, and employees use data to make decisions about operational matters. Unless measures are selected and aligned to provide the right information, at the right time, in the right format, the decisions of the leaders and the employees are likely to be suboptimized. Moreover, although the failure to gather appropriate data tends to reduce decision-making quality, spending resources to gather data and information that do not support decision making throughout the organization (useless data) typically adds unnecessary cost. It is difficult to collect the right data and information if the organization has failed to determine what data are needed to support decision making at all levels. In addition, the failure to collect appropriate information makes it more difficult to monitor performance against goals [Item 4.1b(1)], effectively communicate expectations throughout the organization [Item 1.1a(1)], and deploy actions needed to carry out strategy [Item 2.2a].
4.1a(1)	Strategy identifies the things an organization must do to be successful in the future. Many actions must be taken in an organization to ensure strategic objectives are achieved. Data analysis helps leaders understand critical relationships between actions and outcomes to effectively allocate resources and achieve desired results. The failure to examine and understand the relationship between performance outcomes, action plans, and strategic objectives may cause senior leaders to make inappropriate decisions about the allocation of limited resources. This means that the organization may not realize the maximum benefit from the expenditure of those resources. For example, failing to understand the correlation between product and service quality improvement and improved customer satisfaction and retention may cause the leader to divert resources to less important activities.
4.1a(2)	The failure to collect and effectively use the right comparative data makes it difficult for the organization to learn and take appropriate action. Learning from the best helps provoke an understanding of what systems and processes may be required to make quantum leaps in performance as well as the levels that must be reached to achieve the leadership position projected during the planning process [Item 2.2b]. For example, comparisons showing that the organization's projected performance outpaces the industrial average will have little meaning

Continued

	IF YOU DON'T DO WHAT THE CRITERIA REQUIRE . . . *Continued*
Item Reference	**Possible Adverse Consequences**
	if the best competitor's rate of improvement is greater. Furthermore, if an organization collects comparative data from world-class benchmarks, but does not effectively use comparative data for planning [Item 2.1a(2)], to identify areas needing breakthrough performance, or set improvement priorities [Item 4.1a(2)], then it is simply wasting resources. If an organization does not collect comparative performance outcome data, it is not able to determine if its own rate of progress is sufficient to keep it ahead of the competition or evaluate the strength of its own performance results [required by Category 7].
4.1a(3)	Organizations that fail to improve the speed and accuracy of decision making typically do not perform well in a competitive environment. Without a process to evaluate the information system and how well it responds to the needs of the business, organizations may not know they are collecting insufficient or incorrect data and information. In addition, organizations may not know if the data effectively support daily operations and organizational decision making. They may not know if the resources spent to collect benchmarking and comparison data are producing appropriate benefits.
4.1b(1)	The lack of a system to analyze and make sense out of raw data may make it difficult for senior leaders to understand cause-and-effect relationships, root causes of problems, and the impact of various processes on performance outcomes. This may make it more difficult for leaders to identify specific areas within the organization where improvement is required. It may send a message throughout the organization that performance outcomes are really not that important. If results are not important to top leaders, they may not be considered important to lower levels within the organization and employees at all levels may not contribute optimum effort to achieve these (unimportant) results. It also makes it more difficult for leaders to effectively set priorities. Consider the following examples: a) without a cost–benefit analysis it is more difficult to determine whether project A or project B should receive support, because it is difficult to know which project is likely to be of greater benefit to the organization; b) calculating C_{pk} (the capability of a process) helps leaders understand the extent to which their key processes are in control or need adjustment (the raw run data cannot support this kind of decision making); and c) failing to understand root causes makes it more difficult to prevent problems from recurring, which adds cost but not value.
4.1b(2)	Even if senior leaders have an effective process to review organizational performance, but do not effectively use these review findings to identify priorities for improvement and targets of innovation, they may not be providing appropriate focus and alignment throughout the organization and to affected suppliers and partners. This may make it difficult for workers, managers, partners, and suppliers to make the changes needed to correct problems or comply with the new priorities for improvement, contributing to wasted resources and performance failures. The long-standing failure to identify priorities for improvement or targets of innovation may contribute to the perception that the status quo is acceptable and continuous improvement is not important. This may further contribute to organizational stagnation and may make it difficult to keep pace with competitors and increasing customer requirements.

Continued

IF YOU DON'T DO WHAT THE CRITERIA REQUIRE . . .	Continued

Item Reference	Possible Adverse Consequences
4.1b(2)	Employees and managers at all levels of the organization need useful information to support decision making. The failure to ensure that people at every level understand the impact that their work has on overall organizational performance makes it more difficult for them to identify and understand why they need to perform at certain agreed levels and why change may need to occur. Without this information, employees and managers throughout the organization must rely on intuition or incomplete data to support decision making—typically reducing the accuracy of those decisions and, in some cases, suboptimizing the overall performance of the organization.

4.1 MEASUREMENT, ANALYSIS, AND REVIEW OF ORGANIZATIONAL PERFORMANCE—SAMPLE EFFECTIVE PRACTICES

A. Performance Measurement

- Above all, data and information are favored as a decision-making support tool, rather than a quick and easy reliance on intuition or *gut feel.*

- Data collected at the individual worker level are consistent across the organization to permit consolidation and organization-wide performance monitoring.

- The cost of quality (including rework, delay, waste, scrap, errors) and other financial concerns are measured for internal operations and processes.

- Data are maintained on employee-related issues of satisfaction, morale, safety, education and training, use of teams, and recognition and reward.

- A systematic process exists for data review and improvement, standardization, and easy employee access to data. Training on the use of data systems is provided as needed.

- Data used for management decisions' focus on critical success factors are integrated with work processes for the planning, design, and delivery of products and services.

- A systematic process is in place for identifying and prioritizing comparative information and benchmark targets.

- Research has been conducted to identify best-in-class organizations, which may be competitors or noncompetitors. Critical business processes or functions are the subject of benchmarking. Activities such as those that support the organization's goals and objectives, action plans, and opportunities for improvement and innovation are the subject of benchmarking. Benchmarking also covers key products, services, customer satisfiers, suppliers, employees, and support operations.

- The organization reaches beyond its own business to conduct comparative studies.

- Benchmark or comparison data are used to improve the understanding of work processes and to discover the best levels of performance that have been achieved. Based on this knowledge, the organization sets goals or targets to stretch performance as well as drive innovations.

- A systematic process is in place to improve the use of benchmark or comparison data in the understanding of all work processes.

B. Performance Analysis and Review

- Systematic processes are in place for analyzing all types of data and to determine overall organizational health, including key business results, action plans, and strategic objectives. Part of the process is a method to evaluate the effectiveness of the analysis process and improve upon it.

- Facts, rather than intuition, are used to support most decision making at all levels based on the analyses conducted to make sense out of the data collected.

- The analysis process itself is analyzed to make the results more timely and useful for decision making for quality improvement at all levels.

- Analysis processes and tools, and the value of analyses to decision making, are systematically evaluated and improved.

- Analysis is linked to work groups to facilitate decision making (sometimes daily) throughout the organization.

- Analysis techniques enable meaningful interpretation of the cost and performance impact of organization processes. This analysis helps people at all levels of the organization make necessary trade-offs, set priorities, and reallocate resources to maximize overall organization performance.

- Reviews against measurable performance standards are held frequently.

- Senior leaders base their business decisions on reliable data and facts pertaining to customers, operational processes, and employee performance and satisfaction.

- Senior leaders hold regular meetings to review performance data and set priorities to resolve problems, and improve work.

- Senior leaders conduct monthly reviews of organizational performance. This requires that subordinates conduct biweekly reviews, and workers and work teams provide daily performance updates. Corrective actions are developed to improve performance that deviates from planned performance.

- Customer, performance, and financial data drive priorities for organizational improvement and innovation.

4.2   INFORMATION AND KNOWLEDGE MANAGEMENT: How do you   **PROCESS**
manage organizational information and knowledge? (45 Pts.)

Describe how your organization ensures the quality and availability of needed data and information for employees, suppliers, partners, collaborators, and customers. Describe how your organization builds and manages its knowledge assets.

Within your response, include answers to the following questions:

a. Data and Information Availability

(1) How do you make needed data and information available? How do you make them accessible to employees, suppliers, partners, collaborators, and customers, as appropriate?

(2) How do you ensure that hardware and software are reliable, secure, and user-friendly?

(3) How do you ensure the continued availability of data and information, including the availability of hardware and software systems, in the event of an emergency?

(4) How do you keep your data and information availability mechanisms, including your software and hardware systems, current with business needs and directions and with technological changes in your operating environment?

b. Organizational Knowledge Management

How do you manage organizational knowledge to accomplish the following:

- The collection and transfer of employee knowledge

- The transfer of relevant knowledge from and to customers, suppliers, partners, and collaborators

- The rapid identification, sharing, and implementation of best practices

c. Data, Information, and Knowledge Quality

How do you ensure the following properties of your data, information, and organizational knowledge:

- Accuracy

- Integrity and reliability

- Timeliness

- Security and confidentiality

Notes:

N1   Data and information availability [4.2a] are of growing importance as the Internet, e-business, and e-commerce are used increasingly for business-to-business, organization-to-organization, and business-to-consumer interactions and as intranets become more important as a major source of organization-wide communications.

N2   Data and information access [4.2a(1)] might be via electronic or other means.

The first part of this Item, Data and Information Availability [4.2a], examines how the organization ensures the availability of high-quality, timely data and information for all key users—employees, suppliers/partners, and customers. Top-performing organizations make data and information available and accessible to all appropriate users. The organization's hardware systems and software must be reliable and user friendly, facilitating full access and encouraging routine use. The aim of building and managing knowledge assets is to improve organizational efficiency, effectiveness, and innovation.

As the sources of data and information and the number of users within the organization grow dramatically, systems to manage information technology often require significant resources. Top-performing organizations consider the management of information technology as a strategic imperative. The expanding use of electronic information within organizational operations, more comprehensive knowledge networks, new data from the Internet, and increasing business-to-business and business-to-consumer communications challenges make it absolutely critical that the organization develop systems to ensure data reliability and availability in a user-friendly format.

Plans should address how the organization will continue to provide data and information in the event of either a natural or man-made disaster. These plans should consider the needs of all stakeholders, including employees, customers, and suppliers and partners. Processes should be in place to protect against system failure, which may damage or destroy critical data. This may require redundant systems as well as effective backup and storage of data at remote locations. The plans also should support the organization's overall plan for business continuity [Item 6.2]] and ensuring workplace preparedness for disasters and emergencies [5.3a(2)].

Data and information are especially important in business networks, alliances, and supply chains. Information management systems should facilitate the use of data and information and should recognize the need for rapid data validation and reliability assurance, given the increasing use of electronic data transfer.

As with the other items required for performance excellence, the organization must systematically evaluate and improve data-availability mechanisms, software, and hardware to keep them current with changing business needs and directions.

The second part of this Item, Organizational Knowledge Management [4.2b] recognizes the need for high-performing organizations to focus on the management of knowledge that people need to do their work; that is, to improve processes, products, and services, keep current with changing business needs and directions, and develop innovative, value-added solutions for the customer and the organization. Organizational Knowledge Management [4.2b], addresses the need to transfer knowledge from employees, customers, suppliers, and partners for the benefit of the organization. It also includes the sharing of practices that might benefit the organization and key partners.

The third part of this item, Data, Information, and Knowledge Quality [4.2c], addresses the properties necessary for data and information to meet user needs, including integrity (completeness—tells the whole story), reliability (consistency), accuracy (correctness), timeliness (available when needed), and appropriate levels of security and confidentiality (free from tampering and inappropriate release).

Organizations must ensure data and information reliability since reliability is critical to good decision making, successful monitoring of operations, and successful data integration for assessing overall performance. However, data reliability or consistency is not sufficient. To be useful, data must also be accurate. Consistently incorrect data do not help leaders make consistently good decisions.

- Processes should be in place to protect against external threats, including attacks from hackers, viral infections, power surges, and other storm-related damage.

4.2 Information and Knowledge Management

How the organization ensures the quality and availability of data and information for employees, suppliers and partners, and customers

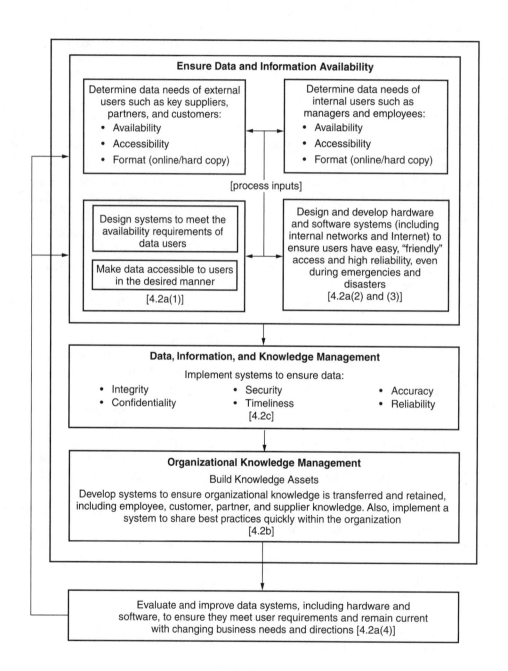

Ensure Data and Information Availability

Determine data needs of external users such as key suppliers, partners, and customers:
- Availability
- Accessibility
- Format (online/hard copy)

Determine data needs of internal users such as managers and employees:
- Availability
- Accessibility
- Format (online/hard copy)

[process inputs]

Design systems to meet the availability requirements of data users

Make data accessible to users in the desired manner

[4.2a(1)]

Design and develop hardware and software systems (including internal networks and Internet) to ensure users have easy, "friendly" access and high reliability, even during emergencies and disasters

[4.2a(2) and (3)]

Data, Information, and Knowledge Management

Implement systems to ensure data:
- Integrity
- Confidentiality
- Security
- Timeliness
- Accuracy
- Reliability

[4.2c]

Organizational Knowledge Management

Build Knowledge Assets

Develop systems to ensure organizational knowledge is transferred and retained, including employee, customer, partner, and supplier knowledge. Also, implement a system to share best practices quickly within the organization

[4.2b]

Evaluate and improve data systems, including hardware and software, to ensure they meet user requirements and remain current with changing business needs and directions [4.2a(4)]

4.2 Information and Knowledge Management Item Linkages

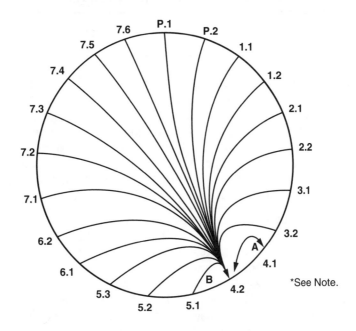

	NATURE OF RELATIONSHIP
A	Information and Knowledge Management [4.2] enables the data flow within the organization and indirectly interacts with all other items (similar to the relationships identified and reported in the Item 4.1 diagram). The simplest way to show these relationships is to tie this Item [4.2] with the Measurement and Analysis of Organizational Performance Item [4.1].
B	To ensure that hardware and software systems are reliable and user friendly [4.2a(2)], information from the following types of system users is gathered: leaders [Category 1]; planners [Category 2]; customer relationships and contact staff [Category 3]; information specialists [Category 4]; human resource personnel, managers, and employees [Category 5]; operations workers, managers, suppliers, and partners [Category 6]; and people who monitor and interpret results [Category 7] for use in decision making.

*Note: Because the information collected and used for decision making links with all other Items, all of the linkage arrows will not be repeated on the other item maps. Only the most relevant will be repeated.

IF YOU DON'T DO WHAT THE CRITERIA REQUIRE . . .	
Item Reference	**Possible Adverse Consequences**
4.2a(1)	Getting the right information to the right people at the right time and in the right format enables effective decision making. Just as different types of employees in an organization need different data to support decision making, they may need to access information in different ways. Similarly, customers and suppliers may need access to information to facilitate ordering and delivery of required products and services. The failure to provide appropriate access to data may make it more difficult for employees to make timely decisions about work, for customers to place orders for products and services, or lead to disruptions in the supply chain. Providing inappropriate access for individuals inside or outside the organization may compromise data confidentiality and security or even violate certain privacy laws.
4.2a(2)	The breadth, depth, and speed of decision making continue to increase as artificial intelligence plays a larger and larger role in our lives. Hardware and software are at the heart of this phenomenon. More people than ever before are being asked to interact with computers. In the best-performing organizations, employees frequently use computers to access data and use them to develop relevant analyses that enable better decisions about their work. People with very little computer literacy must now enter and retrieve data from these systems. A user interface that may be easily understood by information management technicians may be incomprehensible to a line worker, customer, or supplier. The failure to make these systems reliable and easy to use (user friendly) makes it difficult, if not impossible, for some people to use them effectively. This may create significant problems for organizations, particularly those venturing into areas where e-commerce plays a larger and growing role. Consider, for example, a bank that wants to expand and promote distance banking via the Internet or through home-to-bank modem connections. If the software is not reliable and very user friendly, many customers may be unwilling or unable to take advantage of these services. This may limit the organization's ability to achieve strategic and/or market-share goals that should have been considered during the strategy development process [Item 2.1a(2)].
4.2a(3)	The failure to ensure the continued availability of data, hardware, and software systems in an emergency causes reduced decision accuracy and delay at the very least. More typically, in today's world of e-commerce, information system failures can cause the organization to cease work.
4.2a(4)	In a rapidly changing world, access to information and the use of that information to provide insight and help decision making can provide a strategic advantage. Rapid data availability is becoming more and more critical for business success, especially in e-business situations. In some industries such as banking, a few seconds can make the difference between capitalizing on currency rate fluctuations or being hurt by them. As product and delivery cycle times grow shorter, the need for rapid access to information grows greater. Without evaluating the suitability of data and information systems, and making refinements based on this evaluation, the organization leaves itself open to falling behind and not being able to respond rapidly to changing business needs and directions. This Item does not require improvements in software and hardware simply for the sake of buying new gadgets. Improvements should help support changing business needs and directions—as a means to an end, not the end itself.

Continued

	IF YOU DON'T DO WHAT THE CRITERIA REQUIRE . . . *Continued*
Item Reference	**Possible Adverse Consequences**
4.2b(1)	Knowledge is of little or no use unless the people who need it, have it. Knowledge sequestered in one corner of an organization cannot benefit the entire organization unless it is transferred to other employees in other units. The same is true for knowledge held by key customers, suppliers, and partners. Knowledge withheld is knowledge (and resources) wasted. The failure to capture/transfer knowledge from long-standing employees who depart or retire is especially troublesome because they typically possess vast amounts of institutional memory.
4.2b	Decisions that are based on data and information may be compromised if the data are inaccurate or unreliable. For example, when a data-entry error is made and goes unnoticed (sometimes referred to as *garbage in, garbage out*), it could drive decisions to deliver the wrong product at the wrong time to the wrong customer. At the very least this is likely to cause the product to be returned and restocked, adding cost but not value. The lack of timely information may cause decisions to be delayed inappropriately. Consider, for example, an organization that conducts an employee (or customer) satisfaction survey but does not analyze or make the data available for eight months. This not only sends a message to the organization that employee (or customer) concerns are unimportant, it also makes it difficult to identify real problems that may be contributing to customer dissatisfaction, low worker morale, and poor productivity.
4.2c	Concerns about security, data loss, sophisticated hackers, and increased customer requirements for better access and availability place steadily increasing demands on hardware and software systems. The failure to keep these systems current as required by 4.2a(4) may expose them to internal or external threats. For example, the failure to update virus protections frequently and maintain up-to-date, effective firewalls can expose the computer system (and the organization) to catastrophic and costly losses.

4.2 INFORMATION AND KNOWLEDGE MANAGEMENT— SAMPLE EFFECTIVE PRACTICES

A. Data and Information Availability

- Users of data help determine what data systems are developed and how data are accessed.

- A *sunset* review is conducted to determine what data no longer need be collected and can be dropped.

- Every person has access to the data they need to make decisions about their work, from top leaders to individual workers or teams of workers.

- The performance measurement system is systematically evaluated and refined. Improvements have been made to reduce cycle time for data collection and to increase data access, reliability, and use.

- Procedures required to interface with the hardware and software are designed to meet the needs and capabilities of all computer users, to ensure that no one is excluded.

- Data systems are benchmarked against best-in-class systems and continually refined.

B. Organizational Knowledge Management

- All key work processes are documented and stored in a searchable and accessible database and used to share improvements and avoid rework associated with reinventing effective processes.

- A data and knowledge exchange is in place to receive useful knowledge and information from customers, suppliers, partners and other key stakeholders. The system is automated for easy update and access. Face-to-face and/or electronic meetings are held regularly to share information.

C. Data, Information, and Knowledge Quality

- Data are protected against misuse from external sources through encryption and randomly changing user passwords.

- A data reliability (consistency) team routinely and randomly checks data. Systems are in place to minimize or prevent human error in data entry and analysis.

- Disciplined and automatic file backup occurs. Backup data are stored in a secure, external facility.

- Hardware and software systems have been protected against external threats from hackers, viral threats, water, and electrical damage. Protection systems are updated as appropriate (for example, viral updates are made several times daily).

5 Human Resource Focus—85 Points

The **Human Resource Focus** Category examines how your organization's work systems and your employee learning and motivation enable employees to develop and utilize their full potential in alignment with your organization's overall objectives, strategy, and action plans. Also examined are your organization's efforts to build and maintain a work environment and employee support climate conducive to performance excellence and to personal and organizational growth.

Human Resource Focus addresses key human resource practices—those directed toward creating a high-performance workplace and toward developing employees to enable them and the organization to adapt to change. The Category covers human resource development and management requirements in an integrated manner, aligned with the organization's strategic directions and plans. Included in the focus on human resources is a focus on the work environment and the employee-support climate.

To ensure the basic alignment of human resource management with overall strategy, the Criteria also include human resource planning as part of organizational planning in the Strategic Planning Category. Human Resource Focus also evaluates how the organization enables employees to develop and use their full potential.

Work Systems

- Design, organize, and manage work and jobs to optimize employee performance and potential.

- Support objectives for customer satisfaction, high-performance objectives, and employee and organization learning goals with performance feedback to employees and recognition and reward practices

- Identify skills and capabilities needed by potential (future) employees, and then recruit, hire, and effectively retain them.

Employee Learning and Motivation

- Deliver, evaluate, and reinforce appropriate training to achieve action plans and address organization needs including building knowledge, skills, and abilities to improve employee development and performance.

- Enhance employee motivation and career progression.

Employee Well-Being and Satisfaction

- Improve employee safety, well-being, development, and satisfaction and maintain a work environment free from distractions to high performance. Ensure continuing operations in the event of an emergency.

- Systematically evaluate employee well-being, satisfaction, and motivation and identify improvement priorities that promote key business results.

5.1 WORK SYSTEMS: How do you enable employees to accomplish the work of your organization? (35 Pts.)   PROCESS

Describe how your organization's work and jobs enable employees and the organization to achieve high performance. Describe how compensation, career progression, and related workforce practices enable employees and the organization to achieve high performance.

Within your response, include answers to the following questions:

a. Organization and Management of Work

(1) How do you organize and manage work and jobs, including skills, to promote cooperation, initiative, empowerment, innovation, and your organizational culture? How do you organize and manage work and jobs, including skills, to achieve the agility to keep current with business needs and to achieve your action plans?

(2) How do your work systems capitalize on the diverse ideas, cultures, and thinking of your employees and the communities with which you interact (your employee hiring and your customer communities)?

(3) How do you achieve effective communication and skill sharing across work units, jobs, and locations?

b. Employee Performance Management System

How does your employee performance management system, including feedback to employees, support high-performance work and contribute to the achievement of your action plans? How does your employee performance management system support a customer and business focus? How do your compensation, recognition, and related reward and incentive practices reinforce high-performance work and a customer and business focus?

c. Hiring and Career Progression

(1) How do you identify characteristics and skills needed by potential employees?

(2) How do you recruit, hire, and retain new employees? How do you ensure employees represent the diverse ideas, cultures, and thinking of your hiring community?

(3) How do you accomplish effective succession planning for leadership and management positions? How do you manage effective career progression for all employees throughout the organization?

Notes:

N1 "Employees" refers to your organization's permanent, temporary, and part-time personnel, as well as any contract employees supervised by your organization. Employees include team leaders, supervisors, and managers at all levels. Contract employees supervised by a contractor should be addressed in Category 6. *For nonprofit organizations that also rely on volunteers, "employees" also refers to these volunteers.*

N2 "Your organization's work" refers to how your employees are organized or organize themselves in formal and informal, temporary, or longer-term units. This might include work teams, process teams, project teams, customer action teams, problem-solving teams, centers of excellence, functional units, remote workers (, at home), cross-functional teams, and departments—self-managed or managed by supervisors.

"Jobs" refers to responsibilities, authorities, and tasks of individuals. In some work systems, jobs might be shared by a team.

N3 Compensation, recognition, and related reward and incentive practices (5.1b) include promotions and bonuses that might be based on performance, skills acquired, and other factors. *In some governmental organizations, compensation systems are set by law or regulation. Since recognition can include monetary and nonmonetary, formal and informal, and individual and group mechanisms, reward and recognition systems still permit flexibility.*

This Item [5.1] looks at the organization's systems for work and jobs, compensation, career progression, employee-performance management, motivation, recognition, communication, and hiring, with the aim of enabling and encouraging all employees to contribute effectively and to the best of their ability. These systems are intended to foster high performance, to result in individual and organizational learning, and to enable adaptation to change, thereby contributing to organizational sustainability.

Work and jobs should be designed in such a way as to allow employees to exercise optimum discretion and decision making, typically resulting in higher involvement and better performance. *In order to exercise effective decision making, employees need access to appropriate data and analyses concerning their work and possess the knowledge and skills to interpret the data to make good decisions.* (This links to the information and knowledge management systems required in Category 4 and training in Item 5.2.) Unless employees have access to data to support effective decision making and understand how to analyze and interpret data, their decisions, by default, revert to intuition—which is highly variable. Managers are less likely to permit employees to substitute their intuition for that of managers. Therefore, employee decision making is likely to be limited, even if managers were inclined to release decisions to subordinates. Accordingly, systems to promote employee empowerment and agility should ensure employees have the authority to make decisions about their work, as well as data and analysis systems to support effective and consistently good decisions.

Work and job factors important to consider include simplification of job classifications (less specialization and work isolation), which can be addressed by cross-training, job rotation, use of teams (including self-directed teams), and changes in work layout and location. Another important method to combat worker isolation is to foster communication across functions and work units, maintain a focus on customer requirements, and create an environment of knowledge sharing and respect.

High-performance work is also enhanced by systems that promote employee flexibility, innovation, knowledge and skill sharing, alignment with organizational objectives, customer focus, and rapid response to changing business needs and requirements of the marketplace. Work should support the achievement of organizational objectives. Creativity and innovation from all employees should be specifically required, measured, and recognized. Suggestion boxes are not enough. The number of innovative ideas actually *implemented* per person is a better indicator of innovation and idea quality than the number of ideas *proposed*.

Hierarchical, command-and-control management styles work against fast response and high-performance capability. Agility reflects the speed with which employees and the organization do their work, including rapid response to changing needs and requirements. Organizations that are bogged down with bureaucratic inefficiencies cannot be agile. Unnecessary layers of management approval typically add delay and cost but not value.

Developing and sustaining high-performance work systems require ongoing education and training (relates to Item 5.2), and information systems (relates to Category 4) that ensure adequate information availability. To help employees realize their full potential, many organizations use individual development plans prepared with the input of each employee and designed to address their career and learning objectives.

The best organizations put in place an employee-performance management system that provides measurable feedback to employees, and ties reward, recognition, compensation, and/or incentives to the achievement of high-performance objectives and a customer and business focus. Compensation and recognition systems must be matched to support the work necessary for business success. Consistent with this, compensation and recognition might be tied to demonstrated skills and peer evaluations. Compensation and recognition approaches also might include profit sharing, rewarding exemplary team or unit performance, and links to customer-satisfaction and loyalty measures, achievement of organizational strategic objectives, or other business objectives.

Once the organization determines its key strategic objectives, it should review compensation, reward, and recognition systems to ensure they support those objectives. The failure to do this creates an environment where employees are focused on one set of activities (based on their compensation plan), but the organization has determined that another set of activities (the action plans to achieve the strategic objectives) is necessary for success.

The organization must perform effective succession planning for senior leadership and managers at all levels of the organization. The rate of new-knowledge acquisition is increasing throughout the world. Significantly more new knowledge is causing change to occur faster than ever before in history. To manage effectively in this climate of rapid change, the best organizations anticipate future leadership needs and prepare their future leaders, managers, and employees to take over. The best organizations do not wait for vacancies to occur before they think about the requirements and skills needed. Succession planning enables organizations to identify future skill needs against current skill gaps, enabling them to recruit and develop the necessary human resources. Employee hiring and career-progression planning should consider both internal and external candidates with a focus on the future sustainability and growth of the organization.

Finally, organizations must profile, recruit, hire, and retain employees who will meet skill requirements required to position the organization for future success. Obviously, the right workforce is a key driver of high performance. As the pool of skilled talent continues to shrink, it becomes more important than ever for organizations to specifically define the capabilities and skills needed by potential employees and create a work environment to attract them. Accordingly, it is critical to take into account characteristics of diverse populations to make sure appropriate support systems exist that make it possible to attract skilled workers.

5.1 Work Systems

How the organization's work and job-design, compensation, career-progression, and related workforce practices enable and encourage all employees to contribute effectively to achieving high performance

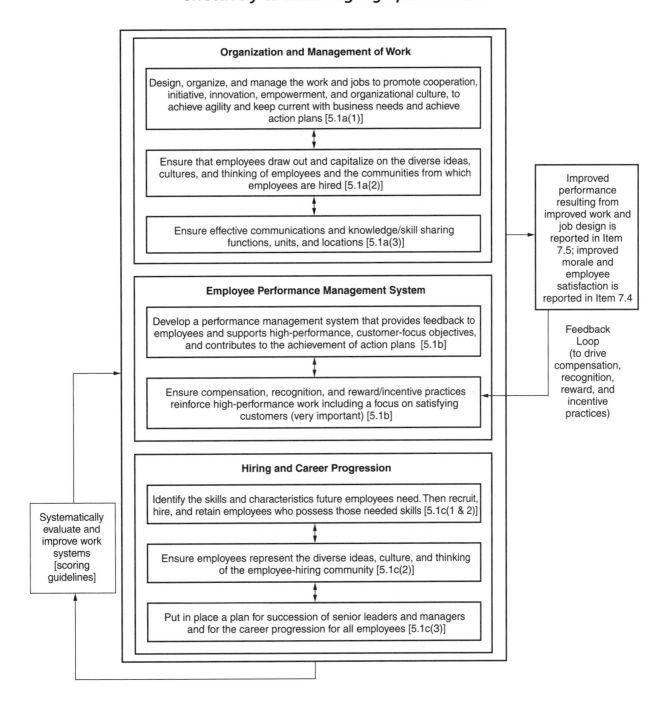

5.1 Work Systems Item Linkages

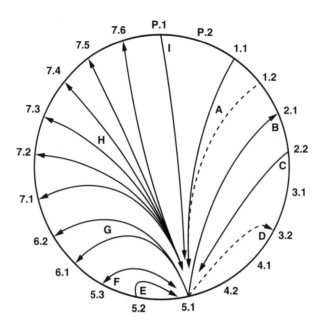

	NATURE OF RELATIONSHIP
A	Senior leaders (and subsequently leaders at all levels) [1.1a(3) and 1.1b(1)] create an environment for employee empowerment, innovation, learning, and organizational agility; set related policies; and role-model appropriate behaviors essential to improving work and job design to optimize performance and productivity [5.1a(1)]. In addition, part of evaluating the performance of the leadership system [1.2a(2)] involves determining the extent to which leaders at all levels helped achieve goals for employee empowerment and other key performance outcomes.
B	Employee diversity, innovation, and related skills [5.1] affect human resource strengths and weaknesses—a factor that should be considered in the planning process [2.1a(2)].
C	Human resource development plans and goals [2.2a(4)] are used to help organize and manage work and jobs [5.1a(1)], align reward and recognition [5.1b], and decide which potential employees need to be recruited to close skill gaps [5.1c(1)].
D	Empowerment, initiative [5.1a(1)], and communication and knowledge sharing [5.1a(3)] are essential to enhance the effectiveness and ability of customer-contact employees to resolve customer concerns promptly [3.2a(3)].
E	Effective training that contributes to achieving action plans [5.2a(1)] with appropriate feedback from employees and managers about their training needs [5.2a(3)] is critical to enable employees/managers at all levels to improve skills and their ability to promote cooperation, initiative, empowerment, and innovation [5.1a(1)] and retain key employees [5.1c(2)] .
F	A safe, secure work climate [5.3] enhances employee motivation, participation, self-direction, and initiative [5.1a] and vice versa.

Continued

NATURE OF RELATIONSHIP	*Continued*
G	High-performance and flexible work systems [5.1a(1)] are essential to improving value-adding and related business processes [6.1]. Effective performance feedback, compensation, and recognition [5.1b] are essential to improving value-creation and support processes [6.1 and 6.2].
H	Compensation, incentives, recognition, and rewards [5.1b] are based in part on performance results [Category 7]. Improvements in work and job design, innovation, empowerment, [5.1a(1)] sharing, and communication [5.1a(3)] can result in improved performance and business results [Category 7]. Processes to improve initiative and empowerment [5.1a(1)] can enhance all performance results [Category 7].
I	Employee characteristics such as educational levels, workforce and job diversity, the existence of bargaining units, the use of contract employees, and other special requirements [P.1a(3)] help set the context for determining the requirements for knowledge and skill sharing across work units, jobs, and locations [5.1a(3)] and skills needed of potential employees [5.1c(1)].

IF YOU DON'T DO WHAT THE CRITERIA REQUIRE . . .	
Item Reference	**Possible Adverse Consequences**
5.1a(1)	The alignment of strategic objectives and the work to accomplish them is vital to the success and optimum performance of the organization. Once strategic objectives, time lines [Item 2.1b(1)], and related actions [Item 2.2a(1)] have been identified and deployed to all levels of the organization, leaders and managers can more effectively organize employees (or they can organize themselves) to carry out the necessary work. In addition, appropriate responsibilities, authorities, and other tasks should be defined to ensure the actions are aligned (consistent) at all levels and effectively carried out. If the organization and management of work and jobs are not aligned to support strategic objectives and related actions, the organization may waste resources by failing to optimize the work that is done.
5.1a(2)	The failure to capitalize on diverse ideas, cultures, and thinking may limit the organization's ability to promote an innovative and empowered workforce [Item 5.1a(1)]. This in turn may limit the organization's ability to meet the challenges of today's highly competitive environment and reduce productivity.
5.1a(3)	The failure to promote cooperation among work units often contributes to redundancy and working at cross-purposes. The failure to promote knowledge and skill sharing often forces the organization to duplicate efforts in the search for more effective and efficient processes. The failure to share knowledge also contributes to isolationism within an organization and prevents *pockets of excellence* from spreading. Frequently, employees working in a hierarchical, command-and-control environment find individual initiative, empowerment, and innovation stifled, reducing morale and further eroding productivity and responsiveness.
5.1b	In order to optimize performance, work throughout the organization must be fully aligned to support strategic objectives, time lines [Item 2.1b(1)], and related action plans [Item 2.2a(1)]. The action plans should be deployed fully throughout the organization at all levels with appropriate quantitative measures developed to monitor progress [Item 2.2a(5)]. The work of individual employees, when taken together, should enable the organization to achieve its

Continued

	IF YOU DON'T DO WHAT THE CRITERIA REQUIRE . . . *Continued*
Item Reference	**Possible Adverse Consequences**
	strategic objectives. There are two questions that are fundamental to the work endeavors that employee feedback should address: 1) are the right things being done (the vital few); and 2) are they being done right (correctly). The failure to provide feedback to employees about their performance may make it more difficult for them to determine if they are doing the right thing in support of business strategy or if they are doing things in the right way (process discipline). It forces them to decide for themselves if they are doing a good job. In addition, the failure to provide feedback causes the organization to miss an opportunity to reinforce a customer and business focus. After all, *what gets measured gets done*. The alignment of what is *expected* and what is *rewarded* sends strong messages throughout the organization about what is really important. Failing to align appropriate compensation, recognition, rewards, and incentives with the strategic objectives may also contribute to a lack of focus within the workforce, forcing employees to substitute their own ideas instead of being driven/guided by management. Many employees equate compensation with the important activities the organization wants to achieve. For example, if achieving profitability is critical for organization success, the organization typically rewards people for achieving financial goals. In this situation, everyone clearly understands the importance of *profit* because their own compensation and rewards are tied to it. Similarly, the failure to provide rewards, recognition, or compensation that support a customer focus may cause employees to believe that customers are unimportant. Rewards (or the absence of them) drive behavior and motivate people to respond in certain ways.
5.1c(1)	Skill mapping is a process that many high-performing organizations practice to compare the skills it needs to achieve strategic objectives with the skills its workforce currently possesses. When a skill gap is identified, organizations are able to more effectively make decisions as to whether they need to recruit, hire, and/or train appropriate employees. The failure to identify characteristics and skills needed by potential employees increases the likelihood of not having appropriate staff in the right places when needed.
5.1c(2)	In a competitive labor market, slowness in recruiting and inefficiencies in hiring may introduce delays that allow competitors to hire the best talent before your organization can act. Inefficient recruitment and bureaucratic bungling in the hiring process also provide a glimpse of the true management system and can scare off the best prospective employees. In addition, the hiring process represents a terrific opportunity to attract and hire employees with diverse ideas and cultures, without which it will be difficult to capitalize on diverse ideas, cultures, and thinking. This in turn may limit the ability of the organization's workforce to be innovative and empowered [Item 5.1a(1)]. Productivity suffers, as does the organization's ability to meet the challenges of today's highly competitive environment.
5.1c(3)	In the face of worldwide shortages of highly skilled employees, an organization's failure to conduct effective succession planning for senior leaders (and for key positions throughout the organization) could threaten organizational stability in the long term and create immediate performance problems in the short term. When critical personnel shortages exist within an organization, it is frequently unable to carry out key objectives. If succession planning does not look ahead at least as far as it might take to acquire or train replacement personnel, the organization may lack the talent it needs to fulfill its promises to customers or other key stakeholders.

5.1 WORK SYSTEMS—SAMPLE EFFECTIVE PRACTICES

A. Organization and Management of Work

- Leaders and managers at all levels require employees to make improvements and innovations to work processes as a basic part of job responsibility.

- Fully using the talents of all employees is a basic organizational value.

- Managers use cross-functional work teams to break down barriers, improve effectiveness, and meet goals.

- Teams have access to data and are authorized to make decisions about their work (not just make recommendations).

- Employee opinion is sought (and obtained) regarding work design and work processes.

- Prompt and regular feedback is provided to teams and individuals regarding their performance. Feedback covers both results and processes.

- Although lower-performing organizations use teams for special improvement projects (while the *regular work* is performed using traditional approaches), higher-performing organizations use teams and self-directed employees as the way regular work is done.

- Self-directed or self-managed work teams are used throughout the organization. They have authority over matters such as budget, hiring, and team membership and roles.

- A systematic process is used to evaluate and improve the effectiveness and extent of employee involvement.

- Many indicators of employee-involvement effectiveness exist, such as the improvements in time or cost reduction produced by teams.

B. Employee Performance Management System

- The performance management system provides feedback to employees that supports their ability to contribute to a high-performing organization.

- Compensation, recognition, and rewards/incentives are provided for generating improvement ideas. In addition, a system exists to encourage and provide rapid reinforcement for submitting improvement ideas.

- Compensation, recognition, and rewards/incentives are provided for results, such as for reductions in cycle time and exceeding target schedules with error-free products or services at less-than-projected cost.

- Employees, as well as managers, participate in creating the compensation, recognition, and rewards/incentives practices and help monitor their implementation and systematic improvement.

- The organization evaluates its approaches to employee performance and compensation, recognition, and rewards to determine the extent to which employees are satisfied with them, the extent of employee participation, and the impact of the system on improved performance (reported in Item 7.4).

- Performance measures exist for employee involvement, self-direction, and initiative. Goals for these measures are expressed in measurable terms. These measurable goals form at least a good part of the basis for performance recognition.

- Recognition, reward/incentives, and compensation are influenced by customer satisfaction ratings as well as other performance measures such as implementing process improvements.

C. Hiring and Career Progression

- Employee skill mapping is in place to define current skills of employees and compare to an analysis of skills that are needed now and in the future. The resulting skill gap or surplus drives decisions to retrain, relocate, or recruit.

- The need for diverse ideas and cultures among employees is specifically considered during the skill-mapping and recruitment process to ensure employees are able to provide the perspective needed to drive innovation and creativity.

- A formal system is in place to develop future leaders. This includes providing training and practice in high-performance leadership tech-

niques. Leaders receive specific training and practice using Baldrige Criteria and performance-improvement systems.

- Demonstrated proficiency in the use of the Baldrige Criteria is a prerequisite to promotion to a leadership position.

- Future leaders serve as examiners in the Baldrige process, state quality award process, or internal award process.

5.2 EMPLOYEE LEARNING AND MOTIVATION: How do you contribute to employee learning and motivate employees? (25 Pts.) PROCESS

Describe how your organization's employee education, training, and career development support the achievement of your overall objectives and contribute to high performance. Describe how your organization's education, training, and career development build employee knowledge, skills, and capabilities.

Within your response, include answers to the following questions:

a. Employee Education, Training, and Development

(1) How do employee education and training contribute to the achievement of your action plans? How do your employee education, training, and development address your key needs associated with organizational performance measurement, performance improvement, and technological change? How does your education and training approach balance short- and longer-term organizational objectives with employee needs for development, ongoing learning, and career progression?

(2) How do employee education, training, and development address your key organizational needs associated with new employee orientation, diversity, ethical business practices, and management and leadership development? How do employee education, training, and development address your key organizational needs associated with employees, workplace, and environmental safety?

(3) How do you seek and use input from employees and their supervisors and managers on education, training, and development needs? How do you incorporate your organizational learning and knowledge assets into your education and training?

(4) How do you deliver education and training? How do you seek and use input from employees and their supervisors and managers in determining your delivery approaches? How do you use both formal and informal delivery approaches, including mentoring and other approaches, as appropriate?

(5) How do you reinforce the use of new knowledge and skills on the job and retain this knowledge for long-term organizational use? How do you systematically transfer knowledge from departing or retiring employees?

(6) How do you evaluate the effectiveness of education and training, taking into account individual and organizational performance?

b. Motivation and Career Development

How do you motivate employees to develop and utilize their full potential? How does your organization use formal and informal mechanisms to help employees attain job- and career-related development and learning objectives? How do managers and supervisors help employees attain job- and career-related development and learning objectives?

Notes:

N1 Many organizations may have unique considerations relative to employee education, training, development, motivation, and career progression. If this is the case for your organization, your response to Item 5.2 should include how you address these considerations. *Nonprofit organizations may have unique considerations relative to the education, training, development, and motivation of volunteers. Nonprofit organizations may need to be sensitive to stakeholder perceptions about ho nonprofit dollars are spent, resulting in limitations on expenses for volunteer training-related activities.*

N2 Education and training delivery (5.2a[4]) might occur inside or outside your organization and involve on-the-job, classroom, computer-based, distance learning, or other types of delivery (formal or informal).

This Item [5.2] looks at the organization's system for workforce education, training, and on-the-job reinforcement of knowledge and skills, as well as systems for motivation and employee career development with the aim of meeting ongoing needs of employees and a high-performance workplace.

To help the organization achieve its high-performance objectives, education and training must be effectively designed, delivered, reinforced on the job, evaluated, and improved. To optimize organization effectiveness, the education and training system should place special emphasis on meeting individual career progression and organizational business needs.

Education and training needs might vary greatly depending on the nature of the organization's work, employee responsibility, and stage of organizational and personal development. These needs might include knowledge-sharing skills, communications, teamwork, problem solving, interpreting and using data, meeting customer requirements, process analysis and simplification, waste and cycle-time reduction, and priority setting based on strategic alignment or cost/benefit analysis. Education needs might include advanced skills in new technologies as well as basic skills, such as reading, writing, language, arithmetic and, increasingly, computer skills.

Organizations should consider job and organizational performance in education and training design and evaluation. Education and training should tie to action plans, and balance short- and longer-term individual and organizational objectives. Employees and their supervisors should help determine training needs and contribute to the design and evaluation of education and training, because these individuals frequently are best able to identify critical needs and evaluate success.

Education and training could be delivered inside or outside the organization and could involve on-the-job, classroom, computer-based, distance learning (including Web-based instruction), or any combination of these. In addition, apprenticeship, internship, and mentoring have proven effective techniques to deliver training and reinforce skills.

All education and training should be evaluated to determine their effectiveness and find ways to improve them. Leaders should identify specific measures of effectiveness prior to conducting an evaluation of training. Such measures might address impact on individual, unit, and organizational performance; impact on customer-related performance; and cost/benefit analysis of the training. Training evaluation should at least cover the extent of knowledge and skills transfer (whether the employees learned anything) and the extent to which they use these new skills and knowledge on the job.

If an objective of the organization is to enhance customer satisfaction and loyalty, it may be critical to identify job requirements for customer-contact employees and then provide them with appropriate training. Such training is increasingly important and common among high-performing organizations that seek to differentiate themselves from competitors. It frequently includes: acquiring critical knowledge and skills with respect to products, services, and customers; learning how to listen to customers; practicing recovery from problems or failures; and learning how to manage customer expectations effectively.

Organizations should ensure that training and education contribute to high performance. This may require organizations to provide training in the use of performance excellence tools. This training may be similar to the *quality* training organizations provided in the past. Training may focus on the use of performance measures, skill standards, quality-control methods, benchmarking, problem-solving processes, and performance improvement techniques such as Six Sigma, Lean manufacturing, and the use of Balanced Scorecards.

This training should also address high-priority needs such as technological change, ethical business practices, management and leadership development, orientation of new employees, safety, diversity, and performance measurement and improvement. Succession planning and leadership development [examined in Items 1.1a(3) and 5.1c(3)] typically require organizations to provide specialized training and development to key individuals identified as possible successors.

Unless knowledge and skills acquired in training are reinforced on the job, they are quickly and easily forgotten—even after a few days. Accordingly, leaders, managers, and supervisors throughout the organization must ensure that employees actually use the skills acquired through recent training. In fact, one of the measures of leadership effectiveness [required by Item 1.2a(2)] may consider the extent to which leaders reinforce these skills among their employees.

High-performing organizations provide mechanisms for sharing the knowledge of employees and the organization to ensure that high-performance work is maintained through personnel and organizational transitions. Systematic processes should be designed and implemented to share information critical to the organization's operations. This is particularly important for knowledge that is personally retained by employees.

To help employees realize their full potential, many organizations prepare individual development plans with every employee to address career and learning objectives. To achieve optimum employee productivity, the organization must understand and address the factors promoting and inhibiting motivation. A better understanding of these factors could be developed through exit interviews with departing employees, as well as through feedback from employee-satisfaction surveys.

All processes associated with education, training, and developing the full potential of employees should be systematically evaluated and ongoing refinements should be made.

5.2 Employee Learning and Motivation

How the organization's education, training, and career development support the achievement of overall objectives, contribute to high performance, and build employee knowledge, skills, and capabilities

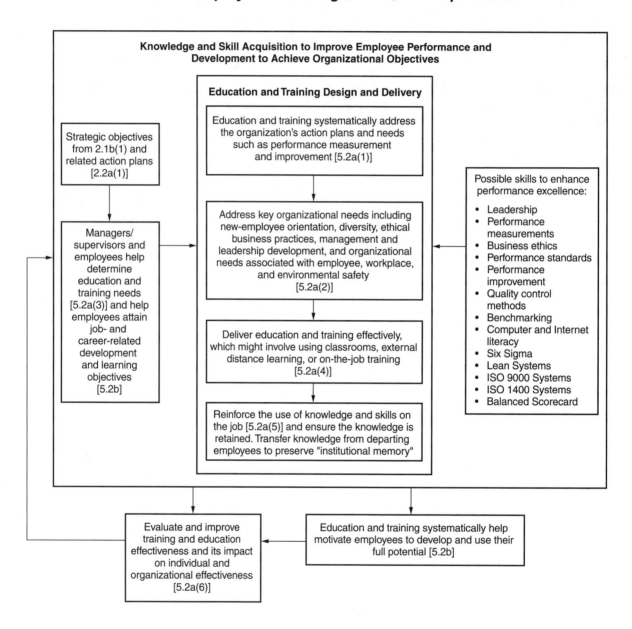

5.2 Employee Learning and Motivation Item Linkages

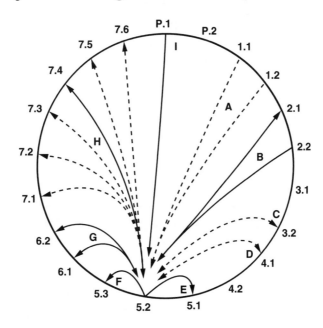

	NATURE OF RELATIONSHIP
A	Leaders [1.1a(3)] are responsible for supporting appropriate skill development of all employees, including future leaders, through training and development systems and reinforcing learning on the job [5.2a(5)]. In addition, specific training may be required to ensure employees understand governance, ethical, and regulatory requirements [1.2a and b].
B	Human resource plans [2.2a(4)] (which were developed to support strategic objectives [2.1b(1)] are used to help align training [5.2a(1)] to ensure employees and managers possess appropriate knowledge, skills, and ability.
C	Training [5.2] can enhance capabilities of customer-contact employees and strengthen customer relationship building [3.2a(2 and 3)].
D	Key measures and benchmarking data [4.1a(2)] are used to improve training [5.2a]. Information regarding training effectiveness [5.2a] is used to support planning and operational decision making [4.1a].
E	Effective training [5.2a] enables managers at all levels to improve their ability to design, organize, and manage better work processes that promote empowerment, innovation [5.1a(1)], creativity, and sharing [5.1a(3)]; make performance feedback and recognition and reward more relevant [5.1b]; enhance succession planning [5.1c(3)]; and recruit and retain the key employees [5.1c(2)].
F	Effective environmental safety training [5.2a(2)] is critical to maintaining and improving a safe, healthful work environment [5.3a] and employee motivation and well-being [5.3b].
G	Training [5.2a(2)] is essential to managing change and improving work effectiveness and innovation [6.1 and 6.2]. In addition, training requirements [5.2] are defined in part by process requirements [6.1 and 6.2].

Continued

	NATURE OF RELATIONSHIP	*Continued*
H	Results of improved training and development [5.2] are reported in 7.4. In addition, results pertaining to product and service quality [7.1], customer satisfaction [7.2], financial and market performance [7.3], organizational effectiveness [7.5], and leadership and social responsibility [7.6] reflect, in part, and are monitored to assess training effectiveness [5.2a(6)].	
I	Employee characteristics such as educational levels, workforce and job diversity, and other special requirements [P.1a(3)] help set the context for determining appropriate training needs by employee segment [5.2a(1)].	

	IF YOU DON'T DO WHAT THE CRITERIA REQUIRE . . .

Item Reference	Possible Adverse Consequences
5.2a(1)	Strategic objectives [Item 2.1b(1)] define what the organization must achieve to be successful in the future. Action plans [Item 2.2a(1)] define the things the organization must do to achieve the strategic objectives. If employees lack the necessary skills to carry out required actions, the strategic plan may fail. Education and training that do not contribute to the achievement of action plans may be a waste of resources. Managers have a responsibility to help employees attain their job- and career-related learning and development objectives [Item 5.2b]. If managers fail to take advantage of appropriate education and training to help employees with work-related development, learning, and career progression, they run the risk of weakening morale and motivation as well as contributing to employee obsolescence. This adversely impacts employee job security and employability and undermines the organization's ability to maintain a viable workforce to compete effectively.
5.2a(2)	Today's best-performing organizations have found that the following four areas are instrumental in optimizing performance and winning in a highly competitive environment: 1) new-employee orientation (acculturation); 2) diversity (capitalizing on diverse thinking, ideas, and cultures); 3) ethical business practices; and 4) management development. The failure to effectively address these factors as a part of employee education, training, and development may adversely affect the organization's ability to achieve its strategic objectives. The failure to provide effective employee orientation may make it difficult to get new employees to achieve organizational objectives. Poor employee orientation may contribute to higher accident rates, higher compensation claims, higher error and rework rates, and lost productivity. The failure to understand and take advantage of diverse ideas and cultures may limit the organization's creativity and innovation and contribute to falling behind competitors. The failure to follow ethical business practices gives rise to corruption, dishonesty, and ultimate business failure (Enron, for example). The failure to develop better managers and leaders may make it more difficult to develop strategic objectives, fully engage employees, and optimize individual or organizational performance.

Continued

	IF YOU DON'T DO WHAT THE CRITERIA REQUIRE . . . *Continued*
Item Reference	**Possible Adverse Consequences**
5.2a(3)	Employees and managers who are closest to the work usually understand best what skills are required (and missing) to do the work effectively. Failing to obtain and use input from these employees and their supervisors may result in the development of inappropriate or ineffective education and training opportunities. Providing ineffective or inappropriate training can waste resources in two ways: 1) the cost of paying employees' salary during training, the cost of facilities, and the cost of instruction; and 2) the cost to the organization of lost productivity while employees are participating in training.
5.2a(4)	The failure to deliver education and training using appropriate methods, consistent with the learning styles and needs of the students, usually suboptimizes the effectiveness of training. If students do not acquire relevant knowledge, skills, or abilities from education and training, the organization has wasted resources. If students do learn new skills and acquire new abilities those new skills and abilities are not used on the job, the organization has also wasted resources. If the students use the new skills and abilities on the job and it makes no difference to organizational performance or career progression, the organization has again wasted resources.
5.2a(5)	If it is worth training an employee to acquire new skills and abilities, it is important to reinforce the use of those new skills when the employee returns to the job and retain this new knowledge for the long term. The failure to reinforce the use of recently acquired knowledge and skills on the job may cause those new skills and abilities to become obsolete and quickly forgotten. Accordingly, the cost of training and the cost of lost productivity while the employee is receiving the training represent wasted resources. Most importantly, when the newly acquired skills are not utilized, the value of those skills and potential productivity gains are lost. Losses of this nature can materially impact an organization's rate of growth and its ability to achieve strategy objectives. A similar problem occurs when valuable organizational knowledge is lost because of employee retirement or attrition.
5.2a(6)	The failure to evaluate and improve the effectiveness of training makes it difficult to optimize individual or organizational performance. Ineffective or inefficient training and education wastes resources directly (cost of training) and indirectly (cost of lost opportunity and productivity while employee is receiving training).
5.2b	An organization that fails to develop and use the full potential of its employees wastes significant resources. This waste can be classified into two categories: 1) the failure to develop existing potential and take advantage of it; and 2) the failure to use skills and abilities that already exist. This waste is equivalent to running an operation at less than optimum capacity; for example, paying an employee for 40 hours of work but asking for only 20, or going out and hiring additional people when the potential for skills development already exists but goes unrecognized. To make matters worse, employees usually recognize when their skills are underused and their productivity suffers further erosion, or they seek job opportunities outside the organization where they can develop and advance more fully, or both.

5.2 EMPLOYEE LEARNING AND MOTIVATION—SAMPLE EFFECTIVE PRACTICES

A. Employee Education, Training, and Development

- Managers and employees conduct systematic needs analyses to ensure that skills required to perform work are routinely assessed, monitored, and maintained.

- Clear linkages exist between strategic objectives and education and training. Skills are developed based on work demands and employee needs.

- Training plans are developed based on employee input.

- Employee career and personal-development options, including development for leadership, diversity, new-employee orientation, and safety are enhanced through formal education and training. Some development uses on-the-job training, including rotational assignments or job exchange programs.

- The organization uses various methods to deliver training to ensure that it is suitable for employee knowledge and skill levels.

- To minimize travel costs, all training is examined to determine if electronic or distance delivery options are viable.

- Training is linked to work requirements, which managers reinforce on the job. Just-in-time training is preferred (rather than just-in-case training) to help ensure that the skills will be used immediately after training.

- Employee feedback on the appropriateness of the training is collected and used to improve course delivery and content.

- The organization systematically evaluates training effectiveness on the job. Performance data are collected on individuals and groups at all levels to assess the impact of training.

- Employee satisfaction with courses is tracked and used to improve training content, training delivery, instructional effectiveness, and the effectiveness of supervisory support for the use of training on the job.

- Training design and delivery are systematically refined and improved based on regular evaluations.

B. Motivation and Career Development

- Formal career plans are in place for each employee. Progress against these plans is evaluated and adjustments are made to ensure they remain relevant.

- Employees receive incentives such as bonuses or other rewards for developing additional career-enhancing skills.

- The organization documents or otherwise captures/stores key knowledge held by employees so that knowledge is not lost when the employee leaves the organization. Proactive sharing of personal knowledge helps preserve the collective knowledge (organizational memory).

5.3 EMPLOYEE WELL-BEING AND SATISFACTION: How do you contribute to employee well-being and grow employee satisfaction? (25 Pts.)   PROCESS

Describe how your organization maintains a work environment and an employee support climate that contribute to the well-being, satisfaction, and motivation of all employees.

Within your response, include answers to the following questions:

a. Work Environment

(1) How do you ensure and improve workplace health, safety, security, and ergonomics in a proactive manner? How do employees take part in these improvement efforts? What are your performance measures or improvement goals for each of these key workplace factors? What are the significant differences in these workplace factors and performance measures or targets if different employee groups and work units have different work environments?

(2) How do you ensure workplace preparedness for disasters or emergencies?

b. Employee Support and Satisfaction

(1) How do you determine the key factors that affect employee well-being, satisfaction, and motivation? How are these factors segmented for a diverse workforce and for different categories and types of employees?

(2) How do you support your employees via services, benefits, and policies? How are these tailored to the needs of a diverse workforce and different categories and types of employees?

(3) What formal and informal assessment methods and measures do you use to determine employee well-being, satisfaction, and motivation? How do these methods and measures differ across a diverse workforce and different categories and types of employees? How do you use other indicators, such as employee retention, absenteeism, grievances, safety, and productivity, to assess and improve employee well-being, satisfaction, and motivation?

(4) How do you relate assessment findings to key business results to identify priorities for improving the work environment and employee support climate?

Notes:

N1   Specific factors that might affect your employees' well-being, satisfaction, and motivation (5.3b[1]) include effective employee problem or grievance resolution; safety factors; employees' views of management; employee training, development, and career opportunities; employee preparation for changes in technology or the work organization; the work environment and other work conditions; management's empowerment of employees; information sharing by management; workload; cooperation and teamwork; recognition; services and benefits; communications; job security; compensation; and equal opportunity.

N2   Approaches for employee support (5.3b[2]) might include providing counseling, career development and employability services, recreational or cultural activities, non-work-related education, day care, job rotation or sharing, special leave for family responsibilities or community service, home safety training, flexible work hours and location, outplacement, and retirement benefits (including extended health care).

N3   Measures and indicators of well-being, satisfaction, and motivation (5.3b[3]) might include data on safety and absenteeism; the overall turnover rate; the turnover rate for customer contact employees; employees' charitable contributions; grievances, strikes, and other job actions; insurance costs; workers' compensation claims; and results of surveys. Survey indicators of satisfaction might include employee knowledge of job roles, employee knowledge of organizational direction, and employee perception of empowerment and information sharing. Your results relative to such measures and indicators should be reported in Item 7.4.

N4   Identifying priorities (5.3b[4]) might draw on your human resource results presented in Item 7.4 and might involve addressing employee problems based on their impact on your business results.

This Item [5.3] looks at the organization's work environment, the employee-support climate, and how employee satisfaction is determined, for the purpose of enhancing the well-being, satisfaction, and motivation of all employees, while recognizing their diverse needs. This Item also looks at the organization's capabilities for handling emergencies or disasters to protect employees and keep the workplace safe.

The first part of this Item [5.3a] looks at systems the organization has in place to provide a safe, secure, and healthful work environment for all employees, taking into account their differing work environments and associated requirements. All organizations, regardless of size, are required to meet minimum regulatory standards for workplace safety; however, high-performing organizations will have processes in place to ensure they not only meet these minimum standards but also go beyond simple compliance. This includes designing proactive processes, with safety and security factors identified by employees directly involved in the work. The organization should identify appropriate measures and targets for key workplace factors so that status and progress can be tracked. The organization should be able to show how it includes such factors in its planning and improvement activities. Important factors in this Area to Address include establishing appropriate measures and targets for employee safety, security, and health. Organizations should also recognize that employee groups might experience very different environments and need different services to ensure workplace safety.

Organizations should also have a workplace preparedness plan in place in case of emergencies or disasters. Part of the plan should focus on ensuring business continuity for the benefit of both employees and customers. Such plans should provide for rapid recovery and minimize disruptions to the work of employees and the products, services, and programs delivered to customers.

The second part of this Item [5.3b] looks at how the organization determines key factors that affect employee well-being, satisfaction, and motivation. The organization must provide appropriate services, benefits, and policies to enhance employee well-being, satisfaction, and motivation. The best organizations develop a holistic view of employees as key stakeholders. Most organizations, regardless of size, have many opportunities to contribute to employees' well-being, satisfaction, and motivation. These organizations place special emphasis on the variety of approaches used to satisfy a diverse workforce with differing needs and expectations in order to reduce attrition and increase motivation.

Examples of services, facilities, activities, and other opportunities are: personal and career counseling; career development and employability services; recreational or cultural activities; formal and informal recognition; non-work-related education; day care; special leave for family responsibilities and/or for community service; home safety training; flexible work hours and benefits packages; outplacement services; and retiree benefits, including extended healthcare and access to employee services. Also, these services might include career-enhancement activities such as skills assessments, helping employees develop learning objectives and plans, and conducting employability assessments.

As the workforce becomes more diverse (including employees who may work in other countries for multinational companies) it becomes more important to consider and support the needs of those employees with different services.

High-performing organizations also use both formal and informal assessment methods and measures to determine employee well-being, satisfaction, and motivation. These methods and measures are tailored to assess the differing needs of a diverse workforce. In addition, indicators other than employee opinion surveys (for example, employee turnover, grievances, complaints, and absenteeism) are used to support the assessment. Taken together, these methods and measures ensure that assessment findings are relevant and relate to key business results in order to identify key priorities for improvement.

Many factors might affect employee motivation, well-being, and satisfaction. Although satisfaction with pay and promotion potential is important, this factor does not fully explain all the variables that contribute to the overall climate for motivation and high performance. For this reason, high-performing organizations usually consider a variety of factors that might affect well-being, satisfaction, and motivation, such as effective employee problem and grievance resolution; safety; employee development and career opportunities; employee preparation for changes in technology or work organization; work environment and management support; workplace safety and security; workload; communication, cooperation, and teamwork; job security; appreciation of the differing needs of diverse employee groups; recognition; benefits; compensation; and organizational support for serving customers.

In addition to direct measurement of employee satisfaction and well-being through formal or informal surveys, some other indicators of satisfaction and well-being might include: absenteeism, turnover, grievances, strikes, accidents, lost-time injuries, and worker's compensation claims.

Information and data on the well-being, satisfaction, and motivation of employees are actually used in identifying improvement priorities. Priority setting might draw upon human resource results reported in Item 7.4 and might involve addressing employee problems based on the actual or potential impact on organizational performance. Factors inhibiting motivation need to be prioritized and addressed. The failure to address these factors is likely to result in even greater problems, which may not only impact human resource results (Item 7.4), but also adversely affect customer satisfaction (Item 7.2), product and service quality (Item 7.1), financial performance (Item 7.3), organizational effectiveness (7.5), and leadership and social responsibility (Item 7.6).

5.3 Employee Well-Being and Satisfaction

How the organization maintains a work environment and employee-support climate that promotes the well-being, satisfaction, and motivation of employees

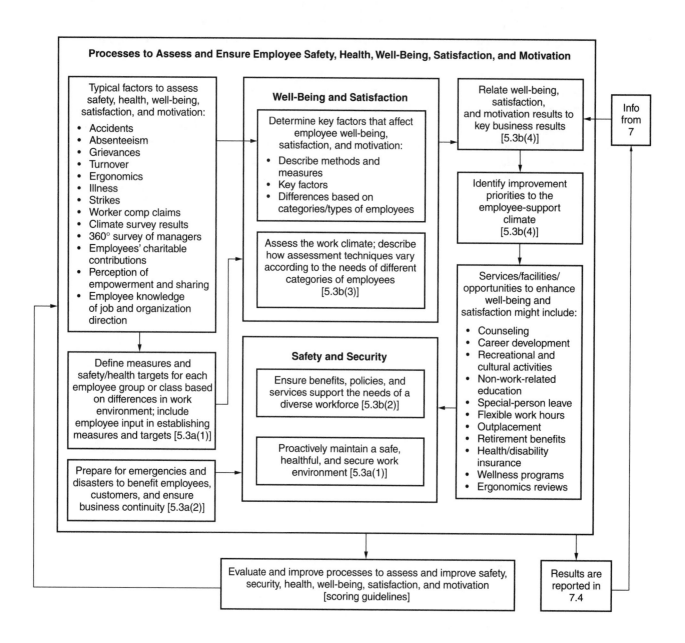

Processes to Assess and Ensure Employee Safety, Health, Well-Being, Satisfaction, and Motivation

Typical factors to assess safety, health, well-being, satisfaction, and motivation:

- Accidents
- Absenteeism
- Grievances
- Turnover
- Ergonomics
- Illness
- Strikes
- Worker comp claims
- Climate survey results
- 360° survey of managers
- Employees' charitable contributions
- Perception of empowerment and sharing
- Employee knowledge of job and organization direction

Define measures and safety/health targets for each employee group or class based on differences in work environment; include employee input in establishing measures and targets [5.3a(1)]

Prepare for emergencies and disasters to benefit employees, customers, and ensure business continuity [5.3a(2)]

Well-Being and Satisfaction

Determine key factors that affect employee well-being, satisfaction, and motivation:

- Describe methods and measures
- Key factors
- Differences based on categories/types of employees

Assess the work climate; describe how assessment techniques vary according to the needs of different categories of employees [5.3b(3)]

Safety and Security

Ensure benefits, policies, and services support the needs of a diverse workforce [5.3b(2)]

Proactively maintain a safe, healthful, and secure work environment [5.3a(1)]

Relate well-being, satisfaction, and motivation results to key business results [5.3b(4)]

Identify improvement priorities to the employee-support climate [5.3b(4)]

Services/facilities/opportunities to enhance well-being and satisfaction might include:

- Counseling
- Career development
- Recreational and cultural activities
- Non-work-related education
- Special-person leave
- Flexible work hours
- Outplacement
- Retirement benefits
- Health/disability insurance
- Wellness programs
- Ergonomics reviews

Info from 7

Evaluate and improve processes to assess and improve safety, security, health, well-being, satisfaction, and motivation [scoring guidelines]

Results are reported in 7.4

5.3 Employee Well-Being and Satisfaction Item Linkages

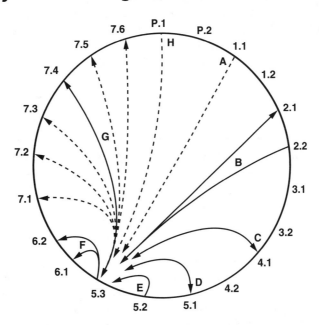

	NATURE OF RELATIONSHIP
A	Leaders [1.1a(3)] are responsible for creating an environment that fosters employee empowerment, innovation, and organizational agility, consistent with effective systems to enhance employee health, safety, security, satisfaction, well-being, and motivation [5.3a].
B	Human resource development plans [2.2a(4)] typically address or set the context for safety, security, motivation, satisfaction, and well-being systems [5.3]. Employee motivation and satisfaction, safety, security, and disaster-recovery processes [5.3] may be important to consider in the process of developing strategy [2.1a(2)].
C	Key benchmarking data [4.1a(2)] are used to design processes to enhance employee motivation and well-being [5.3b]. Information regarding employee well-being and motivation [5.3b(3)] is analyzed to gain a better understanding of problems and performance capabilities to support strategic planning [4.1b(1)].
D	High motivation [5.3] enhances employee empowerment, initiative (self-direction), and innovation [5.1a(1)], and vice versa.
E	Effective training [5.2] is critical to maintaining and improving a safe, secure, healthful work environment and providing an appropriate emergency or disaster response [5.3a(2)] and improved employee motivation, satisfaction, and well-being [5.3b].
F	A safe, healthful work environment [5.3a] contributes to higher performance and productivity, with fewer errors and rework [6.1].
G	Systems that enhance employee motivation, satisfaction, and well-being [5.3] can boost financial and market performance [7.3], product and service quality [7.1], customer satisfaction [7.2], organizational effectiveness and productivity [7.5], and leadership and social responsibility [7.6]. Specific results of employee well-being and satisfaction systems are reported in 7.4.

Continued

	NATURE OF RELATIONSHIP	*Continued*
H	Employee characteristics such as educational levels, workforce and job diversity, the existence of bargaining units, the use of contract employees, and other special requirements [P.1a(3)] may help set the context for tailoring benefits, services, and satisfaction assessment methods for employees according to various types and categories [5.3a and b(1, 2, and 3)].	

IF YOU DON'T DO WHAT THE CRITERIA REQUIRE . . .

Item Reference	Possible Adverse Consequences
5.3a	The failure to improve workplace health, safety, security, and ergonomics may increase employee accidents and illness, reduce employee effectiveness, and negatively impact morale and motivation. Poor working conditions distract employees, reduce productivity, and increase errors, rework, cycle time, and waste, to name a few. Failing to involve employees in the identification of potential health, safety, security, and ergonomics issues may cause the organization to overlook and fail to correct those problems. If significant variation exists in the work environment for different employee groups or work units, employees are likely to face different workplace health, safety, security, and ergonomic issues. For example, carpal tunnel syndrome may be a problem for those who do substantial keypunching but not for certain employees on the shop floor. Those employees may be more concerned about injury from lifting heavy objects. Accordingly, the failure to define performance measures and establish targets for each key environmental factor and each distinct employee group increases the likelihood the problems will go unnoticed and those employees will be distracted from their work, suboptimizing performance. In addition, the failure to plan and prepare for emergencies and disasters makes the organization vulnerable to serious disruptions of service, which may hurt both employees and customers, and damage the stability and continuity of the business.
5.3b(1)	Factors that affect employee well-being, satisfaction, and motivation can vary significantly from organization to organization or within an organization from site to site, or among different groups of employees in the same organization. The failure to determine the key factors affecting employee well-being, satisfaction, and motivation for each employee or segment may make it difficult to identify key problems and take appropriate corrective action. The inability to identify and correct these problems can reduce employee morale and motivation, which, in turn, hurts productivity and ultimately customer satisfaction.
5.3b(2)	Just as different employee groups may have different needs for safety, different groups of employees may need different support services and benefits to keep them from being distracted in their work. For example, in one company employees located in an extremely rural area lost an entire day of work traveling to a dentist or physician to deal with a toothache or a minor medical problem. Positioning a trailer with dental and health professionals near the plant entrance minimized the time employees had to be absent from work due to a medical problem. A sister plant in the same company, located near a major metropolitan area, had plenty of dentists and physicians nearby and determined that its employees would be better served by an in-house exercise and wellness program. When an organization fails employees would be better served by an in-house exercise and wellness program. When an organization fails to identify and tailor benefits and services to the needs of its diverse workforce, it may

Continued

	IF YOU DON'T DO WHAT THE CRITERIA REQUIRE . . . *Continued*
Item Reference	**Possible Adverse Consequences**
	increase distractions and reduce optimum employee participation and performance. Suboptimum employee performance hurts productivity.
5.3b(3)	Because the factors that affect employee well-being, satisfaction, and motivation can vary significantly among the diverse groups of employees, if an organization fails to differentiate assessment methods and measures it may not be able to determine accurately the existence of problems and take appropriate corrective action. The failure to identify and correct a problem that adversely affects employee well-being, satisfaction, and motivation can contribute to operational inefficiency, waste resources, and reduce product and service quality and customer satisfaction. Failing to consider data that relate to employee well-being and satisfaction such as absenteeism, grievances, and undesired employee attrition may also prevent a problem from being identified and corrected. Finally, the *one-size-fits-all* method of assessing employee well-being and satisfaction (such as the *annual* climate survey) may fail to take into account parts of the organization that may be undergoing change and facing more turmoil than other parts of the organization. For organizations that are relatively stable, an annual survey may be appropriate. However, for organizations (or parts of organizations) that face a more volatile, unstable environment, more frequent assessments may be required. The failure to ask the right questions, at the right time, and in the right manner may prevent the organization from learning about and correcting serious problems that may adversely affect performance and productivity.
5.3b(4)	When deciding what actions to take to improve the work environment (based on the results of appropriate surveys and related data), organizations may waste resources if they do not set priorities for improvement that are likely to optimize business results. In the example above [5.3b(2)], the plant manager could have installed a workout room and shower facilities rather than a health services trailer. However, analysis revealed that exercise facilities would have minimum impact on productivity, whereas the healthcare trailer would save hundreds of days each year in lost time due to employee absenteeism. Organizations risk wasting resources if they fail to understand the likely impact on business results of the improvement priorities they set in response to employee satisfaction assessment findings.

5.3 EMPLOYEE WELL-BEING AND SATISFACTION—SAMPLE EFFECTIVE PRACTICES

A. Work Environment

- Issues and concerns relating to employee health, safety, security, and workplace environment are used to design the work environment for all groups of employees. Plans exist and processes are in place to optimize working conditions and eliminate adverse conditions.

- Root causes for health, safety, and security problems are systematically identified and eliminated. Corrective actions are communicated widely to help prevent the problem in other parts of the organization.

- Targets are set and reviewed for all key health, safety, security, and ergonomic factors affecting the employees' work environment. Employees are directly involved in setting these targets.

- A documented and tested emergency-recovery plan is in place and all employees are trained and understand the processes they will follow.

- Disaster-recovery processes are in place and serious tests (drills) are conducted to simulate emergency response to minimize problems and risks to employees and customers in the event of a real crisis. These procedures were developed based on benchmarking other organizations that faced crises.

B. Employee Support and Satisfaction

- Special activities and services are available for employees. These are quite varied, depending on the needs of different employee categories. Examples include the following:
  - Flexible benefits plan including: healthcare, on-site day care, dental, portable retirement, education (both work and non-work-related), maternity, paternity, and family-illness leave
  - Group-purchasing-power program where the number of participating merchants is increasing steadily
  - Special facilities for employee meetings to discuss their concerns

- Senior leaders build a work climate that addresses the needs of a diverse workforce. Recruitment and training are tools to enhance the work climate.

- Key employee-satisfaction opinion indicators are gathered periodically based on the stability of the organization (organizations in the midst of rapid change conduct assessments more frequently). Supervisors, managers, and leaders take consistent and prompt action to improve conditions identified through these employee-satisfaction surveys.

- On-demand electronic surveys are available for quick response and tabulations any time managers need employee-satisfaction feedback. Whenever the survey is completed, managers always follow up promptly to make improvements identified by the survey that relate to key business results.

- Satisfaction data are derived from employee focus groups, employee-satisfaction survey results, turnover, absenteeism, and other data that reflect employee satisfaction.

- Managers use the results of these surveys to focus improvements in work systems and enhance employee satisfaction. Actions to improve satisfaction are clearly tied to assessments so employees understand the value of the assessment, and the improvement initiatives do not appear random or capricious.

- Employee-satisfaction indicators are correlated with drivers of business success to help identify where resources should be placed to provide maximum business benefit.

- Methods to improve how employee satisfaction is determined are systematically evaluated and improved. Techniques to actually improve employee satisfaction and well-being are themselves evaluated and refined consistently.

6 Process Management—85 Points

*The **Process Management** Category examines the key aspects of your organization's process management, including key product, service, and organizational processes for creating customer and organizational value and key support processes. This Category encompasses all key processes and work units.*

Process Management is the focal point within the Criteria for all key work processes. Built into the Category are the central requirements for efficient and effective process management: effective design, a prevention orientation, linkage to customers, suppliers, and partners, a focus on value creation for all stakeholders, supply chain integration, operational and financial performance, cycle time, evaluation, continuous improvement, and organizational learning.

Organizational agility, cost reduction, and cycle-time reduction are increasingly important in all aspects of process management and organizational design. Agility refers to an organization's ability to adapt quickly, flexibly, and effectively to changing requirements. Depending on the nature of the organization's strategy and markets, agility might mean rapid changeover from one product to another, rapid response to changing demands, or the ability to produce a wide range of customized services. Agility also increasingly involves outsourcing decisions, agreements with key suppliers, and novel partnering arrangements. It typically involves the elimination of unnecessary levels of review and approval prior to a decision; the increased empowerment of employees to make more decisions about their work; and eliminating general bureaucratic barriers to efficiency. Flexibility might demand special strategies such as implementing modular designs, sharing components, sharing manufacturing lines, and providing specialized training.

- Cost and cycle-time reduction often involve many of the same process management strategies as achieving agility, including Lean process improvement techniques. Thus, it is crucial to utilize key measures for these requirements in the overall process management.

Process Management contains two Items that evaluate the management of product and service processes (including key business processes) and support processes.

Value Creation Processes

These are core and key business processes required to produce and deliver the organization's products and services, deliver value to customers and key stakeholders, and improve market and financial position.

- Design, develop, and introduce products and services to meet customer requirements, operational-performance requirements, and market requirements

- Use customer feedback, supplier feedback, and in-process measures to control and improve the performance of these processes

- Manage and continuously improve these processes

Support Processes

These are processes that support value creation and business operations.

- Design, develop, and provide products and services to meet internal and external customer requirements in support of value creation processes

- Use customer feedback and in-process measures to control and improve the performance of these processes

- Ensure adequate financial resources are available to support operations

- Ensure continuity of operations in an emergency

6.1 VALUE CREATION PROCESSES: How do you identify and manage your key processes? (45 Pts.)

PROCESS

Describe how your organization identifies and manages its key value creation processes for delivering customer value and achieving organizational success and growth.

Within your response, include answers to the following questions:

a. Value Creation Processes

(1) How does your organization determine its key value creation processes? What are your organization's key product, service, and business processes for creating or adding value? How do these processes contribute to profitability, sustainability, and organizational success, as appropriate?

(2) How do you determine key value creation process requirements, incorporating input from customers, suppliers, partners, and collaborators, as appropriate? What are the key requirements for these processes?

(3) How do you design these processes to meet all the key requirements? How do you incorporate new technology, organizational knowledge, and the potential need for agility into the design of these processes? How do you incorporate cycle time, productivity, cost control, and other efficiency and effectiveness factors into the design of these processes? How do you implement these processes to ensure they meet design requirements?

(4) What are your key performance measures or indicators used for the control and improvement of your value creation processes? How does your day-to-day operation of these processes ensure meeting key process requirements? How are in-process measures used in managing these processes? How is customer, supplier, partner, and collaborator input used in managing these processes, as appropriate?

(5) How do you minimize overall costs associated with inspections, tests, and process or performance audits, as appropriate? How do you prevent defects, service errors, and rework, and minimize warranty costs, as appropriate?

(6) How do you improve your value creation processes to achieve better performance, to reduce variability, to improve products and services, and to keep the processes current with business needs and directions? How are improvements and lessons learned shared with other organizational units and processes to drive organizational learning and innovation?

Notes:

N1 Your key value creation processes are those most important to "running your business" and maintaining or achieving a sustainable competitive advantage. They are the processes that involve the majority of your organization's employees and produce customer, stakeholder, and stockholder value. They include the processes through which your organization adds the greatest value to its products and services. They also include the business processes most critical to adding value to the organization itself, resulting in success and growth.

N2 Key value creation processes differ greatly among organizations, depending on many factors. These factors include the nature of your products and services, how they are produced and delivered, technology requirements, customer and supplier relationships and involvement, outsourcing, the importance of research and development, the role of technology acquisition, information and knowledge management, supply chain management, mergers and acquisitions, global expansion, legislative mandates, and sales and marketing. Responses to Item 6.1 should be based on the most critical requirements and processes for your products, services, and business.

N3 To achieve better process performance and reduce variability, you might implement approaches such as a Lean Enterprise System, Six Sigma methodology, use of ISO 9000:2000 standards, or other process improvement tools.

Continued

> **Notes:**   *Continued*
>
> N4   To provide as complete and concise a response as possible for your key value creation processes, you might
>   want to use a tabular format identifying the key processes and the attributes of each as called for in questions
>   6.1a(1)–6.1a(6).
>
> N5   The results of improvements in product and service performance should be reported in Item 7.1. All other
>   process performance results should be reported in Item 7.5.

This Item [6.1] looks at two main areas responsible for value creation: (a) key design processes for products and services that meet or exceed customer requirements and (b) processes to deliver value for the organization, its customers, and stakeholders. Together, these processes can create a competitive advantage and improve market and operational performance. Organizations must define their key processes and specific requirements, and explain how performance relative to these requirements is determined and maintained. Typically, these requirements reflect the need for increasing agility—speed and flexibility—to adapt to change more quickly than competitors.

Design approaches could differ significantly depending upon the nature of products and services—whether the products/services are entirely new, variants, or involve major or minor process changes.

- Factors organizations might consider in design include: safety, long-term performance, environmental impact, *green* manufacturing, measurement capability, process capability, manufacturability, maintainability, variability in customer expectations requiring product/service options, supplier capability, and documentation. Detailed mapping of manufacturing or service processes and redesigning or reengineering those processes to achieve higher levels of efficiency and to meet changing customer requirements may be helpful but are not required.

- Factors organizations must consider in design include cycle time and efficiency of production and delivery processes. The best-performing organizations accurately and completely define key production/delivery processes, their key performance requirements, and key performance measures. These requirements and measures

provide the basis for maintaining and improving products, services, and production/delivery processes. These organizations also define how performance relative to these requirements is determined and maintained. Increasingly, these requirements usually include the need for agility—speed and flexibility—to adapt to change. New technology, including e-technology, should be incorporated into the design of products and services. The use of e-technology might include new ways of electronically sharing information with suppliers/partners, communicating with customers and giving them continuous (24/7) access, and transferring automated information for products requiring maintenance in the field.

Frequently, defective design processes require organizations to capture information from customer complaint data using the processes described in Item 3.2a. Immediate access to customer-complaint data allows the organization to make design or production complaint changes quickly to prevent problems from occurring or recurring.

The best-performing organizations consider requirements of suppliers and/or business partners at the design stage. This minimizes the chances that important design issues are not achievable because of supplier and/or partner limitations. Similarly, effective design systems take into account all stakeholders in the value chain.

To enhance design-process efficiency, all related design and production activities should be coordinated within the organization. Coordination of design, production, and delivery processes involves all work units and/or individuals who take part in production/delivery and whose performance materially affects overall process outcome. This might include key business functions or processes such as R&D, marketing, design, product/process engineering, and key suppliers. If many design projects are carried out in parallel, or if the organization's products require parts, equipment, and facilities that are used for other products, coordination of resources frequently provides a means to significantly reduce unit costs and time to market.

- Design processes should cover all key operational performance requirements and appropriate coordination and testing to ensure effective product/service launch without need for rework.

Top organizations minimize the need for inspections, tests, and audits to avoid rework and warranty costs, because they have implemented processes to prevent problems from occurring in the first place. Sometimes these processes involve error-proofing, which makes it impossible to do the wrong thing the wrong way (for example, electrical cords on today's appliances have one plug blade wider than the other to prevent the plug from being inserted incorrectly into a wall outlet).

The best way to minimize the need for tests, inspections, and audits is to consistently, without fail, produce desired outcomes. To help minimize unacceptable variation (errors), organizations use key measurements, observations, or interactions at the earliest points possible in processes. Consistently achieving expected performance frequently requires setting in-process performance levels or standards to guide decision making. When deviations occur, corrective action is taken to restore the performance of the process to its design specifications. Depending on the nature of the process, the corrective action could involve technical and/or human considerations. Proper corrective action involves changes at the source (root cause) of the deviation. Effective corrective action minimizes the likelihood of this type of deviation occurring again or anywhere else in the organization.

The best-performing organizations have a system in place to evaluate and improve production/delivery processes to achieve better process efficiency and better products and services. Better performance means not only better quality from the customers' perspective but also results in better financial and operational performance—such as productivity. A variety of process improvement approaches are commonly used. These approaches include:

- Sharing successful techniques across the organization to improve learning and innovation

- Process analysis and research (for example, process mapping, optimization experiments, and error-proofing)

- Technical and business research and development

- Benchmarking

- Using alternative technology

- Using information from customers of the processes—within and outside of the organization

New process improvement approaches might also involve the use of cost data to evaluate alternatives and set improvement priorities. Taken together, these approaches offer a wide range of possibilities, including complete redesign of key processes to achieve new levels of operational excellence.

In addition to designing and delivering core value creation products and services, this Item [6.1] also covers the design and delivery of key business processes. Business processes include the organization's key nonproduct and nonservice processes. A nonproduct/nonservice business process is one that is critical to the future success and business growth of the organization but does not involve actually producing products or services for end users (value-creation products and services). Key business processes frequently relate to an organization's strategic objectives and critical success factors. As such, it might be useful to consider them as *strategic business processes.* These are not core business activities. However, they may be considered as more critical than ordinary support activities (which are examined in Item 6.2). The diverse nature of these processes might result in significant variations in requirements and performance characteristics for different processes.

Key business processes might include the following:

- Processes for innovation, including empowering employees to generate and implement new ideas.

- R&D, involving dedicated units and distributing R&D responsibility throughout the organization.

- Technology acquisition (which may involve partnering), acquisitions, mergers, invention, or other techniques.

- Information and knowledge management, which goes beyond traditional information technology or information-management activities. Knowledge management often supports knowledge transfer and knowledge sharing among all organizational units at all levels and sites within an organization.

- Mergers and acquisitions, including global expansion initiatives.

- Project management, to ensure on-time and consistent development of new programs, products, and services.

- Sales and marketing, to strengthen and expand new markets, including e-commerce.

- Supply-chain management, supplier partnering, and outsourcing. For many organizations, supply-chain management is an increasingly important factor in achieving productivity and profitability goals and overall business success. Suppliers and partners are receiving increasing strategic attention as organizations reevaluate and outsource their core functions. Supply-chain management processes typically fulfill two purposes: to help improve the performance of suppliers and partners and, in turn, contribute to better internal operational performance. Supply chain management might include processes for supplier selection, with the aim of reducing the total number of suppliers and increasing preferred supplier and partnering agreements.

6.1 Value Creation Processes

How the organization identifies and manages its key processes for creating customer value and achieving business success and growth

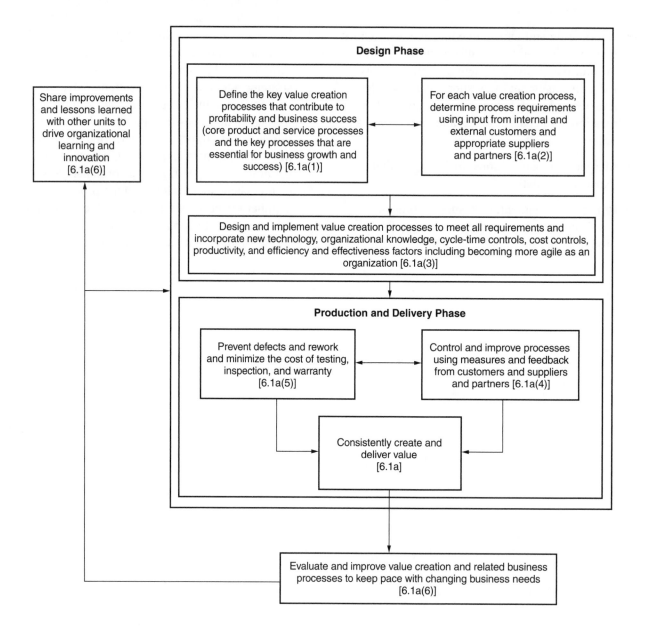

Design Phase

Define the key value creation processes that contribute to profitability and business success (core product and service processes and the key processes that are essential for business growth and success) [6.1a(1)]

For each value creation process, determine process requirements using input from internal and external customers and appropriate suppliers and partners [6.1a(2)]

Design and implement value creation processes to meet all requirements and incorporate new technology, organizational knowledge, cycle-time controls, cost controls, productivity, and efficiency and effectiveness factors including becoming more agile as an organization [6.1a(3)]

Production and Delivery Phase

Prevent defects and rework and minimize the cost of testing, inspection, and warranty [6.1a(5)]

Control and improve processes using measures and feedback from customers and suppliers and partners [6.1a(4)]

Consistently create and deliver value [6.1a]

Share improvements and lessons learned with other units to drive organizational learning and innovation [6.1a(6)]

Evaluate and improve value creation and related business processes to keep pace with changing business needs [6.1a(6)]

6.1 Value Creation Processes Item Linkages

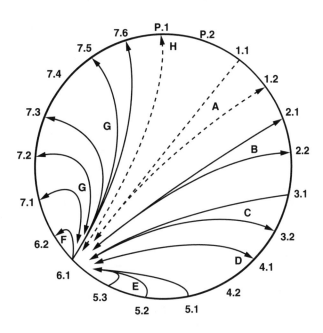

	NATURE OF RELATIONSHIP
A	Senior leaders [1.1] and the governance system [1.2a] have a responsibility for ensuring that value creation and business processes critical for growth and success are designed [6.1a(2)] consistent with the organization's vision and values, including those relating to social responsibility and good corporate citizenship [1.2a].
B	Organizational value creation process strengths and weaknesses [6.1] are considered as part of the planning process [2.1a(2)]. Action plans, deployed to the workforce [2.2a], are used to align actions to design [6.1a(1, 2, and 3)] and perform critical value creation and business services [6.1a(4)].
C	Customer requirements and preferences [3.1a(2)], customer questions [3.2a(2)], complaints/complaint resolution [3.2a(3)], and satisfaction/dissatisfaction [3.2b(1, 2, and 3)] are used to identify requirements for critical value creation and business processes [6.1a(2)] and determine areas needing improvement [6.1a(4)].
D	Key business processes such as R&D, knowledge management, and information technology [6.1] are used to help identify and prioritize benchmarking targets [4.1a(2)]. Benchmarking data [4.1a(2)] are used to improve key value creation and business processes [6.1].
E	High-performance, flexible work systems [5.1a(1)], effective recognition [5.1b], training [5.2], and a safe, healthful work climate [5.3] are essential to improving value-adding and related business processes [6.1].
F	Value creation processes [6.1], as customers of support processes [6.2], help define requirements and set priorities for support processes.

Continued

	NATURE OF RELATIONSHIP	*Continued*
G	Information about product and service quality [7.1] and customer satisfaction [7.2] outcomes is used to target improvement efforts in key value creation and business processes [6.1a(4) and (6)]. Improved value creation and business processes [6.1] can be reflected in better customer satisfaction [7.2] and better product and service quality [7.1], better financial results [7.3], operational efficiency [7.5a(1 and 2)], and social responsibility/regulatory compliance [7.6a(4)].	
H	Information in P.1a(1) derives from the value creation processes [6.1] and helps set the context for examiner review of these processes.	

	IF YOU DON'T DO WHAT THE CRITERIA REQUIRE . . .
Item Reference	**Possible Adverse Consequences**
6.1a(1)	The requirements of design processes can vary significantly within an organization depending on the nature of the products and services being delivered to customers. Design processes may also vary based on whether the products and services are new or only involve minor variations to current product and service offerings. In any event, a design process that fails to consider the key requirements for products and services, and other factors such as environmental impact, process capability, measurement capability, customer service expectations, supplier capability, and customer documentation requirements (such as found in ISO 9000), may make it difficult or impossible for the organization to achieve desired results (satisfy customers) in an efficient and cost-effective (profitable) manner. In an effort to ensure the design process is consistent and effective, organizations frequently develop checkpoints or *gates* that must be passed as part of bringing a new product or service into the marketplace. The gates serve a twofold purpose: (1) assuring the focus on customer requirements is maintained throughout the design process and responds to changing customer and market demands; and (2) assuring design maturity is on track. The first deals with fully responding to customer requirements by providing value in the eyes of the customer. The second addresses the ability of the organization to do this in an efficient and effective manner. Design processes that are not capable of incorporating changing customer or market requirements into products and services in a timely fashion are not sufficiently agile and may find it difficult to remain competitive. An organization that receives customer change requirements at a faster pace than they can implement the changes can be virtually paralyzed. Unwieldy design systems often lead to frustrated employees, excessive delay, and ultimately dissatisfied customers and lost business. When faced with rapidly changing technology, customer requirements, or market demands, inflexible or cumbersome design processes can render a once-good design obsolete before it ever gets to market.
6.1a(2)	An organization that fails to accurately identify the performance requirements of its value creation and related key business processes may find it difficult to design and deliver products and services to meet customer expectations. Design flaws produce undesired results and nonconforming products and services. This, in turn, requires even more rework or more people-intensive services, which can add significant delay and cost and prevent the organization from achieving its objectives. When these processes fail to meet requirements, resources are wasted and the objectives of the organization may be jeopardized.

Continued

	IF YOU DON'T DO WHAT THE CRITERIA REQUIRE . . . *Continued*
Item Reference	**Possible Adverse Consequences**

6.1a(3)	Organizations that fail to consider all key operational performance requirements when designing key business processes find that the system they designed is not optimum. Design flaws produce undesired results, as well as nonconforming products and services. These, in turn, require even more rework to correct. The failure to identify and address all of the requirements of customers may increase the likelihood of downstream problems with the design, production, and delivery of core products and services.
	
	    In today's highly competitive global economy, speed and agility are important factors that distinguish the best-performing organizations from the rest. The best-performing organizations provide their customers with more value at a faster pace (speed), and across a wider range of areas (agility) than their competition. The speed and agility offered by new technologies typically enhance value. Consequently, the leaders are able to distinguish their organizations in chosen markets, keeping their current customers and acquiring new ones. Increasingly, the failure to use the appropriate technologies limits the organization's ability to keep pace with aggressive competitors. These organizations may have the latest computers, but those computers may not be used effectively to accelerate delivery of the things that are important to customers. One *Fortune 500* company, learning that its customers placed a premium on accurate bills being delivered on time, acquired and implemented new technology to dramatically speed up its billing cycle. Unfortunately, the billing process itself was not capable of rendering an accurate invoice. Customers received their inaccurate invoices faster than ever. Using technology to accelerate a bad process only produces unsatisfactory results faster. The failure to incorporate the technology appropriately can have significant adverse effects on an organization's ability to bring value to its customers and to operate in an efficient and effective manner.
	
	    Eliminating unnecessary steps in any work process tends to reduce variation (increasing quality), reduce cycle time, and reduce cost. In addition, sharing knowledge and learning from the successes and mistakes of others helps prevent employees from repeating the same problems (which add rework, waste, and delay). When designing new products and services and related production and delivery systems, the failure to consider factors such as cost control, new technology, variability, and ways to enhance productivity and efficiency typically adds unnecessary cost, delay, and rework, making it more difficult to meet increasing demands of customers and the marketplace.

6.1a(4)	The best-performing organizations are able to consistently deliver products and services that meet key performance requirements. They do this by identifying key processes, monitoring them regularly, and improving then continuously. The failure to ensure consistent day-to-day operation of production and delivery processes increases the likelihood of defects, which contribute to rework, waste, delay, and excessive costs. Organizations can always tell if a process is producing desired results by waiting for those results and checking to see if the end product and service meet customer and operational requirements. Unfortunately, waiting for the end of the process to learn that it has not produced desired results is time-consuming and expensive, since most costs may have already been sunk. The earlier an organization can determine if a process is not likely to produced desired results, the earlier it can take corrective action to minimize rework, scrap, delay, and unnecessary cost. In addition, the failure to collect and analyze in-process data makes it more difficult for employees to know when to adjust a process to make it work better.

Continued

	IF YOU DON'T DO WHAT THE CRITERIA REQUIRE . . . *Continued*
Item Reference	**Possible Adverse Consequences**
	Inappropriate or unnecessary adjustments can actually increase variation and decrease productivity quality. Customers can usually determine quickly if the products and services they receive meet (or exceed) their requirements. They are in a good position to provide near-real-time feedback that will enable employees to make adjustments to meet requirements. The failure to gather and use this information makes it more difficult for organizations to make timely changes to reduce rework costs and increase customer satisfaction.
6.1a(5)	High-performing organizations do not rely on excessive inspection and testing to determine if process requirements are likely to be met. Conceptually, the only time to inspect is when the outcome is not known. Instead, these organizations design process controls that let them know how well the process is performing during each of its critical steps. They develop processes that prevent problems using tools and techniques such as error-proofing. The best that testing or inspection can hope to accomplish is to uncover and correct a problem before the customer is disrupted. Although this is better than causing problems for customers, it is still more costly to fix the problem than to prevent it from happening in the first place.
6.1a(6)	Organizations that fail to systematically evaluate and improve production and delivery systems and processes often seem to lag behind the competition. Consider two comparable organizations, each using similar processes to develop and deliver similar products and services. Let's also assume that the organizations are equally competitive today. However, one organization has embedded into its work processes an ongoing evaluation and improvement of its design, production, and delivery systems; the other has not. As time passes the first organization begins to see the impact of improved work processes. It is able to produce goods and services faster, better, and cheaper than its competitor. It has been able to pass a portion of its cost savings on to its customers (lowering prices), keeping the rest as increased profit. As a result of better, more timely, and less-expensive products, it is acquiring greater market share—at the expense of its competitor—and making its stockholders exceedingly happy as its share price increases. In addition, the first organization has been able to accelerate performance by sharing improvements with other organizational units so they can get better as well. The organization that does not systematically improve continues to fall further and further behind in a highly competitive environment (or as the popular adage acclaims: today, if you're standing still, you're falling behind). The failure to share effective practices with other organizational support units may cause them to waste time and other resources in redundant work—work that adds cost but not value.

6.1 VALUE CREATION PROCESSES— SAMPLE EFFECTIVE PRACTICES

A. Value Creation Processes (Which Includes Key Business Processes)

- A systematic, iterative process (such as quality function deployment) is used to maintain a focus on the voice of the customer and convert customer requirements into product or service design, production, and delivery.

- Product-design requirements are systematically translated into process specifications, with measurement plans to monitor process consistency.

- The work of various functions is coordinated to bring the product or service through the design-to-delivery phases. Functional barriers between units have been eliminated organization-wide.

- Concurrent engineering is used to operate several processes (for example, product and service planning, R&D, manufacturing, marketing, supplier certification) in parallel as much as possible, rather than operating in sequence. All activities are closely coordinated through effective communication and teamwork.

- Internal process capacity and supplier capability, using measures such as C_{pk}, are reviewed and considered before production and delivery-process designs or plans are finalized.

- Market, design, production, service, and delivery reviews occur at defined intervals or as needed.

- Steps are taken (such as design testing or prototyping) to ensure that the production and delivery process will work as designed, and will meet customer requirements.

- Design processes are evaluated and improvements are made so that future designs are developed faster (shorter cycle time), at lower cost, and with higher quality, relative to key product or service characteristics that predict customer satisfaction.

- Performance requirements and customer requirements are set using facts and data and are monitored using statistical or other process-control techniques.

- Value creation delivery processes are measured and tracked. Measures (quantitative and qualitative) should reflect or assess the extent to which customer requirements are met, as well as production consistency.

- For processes that produce defects (out-of-control processes), root causes are quickly and systematically identified and corrective action is taken to prevent their recurrence.

- Corrections are monitored and verified. Improvements are shared throughout the organization.

- Processes are systematically reviewed to improve productivity, reduce cycle time and waste, and increase quality.

- Tools—such as flowcharting, work redesign, and reengineering—are used throughout the organization to improve work processes.

- Benchmarking, competitive comparison data, or information from customers of the process (in or out of the organization) are used to gain insight to improve processes.

- Information about customer requirements, complaints, concerns, and reactions to products and services are captured *near-real time* and used directly by workers to improve the value creation and delivery processes.

- Key business processes, which are critical to the success of the organization and support core production and delivery activities, are formally identified. For each of these key business processes, a formal process exists to understand customer requirements, translate those requirements into efficient processes, measure their effectiveness, and systematically improve.

- Improvements in key business processes are made with the same rigor and concern for the internal and external customer as improvements in value creation processes.

- All key business processes are subject to continuous review and improvements in performance and customer satisfaction.

- Key business processes are systematically reviewed to improve productivity, reduce cycle time and waste, and increase quality. Improvements in these processes are shared throughout the organization.

6.2 SUPPORT PROCESSES AND OPERATIONAL PLANNING: How do you identify and manage your support processes and accomplish operational planning? (40 Pts.) PROCESS

Describe how your organization manages its key processes that support your value creation processes. Describe your processes for financial management and continuity of operations in an emergency.

Within your response, include answers to the following questions:

a. Support Processes

(1) How does your organization determine its key support processes? What are your key processes for supporting your value creation processes?

(2) How do you determine key support process requirements, incorporating input from internal and external customers, suppliers, partners, and collaborators, as appropriate? What are the key requirements for these processes?

(3) How do you design these processes to meet all the key requirements? How do you incorporate new technology, organizational knowledge, and the potential need for agility into the design of these processes? How do you incorporate cycle time, productivity, cost control, and other efficiency and effectiveness factors into the design of these processes? How do you implement these processes to ensure they meet design requirements?

(4) What are your key performance measures or indicators used for the control and improvement of your support processes? How does your day-to-day operation of key support processes ensure meeting key performance requirements? How are in-process measures used in managing these processes? How is customer, supplier, partner, and collaborator input used in managing these processes, as appropriate?

(5) How do you minimize overall costs associated with inspections, tests, and process or performance audits, as appropriate? How do you prevent defects, service errors, and rework?

(6) How do you improve your support processes to achieve better performance, to reduce variability, and to keep the processes current with business needs and directions? How are improvements and lessons learned shared with other organizational units and processes to drive organizational learning and innovation?

B. Operational Planning

(1) How does your organization ensure adequate financial resources are available to support your operations? How do you determine the resources needed to meet current financial obligations? How do you ensure adequate resources are available to support major new business investments, as appropriate? How do you assess the financial risks associated with your current operations and major new business investments?

(2) How do you ensure continuity of operations in the event of an emergency?

Notes:

N1   Your key support processes (6.2a) are those that are considered most important for support of your organization's value creation processes, employees, and daily operations. These might include facilities management, legal, human resource, project management, and administration processes.

N2   An emergency (6.2b[2]) might be weather-related, utility-related, or due to a local or national emergency.

N3   Your financial management results should be reported in Item 7.3. Other results related to your key support processes and operational planning should be reported in Item 7.5.

This Item [6.2] looks at the organization's key support processes and operational planning with respect to financial management and planning for continuity of operations, in order to improve overall operational performance. The organization must ensure its key support processes are designed to meet all internal operational and customer requirements.

The requirements of this Item are similar to the requirements in Item 6.1.

Support processes are those that support daily operations and product and/or service delivery but are not usually designed in detail with the products and services. The support process requirements usually do not depend significantly upon product and service characteristics. Instead, support process design requirements usually depend mainly upon internal customer requirements, and they must be coordinated and integrated to ensure efficient and effective linkage and performance.

Support processes might include finance and accounting, software or information-technology services, public relations, transportation services, food services, human resource services, legal services, plant and facilities management, and secretarial and other administrative services.

As with value creation processes described in Item 6.1, the organization must ensure that the day-to-day operation of its key support processes consistently meets the key performance requirements. To do this, in-process measures are defined to permit rapid identification and correction of potential problems. Just as with other work processes, key support processes should incorporate mechanisms to obtain and use customer feedback to help identify problems and take prompt, corrective action. The organization should also minimize costs associated with inspection, tests, and audits through use of prevention-based processes, as in Item 6.1.

Different types of analyses can be used to ensure adequate financial resources are available to support current operations and new business investments, and to assess associated financial risks. For current operations, these analyses might examine cash flows, net income statements, and current liabilities versus current assets. Analyses associated with business investments may look at discounted cash flows, return on investment (ROI), or return on invested capital (ROIC). Different organizations may utilize different specific types of analyses, but whatever analyses are selected should help the organization assess the financial viability of current operations and the potential viability of and risks associated with new business initiatives.

Finally, organizations should systematically evaluate and improve key support processes to achieve better performance and to keep them current with changing business needs and directions. Top organizations evaluate and improve the performance of key support processes and share information between organizational units to drive learning and innovation. A variety of approaches to evaluating and improving support processes are frequently used:

– Process analysis and research

– Benchmarking

– Use of alternative technology

– Use of information from customers of the processes

– Sharing successful techniques across the organization to improve learning and innovation

As with value creation processes, a systematic, fact-based approach to improving support processes presents a wide range of possibilities, ranging from minor process modification to complete redesign of key processes or steps within the processes.

Ensuring continuity of operations in an emergency requires consideration of all facets of an organization that are needed to provide required products or services to customers, as required, every time. Operational planning should address both value creation and key support processes. The specific level of service required is usually guided by the organization's type of business and customers' needs and requirements. For example, a public utility will likely have a higher need for services than businesses that do not provide an essential function. Continuity of operations efforts should also be coordinated with efforts to ensure data and information availability (Item 4.2) and workplace preparedness (Item 5.3a).

6.2 Support Processes and Operational Planning

How the organization identifies and manages its key processes that support value creation processes, ensures availability of financial resources, and provides for continuity of operations in emergencies

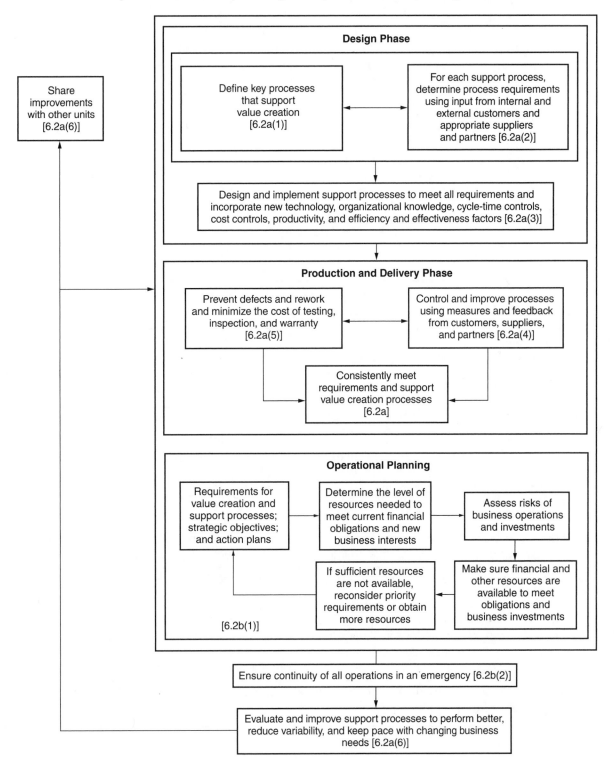

6.2 Support Processes and Operational Planning Item Linkages

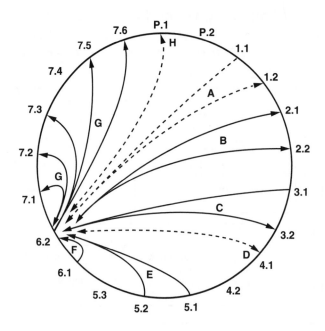

	NATURE OF RELATIONSHIP
A	Senior leaders [1.1] and the governance system [1.2a] have a responsibility for ensuring that support processes are designed [6.2a(2)] consistent with the organization's vision and values, including those relating to social responsibility and good corporate citizenship [1.2].
B	Organizational support process strengths and weaknesses [6.2] are considered as part of the planning process [2.1a(2)]. Action plans, deployed to the workforce [2.2a], are used to align actions to help ensure that support services [6.2] meet the requirements needed to carry out the action plans.
C	Customer complaints [3.2a(3)], and satisfaction/dissatisfaction [3.2b(1 and 2)] may be used to identify requirements for support processes [6.2a(2)] or provide feedback to help manage those processes [6.2a(4)] and determine areas needing improvement [6.1a(4)].
D	Critical support processes [6.2a] may be used to help identify and prioritize benchmarking targets [4.1a(2)]. Benchmarking data [4.1a(2)] are used to improve support work processes [6.2].
E	High-performance work systems [5.1a(1)] and effective recognition [5.1b], training [5.2a], and a safe, healthful work climate [5.3] are essential to improving support work processes [6.2].
F	Value creation processes [6.1], as customers of support processes [6.2], help define requirements and set priorities for support processes.
G	Information about product and service quality [7.1] and customer satisfaction [7.2] can be used to target improvement efforts in support processes [6.2a(4) and (6)]. Improved support processes [6.2] can be reflected in better customer satisfaction [7.2], product and service quality [7.1], financial results [7.3], operational efficiency [7.5], and social responsibility/regulatory compliance [7.6a(4)].
H	Information in P.1a(1) derives in part from the support processes [6.2] and helps set the context for examiner review of these processes.

IF YOU DON'T DO WHAT THE CRITERIA REQUIRE . . .	
Item Reference	**Possible Adverse Consequences**
6.2a(1)	The requirements of support processes can vary significantly within an organization depending on the nature of the core products and services that these business processes must support. If a work process has not been identified as a value creation process or key business process, it is a support process, reviewed under the requirements of Item 6.2.
6.2a(2)	An organization that fails to accurately identify the performance and operational requirements of its support processes may find it difficult to design those processes to meet internal customer expectations. When support processes fail to meet requirements, resources are wasted and the achievement of objectives may be jeopardized.
6.2a(3)	Organizations that fail to consider all key operational performance requirements when designing support processes frequently find that the system they design does not meet internal customer requirements. Design flaws produce undesired results and nonconforming support products and services. This, in turn, usually requires even more rework and disrupts core work processes.
6.2a(4)	The failure to consistently meet the requirements of support process customers may increase the likelihood of downstream problems with the design, production, and delivery of core (value creation) products and services. Without key measures or indicators of process performance, it is difficult for employees to determine if a process is working as it should. Without in-process measures, employees must generally wait until they get the results at the end of the line to determine if the support processes worked as intended. The failure to collect and analyze in-process data makes it more difficult for employees to know when to adjust a process to make it work better. Inappropriate or unnecessary adjustments can actually increase variation and decrease product quality. Internal customers can usually determine quickly if the products and services they receive meet requirements. The failure to gather and make timely use of feedback from internal customers makes it more difficult for organizations to reduce rework costs and increase customer satisfaction.
6.2a(5)	High-performing organizations do not rely on excessive inspection and testing to determine if support process requirements are likely to be met. Instead, these organizations develop processes that prevent problems using tools and techniques such as error-proofing. The best that testing or inspection can hope to accomplish is to uncover and correct a problem before the internal customer is disrupted. However, it is still more costly to fix the problem than to prevent it from happening in the first place.
6.2a(6)	Support processes that do not improve may cause the support function to become so ineffective that it becomes a good target for outsourcing. These support process units may not be able to effectively provide critical support to core product and service delivery units within the parent organization and may contribute to the erosion of overall capability in the parent organization. The failure to share effective practices with other organization support units may cause them to waste time and other resources in redundant work—work that adds cost but not value.

Continued

	IF YOU DON'T DO WHAT THE CRITERIA REQUIRE . . . *Continued*
Item Reference	**Possible Adverse Consequences**
6.2b(1)	The failure to ensure adequate financial resources are available to support all operations makes it difficult to meet goals and objectives. Unless processes are changed incrementally or radically through innovation, the organization will not be successful. By changing processes to make them more efficient and effective, the organization may require fewer resources. This may bring the organization back into equilibrium—it possesses resources that are now sufficient to meet obligations. The failure to assess financial risks accurately may cause leaders to overestimate available resources and overcommit operationally. This, too, may lead to operational failure.
6.2b(2)	Emergencies and disasters are usually difficult to predict. The stress and confusion created by a disaster or emergency can cause a normally efficient operation to become dysfunctional and fail. It is difficult to change processes *during* a disaster, which makes recovery nearly impossible, until the emergency passes. Although the timing of disasters is difficult to predict, the possibility of one occurring is great enough to cause the best performing organizations to prepare, in advance, to minimize the adverse impact. Failure to prepare (in advance) increases the possibility of catastrophic failure which many organizations may not survive.

6.2 SUPPORT PROCESSES AND OPERATIONAL PLANNING— SAMPLE EFFECTIVE PRACTICES

A. Support Processes

- A formal process exists to understand internal customer requirements for all support processes, translate those requirements into efficient service delivery, and measure their effectiveness.

- Specific improvements in support services are made with the same rigor and concern for the internal and external customer as improvements in value creation processes.

- All key support services are subject to continuous review and improvements in performance and customer satisfaction.

- Systems are in place to ensure process performance is maintained and customer requirements are met. In-process measures are defined and monitored to ensure early alert of problem.

- Root causes of problems are systematically identified and corrected for processes that produce defects.

- Corrections are monitored and verified. Processes used and results obtained should be systematic and integrated throughout the organization.

- Support processes are systematically reviewed to improve productivity, reduce cycle time and waste, and increase quality. Improvement ideas are routinely implemented and shared throughout the organization.

- Work-process simplification and performance improvement tools are applied to support processes with measurable sustained results.

- Measurable goals and related actions are used to drive higher levels of support process performance.

- Benchmarking, competitive comparison data, or information from customers of the process (in or out of the organization) are used to gain insight to improve processes.

B. Operational Planning

- A formal process exists to conduct emergency and disaster-scenario analysis and planning.

- Disaster and emergency plans are recorded and coordinated with relevant public and private organizations such as the Red Cross, local law enforcement, National Guard, Coast Guard, hospitals, utility companies, schools, and federal agencies.

- Partnering agreements are in place to run many operations remotely, such as redundant information systems located geographically apart to minimize/localize the adverse impact of a disaster.

- Early in every design stage for every value creation, business, and support service, a cost analysis is completed with low, medium, and high estimate. Based on each scenario, financial resources are identified. If surplus resources are not available, plans have been developed for changing the scope or reallocating resources from other activities. A contingency plan for every plausible worst-case scenario has been developed and is easily set in motion.

- As a part of due diligence for every new business investment, including acquisitions, a Baldrige analysis is completed to determine the level of risk/threat. Key opportunities for improvement are identified and included in the contingency plan.

7 Results—450 Points

*The **Results** Category examines your organization's performance and improvement in all key areas—product and service outcomes, customer satisfaction, financial and marketplace performance, human resource outcomes, operational performance, and leadership and social responsibility. Performance levels are examined relative to those of competitors and other organizations providing similar products and services.*

The Results Category provides a results focus that encompasses both the organization's and its customers' evaluations of the organization's products and services, overall financial and market performance, the results of all key processes and process improvement activities, fiscal accountability, leadership system, and ethical behavior as a part of practicing good citizenship.

Through this focus, the Criteria's purposes—superior value of offerings as viewed by customers and by the marketplace, superior organizational performance reflected in operational, legal, ethical, and financial indicators, and organizational and personal learning—are established and maintained. Category 7 can provide *real-time* information (measures of progress) for evaluation and improvement of processes, products, and services, aligned with overall organizational strategy.

Taken together, the Results Category presents a balanced scorecard of organizational performance. Historically, businesses have been far too preoccupied with financial performance. Many performance reviews focused almost exclusively on achieving (or failing to achieve) expected levels of financial performance. As such, these results were considered *unbalanced.*

- Financial results are considered *lagging* indicators of business success. Financial results are the net of all the good processes, bad processes, satisfied customers, dissatisfied customers, motivated employees, disgruntled employees, effective suppliers, and sloppy suppliers, to name a few. By the time financial indicators become available, bad products and dissatisfied customers have already occurred.

- The second most lagging indicator is customer satisfaction. By definition, customers must experience the product or service before they are in a position to comment on their satisfaction with that product or service. As with financial results, customer satisfaction is affected by many variables including process performance, employee motivation and morale, and supplier performance.

- On the other hand, leading indicators help organizations predict subsequent customer satisfaction and financial performance. Leading indicators include operational effectiveness and employee well-being and satisfaction. Supplier and partner performance, because it affects an organization's own operating performance, is also a leading indicator of customer satisfaction and financial performance.

Taken together, these measures represent a balance between leading and lagging indicators and enable decision makers to identify problems early and take corrective action.

Category 7 requires organizations to report current levels and improvement trends for the following:

- Product and service performance important to customers

- Customer satisfaction and dissatisfaction and customer-perceived value broken out by appropriate customer groups and market segments

- Financial and marketplace performance

- Human resource performance including work systems, employee learning, and employee well-being and satisfaction

- Operational performance key-value creation and other processes, such as cycle time, productivity, and supplier and partner performance

- Leadership and social responsibility including the accomplishment of organizational strategy and action plans, fiscal accountability, ethical behavior, regulatory and legal compliance, and support of key communities

For all of these areas, organizations must include appropriate comparative data to enable examiners to define what *good* means. Otherwise, even though performance may be improving, it is difficult to determine whether the level of performance is good.

**7.1   PRODUCT AND SERVICE OUTCOMES: What are your product and   RESULTS
service performance results? (100 Pts.)**

Summarize your organization's key product and service performance results. Segment your results by product and service types and groups, customer groups, and market segments, as appropriate. Include appropriate comparative data.

Provide data and information to answer the following questions:

a. Product and Service Results

What are your current levels and trends in key measures or indicators of product and service performance that are important to your customers? How do these results compare with the performance of your competitors and other organizations providing similar products and services?

Notes:

N1   Product and service results reported in this Item should relate to the key product, program, and service features identified as customer requirements or expectations in P.1b(2), based on information gathered in Items 3.1 and 3.2. The measures or indicators should address factors that affect customer preference, such as those included in Item P.1, Note 3, and Item 3.1, Note 3.

N2   *For some nonprofit organizations, product or service performance measures might be mandated by your funding sources. These measures should be reported and identified in your response to this Item.*

Item 7.1 looks at the organization's product and service-quality results to demonstrate how well the organization has been delivering products and services that lead to satisfaction, loyalty, and positive referral.

Organizations must provide data to demonstrate current levels, trends, and appropriate comparisons for key measures and/or indicators of product and service performance relating to key drivers of customers' satisfaction and retention as well as indicators of customers' views and decisions relative to future purchases and relationships. These measures of product and service performance are derived from customer-related information gathered in Items 3.1 and 3.2.

The correlations between product and service performance and customer indicators are a critical tool that helps managers:

- Define and focus on key quality and customer requirements.

- Identify product and service differentiators in the marketplace.

- Determine cause–effect relationships between the organization's product and service attributes

and evidence of customer satisfaction and loyalty, as well as positive referrals.

The correlations might reveal emerging or changing market segments, the changing importance of requirements, or even the potential obsolescence of offerings.

Product/service performance results appropriate for recording in this Item might be based upon one or more of the following:

- Internal (organizational) quality measurements

- Field performance of products, defect levels, and response time.

- Data collected from customers by the organization or for the organization.

- Customer surveys on product and service performance

- Attributes that cannot be accurately assessed through direct measurement (for example, ease of use) or when variability in customer expectations makes the customer's perception the most meaningful indicator (for example, courtesy)

7.1 Product and Service Outcomes

Key product and service performance results segmented by product groups, customer groups, and market segments

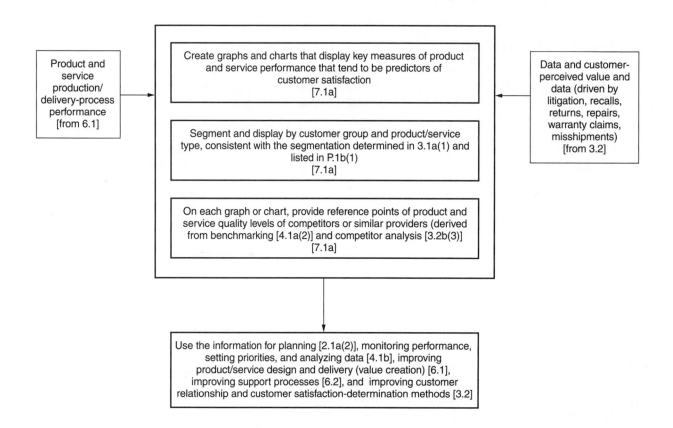

Product and service production/ delivery-process performance [from 6.1]

Create graphs and charts that display key measures of product and service performance that tend to be predictors of customer satisfaction
[7.1a]

Segment and display by customer group and product/service type, consistent with the segmentation determined in 3.1a(1) and listed in P.1b(1)
[7.1a]

On each graph or chart, provide reference points of product and service quality levels of competitors or similar providers (derived from benchmarking [4.1a(2)] and competitor analysis [3.2b(3)])
[7.1a]

Data and customer-perceived value and data (driven by litigation, recalls, returns, repairs, warranty claims, misshipments)
[from 3.2]

Use the information for planning [2.1a(2)], monitoring performance, setting priorities, and analyzing data [4.1b], improving product/service design and delivery (value creation) [6.1], improving support processes [6.2], and improving customer relationship and customer satisfaction-determination methods [3.2]

7.1 Product and Service Outcomes Item Linkages

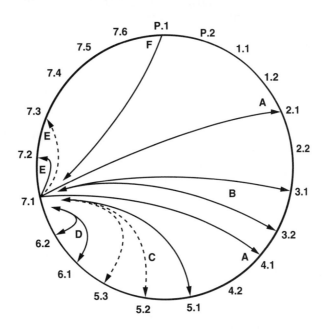

	NATURE OF RELATIONSHIP
A	Data on product and service quality [7.1] are monitored by senior leaders [4.1b(1)] and are used for strategic planning [2.1a(2)] and to set priorities for improvement and innovation [4.1b(2)].
B	Processes used to gather intelligence about current customer requirements [3.1a(2)], strength of customer relations [3.2a(1)], and to determine customer satisfaction [3.2b(1)] produce product and service outcomes data [7.1]. In addition, product and service quality outcomes [7.1] are used to help set customer-contact requirements (service standards) [3.2a(2)] and better understand customer requirements and preferences [3.1a(2)].
C	Recognition and rewards [5.1b] should be based, in part, on product and service quality outcomes [7.1]. Innovation, empowerment, and initiative developed by effective work systems [5.1a] can foster better product and service quality [7.1] Product and service quality data [7.1] are monitored, in part, to assess training effectiveness [5.2]. In addition, results pertaining to product and service quality [7.1] can be improved with effective training [5.2]. Systems to enhance employee motivation, satisfaction, and well-being (including disaster-prevention and recovery systems) [5.3] can produce higher levels of product and service quality [7.1]. Improved product and service quality can affect the morale and motivation of customer-contact employees.
D	Data on product and service quality [7.1] may be used to help design and improve value creation [6.1] and support [6.2] processes. These processes [6.1 and 6.2] can have a direct effect on product and service quality [7.1].
E	Better product and service results [7.1] can enhance customer satisfaction results [7.2] and can improve financial and market performance [7.3]. Better organizational effectiveness [7.5] can improve product and service results [7.1].
F	The information in P.1b(2) helps examiners identify the kind of product and service quality outcomes, broken out by customer and market segment, that should be reported in Item 7.1.

IF YOU DON'T DO WHAT THE CRITERIA REQUIRE . . .	
Item Reference	**Possible Adverse Consequences**
7.1	Failing to provide comparison data makes it difficult for leaders (or Baldrige examiners) to determine if the level of performance reported is good or not. Failing to provide results data for at least most areas of importance to the organization makes it difficult to determine if performance is getting better in key areas. Finally, the failure to provide this information as part of a Baldrige Award assessment is likely to reduce the score and may even prevent an organization from receiving a site visit (during which time additional results data are usually obtained).

7.1 PRODUCT AND SERVICE OUTCOMES—SAMPLE EFFECTIVE RESULTS

A. Product and Service Results

- Data are presented for the most relevant product or service-quality indicators collected through the processes described in Item 3.2 (some of which may be referenced in the Organizational Profile).

- Operational data are presented that correlate with, and help predict, customer satisfaction. These data show consistently improving trends and levels that compare favorably with competitors.

- All indicators show steady improvement. (Indicators include data collected in Item 6.1, such as product and service-quality levels and on-time delivery.)

- All or most indicators compare favorably to competitors or similar providers.

- Graphs and information are accurate and easy to understand.

- Data are not missing.

7.2 CUSTOMER-FOCUSED OUTCOMES: What are your customer-focused performance results? (70 Pts.)   **RESULTS**

Summarize your organization's key customer-focused results, including customer satisfaction and customer-perceived value. Segment your results by product and service types and groups, customer groups, and market segments as appropriate. Include appropriate comparative data.

Provide data and information to answer the following questions:

a. Customer-Focused Results

(1) What are your current levels and trends in key measures or indicators of customer satisfaction and dissatisfaction? How do these results compare with the customer satisfaction levels of your competitors and other organizations providing similar products and services?

(2) What are your current levels and trends in key measures or indicators of customer-perceived value, including customer loyalty and retention, positive referral, and other aspects of building relationships with customers, as appropriate?

Notes:

N1   Customer satisfaction and dissatisfaction results reported in this Item should relate to the customer groups and market segments discussed in P.1b(2) and Item 3.1 and to the determination methods and data described in Item 3.2.

N2   Measures and indicators of customers' satisfaction with your products and services relative to customers' satisfaction with competitors and comparable organizations might include objective information and data from your customers and from independent organizations.

Item 7.2 looks at the organization's customer-focused performance results to demonstrate how well the organization has been satisfying its customers and delivering product and service quality that lead to satisfaction, loyalty, and positive referral.

Top-performing organizations use all relevant data to determine and help predict the organization's performance as viewed by customers. Relevant data and information include:

- Customer satisfaction and dissatisfaction

- Retention, gains, and losses of customers and customer accounts

- Customer complaints, complaint management, complaint resolution, and warranty claims

- Customer-perceived value based on quality and price

- Customer assessment of access and ease of use (including courtesy in-service interactions)

- Awards, ratings, and recognition from customers and independent rating organizations

This Item emphasizes customer-focused results that go beyond satisfaction measurement because loyalty, repeat business, and longer-term customer relationships are better indicators and measures of future success in the marketplace and of organizational sustainability.

Organizations should provide appropriate comparisons for key measures and/or indicators to permit the assessment of the strength or *goodness* of the organization's performance.

7.2 Customer-Focused Outcomes

The organization's key customer-focused results, customer satisfaction, and customer-perceived value

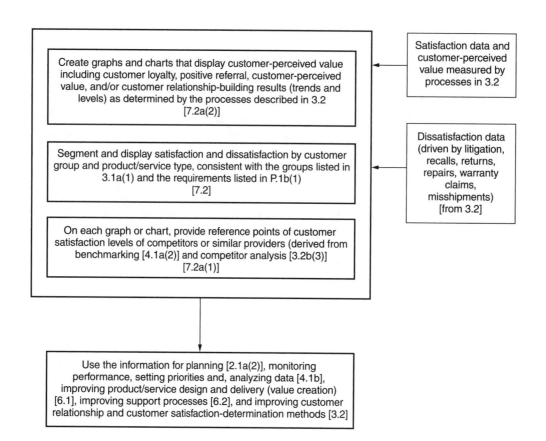

Create graphs and charts that display customer-perceived value including customer loyalty, positive referral, customer-perceived value, and/or customer relationship-building results (trends and levels) as determined by the processes described in 3.2 [7.2a(2)]

Segment and display satisfaction and dissatisfaction by customer group and product/service type, consistent with the groups listed in 3.1a(1) and the requirements listed in P.1b(1) [7.2]

On each graph or chart, provide reference points of customer satisfaction levels of competitors or similar providers (derived from benchmarking [4.1a(2)] and competitor analysis [3.2b(3)] [7.2a(1)]

Satisfaction data and customer-perceived value measured by processes in 3.2

Dissatisfaction data (driven by litigation, recalls, returns, repairs, warranty claims, misshipments) [from 3.2]

Use the information for planning [2.1a(2)], monitoring performance, setting priorities and, analyzing data [4.1b], improving product/service design and delivery (value creation) [6.1], improving support processes [6.2], and improving customer relationship and customer satisfaction-determination methods [3.2]

7.2 Customer-Focused Outcomes Item Linkages

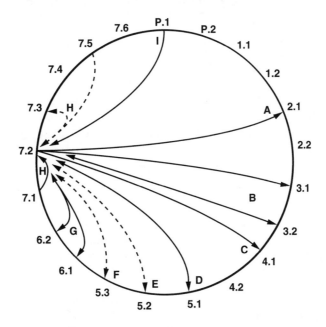

	NATURE OF RELATIONSHIP
A	Data on customer satisfaction and loyalty [7.2a(2)] are used for strategic planning [2.1a(2)].
B	Processes used to gather intelligence about current customer requirements [3.1a(2)], strength of customer relations [3.2a(1)], and to determine customer satisfaction [3.2b(1)] produce customer satisfaction results data [7.2a]. In addition, customer satisfaction results [7.2] are used to help set customer-contact requirements (service standards) [3.2a(2)] and better understand customer requirements and preferences [3.1a(2)].
C	Data on levels of satisfaction of customers [7.2] are monitored by senior leaders [4.1b].
D	Recognition and rewards [5.1b] should be based, in part, on customer satisfaction results [7.2]. Innovation, empowerment, and initiative developed by effective work systems [5.1a] can foster better customer satisfaction [7.2].
E	Customer satisfaction data [7.2] are monitored, in part, to assess training effectiveness [5.2a(6)]. In addition, results pertaining to customer satisfaction [7.2] can be improved with effective training [5.2].
F	Systems to enhance employee motivation, satisfaction, and well-being (including disaster prevention and recovery systems) [5.3] can produce higher levels of customer satisfaction [7.2]. Improved customer satisfaction can affect the morale and motivation of customer-contact employees.
G	Data on satisfaction and dissatisfaction of customers [7.2a(1) and (2)] are used to help design and improve value creation [6.1] and support [6.2] processes respectively. These processes [6.1 and 6.2] have a direct effect on customer satisfaction/dissatisfaction and loyalty [7.2a(1) and (2) respectively].
H	Better product and service quality [7.1] and operational [7.5a] results can enhance customer-focused results [7.2]. Better customer satisfaction [7.2] can improve financial and market performance [7.3].
I	The information in P.1b(2) helps examiners identify the kind of results, broken out by customer and market segment, that should be reported in Item 7.2.

IF YOU DON'T DO WHAT THE CRITERIA REQUIRE . . .	
Item Reference	**Possible Adverse Consequences**
7.2	Failing to provide comparison data makes it difficult for leaders (or Baldrige examiners) to determine if the level of performance reported is good. Failing to provide results data for at least most areas of importance to the organization makes it difficult to determine if performance is getting better in key areas. Finally, the failure to provide this information as part of a Baldrige Award assessment is likely to reduce the score and may even prevent an organization from receiving a site visit (during which time additional results data are usually obtained).

7.2 CUSTOMER-FOCUSED OUTCOMES—SAMPLE EFFECTIVE RESULTS

A. Customer-Focused Results

- Trends and indicators of customer satisfaction and dissatisfaction (including complaint data), segmented by customer groups, are provided in graph and chart form for all key measures. Multiyear data are provided.

- All indicators show steady improvement. (Indicators include data collected in Area 3.2b, such as customer assessments of products and services, customer awards, and customer retention.)

- All indicators compare favorably to competitors or similar providers.

- Graphs and information are accurate and easy to understand.

- Data are not missing.

- Results data are supported by customer feedback, customers' overall assessments of products and services, customer awards, and indicators from design and production/delivery processes of products and services.

7.3 FINANCIAL AND MARKET OUTCOMES: What are your financial and market results? (70 Pts.)   RESULTS

Summarize your organization's key financial and marketplace performance results by customer or market segments, as appropriate. Include appropriate comparative data.

Provide data and information to answer the following questions:

a. Financial and Market Results

(1) What are your current levels and trends in key measures or indicators of financial performance, including aggregate measures of financial return and economic value or budgetary measures, as appropriate?

(2) What are your current levels and trends in key measures or indicators of marketplace performance, including market share or position, growth, and new markets entered, as appropriate?

Notes:

N1 Responses to 7.3a(1) might include aggregate measures such as return on investment (ROI), asset utilization, operating margins, profitability, profitability by market or customer segment, liquidity, debt-to-equity ratio, value added per employee, and financial activity measures. Measures should relate to the financial management approaches described in Item 6.2. *For nonprofit organizations, additional measures might include performance to budget, reserve funds, cost avoidance or savings, administrative expenditures as a percentage of budget, and cost of fundraising versus funds raised.*

N2 *For nonprofit organizations, responses to 7.3a(2) might include measures of charitable donations or grants and the number of new programs or services offered.*

Item 7.3 looks at the organization's key financial and market results to provide a complete picture of financial sustainability and marketplace success and challenges.

Organizations should provide data demonstrating levels, trends, and appropriate comparisons for key financial, market, and business indicators. Measures reported in this Item are used by senior leaders to assess organization-level performance.

- Appropriate financial measures and indicators might include:

  - Revenue

  - Profits or losses

  - Market position

  - Order-to-cash cycle time

  - Cost per person served

  - Earnings per share

  - Financial returns

- Marketplace performance measures might include:

  - Market share

  - Measures of business growth

  - New products or services and and markets entered (including exports)

  - Entry into e-commerce markets

  - Percent of sales from new products

Organizations should provide appropriate comparisons for key measures and/or indicators to permit the assessment of the strength or *goodness* of the organization's performance.

7.3 Financial and Market Outcomes

Results of improvement efforts using key measures and/or indicators of financial and market performance

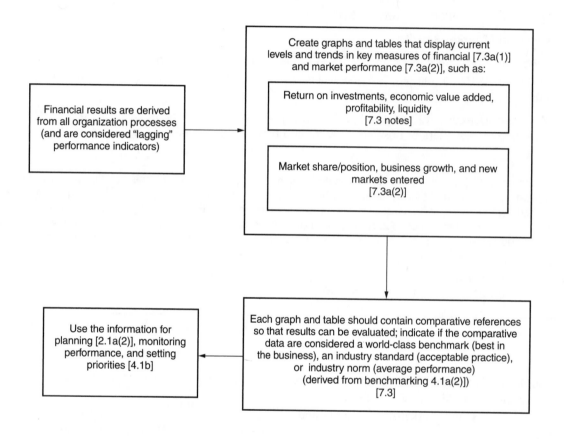

Financial results are derived from all organization processes (and are considered "lagging" performance indicators)

Create graphs and tables that display current levels and trends in key measures of financial [7.3a(1)] and market performance [7.3a(2)], such as:

Return on investments, economic value added, profitability, liquidity
[7.3 notes]

Market share/position, business growth, and new markets entered
[7.3a(2)]

Use the information for planning [2.1a(2)], monitoring performance, and setting priorities [4.1b]

Each graph and table should contain comparative references so that results can be evaluated; indicate if the comparative data are considered a world-class benchmark (best in the business), an industry standard (acceptable practice), or industry norm (average performance) (derived from benchmarking 4.1a(2)])
[7.3]

7.3 Financial and Market Outcomes Item Linkages

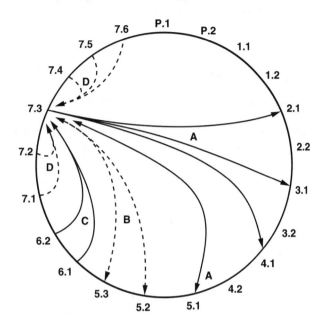

	NATURE OF RELATIONSHIP
A	Financial [7.3a(1)] and market [7.3a(2)] results are used for strategic planning [2.1a(2)]; understanding market requirements and customer preferences [3.1a(2)]; and leadership monitoring [4.1b(1)], priority setting, and analysis [4.1b(2)] as well as contributing to employee feedback and reward [5.1b].
B	Financial results [7.3a(1)] and market results [7.3a(2)] are monitored, in part, to assess training effectiveness [5.2] and could be used as a partial basis for compensation, recognition, and reward [5.1b]. In addition, results pertaining to financial and market performance [7.3a], reflect, in part, training effectiveness [5.2]. Employee motivation and well-being [5.3] affect financial and market performance results [7.3a], and vice versa.
C	Financial [7.3a(1)] and market [7.3a(2)] results are enhanced by improvements in value creation processes [6.1] and support processes [6.2]. Those processes may be modified or improved based on financial and market performance.
D	Better financial [7.3a(1)] and market [7.3a(2)] results (lagging indicators) can be driven by better customer satisfaction [7.2], product and service quality [7.1], employee motivation and morale [7.4], operational effectiveness [7.5] results, and compliance with laws and regulations and good ethical behavior [7.6].

IF YOU DON'T DO WHAT THE CRITERIA REQUIRE . . .	
Item Reference	**Possible Adverse Consequences**
7.3	Failing to provide comparison data makes it difficult for leaders (or Baldrige examiners) to determine if the level of performance reported is good. Failing to provide results data for at least most areas of importance to the organization makes it difficult to determine if performance is getting better in key areas. Finally, the failure to provide this information as part of a Baldrige Award assessment is likely to reduce the score and may even prevent an organization from receiving a site visit (during which time additional results data are usually obtained).

7.3 FINANCIAL AND MARKET OUTCOMES—SAMPLE EFFECTIVE RESULTS

A. Financial and Market Results

- Key measures and indicators of organization market and financial performance address the following areas:

  - Effective use of materials, energy, capital, and assets

  - Asset utilization

  - Market share, business growth, new markets entered, and market shifting

  - Return on equity

  - Operating margins

  - Pre-tax profit

  - Earnings per share

  - Generating enough revenue to cover expenses (not-for-profit and public sector)

  - Operating within budget (government sector)

- Measures and indicators show steady improvement.

- All key financial and market data are presented.

- Comparative data include industry-best, best-competitor, and other appropriate benchmarks.

7.4 HUMAN RESOURCE OUTCOMES: What are your human resource results? RESULTS (70 Pts.)

Summarize your organization's key human resource results, including work system performance, and employee learning, development, well-being, and satisfaction. Segment your results to address the diversity of your workforce and the different types and categories of employees, as appropriate. Include appropriate comparative data.

Provide data and information to answer the following questions:

a. Human Resource Results

(1) What are your current levels and trends in key measures or indicators of work system performance and effectiveness?

(2) What are your current levels and trends in key measures of employee learning and development?

(3) What are your current levels and trends in key measures or indicators of employee well-being, satisfaction, and dissatisfaction?

Notes:

N1 Results reported in this Item should relate to activities described in Category 5. Your results should be responsive to key process needs described in Category 6 and to your organization's action plans and human resource plans described in Item 2.2.

N2 Appropriate measures and indicators of work system performance and effectiveness [7.4a(1)] might include simplification of jobs and job classifications, job rotation, work layout improvement, employee retention and internal promotion rates, and changing supervisory ratios.

N3 Appropriate measures and indicators of employee learning and development [7.4a(2)] might include innovation and suggestion rates, courses completed, learning, on-the-job performance improvements, and cross-training rates.

N4 For appropriate measures of employee well-being and satisfaction [7.4a(3)], see Item 5.3 Notes.

N5. *Nonprofit organizations that rely on volunteers to supplement the work of their employees should include results for their volunteer workforce, as appropriate.*

Item 7.4 looks at the organization's human resource results to demonstrate how well the organization has created, maintained, and enhanced a positive, productive, learning, and caring work environment.

Organizations should provide data demonstrating current levels, trends, and appropriate comparisons for key measures and/or indicators of employee well-being, satisfaction, dissatisfaction, and development.

Organizations should also provide data and information on the organization's work-system performance and effectiveness, showing favorable comparisons with industry leaders.

Results measures reported for work-system performance might include: improvement in job classification, job rotation, work layout, and improved employee decision making (both decision quality and increased decision-making authority). Results reported might include input data, such as extent of training, but the emphasis should be on data that show effectiveness and improvement of outcomes. For example, one measure might be productivity enhancements or cost savings realized from the redesign of work processes by employee work teams.

Results reported for employee learning and development might include extent of training or cross-training, new skills acquired, pre-training/post-training knowledge acquisition, and increased use of new skills on the job.

Results reported for employee well-being, satisfaction and dissatisfaction might include: safety, absenteeism, turnover, satisfaction ratings of work climate, and complaints (grievances). Other factors important to employees, such as data on wage-scale comparisons with industry standards, or perceived job security may be important to report. For measures such as absenteeism and turnover, local or regional comparisons may be most appropriate.

Organizations should provide appropriate comparisons for key measures and/or indicators to permit the assessment of the strength or *goodness* of the organization's performance.

7.4 Human Resource Outcomes

Results of human resource improvement efforts using key measures and/or indicators of such performance

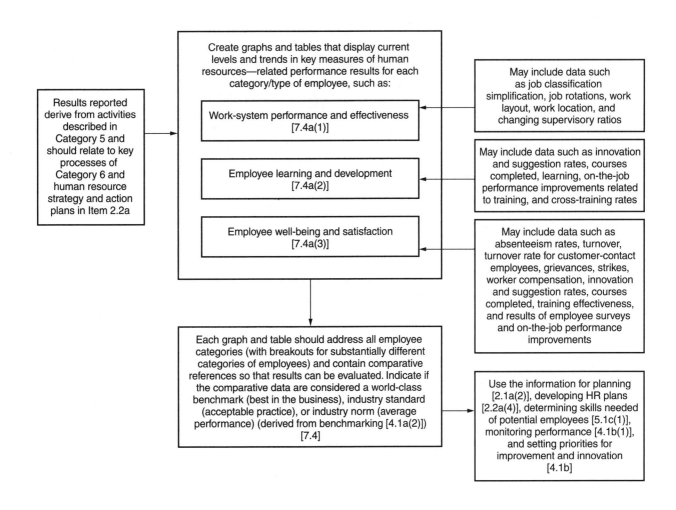

Results reported derive from activities described in Category 5 and should relate to key processes of Category 6 and human resource strategy and action plans in Item 2.2a

Create graphs and tables that display current levels and trends in key measures of human resources—related performance results for each category/type of employee, such as:

Work-system performance and effectiveness [7.4a(1)]

Employee learning and development [7.4a(2)]

Employee well-being and satisfaction [7.4a(3)]

May include data such as job classification simplification, job rotations, work layout, work location, and changing supervisory ratios

May include data such as innovation and suggestion rates, courses completed, learning, on-the-job performance improvements related to training, and cross-training rates

May include data such as absenteeism rates, turnover, turnover rate for customer-contact employees, grievances, strikes, worker compensation, innovation and suggestion rates, courses completed, training effectiveness, and results of employee surveys and on-the-job performance improvements

Each graph and table should address all employee categories (with breakouts for substantially different categories of employees) and contain comparative references so that results can be evaluated. Indicate if the comparative data are considered a world-class benchmark (best in the business), industry standard (acceptable practice), or industry norm (average performance) (derived from benchmarking [4.1a(2)]) [7.4]

Use the information for planning [2.1a(2)], developing HR plans [2.2a(4)], determining skills needed of potential employees [5.1c(1)], monitoring performance [4.1b(1)], and setting priorities for improvement and innovation [4.1b]

7.4 Human Resource Outcomes—Item Linkages

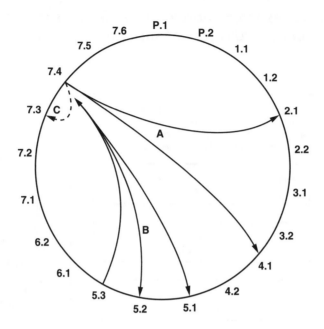

	NATURE OF RELATIONSHIP
A	Human resource results [7.4] are reported and used for planning [2.1a(2)], for monitoring organizational performance [4.1b], and for analysis [4.1b].
B	Human resource results derive from and are enhanced by improving work systems and enhancing flexibility, and by strengthening employee recognition systems [5.1], training [5.2], and well-being and satisfaction [5.3]. In addition, human resource results data [7.4] are monitored, in part, to assess training effectiveness [5.2].
C	Better financial [7.3a] and market [7.3b] results (lagging indicators) can be driven by better employee motivation and morale [7.4].

IF YOU DON'T DO WHAT THE CRITERIA REQUIRE . . .	
Item Reference	**Possible Adverse Consequences**
7.4	Failing to provide comparison data makes it difficult for leaders (or Baldrige examiners) to determine if the level of performance reported is good or not. Failing to provide results data for at least most areas of importance to the organization makes it difficult to determine if performance is getting better in key areas. Finally, the failure to provide this information as part of a Baldrige Award assessment is likely to reduce the score and may even prevent an organization from receiving a site visit (during which time additional results data are usually obtained).

7.4 HUMAN RESOURCE OUTCOMES—SAMPLE EFFECTIVE RESULTS

A. Human Resource Results

- The results reported in Item 7.4 derive from activities described in Category 5 and the human resource plans from Item 2.2a(4).

- Multiyear data are provided to show sustained performance.

- All results show steady improvement.

- Data are not missing. If human resource results are declared important, related data are reported.

- Comparison data for benchmark or competitor organizations are reported, and the organization compares favorably.

- Trend data are reported for employee satisfaction with working conditions, safety, retirement package, and other employee benefits. Satisfaction with management is also reported.

- Trends for declining absenteeism, grievances, employee turnover, strikes, and worker compensation claims are reported.

- Data reported are segmented for all employee categories.

- Being recognized as one of the top organizations in America to work for provides some evidence of excellent human resource results.

**7.5   ORGANIZATIONAL EFFECTIVENESS OUTCOMES: What are your   RESULTS
organizational effectiveness results? (70 Pts.)**

Summarize your organization's key operational performance results that contribute to the improvement of organizational effectiveness. Segment your results by product and service types and groups and by market segments, as appropriate. Include appropriate comparative data.

Provide data and information to answer the following questions:

a. Organizational Effectiveness Results

   (1) What are your current levels and trends in key measures or indicators of the operational performance of your key value creation processes? Include productivity, cycle time, supplier and partner performance, and other appropriate measures of effectiveness and efficiency.

   (2) What are your current levels and trends in key measures or indicators of the operational performance of your other key processes? Include productivity, cycle time, supplier and partner performance, and other appropriate measures of effectiveness and efficiency?

Notes:

   N1   Results reported in Item 7.5 should address your key operational requirements as presented in the Organizational Profile and in Items 6.1 and 6.2. Include results not reported in Items 7.1–7.4.

   N2   Results reported in Item 7.5 should provide key information for analysis and review of your organizational performance [Item 4.1] and should provide the operational basis for product and service outcomes [Item 7.1], customer-focused outcomes [Item 7.2], and financial and market outcomes [Item 7.3].

Item 7.5 looks at the organization's key operational performance results to demonstrate organizational effectiveness in both value creation and support processes and the achievement of key goals and strategic objectives. Organizations should provide data in this item if it does not belong in other Category 7 Items (7.1, 7.2, 7.3, 7.4, or 7.6).

This item encourages the organization to develop and include unique and innovative measures to track business development, key processes, and operational improvement. However, all key areas of business and operational performance should be covered by measures that are relevant and important to the organization.

Measures and/or indicators of operational effectiveness and efficiency might include:

• Cycle-time reduction, production flexibility, lead times, set-up times, and time to market

• Business-specific indicators such as innovation rates and increased use of e-technology, product and process yields, Six Sigma and Lean initiative results, and on-time delivery performance to request

• Supply-chain indicators such as reductions in inventory and incoming inspections, increases in quality and productivity, improvements in electronic data exchange, and reductions in supply-chain management costs

• Valid third-party assessment results such as ISO 9001 audits.

Organizations should provide appropriate comparisons for key measures and/or indicators to permit the assessment of the strength or *goodness* of the organization's performance.

Do not report results in 7.5 that belong elsewhere. For example, if on-time delivery is a key customer requirement, it should be reported in 7.1.

7.5 Organizational Effectiveness Outcomes

Results of improvement efforts that contribute to achievement of organizational effectiveness

Organizational Effectiveness Results

Create graphs and tables that display current levels of sustained trends of key operational performance results that contribute to strategic objectives

Key process-performance improvement results are derived from *value creation* processes in Items 6.1, including productivity, cycle time, supplier and partner performance, and other efficiency and effectiveness measures important to the organization
[7.5a(1)]

Key process-performance improvement results are derived from *support* processes in Items 6.2, including productivity, cycle time, supplier and partner performance, and other efficiency and effectiveness measures important to the organization
[7.5a(2)]

Each graph and table should contain comparative references so that results can be evaluated; indicate if the comparative data are considered a world-class benchmark (best in the business), or industry norm (average performance) (derived from benchmarking [4.1a(2)])
[7.5]

Results provide data for analysis and performance review
[4.1b]

7.5 Organizational Effectiveness Outcomes Item Linkages

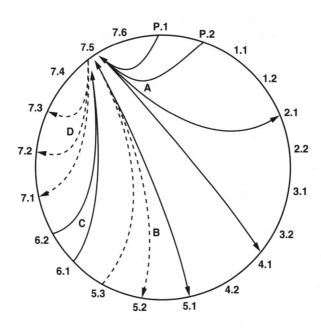

NATURE OF RELATIONSHIP	
A	Organizational effectiveness results [7.5] are reported and used for planning [2.1a(2)], management improvement, performance monitoring and priority setting [4.1b]. Performance related to the key suppliers and distributors listed in P.1b(2) should be reported in 7.5a(1)].
B	Organizational effectiveness results [7.5] are used to provide employee feedback and drive rewards and recognition [5.1b] and identify areas to emphasize in training and employee development [5.2]. Processes to improve employee initiative and flexibility [5.1a(1)] and employee safety, security, morale, motivation, and well-being [5.3], and better align recognition and reward to desired performance outcomes [5.1b] may enhance organizational effectiveness results [7.5].
C	Designing value creation processes to meet customer requirements [6.1a(3)] and improving product and service delivery and consistency [6.1a(4)] and support service processes [6.2] should affect organizational effectiveness performance outcomes [7.5].
D	Organizational effectiveness results [7.5] contribute to financial and market results [7.3], product and service quality [7.1], and customer-focused results [7.2].

IF YOU DON'T DO WHAT THE CRITERIA REQUIRE . . .	
Item Reference	**Possible Adverse Consequences**
7.5	Failing to provide comparison data makes it difficult for leaders (or Baldrige examiners) to determine if the level of performance reported is good. Failing to provide results data for at least most areas of importance to the organization makes it difficult to determine if performance is getting better in key areas. Finally, the failure to provide this information as part of a Baldrige Award assessment is likely to reduce the score and may even prevent an organization from receiving a site visit (during which time additional results data are usually obtained).

7.5 ORGANIZATIONAL EFFECTIVENESS OUTCOMES— SAMPLE EFFECTIVE RESULTS

A. Organizational Effectiveness Results

- Indices and trend data are provided in graph and chart form for all operational performance measures identified in 1.1, 6.1, and 6.2, and the key business factors identified in the Organizational Profile and not reported elsewhere in Category 7. Multiyear data are reported.

- Most to all indicators show steady improvement.

- Product and service-quality measures and indicators address requirements such as accuracy, timeliness, and reliability. Examples include defect levels, repeat services, meeting product or service delivery or response times, and availability levels. However, if these measures predict customer satisfaction, they should be moved to Item 7.1.

- Operational performance measures address:

  - Productivity, efficiency, and effectiveness, such as productivity indices, and product/service design-improvement measures

  - Cycle-time reductions

- Comparative data include industry best, best competitor, industry average, and appropriate benchmarks. Data are also derived from independent surveys, studies, laboratory testing, or other sources.

- Data are not missing. (For example, do not show a steady trend from 2001 to 2005 but leave out 2004.)

- Data are not aggregated, since aggregation tends to hide poor performance by blending it with good performance. Charts and graphs break out and report trends separately.

7.6 LEADERSHIP AND SOCIAL RESPONSIBILITY OUTCOMES: What are your leadership and social responsibility results? (70 Pts.)   RESULTS

Summarize your organization's key governance, senior leadership, and social responsibility results, including evidence of ethical behavior, fiscal accountability, legal compliance, and organizational citizenship. Segment your results by organizational units, as appropriate. Include appropriate comparative data.

Provide data and information to answer the following questions:

a. Leadership and Social Responsibility Results

(1) What are your results for key measures or indicators of accomplishment of your organizational strategy and action plans?

(2) What are your results for key measures or indicators of ethical behavior and of stakeholder trust in the senior leaders and governance of your organization? What are your results for key measures or indicators of breaches of ethical behavior?

(3) What are your key current findings and trends in key measures or indicators of fiscal accountability, both internal and external, as appropriate?

(4) What are your results for key measures or indicators of regulatory and legal compliance?

(5) What are your results for key measures or indicators of organizational citizenship in support of your key communities?

Notes:

N1   For examples of measures of ethical behavior and stakeholder trust [7.6a(2)], see Item 1.2, Note 4.

N2   Responses to 7.6a(3) might include financial statement issues and risks, important internal and external auditor recommendations, and management's responses to these matters. *For some nonprofit organizations, results of IRS 990 audits also might be included.*

N3   Regulatory and legal compliance results [7.6a(4)] should address requirements described in 1.2b. Employee related occupational health and safety results (for example, OSHA-reportable incidents) should be reported in 7.4a(3).

N4   Organizational citizenship results [7.6a(5)] should address support of the key communities discussed in 1.2c.

Item 7.6 looks at key results in the areas of leadership and social responsibility that reflect the behavior of a fiscally sound and ethical organization that is a good citizen in its communities. In this Item, provide data and information on key measures or indicators of organizational accountability, stakeholder trust, and ethical behavior as well as regulatory and legal compliance and citizenship.

Lack of appropriate measures can be challenging for many organizations seeking to determine their progress in accomplishing strategic objectives. Often, these progress measures can be discerned by first defining the results that would indicate end-goal success in achieving the strategic objective and then using that measure to define intermediate measures.

In any case, data showing progress toward achieving outcome-oriented strategic objectives should be reported. Although there is an increased focus nationally on issues of governance, ethics, and board and leadership accountability, the best-performing organizations practice and demonstrate high standards of overall conduct. The failure to do so may threaten an organization's public trust, which may threaten its long-term success, if not its survival. Boards and senior leaders should track performance measures that relate to governance and social responsibility on a regular basis and emphasize this performance in stakeholder communications.

Measures should include environmental, legal, and regulatory compliance and highlight noteworthy achievements in these areas, as appropriate. Reduced emission levels, waste-stream reductions, by-product use, recycling, and OSHA compliance, to name a few

Summarize and report any sanctions or adverse findings (including independent audit findings) under law, regulation, or contract the organization has received during the past three years, including the nature of the incidents and their current status.

Results also should include indicators of support for key communities and other public purposes. These might include charts showing increased levels of time that managers and employees commit to volunteer activities, increased levels of business support to community-based service organizations, and increased support for community healthcare, education, and the arts, to name a few.

Organizations should provide appropriate comparisons for key measures and/or indicators to permit the assessment of the strength or *goodness* of the organization's performance.

7.6 Leadership and Social Responsibility Outcomes

Results of improvement efforts that contribute to achievement of key leadership and social responsibility results, including strategy and action plans, fiscal accountability ethical behavior, legal compliance, and organizational citizenship

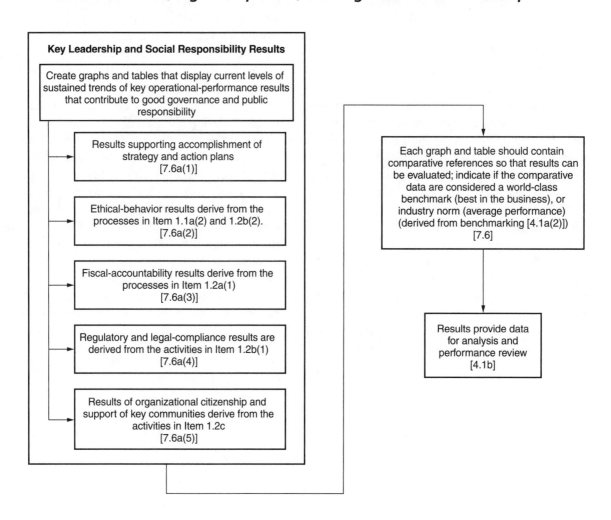

7.6 Leadership and Social Responsibility Outcomes Item Linkages

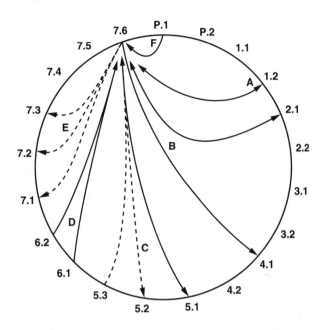

	NATURE OF RELATIONSHIP
A	Results for regulatory and legal compliance and citizenship, related to the activities in Item 1.2, should be reported in 7.5a(4). In addition, these results are monitored to determine if process changes are needed.
B	Leadership and social responsibility results that relate to ethical behavior, fiscal accountability, and regulatory compliance [7.6a(2, 3, and 4)] are used for planning [2.1a(2)], and management improvement, performance monitoring, and priority setting [4.1b]. Progress in addressing strategic objectives listed in 2.1b(1), should be reported in Item 7.6a(1).
C	Employee motivation, satisfaction, and well-being [5.3] affect social responsibility results and may affect ethical behavior and regulatory compliance [7.6a(2 and 4)]. In addition, results pertaining to these key areas [7.6] should be reflected, in part, in employee feedback [5.1b] and are monitored to identify training needs and assess training effectiveness [5.2].
D	Value creation [6.1] and support service processes [6.2] affect regulatory compliance and possible ethical behavior [7.6a(4 and 2)].
E	Leadership and social responsibility results [7.6] may affect financial and market results [7.3], product and service quality [7.1], and customer-focused results [7.2].
F	The regulatory requirements described in P.1a(5) define the related performance results that should be reported in 7.6a(4).

IF YOU DON'T DO WHAT THE CRITERIA REQUIRE . . .	
Item Reference	**Possible Adverse Consequences**
7.6	Failing to provide comparison data makes it difficult for leaders (or Baldrige examiners) to determine if the level of performance reported is good. Failing to provide results data for at least most areas of importance to the organization makes it difficult to determine if performance is getting better in key areas. Finally, the failure to provide this information as part of a Baldrige Award assessment is likely to reduce the score and may even prevent an organization from receiving a site visit (during which time additional results data are usually obtained).

7.6 LEADERSHIP AND SOCIAL RESPONSIBILITY OUTCOMES— SAMPLE EFFECTIVE RESULTS

A. Leadership and Social Responsibility Results

- Indices and trend data are provided in graph and chart form for all regulatory and legal compliance requirements identified in Item 1.2b(1) and P.1a(5) and relevant organizational goals (2.2) and strategic objectives (2.1b).

- Results address public responsibilities such as environmental improvements and the increased use of technologies, materials, and work processes that are environmentally friendly.

- Ethical behavior is demonstrated by a large percentage of independent board members. In addition, independent audits demonstrate full compliance with ethics rules established by the organization.

- Areas of community support demonstrate increasing efforts to strengthen local community services, education, and healthcare, the environment, and related trade and business associations.

- Data indicate most measures of regulatory compliance exceed requirements. Performance is leading the industry. No sanctions or violations have been reported.

- Data show sustained improvements in waste reduction and energy efficiency.

- Resources allocated to support key communities, consistent with business strategy, demonstrate positive desired results, increasing in effectiveness over time.

- Most to all indicators show steady improvement.

- Comparative data include industry best, best competitor, industry average, and appropriate benchmarks. Data are also derived from independent surveys, studies, laboratory testing, or other sources.

- Data are not missing. (For example, do not show a steady trend from 2001 to 2005, but leave out 2004.)

- Data are not aggregated, since aggregation tends to hide poor performance by blending it with good performance. Charts and graphs break out and report trends separately.

Tips on Preparing a Baldrige Award Application

Applications are put together by every conceivable combination of teams, committees, and individual efforts, including consultants. There is no *right* or *best* way to do it. There are, however, lessons that have been learned and are worth considering because they contribute to people and organizations growing and improving.

Author's note: Gathering process information from across the organization is essential to prepare an accurate and complete Baldrige application. Over the past several years, I have helped many organizations conduct assessments and apply for awards. During this time, I have prepared a Microsoft Word template to help writing teams gather information and prepare to write. The application template provided on the CD that is included with this book facilitates the collection of critical information and makes it easier to write a Baldrige application. A sample of the completed portion of the template appears in Figure 32 on the next page. Templates are available for education and health care as well.

The thoughts that follow are intended to generate conversation and learning. They are not intended to present a comprehensive treatment of the subject.

Getting the Fingerprints of the Organization on the Application

How do we put together a *good* application? To be *good* from a technical perspective, it must both be accurate and respond fully to the multiple requirements of the Criteria. It must convey to examiners a succinct description of the organization's management system. It must be clear and internally consistent.

To be effective, the application must be more than technically accurate. The organization must reflect a sense of commitment and ownership for the application. Ownership requires a role for people throughout the organization as well as top leadership. The actual *putting of words on paper* can be accomplished in a variety of ways. However, ignoring this larger question of ownership exposes the organization to developing a sterile, disjointed, or unrecognizable document that diminishes its value as a vehicle of growth.

The Spirit and Values in an Application

Like it or not, the team or individual that is responsible for developing an application will be closely watched by everyone in the organization. The people coordinating the development of the application need to be perceived as *walking the talk*. They need to be seen as believers and role models for what is being written. The application should reflect the following:

- *Continuous improvement must be fully embedded into all management processes and work processes.* Do not make the common mistake of only describing how the processes work today. Make sure that the methods used to evaluate each key process are briefly described. Then list the key requirements that were made to the process based on the evaluation.

- The application describes the system used to run the business. This includes not just a description of the pieces, but also the linkages among the activities that make the organization function effectively.

- Put your best foot forward, but do not exaggerate.

Core Values and Recurring Themes

In a document as complex and fact-filled as a Baldrige Award application, make sure key messages are clearly communicated. There are 11 Core Values and the application must address all of them. The organization needs to decide at the onset what key

2006 Baldrige Application Development Template
Item 1.1a—Vision and Values

How Senior Leaders:	Set
Organizational Values	Initially set by a cross-functional working group of top leaders, board members, customers, suppliers, and employees at a planning retreat organized by the leadership team. The application of values is reviewed at quarterly progress reviews and updated annually in planning process
Vision	Set as part of the strategic planning process (step 1) and validated by the board of directors and the executive steering committee

How Senior Leaders:	Deploy Vision and Values though the Leadership System
To All Employees	All-hands meetings with a discussion and examples of vision and values on the agenda. A discussion of progress toward vision during each employee performance review and during the two-way *skip-a-level* semiannual meetings
To Key Suppliers	During the annual supplier/partner excellence forum conducted by top leaders and as needed based on performance
To Partners	During the annual supplier/partner excellence forum conducted by top leaders and as needed based on performance
To Customers	During rotating customer-appreciation meetings. Meetings with each key customer are held at least quarterly, more often for major customers. Smaller customers receive reminder tokens such as desk calendars, pens, letter openers, and so on, with values and vision featured as well as hot line access numbers

How Personal Actions of Senior Leaders Reflect Organizational Values	Behavior
Value 1: We are Customer-Focused	• Personally meets with key customers every week • Every meeting agenda has a section relating to progress in meeting and exceeding customer requirements • Customer satisfaction is a required key performance element for all managers and supervisors • No manager can be considered for promotion or pay raises unless his or her customer satisfaction target has been met (both internal and external customers)
Value 2: Innovation is Everyone's Responsibility	• Have set a requirement that every manager and employee, as a part of normal work, must improve one aspect of work each year. This is a part of every performance plan and appraisal. Employee or manager cannot fully meet expectations without improving one aspect of his or her work
Value 3: Value Employees and Promote Empowerment	• Conducts an annual review of decisions and decision authority. Requires managers to develop the decision skills of subordinates and increase the number of decisions made at lower levels. This is a part of the senior leader's personal performance plan and the plan of every manager and supervisor. Top leaders monitor progress quarterly and provide counseling to managers who are not meeting expectations • Conducts pulse survey of employee satisfaction in a different part of the organization each month and works with managers to improve weakest areas • Personally receives employee feedback on aspects of personal leadership effectiveness including fairness, communication, commitment to values, accessibility, and openness to new ideas

Figure 32 Example of Completed Section of the Application Development Template for Item 1.1a(1).

*Note: See the CD-ROM in the back of this book for the complete Baldrige Application Development Templates.

messages reflect the drivers of business success. These key messages should be reflected in each Category and tie together the entire application. This is one of the reasons it becomes so important to design and write the Organizational Profile early and well. Too many applicants ignore the importance of the Organizational Profile as a tool for ensuring alignment and integration within the application. An effective Organizational Profile clearly identifies those things that are important to the organization, its customers and stakeholders, and future success. These selected themes guide the development of the application. We are often asked, "How many themes should an organization include?" The answer depends on how many the organization actually uses. Try starting with three.

It is important to remember that the information presented in the Organizational Profile causes examiners to *expect* certain things in the application. For example, if the organization states it has three customer groups, examiners expect to see processes the organization uses to understand the requirements of all three [3.1a(2)]; assess the satisfaction of all three [3.2b(1)]; and report results of product and service quality [7.1] and satisfaction [7.2] of all three.

Interim Review and Feedback

During the development of an application, conduct *tests* periodically with two groups of people: the senior executive team and customer-contact or individual contributor (front-line) employees.

With senior executive teams, the issue is the rate of growth of those items undergoing intensive improvement efforts and under the direct sponsorship of senior executives. Every Baldrige application effort should use the occasion to drive significant process improvements throughout the organization. The development of an application offers an opportunity to review and improve these initiatives. Each improvement of an existing process is a candidate for inclusion in the application to demonstrate progress.

At the customer-contact or front-line employee level, conduct a *reality check.* Determine whether the application as written reflects the way the organization is actually run. When people are given the opportunity to review an application during the developmental stages, several things happen:

- Front-line people can comment on how closely the write-up reflects reality. It provides the writer(s) an opportunity to calibrate those words with reality.

- It allows employees to take a top-level view—which can be a learning experience in itself.

- It forces the writers to walk in the shoes of the individual contributor—again learning.

Test the Application

As an application comes together, a question asked by everyone—particularly the leadership team—is, "How well are we doing; what's the score?" Although the real value of an application is identifying opportunities for improvement, the competitive nature of people typically comes to the forefront. After all, that spirit helps drive people to higher levels of excellence. Nurture that spirit.

The best means of getting an objective review is to have people familiar with the Baldrige process, but unbiased with respect to the organization and its processes, examine the application. It is surprising how differently outsiders view the workings of the organization. The important aspect of this review is obviously the skill of the reviewers or examiners. The value to the organization is threefold:

- An early assessment—which sets expectations and eliminates surprises

- An opportunity for an early start on improvement initiatives

- A test of understandability by outsiders—which every application ultimately has to pass

Take Time to Celebrate/ Continuously Improve

Developing an application is tough work. At the end of the day, the application represents: 1) a document highlighting the accomplishments and future aspirations of the organization; 2) a plan for getting there; and 3) an operations manual for the organization.

At key milestones in the development of an application, it is important to take time to celebrate the accomplishments just completed. The celebration should be immediate, inclusive, and visible. Such a celebration raises questions within the organization, and it raises expectations—all of which are critical when trying to change and improve the overall performance of the organization. It also presents an ideal opportunity to promote improvement initiatives.

In the words of David Kearns, former CEO of Xerox and one of the greatest leaders of performance excellence in the world, "Quality is a journey without an end." Every company today is faced with the struggle to bring about change—and the pace quickens each year. The Baldrige application is a mechanism that can help focus the energy for change in a most productive manner. Used properly, it can help companies break out of restrictive paradigms and continue on the journey to top levels of performance excellence.

2006 CRITERIA RESPONSE GUIDELINES

The guidelines given in this section are offered to assist Criteria for Performance Excellence users in responding most effectively to the requirements of the 19 Criteria Items. Writing an application for the Baldrige Award involves responding to these requirements in 50 or fewer pages.

The guidelines are presented in three parts:

1. General guidelines regarding the Criteria booklet, including how the Items are formatted

2. Guidelines for responding to Process Items

3. Guidelines for responding to Results Items

General Guidelines

Read the Entire Criteria Booklet

The main sections of the booklet provide an overall orientation to the Criteria, including how responses are to be evaluated for self-assessment or by award examiners. Become thoroughly familiar with the following Criteria booklet sections:

- Criteria for Performance Excellence (also see the Notes below each Item and the Application Development Templates contained on the CD-ROM accompanying this book)

- Scoring System (also see the Scoring Calibration Guide on the CD-ROM)

- Glossary of Key Terms (also see the explanation of confusing terms on page 337 of this book)

- Category and Item Descriptions (also see the flow charts and linkage diagrams and sample effective practices in this book)

Review the Item format and understand how to respond to the Item requirements.

The Item format shows the different parts of Items, the role of each part, and where each part is placed. It is especially important to understand the multiple requirements in the Areas to Address. Item Notes are there to help users understand the Areas.

Each Item is classified as either Process (Categories 1 through 6) or Results (Category 7), depending on the type of information required. Item requirements are presented in question format. Areas to Address include multiple questions. Responses to an Item should answer all questions (however, each question need not be answered separately). Responses to multiple questions within a single Area to Address may be grouped, as appropriate to the organization. These multiple questions serve as a guide in understanding the full meaning of the information being requested.

Carefully read the information describing the linkages, sample effective practices, and process-flow diagrams presented in this book. In particular, be certain to understand how the various requirements of the Criteria are integrated into a comprehensive management system. Then gather data using the electronic application template provided with this book on the accompanying CD-ROM.

Start by Preparing the Organizational Profile

The Organizational Profile is the most appropriate starting point. The Organizational Profile is intended to help everyone—including organizations using the Criteria for self-assessment, application writers, and reviewers—to understand what is most relevant and important to the organization's mission and performance requirements.

Guidelines for Responding to Process Items

Although the Criteria focus on key performance results, these results by themselves offer little diagnostic value. If some results are poor or are improving at rates slower than your competitors' or comparable organizations, it is important to understand why this is so and what might be done to accelerate improvement. The answers to the Process Item questions permit the diagnosis of the organization's most important processes—the ones that yield fast-paced organizational performance improvement and contribute to key outcomes or performance results. Diagnosis and feedback depend heavily on the content and completeness of Item responses. For this reason, it is important to respond to these Items by providing clear, complete key process information.

Understand the Meaning of "How"

Process Items include questions that begin with the word *how*. Responses should outline key process steps that addresses approach, deployment, learning, and integration. Responses lacking such process detail, or merely providing an example, are referred to in the Scoring Guidelines as *anecdotal information,* and will score very low.

Understand the Meaning of "What"

Two types of questions in Process Items begin with the word *what*. Answers to these questions provide examiners with background information to help set a context for the assessment they are about to perform. This type of question requests basic information on the elements or components of key processes. Although it may be helpful to include who performs the work, merely stating who does not permit effective diagnosis or feedback. This type of question may also request information on key findings, plans, objectives, goals, or measures. This latter type of question sets the context for showing alignment and integration in the performance management system.

For example, when key strategic objectives, action plans, human resource development plans, and key performance measures are identified in Categories 1 through 6, examiners will expect to find related results reported. If these expected results are not presented, examiners may assume they are missing and reduce the score accordingly.

The linkage (circle) diagrams in this book will help identify the systems and processes that interrelate and should be clearly aligned in the application.

Show That Processes Are Systematic

Ensure that the response describes a systematic approach, not merely an anecdotal example. Systematic approaches are disciplined, consistent, repeatable, and predictable. At the higher scoring levels it is expected that systematic approaches involve the use of data and information for evaluation, subsequent improvement, and sharing across the organization. In other words, the approaches are consistent over time, build in learning, evaluation, improvement, innovation, and sharing, and demonstrate maturity. Scores above 50 percent rely on clear evidence that approaches are systematic, evaluated, and refined.

Show Deployment

Ensure that the response gives clear and sufficient information on deployment in different parts of the organization. One must be able to distinguish from a response whether an approach described is used in one, some, most, or all parts of the organization. If the process is widely used in the organization, be sure to state where it is deployed.

Deployment can be shown compactly by using summary tables that outline what is done in different parts of the organization. *This is a particularly effective supplement when the systematic approach is described in a narrative.*

Show Evidence of Learning

Processes should include fact-based evaluation *and* improvement cycles that are based on the the evaluation. Process improvements should be shared with other appropriate units of the organization to enable organizational learning. Each key process should include a brief explanation of how fact-based evaluations occur, what is covered, a list of refinements that have been made based on the evaluations, and how those refinements have been implemented throughout the organization, as appropriate.

Show Integration

Integration shows process, plan, measures, and action alignment and harmonization that generate organizational effectiveness and efficiencies. For example, strategic objectives listed in 2.1b(1) must address challenges in P2b [2.1b(2)] and timetables for implementation [2.1b(1)] must be consistent with the measures of organizational performance [4.1a(1)] and the frequency of senior leader reviews [4.1b]. If senior leaders review progress toward a specific customer-satisfaction objective each quarter, then customer-satisfaction data must be collected at least quarterly, and timetables in 2.1b(1) should indicate the desired progress expected each quarter. Otherwise, leaders will have no fact-basis for determining whether the organization is on track or not. This lack of alignment between senior leader review frequency and projected time lines is a failure of integration.

Show Focus and Consistency

The response demonstrates that the organization is focused on key processes and on improvements that offer the greatest potential to improve business performance and accomplish organization action plans.

There are four important factors to consider regarding focus and consistency:

1. The Organizational Profile should make clear what is important.

2. Strategic objectives and action plans should highlight areas of greatest focus and describe how deployment is accomplished.

3. Descriptions of organizational-level analysis and review (Item 4.1) should show how the organization uses performance information to set priorities for improvement.

4. The Process Management Category should highlight product, service, support, and supplier processes that are key to overall performance

and show how they are used to achieve strategic objectives.

Showing focus and consistency in the Process Items and tracking corresponding measures in the Results Items should help align (and possibly improve) organizational performance.

Respond Fully to Item Requirements

Ensure that the response fully addresses all important parts of each Item and each Area to Address. Missing or incomplete information will be interpreted by examiners as a system deficiency—a gap and potential opportunity for improvement. All Areas to Address should be included in the application. Individual components of an Area to Address (subparts) may be addressed individually or together. When using the Application Development Template in this book it is easy to see where gaps exist. Organizations can use this information to begin closing gaps even before the examiners conduct their analysis and prepare the feedback report.

Cross-Reference When Appropriate

Although each Item response should be self-contained, some responses to different Items might be mutually reinforcing. For example, leaders may use parts of the strategy development process to set vision [1.1]. It is best to refer to the other responses, rather than to repeat information.

Use a Compact Format

Applicants should make the best use of the 50 application pages permitted. Complete sentences are not required when lists convey the information just as well. Use flowcharts, tables, and *bulletized* text to present information concisely. Use color to focus attention. For example, whenever an improved process is described, use blue-colored text.

Refer to the Scoring Calibration Guidelines

The evaluation of Process Item responses is accomplished by consideration of the Criteria Item requirements and the maturity of the organization's approaches, breadth of deployment, extent of learning.

and integration of other elements of the performance management system, as described in the Scoring Guidelines and clarified in the Scoring Calibration Guide contained in this book and on the accompanying CD. Therefore, applicants should consider both the Criteria and the Scoring Guidelines in preparing responses. *In particular, remember that in order to score over 50 percent, organizations must have in place a fact-based evaluation process and corresponding improvements for all of the basic Item requirements and some of the overall requirements. The Scoring Guidelines make this requirement applicable to all items in Categories 1 through 6. Even if the Criteria questions for the Item do not ask for a description of evaluation and improvement techniques, it will help the examiners give you full credit for your processes if an explanation is provided to show how the processes are systematically evaluated and subsequently refined. List the process improvements that have been made during the last three to four years and use a colored font.*

GUIDELINES FOR RESPONDING TO RESULTS ITEMS

The Baldrige Criteria place great emphasis (and 45 percent of the score) on results. Category 7 Items call for results related to all key requirements, stakeholders, and goals. Examiners are likely to prepare a list of results they expect to find in Category 7 based on process details contained in Categories 1–6.

Focus on Reporting the Most Critical Organizational Results

Results reported should cover the most important requirements for success highlighted in the Organizational Profile and the Strategic Planning, Customer and Market Focus, and Process Management Categories, and included in responses to other Items, such as Human Resource Focus (Category 5) and Process Management (Category 6).

Four key requirements for effective reporting of results data include the following:

- Results show performance levels on a meaningful measurement scale.

- Trends to show directions of results and rates of change, together with an indicator of the desired direction.

- Data to show how results compare with those of other, relevant organizations.

- Breadth and importance of results to show that all important results are included and segmented, that is, by important customer, employee, process, and product-line groups.

Complete Data

Be sure that results data are displayed for all relevant customer, financial, market, human resource, operational performance, and supplier-performance characteristics. If you identify relevant performance measures and goals in other parts of the analysis (for example, Categories 1 through 6), be sure to include the results of these performance characteristics in Category 7. As each relevant performance measure is identified in the assessment process, create a blank chart and label the axes. Define all units of measure, especially if they are industry-specific or unique to the applicant. As data are collected, populate the charts. If expected data are not provided in the application, examiners may assume that the trends or levels are not good. Missing data drive the score down in the same way that poor trends do.

After you complete all of the data in Category 7, review the Organizational Profile and the processes described in Categories 1 through 6. Make a list of all of the results that an examiner would expect to find in Category 7. Then, cross-check this list with the data provided in Category 7. If any *expected* data are missing, be sure to add the appropriate charts or graphs.

Many examiners actually prepare a list of results that appear to be relevant based on information provided in the application. I refer to this list as a *table of expected results.* (See pages 328–329)

Actual Time Periods for Tracking Trends

No minimum period of time is required for trend data. Reporting-time intervals between data points should be meaningful for the specific measures reported. Trends might be much shorter for some of the organization's more recent improvement activities and span several years for others. Because of the importance of showing deployment and focus, new data should be included even if trends and comparisons are not yet well established. It is better to report four quarterly measures covering a one-year period than two measures for the beginning and end of the year. The four measures may help to demonstrate a sustained trend (if one exists, the data points cannot be considered a trend).

Compact Presentation

Results should be reported compactly by using graphs and tables. Graphs and tables should be labeled for easy interpretation. Results over time or compared with others should be *normalized*—presented in a way (such as with the use of ratios) that takes into account various size factors. For example, reporting safety trends in terms of lost workdays per 100,000 employee-hours worked would be more meaningful than total lost workdays, if the number of employees has varied over the reporting period or if comparison organizations are different in terms of size, volume, and other key factors. When reporting cost data over many years, it may be appropriate to show constant (for example, 2001) dollars.

Integrate Results with Text

Descriptions of results and the results themselves should be in close proximity in the Award application. Trends that show a significant positive or negative change should be explained. Use figure numbers that correspond to Items. For example, the third figure for Item 7.1 should be 7.1-3 (see Figure 33).

Figure 33 illustrates data an applicant might present as part of a response to Item 7.1, Product and Service Results. In the Organizational Profile, in Item 2.1b(1), and in Item 3.1, the applicant has indicated on-time delivery as a key customer requirement.

Using the graph, the following characteristics of clear and effective data presentation are illustrated:

- A figure number is provided for reference to the graph in the text.

- Both axes and units of measure are clearly labeled.

- Trend lines report data for a key business requirement—on-time delivery.

- Results are presented for several years.

- Appropriate comparisons are clearly shown.

- The organization shows, using a single graph, that its three divisions separately track on-time delivery.

- If different segments or components exist, show each as a separate measure. Avoid aggregating data when the segments are meaningful.

- An upward-pointing arrow appears on the graph, indicating that increasing values are *good*. (A downward-pointing arrow would indicate that decreasing values are *good*.) The *desired direction* arrows may seem obvious to the authors of the application, but some desired directions are not obvious to examiners who are not familiar with certain data displays.

To help interpret the Scoring Guidelines, the following comments on the graphed results in the previous sample would be appropriate.

- The current overall organization performance level is excellent. This conclusion is supported by the comparison with competitors and with a *world-class* level.

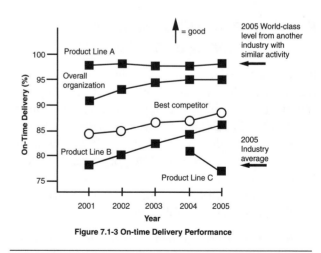

Figure 7.1-3 On-time Delivery Performance

Figure 33 Linking results with text.

- The organization exhibits excellent improvement trends.

- Product Line A is the current performance leader—showing sustained high performance and a slightly positive trend. Product Line B shows rapid improvement. Its current performance is near that of the best industry competitor but trails the world-class level.

- Product Line C—a new product—is having early problems with on-time delivery. (The applicant should analyze and explain the early problems in the application text.) Its current performance is not yet at the level of the best industry competitor.

Break Out Data

This point, mentioned earlier, bears repeating: avoid aggregating the data. Where appropriate, break data into meaningful components. If you serve several different customer groups, display performance and satisfaction data for each group. As Figure 34 demonstrates, only one of the three trends is positive, although the average is positive. Examiners will seek component data when aggregate data are reported. Presenting aggregate data instead of meaningful component data is likely to reduce the score.

Data and Measures

Comparison data are required for all items in Category 7. These data are designed to demonstrate how well the organization is performing. To judge performance excellence, one must possess comparison data. In Figure 35, performance is represented by the line connecting the squares. Clearly the organization is improving, but how *good* is it? Without comparison data, answering that question is difficult.

Now consider the chart with comparison data added (Figure 36).

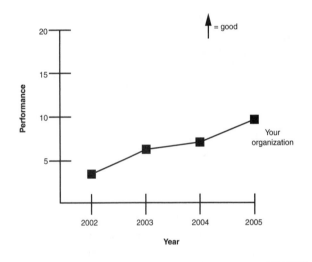

Figure 35   Getting better.

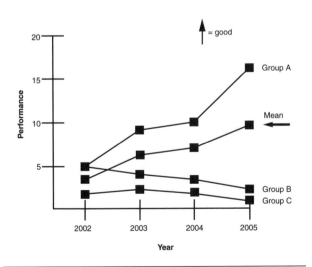

Figure 34   Breakout group data.

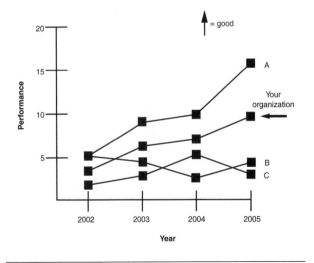

Figure 36   Comparison data.

Note the position of three hypothetical comparisons, represented by the letters A, B, and C. Consider the following two scenarios:

1. If A represents the industry average and both B and C represent competitors, then examiners would conclude that your organization's performance was substandard, even though it is improving.

2. If A represents a best-in-class (benchmark) organization and B represents the industry average, then examiners would conclude that your organizational performance is very good.

In both scenarios, the organizational performance remained the same, but the examiner's perception of it changed based on changes in comparison data.

Measures

Agreeing on relevant measures is difficult for organizations in the early phases of quality and performance improvement. The task is easier if the following guidelines are considered:

- *Clearly define customer requirements.* Clear customer requirements are easier to measure. Clearly defined customer requirements require probing and suggesting. For example, the customer of a new computer wants the equipment to be reliable. After probing to find what *reliable* means, we discover that: a) the customer expects it to work all of the time; b) prompt appearance by a repair technician at the site if it does stop working; c) immediate access to parts; and d) the ability to fix it right the first time.

- *For each of the four requirements defined, identify a measure.* For example, mean time between failures is one indicator of reliability, but it does not account for all of the variation in customer satisfaction. Since the customer is concerned with run time, we must assess how long it took the repair technician to arrive at the site, diagnose the problem, and fix it. Measures include time in hours, days, weeks between failures, time in minutes between the service call and the computer regaining capability (time to fix), time in minutes waiting for parts, and the associated costs in terms of cash and worker effort.

- *Collect and report data.* Several charts might be required to display these factors, or one chart with several lines.

Refer to the Scoring Guidelines

Considerations in the evaluation of Results Item responses include the Criteria Item requirements and the significance of the results trends, actual performance levels, relevant comparative data, alignment with important elements of your performance management system, and the strength of the improvement process relative to the Scoring Guidelines. Therefore, you need to consider both the Criteria and the Scoring Guidelines.

Scoring System

Scoring dimensions are classified according to the kinds of information and/or data being reviewed. The two types of Items and their designations are:

1. Process (for the 13 Items in Categories 1 through 6)

2. Results (for the six Items in Category 7)

Applicants should furnish information relating to these dimensions. Specific factors for these dimensions are described in the following paragraphs.

Process

Process refers to the methods the organization uses and improves to address the Item requirements in Categories 1–6. The four factors used to evaluate process are Approach, Deployment, Learning, and Integration (A–D–L–I).

Approach refers to:

- The methods used to accomplish the process

- The appropriateness of the methods to the Item requirement.

- The effectiveness of use of the methods

- The degree to which the approach is repeatable and based on reliable data and information (for example, systematic)

Deployment refers to the extent to which:

- The approach is applied in addressing Item requirements relevant and important to the organization

- The approach is applied consistently

- The approach is used by all appropriate work units

Learning refers to:

- Refining the approach through cycles of evaluation and improvement

- Encouraging breakthrough change to the approach through innovation

- Sharing of refinements and innovation with other relevant work units and processes in the organization

Integration refers to the extent to which:

- The approach is aligned with the organizational needs identified in other Criteria Category or Item requirements

- The measures, information, and improvement systems are complementary across processes and work units

- The plans, processes, results, analysis, learning, and actions are harmonized across processes and work units to support organization-wide goals

For Process Items (Categories 1–6), approach–deployment–learning–integration are linked to emphasize that descriptions of approach should always indicate the deployment—consistent with the specific requirements of the Item. As processes mature, their description also should indicate how cycles of learning, as well as integration with other processes and work units, occur. Although the approach–deployment–learning–integration factors are linked, feedback to Award applicants reflects strengths and/or opportunities for improvement in any or all of these factors.

Results

Results refers to the organization's outputs and outcomes in achieving the requirements in Items 7.1–7.6. The four factors used to evaluate results include:

- Current level of performance

- Rate (that is, slope of trend data) and breadth (how widely deployed and shared) of the organization's performance improvements

- Performance relative to appropriate comparisons and/or benchmarks

- Linkage of results measures (often through segmentation) to important customer, product and service, market, process, and action-plan performance requirements identified in the Organizational Profile and in Process Items

Results Items call for data showing performance levels, improvement rates, and relevant comparative data for key measures and indicators of organizational performance. Results Items also call for data on breadth of performance improvements. This is directly related to deployment and organizational learning; if improvement processes are widely shared and deployed, there should be corresponding results. A score for a Results Item is thus a composite based upon overall performance, taking into account the rate and breadth of improvements and their importance to the Item requirements and your business or mission.

"Importance" As a Scoring Factor

The Process and Results evaluation dimensions described previously are critical to evaluation and feedback. However, another key consideration in evaluation and feedback is the importance of key process and results to key business factors. The areas of greatest importance should be identified in the Organizational Profile and in Items such as 2.1, 2.2, 3.1, 5.1, and 6.1. Key customer requirements, competitive environment, key strategic objectives, and action plans are particularly important.

Assignment of Scores

The following guidelines should be observed in assigning scores to Item responses:

- All Areas to Address should be included in Item responses. Also, responses should reflect what is important to the organization.

- In assigning a score to an Item, examiners first decide which scoring range (for example, 50 to 65 percent) is most descriptive of the organization's achievement level as presented in the Item response. *Most descriptive of the organization's achievement level* represents the best fit and can include some gaps in one or more of the A-D-L-I (process) factors or results factors for the chosen scoring range. An organization's achievement level is based on a holistic view of either the four process or four results factors in aggregate and not on a tallying or averaging of independent assessments against each of the four factors. Every requirement in a scoring range does not have to be met to score in that range. All requirements in a scoring range would have to be met to score at the top of that scoring range. Assigning the actual score within the chosen range requires evaluating whether the Item response is closer to the statements in the next-higher or next-lower scoring range.

- A Process Item score of 50 percent represents an approach that meets the overall requirements of the Item, that is deployed consistently and to most work units covered by the Item, that has been through some cycles of improvement and learning, and that addresses the key organizational needs. Higher scores reflect greater achievement, demonstrated by broader deployment, significant organizational learning, and increased integration.

- A Results Item score of 50 percent represents a clear indication of improvement trends and/or good levels of performance with appropriate comparative data in the results areas covered in the Item and important to the organization's business or mission. Higher scores reflect better improvement rates and/or levels of importance, better comparative performance, and broader coverage and integration with business or mission requirements.

Calibration Guidelines

Defining scoring terms may help reduce unnecessary variability. I have frequently asked examiners to define, in terms of percent, the meaning of *most*. Some define *most* as 51 percent. Others have a higher standard, even up to 90 percent. Defining *good* and *very good* is even more difficult. To reduce this variability, the following guidelines are suggested:

Few:	Up to 15 percent (major gaps in deployment exist)
Some:	Greater than 15 percent to 30 percent (deployed, although in the early stages)
Many:	Greater than 30 percent to 50 percent (well-deployed, although deployment may vary in some areas)
Most:	Greater than 50 percent to 80 percent (well-deployed, with no apparent gaps in most areas)
Nearly All:	Greater than 80 percent to less than 100 percent (fully deployed, with no significant gaps in any areas or work units)
All:	100 percent
Good:	*For example, better than average for relevant competitors or similar providers; above industry average.*
Very Good:	*For example, in the top quartile of competitors or similar providers.*
Excellent:	*For example, at or near the top of competitors or similar providers; top 5 percent; best benchmark; better than best competitor.*

Score	Baldrige Scoring Guidelines For Use With Categories 1–6 Process
0% or 5%	• No systematic approach is evident; information is anecdotal. (A) • Little or no deployment of an approach is evident. (D) • An improvement orientation is not evident; improvement is achieved through reacting to problems. (L) • No organizational alignment is evident; individual areas or work units operate independently. (I)
10%, 15%, 20%, or 25%	• The beginning of a systematic approach to the basic requirements of the Item is evident. (A) • The approach is in the early stages of deployment in most areas or work units, inhibiting progress in achieving the basic requirements of the Item. (D) • Early stages of a transition from reacting to problems to a general improvement orientation are evident. (L) • The approach is aligned with other areas or work units largely through joint problem solving. (I)
30%, 35%, 40%, or 45%	• An effective, systematic approach, responsive to the basic requirements of the Item, is evident. (A) • The approach is deployed, although some areas or work units are in early stages of deployment. (D) • The beginning of a systematic approach to evaluation and improvement of key processes is evident. (L) • The approach is in early stages of alignment with your basic organizational needs identified in response to the other Criteria Categories. (I)
50%, 55%, 60%, or 65%	• An effective, systematic approach, responsive to the overall requirements of the Item, is evident. (A) • The approach is well deployed, although deployment may vary in some areas or work units. (D) • A fact-based, systematic evaluation and improvement process and some organizational learning are in place for improving the efficiency and effectiveness of key processes. (L) • The approach is aligned with your organizational needs identified in response to the other Criteria Categories. (I)
70%, 75%, 80%, or 85%	• An effective, systematic approach, responsive to the multiple requirements of the Item, is evident. (A) • The approach is well deployed, with no significant gaps. (D) • Fact-based, systematic evaluation and improvement and organizational learning are key management tools; there is clear evidence of refinement and innovation as a result of organizational-level analysis and sharing. (L) • The approach is integrated with your organizational needs identified in response to the other Criteria Items. (I)
90%, 95%, or 100%	• An effective, systematic approach, fully responsive to the multiple requirements of the Item, is evident. (A) • The approach is fully deployed without significant weaknesses or gaps in any areas or work units. (D) • Fact-based, systematic evaluation and improvement and organizational learning are key organization-wide tools; refinement and innovation, backed by analysis and sharing, are evident throughout the organization. (L) • The approach is well integrated with your organizational needs identified in response to the other Criteria Items. (I)

Score	Baldrige Scoring Guidelines For Use With Category 7 Results
0% or 5%	• There are no organizational performance results or poor results in areas reported. • Trend data are either not reported or show mainly adverse trends. • Comparative information is not reported. • Results are not reported for any areas of importance to your organization's key mission or business requirements.
10%, 15%, 20%, or 25%	• A few organizational performance results are reported; there are some improvements and/or early good performance levels in a few areas. • Little or no trend data are reported. • Little or no comparative information is reported. • Results are reported for a few areas of importance to your organization's key mission or business requirements.
30%, 35%, 40%, or 45%	• Improvements and/or good performance levels are reported in many areas addressed in the Item requirements. • Early stages of developing trends are evident. • Early stages of obtaining comparative information are evident. • Results are reported for many areas of importance to your organization's key mission or business requirements.
50%, 55%, 60%, or 65%	• Improvement trends and/or good performance levels are reported for most areas addressed in the Item requirements. • No pattern of adverse trends and no poor performance levels are evident in areas of importance to your organization's key mission or business requirements. • Some trends and/or current performance levels—evaluated against relevant comparisons and/or benchmarks—show areas of good to very good relative performance. • Organizational performance results address most key customer, market, and process requirements.
70%, 75%, 80%, or 85%	• Current performance is good to excellent in most areas of importance to the Item requirements. • Most improvement trends and/or current performance levels are sustained. • Many to most reported trends and/or current performance levels—evaluated against relevant comparisons and/or benchmarks—show areas of leadership and very good relative performance. • Organizational performance results address most key customer, market, process, and action plan requirements.
90%, 95%, or 100%	• Current performance is excellent in most areas of importance to the Item requirements. • Excellent improvement trends and/or sustained excellent performance levels are reported in most areas. • Evidence of industry and benchmark leadership is demonstrated in many areas. • Organizational performance results fully address key customer, market, process, and action plan requirements.

PROCESS TERMS

Systematic

Look for evidence of a system—a repeatable, predictable process that uses data and information to promote improvement and learning—that is used to fulfill the requirements of the Item. The application should briefly describe the system, explain how it works, how it is evaluated, and what refinements have been made as a result. The application must communicate the nature of the system to people who may not be familiar with it.

Integrated

Determine the extent to which the system is integrated or interconnected with other elements of the overall management system. Show the linkages across categories for key themes such as those displayed earlier for each Item. Consider the extent to which the work of senior leaders is integrated. For example:

1. Senior executives (Item 1.1) are responsible for shaping and communicating the organization's values and performance expectations throughout the leadership system and workforce.

2. They develop relationships with key customers (Item 3.2) and monitor customer satisfaction (Item 7.2), related product and service quality (Item 7.1), and organization performance results (Items 7.3, 7.4, 7.5, and 7.6).

3. With this in mind, senior executives participate in strategy development (Item 2.1) and ensure the alignment of the workplace to achieve strategic objectives (Item 2.2).

4. Leaders must convert goals and strategic objectives into measurable milestones and time lines [Item 2.1b(1)] to serve as a basis for monitoring performance [Item 4.1b(1)] and setting improvement priorities [Item 4.1b(2)]. (Time lines [2.1b(1)] should be set to coincide with the review cycle of senior leaders. If they review progress quarterly, then quarterly time lines or milestones should be set.)

5. This information, when properly collected and analyzed (Item 4.1), helps leaders plan and monitor progress effectively and make more informed decisions to optimize customer satisfaction and operational and financial performance.

6. Senior executives may also become involved in supporting new structures to improve employee performance and motivation (Item 5.1), training effectiveness (Item 5.2), and employee well-being and satisfaction (Item 5.3).

Similar relationships (linkages) exist between other items. In the application, highlight these linkages using cross-references to demonstrate integration.

Prevention-Based

Prevention-based systems are characterized by actions to minimize or prevent the existence or recurrence of problems. In an ideal world, all systems would produce perfect products and flawless service. Since that rarely happens, high-performing organizations are able to act quickly to recover from a problem (fight the fire) and then take action to identify the root cause of the problem and prevent it from surfacing again. The nature of the problem, its root cause, and appropriate corrective action are communicated to all relevant employees so that they can implement the corrective action in their area before the problem arises.

Continuous Improvement

Continuous improvement is a bedrock theme for top-performing organizations. It is the method that helps organizations establish and keep their competitive edge. Continuous improvement involves the fact-based evaluation and improvement of processes crucial to organizational success. Evaluation and improvement completes the high-performance management cycle. Fact-based evaluations can be complex statistical processes, or as simple as a focus group discussing and recording what went right, what went wrong, and how it could be done better. The key to optimum performance lies in the pervasive evaluation and improvement of all processes. By practicing systematic, pervasive, continuous improvement, time becomes the organization's ally. Consistent fact-based evaluation and refinement practices with correspondingly good deployment can drive the score to 60 percent or 70 percent, and higher. Without evaluation and refinement it is difficult to score above 45 to 55 percent.

Complete

Each Item contains one or more Areas to Address. Many Areas to Address contain several subparts. Failure to address all Areas and subparts can push the score lower. If an Area to Address or part of an Area does not apply to an organization, it is important to explain why. Otherwise, examiners may conclude that the system is incomplete.

Anecdotal

If the application narrative describes a process or procedure that is random, ad hoc, or anecdotal and does not address the Criteria in a predictable, disciplined manner, it is worth very little (zero to five points).

Deployment

The extent to which processes are widely used by organization units affects scoring. For example, a systematic approach that is well-integrated, evaluated consistently, and refined routinely may be worth 70 percent or more. However, if that process is not in place in all key parts of the organization, the score may be reduced, perhaps significantly, depending on the nature and extent of the deployment gap.

Major gaps are expected to exist at the 5 percent to 25 percent level. At the 30 percent and higher levels, no major gaps exist, although some units may still be at the early stages of development. At the 70 percent to 85 percent level, no major gaps exist and the approach is well-integrated with organizational needs identified in other parts of the Criteria.

Summary

For each Item examined, the process is rated as follows:

- Anecdotal: zero percent to 5 percent

- Beginnings of a systematic approach to meet basic Item requirements (perhaps recently piloted or implemented process): 10 percent to 25 percent

- Effective, systematic approach in place to meet basic Item requirements: 30 to 35 percent

- Effective, systematic approach in place to meet basic Item requirements, with the beginnings (planned or piloted) of a process to evaluate and improve: 40 to 45 percent

- Effective, systematic approach in place to meet overall Item requirements, with fact-based evaluation process in place: 50 percent

- Effective, systematic approach in place to meet overall Item requirements, with fact-based evaluation process in place and at least one cycle of refinements based on the evaluation: 60 to 65 percent

- Effective, systematic approach in place to meet multiple Item requirements, with fact-based evaluation process in place and multiple cycles of refinement, innovation, and integration based on the evaluation: 70 percent to 85 percent

- Integrated: 70 percent to 100 percent

- Refined: 60 percent to 100 percent

- Widely used, with no significant gaps in deployment: 70 percent or greater

Systematic, integrated, prevention-based, and continuously improved systems that are widely used are generally easier to describe than undeveloped systems. Moreover, describing activities or anecdotes does not convince examiners that an integrated, systematic process is in place. In fact, simply describing activities and anecdotes suggests that an integrated system does not exist. However, by tracing critical success threads through the relevant Items in the Criteria, the organization demonstrates that its system is integrated and fully deployed.

To demonstrate system integration, pick several critical success factors and show how the organization manages them. For example, trace the leadership focus on performance.

- Identify performance-related data that are collected to indicate progress against goals [Item 4.1].

- Show how performance data are analyzed and reviewed by senior leaders [Item 4.1b], and used to set priorities for work and resources [Item 4.1b(2)].

- Show how performance effectiveness is considered in the planning process [Item 2.1a] and how work at all levels is aligned to increase performance [Item 2.2a].

- Demonstrate the impact of human resource management [Item 5.1] and training [Item 5.2] on performance and show how both tie to the strategy and human resource plans [Item 2.2a(4)].

- Show how value creation and support processes [Items 6.1 and 6.2] are enhanced to improve results.

- Report the results of improved performance [Items 7.1, 7.2, 7.3, 7.4, 7.5, and 7.6] and be sure all key results are reported with key comparative or benchmark data included.

- Determine how improved product and service quality [Item 7.1] affects customer satisfaction levels [Item 7.2].

- Show how customer requirements and preferences [Item 3.1] and concerns [Item 3.2] are used to drive the selection of key measures [Item 4.1] and impact design and delivery processes [Items 6.1 and 6.2].

Note that the application is limited to 50 pages, not including the five-page Organizational Profile. This may not be sufficient to describe in great detail the process, results, integration, and refinement of all systematic critical success factors, goals, or processes. Thus, it is better to pick the most important few, indicate them as such, and then thoroughly describe the threads and linkages throughout the application.

Clarifying the Baldrige Scoring Requirements

INTRODUCTION

The Baldrige Criteria, together with the Scoring Guidelines, are supposed to help examiners identify the key strengths and vital few areas needing improvement to help leaders focus their resources on the steps needed to get to the next developmental level. Unfortunately, for several years, national and state examiners have tended to *nit-pick* applicants by citing minute, inconsequential opportunities for improvement—even when basic or fundamental processes were not in place. Because of the tendency to *nit-pick*, scores were inappropriately low and comments were not properly focused.

To avoid this problem, the Baldrige Award office redefined the Scoring Guidelines to focus attention on a hierarchy of requirements moving from *basic* to *overall* to *multiple*. The purpose of this hierarchy was to keep examiners focused on the most important factors each applicant needed to put in place to get to the next level and not turn the examination process into a compliance checklist.

In other words, the strengths comments were supposed to describe the processes and systems an applicant had in place that supported or justified the score assigned. The opportunities for improvement were supposed to identify the processes or systems that were not in place that kept the organization from moving to the next higher level. By listing insignificant issues (nits) in the feedback report, an applicant might spend resources fixing a problem that had relatively low impact and overlook a key area essential for growth and improvement.

I believe that the Baldrige Award office was correct in identifying the need to prevent examiners from *nit-picking* while getting them to focus on the vital few issues. To achieve this objective, *it is essential that all examiners reviewing applications for a state, regional, or "in-house" Baldrige-based recognition program interpret the Criteria and scoring guidelines consistently.* Unfortunately, the process and definitions presented in the 2003 to 2006 Criteria and Scoring Guidelines do not achieve this objective.

From my experience in training thousands of examiners *each year* on the use of the Baldrige criteria, I have found that the greatest source of unacceptable variation is caused by examiners who each believe different aspects of the Criteria are *most important*. The lack of clarity in defining precisely what systems and/or processes are required for each scoring level and for each Item forces examiners to decide for themselves the elements of each Item they deem more critical than others. With many different opinions of what constitutes *basic* and *overall* requirements, examiners' comments and scores have not been consistent, either from team to team or examiner to examiner. For example, in recent examiner training classes conducted, I asked the examiners to follow the Baldrige definitions and list the factors they would look for as a basic requirement of *Senior Leadership [Item 1.1]* of the business criteria. Each class generated a list similar to the following.

The applicant organization and its senior leaders must have in place processes to:

- *Set values and vision*

- *Empower employees*

- *Focus on customers*

- *Deploy vision and values to all employees*

- *Deploy values to key partners, suppliers, and customers*

- *Require legal and ethical behavior*

- *Encourage two-way communication with employees and customers*

- *Make sure their actions match their values*

- *Ensure steady performance improvement, innovation, and agility throughout the organization*

- *Personally participate in succession planning*

- *Develop future leaders*

- *Reinforce high performance and a customer and business focus by actively rewarding and recognizing employees*

- *Focus on improving performance*

- *Balance value for customers and stakeholders*

The list of *basic* requirements that the individual examiners produced (required for a score of 10 to 45 percent) more accurately defines most of the *multiple-level* requirements (needed for a score of 70 to 100 percent). With this kind of variation in defining the *basic* requirements of Item 1.1, a relatively straightforward Item, imagine the differences a team of six to 10 examiners will have interpreting the requirements of the 13 Items in Categories 1 through 6 that use the Process Scoring Guidelines. It is difficult to conduct a consistently accurate assessment when each examiner's interpretation of the *basic* and *overall* requirements is so varied.

During the past three years, many state and in-house organizational award programs tested and subsequently implemented a new approach to scoring that produces more consistently accurate assessments in both the government and private sectors. This technique provides examiners with a more precise and consistent definition of *basic* and *overall* requirements for each Item (the multiple-level requirements are already precise).

By providing clearer definitions of Criteria requirements, examiners have been able to more accurately and consistently assess, score, and provide meaningful feedback to participating organizations or quality award applicants.

Official Baldrige Definitions

This section presents the actual definitions (in italic type) from the Baldrige Award Office that created the confusion.

Basic Requirements

The term "basic requirements" refers to the topic Criteria users need to address when responding to the most central concept of an Item. Basic requirements are the fundamental theme of that Item. In the Criteria, the basic requirements of each Item are presented as the Item title question.

Only meeting the basic requirements of the Item could result in a score at the 10 to 45 percent levels depending on the level of development of the basic systems and on the extent of deployment of those systems.

Accordingly, for Item 1.1, an organization can meet the *basic* requirements by providing *Senior Leadership* (the title of item 1.1). For Item 2.1, the organization must have a process for *Strategy Development* (also undefined). What do these terms mean? What does "strategy development process" include? There is simply not enough information presented by these terms to ensure a consistent review, which is critical to ensure appropriate feedback and an accurate score.

Overall Requirements

The term "overall requirements" refers to the topics Criteria users need to address when responding to the central theme of an Item. Overall requirements address the most significant features of the Item requirements. In the Criteria, the overall requirements of each Item are presented in one or more introductory sentences printed in bold.

Meeting the overall requirements of the Item could result in a score at the 50, 55, 60, or 65 percent level depending on the maturity of the overall systems, the extent of deployment of those systems, and the extent of systematic evaluation, refinement, and integration of those systems.

More detail is provided to define the *overall* level than is provided for the *basic* level. However, the explanation is still too limited to enable examiners to provide a consistent review, appropriate feedback, and an accurate score.

For example, under the requirements of Item 4.1, the organization must measure, analyze, align, review, and improve its performance at all levels and in all parts of the organization. Under Item 2.1, the organization must have a system in place to establish its strategy and strategic objectives and address its strategic challenges. Ask any five people what systems might be needed to meet these requirements and you will receive five different answers.

Multiple Requirements

The term "multiple requirements" refers to the individual questions Criteria users need to answer within each Area to Address. These questions constitute the details of an Item's requirements. They are presented in black text under each Item's Area(s) to Address.

Meeting the multiple requirements of the Item could result in a score at the 70 to 100 percent levels, depending on the maturity of the multiple systems, the extent of deployment of those systems, and the extent of systematic evaluation, refinement, innovation, and improved integration of those systems.

Unlike the *basic* and *overall* definitions, the *multiple*-level definitions are quite clear. Sufficient detail is provided to enable examiners to identify the elements of management systems and processes that must be in place to score at the 70 percent or higher level.

Importance As a Scoring Factor

Examiners must determine the extent to which the management systems and processes are responsive to the organization's *key business requirements* and *changing business needs* (especially at the 50 percent and higher scoring bands). Accordingly, examiners should consider the extent to which processes in the application appear to support or respond to key business needs that were expressed in the Organizational Profile and in Items such as:

- 2.1 Strategic objectives

- 2.2 Action plans and measures that derive from the strategic objectives and are deployed to all levels of the organization

- 3.1 The definition of customer segments, their requirements, and preferences for products and services that are most likely to drive loyalty

- 5.1 Work systems and systems to align employee feedback, reward, recognition, and compensation with high-performance, business, and customer-focused objectives

- 5.2 Training and education supports strategy and action plans.

- 6.1 Key value creation and business processes critical to organizational success and growth

Key customer requirements, competitive environment, strategic objectives, and action plans are particularly important to consider when determining the relevance of the systems and processes described in the application.

Clarifications for Scoring

The definitions on the following pages are intended to help improve consistency of interpretation and are offered as guidelines only. Prior to using these clarifying statements, the cognizant award program should reach consensus that the Basic, Overall, and Multiple requirements listed on the following pages appropriately capture the levels and meaning of the Criteria. Examiners please remember that the notes at the end of each Item provide additional clarification about information that is expected as part of the review. The full version of the Scoring Calibration Guide, which is on the CD-ROM included with this book, includes cross-referenced Notes for each Criteria Item.)

- The word *should* creates an expectation that the process is in place. For example, Note 1 for Item 1.1 indicates that, "Organizational vision [1.1a(1)] should set the context for strategic objectives and action plans, which are described in Items 2.1 and 2.2." This means that examiners will be looking for, and expect to find these linkages.

- The word *might* is meant to suggest alternatives or examples, but not establish the expectation that the process is required. For example, Note 3 in 1.1 indicates that "A focus on action

[1.1b(2)] considers both the people and the hard assets of the organization. It includes ongoing improvements in productivity that may be achieved through eliminating waste or reducing cycle time, and it might use techniques such as Six Sigma and Lean Production. It also includes the actions to accomplish the organization's strategic objectives." This means that examiners cannot require techniques such as Six Sigma and Lean Production and they must not write an Opportunity for Improvement comment or lower the score if the organization does not use such approaches.

To make the following clarifying tables more complete, for the process Items in Categories 1 through 6 the Best Fit Scoring Guidelines are presented in the first column as a reminder of the key points in the scoring for each level. The process-scoring guidelines for the 70-85 percent level and the 90-100 percent levels have been grouped together in the tables because these scoring levels all require the multiple-level requirements to be met. For results Items in Category 7, the overall requirements of each Item are presented, followed by the scoring calibration statements and corresponding actual scoring guidelines that apply to all the Category 7 Items.

Remember, the following analysis is presented only as a guideline that state, local, and in-house recognition programs may want to consider in order to help their examiners provide more consistent and meaningful scoring and feedback to applicants.

1.1 Senior Leadership *(70 points possible)*	
Best Fit Scoring Guidelines	**Expected Findings**
0-5% If examiners observe the applicant is not responsive to the requirements of an Item or provides no information, the score should be zero. If the applicant provides only anecdotal information, but no indication that a systematic approach has begun (even though deployment is very limited) the score should be 5%.	***0-5% Scoring Band: No Systems to Meet Requirements*** ***1.1 Senior Leadership.*** Senior leaders have no effective processes to lead the organization such as providing clear guidance [1.1a(1)] and communicating with employees [1.1b(1)] (A). *The values and a clear direction to guide the organization and its senior leaders have not been deployed (D). Reacting to problems is the normal way of approaching work and no consistent effort is made to prevent problems (L). There is no effective alignment in the organization among leaders related to values and direction and people and/or units seem to operate independently (I).*
10-25%. If examiners observe the applicant is barely doing the things described in the 10-25% scoring band, the score should be in the lower part of this band. If they observe the applicant is doing everything in the 10-25% band, but nothing in the next higher 30-45% band, the score should be 25%.	***10-25% Scoring Band: Beginning to Meet Basic Requirements*** ***1.1 Senior Leadership.*** Senior leaders are in the beginning stages of establishing effective processes to lead the organization such as providing clear guidance [1.1a(1)] and communicating with employees [1.1b(1)] (A). *The values and approaches that guide the organization and its senior leaders are not widely understood (D). Reacting to problems is widespread; working to prevent problems is in the beginning stages (L). Some joint problem-solving activities are used to help promote alignment within the organization (I).*
30-45%. If examiners observe the applicant is doing everything described in the 10-25% scoring band, and a few additional things in the next higher 30-45% band, the score should be in the lower part of the 30-45% band. If they observe the applicant is doing everything in the 30-45% band, but nothing in the next higher 50-65% band, the score should be 45%.	***30-45% Scoring Band: Systematically Meeting Basic Requirements*** ***1.1 Senior Leadership.*** Senior leaders have effective, systematic processes in place to lead the organization, which may include providing clear guidance [1.1a(1)] and communicating with employees [1.1b(1)] (A). *The values and approaches that guide the organization and its senior leaders are generally understood (D). Senior leaders are beginning to evaluate some of these processes and may or may not have made improvements based on the evaluation (L). The values and directions are generally consistent with organization priorities such as those set forth in the organization's mission and vision and the requirements set forth in other Criteria Categories (I).*
50-65%. If examiners observe the applicant is doing everything described in the 30-45% scoring band, and a few additional things in the next higher 50-65% band, the score should be in the lower part of the 50-65% band. If they observe the applicant is doing everything in the 50-65% band, but nothing in the next higher 70-85% band, the score should be 65%.	***50-65% Scoring Band: Systematically Meeting Overall Requirements*** ***1.1 Senior Leadership.*** Senior leaders have effective, systematic processes in place to do the following: ***a. Vision and Values.*** Guide the organization [1.1a(1)] and sustain organizational success by ensuring it is capable of addressing current business needs and preparing for future challenges using techniques such as fact-based evaluation and improvement of some key processes [1.1a(3)] (A). ***b. Communication and Organizational Performance.*** Communicate with and motivate employees to encourage high performance [1.1b(1)] (A). *Some relatively minor gaps may exist in the deployment of these processes in some parts of the organization (D). There is a systematic, fact-based process in place to evaluate and improve the efficiency/ effectiveness of some of the key elements of (a) and/or (b) above (L). The leadership processes are generally aligned with organizational needs and the requirements set forth in other Criteria Categories. (I)*

Continued

1.1 Senior Leadership *(70 points possible)*	*Continued*
Best Fit Scoring Guidelines	**Expected Findings**

<table>
<tr>
<td valign="top">

70-85% If examiners observe the applicant is doing everything described in the 50-65% Overall Requirements scoring band, and a few additional things in the 70-100% Multiple Requirements scoring band, the score should be in the lower part of the Multiple Requirements) scoring band (for example, 70-75%). If they observe the applicant is meeting many to most requirements in the 70-100% Multiple Requirements scoring band the score should be 85%.

90-100% If examiners observe the applicant is doing nearly everything described in the 70-100% Multiple Requirements scoring band, the score should be 90-95%. If examiners observe the applicant is meeting all of the requirements in the 70-100% Multiple Requirements band, the score should be 100%.

Note: *A score of 100% is possible only if **all** requirements are met and no Opportunities for Improvement can be identified. In addition, examiners must observe full deployment, extensive and ongoing evaluation, improvement, organizational learning, innovation, and knowledge sharing throughout the organization. Required approaches must be well integrated with organizational needs identified in response to the other Criteria Items.*

</td>
<td valign="top">

70-85% and 90-100% Scoring Bands: Multiple Requirements

1.1 Senior Leadership (70 pts.) Senior leaders guide and sustain the organization, communicate effectively with employees, and encourage high performance.

a. Vision and Values

1. Senior leaders have an effective process in place to set and deploy organizational vision and values through the leadership system, to all employees, key suppliers and partners, customers, and other stakeholders, as appropriate. Their personal actions reflect a commitment to the organization's values.

2. Senior leaders have an effective process in place to promote an environment that fosters and requires legal and ethical behavior.

3. Senior leaders have an effective process in place to create a sustainable organization. They have created an environment for performance improvement, accomplishment of mission and strategic objectives, innovation, organizational agility, and organizational and employee learning. They personally participate in succession planning and the development of future organizational leaders.

b. Communication and Organizational Performance

1. Senior leaders have an effective process in place to communicate with, empower, and motivate all employees throughout the organization. They have an effective process in place to encourage frank, two-way communication throughout the organization. They take an active role in employee reward and recognition to reinforce high performance and a customer and business focus.

2. Senior leaders have an effective process in place to create a focus on action to accomplish the organization's objectives, improve performance, and attain the organization's vision. The process ensures a focus on creating and balancing value for customers and other stakeholders in their organizational performance expectations.

The approach is well deployed with no significant gaps (D). There is a systematic, fact-based process in place to evaluate and improve elements of (a) and (b) above with clear evidence of innovation, learning, and organizational sharing, which results in refinements and improved integration organizationwide (L). The approach is integrated and consistent with the organizational needs identified in other Criteria Items (such as strategic objectives, customer requirements, and performance-review and improvement systems (I).

</td>
</tr>
</table>

1.2 Governance and Social Responsibilities *(50 points possible)*	
Best Fit Scoring Guidelines	**Expected Findings**
0-5% If examiners observe the applicant is not responsive to the requirements of an Item or provides no information, the score should be zero. If the applicant provides only anecdotal information, but no indication that a systematic approach has begun (even though deployment is very limited) the score should be 5%.	*0-5% Scoring Band: No Systems to Meet Requirements* *1.2 Governance and Social Responsibilities.* The organization has no effective processes to provide governance [1.2a(1)] and meet its social responsibilities [1.2b(1)] *(A). The processes to promote effective governance and exhibit good citizenship have not been deployed (D). Reacting to problems is the normal way of approaching work and no consistent effort is made to prevent problems (L). There is no effective alignment in the organization related to governance and meeting social responsibilities and people and/or units seem to operate independently (I).*
10-25%. If examiners observe the applicant is barely doing the things described in the 10-25% scoring band, the score should be in the lower part of this band. If they observe the applicant is doing everything in the 10-25% band, but nothing in the next higher 30-45% band, the score should be 25%.	*10-25% Scoring Band: Beginning to Meet Basic Requirements* *1.2 Governance and Social Responsibilities.* The organization is in the beginning stages of establishing processes to provide effective governance (such as ensuring management accountability) [1.2a(1)] and to meet its social responsibilities (such as complying with laws and regulations) [1.2b(1)] *(A). Major gaps exist where the processes do not provide effective governance or ensure compliance with key regulatory or legal requirements in most parts of the organization (D). Reacting to problems related to governance and social responsibility is common, and working to prevent problems is in the beginning stages (L). Some joint problem-solving activities are used to help promote alignment within the organization (I).*
30-45%. If examiners observe the applicant is doing everything described in the 10-25% scoring band, and a few additional things in the next higher 30-45% band, the score should be in the lower part of the 30-45% band. If they observe the applicant is doing everything in the 30-45% band, but nothing in the next higher 50-65% band, the score should be 45%.	*30-45% Scoring Band: Systematically Meeting Basic Requirements* *1.2 Governance and Social Responsibilities.* The organization has systematic processes in place to provide effective governance (such as ensuring management accountability) [1.2a(1)] and meet its social responsibilities (such as complying with laws and regulations) [1.2b(1)] *(A) in most parts of the organization (D). The organization is beginning to evaluate some of these processes and may or may not have made improvements based on the evaluation (L). The value and directions are generally consistent with organization priorities such as those set forth in the organization's business plans and the requirements set forth in other Criteria Categories (I).*
50-65%. If examiners observe the applicant is doing everything described in the 30-45% scoring band, and a few additional things in the next higher 50-65% band, the score should be in the lower part of the 50-65% band. If they observe the applicant is doing everything in the 50-65% band, but nothing in the next higher 70-85% band, the score should be 65%.	*50-65% Scoring Band: Systematically Meeting Overall Requirements* *1.2 Governance and Social Responsibilities.* The organization has effective, systematic processes in place to do the following: a. *Organizational Governance.* Govern the organization to ensure, for example, accountability for management actions. [1.2a(1)] *(A).* b. *Legal and Ethical Behavior.* Address responsibilities to the public (to ensure, for example, that the organization meets regulatory and legal requirements [1.1b(1)]; promote ethical behavior throughout the organization). [1.2b(2)] *(A).* c. *Support of Key Communities.* Practice good citizenship (for example, by actively supporting key communities). [1.2c] *(A).* *Some relatively minor gaps may exist in the deployment of these processes in some parts of the organization (D). However, there is a systematic, fact-based process in place to evaluate and improve the efficiency/effectiveness of some of the key elements of (a), (b), and/or (c) above (L). The governance and social responsibility processes are generally aligned with organizational needs such as those set forth in the organization's vision, values, and plans and the requirements set forth in other Criteria Categories (I).*

Continued

1.2 Governance and Social Responsibilities *(50 points possible)*	*Continued*
Best Fit Scoring Guidelines	**Expected Findings**

70-85% If examiners observe the applicant is doing everything described in the 50-65% Overall Requirements scoring band, and a few additional things in the 70-100% Multiple Requirements scoring band, the score should be in the lower part of the Multiple Requirements) scoring band (for example, 70-75%). If they observe the applicant is meeting many to most requirements in the 70-100% Multiple Requirements scoring band the score should be 85%.
 	
90-100% If examiners observe the applicant is doing nearly everything described in the 70-100% Multiple Requirements scoring band, the score should be 90-95%. If examiners observe the applicant is meeting all of the requirements in the 70-100% Multiple Requirements band, the score should be 100%.
 	
Note: *A score of 100% is possible only if **all** requirements are met and no Opportunities for Improvement can be identified. In addition, examiners must observe full deployment, extensive and ongoing evaluation, improvement, organizational learning, innovation, and knowledge sharing throughout the organization. Required approaches must be well integrated with organizational needs identified in response to the other Criteria Items.*
	1.2 Governance and Social Responsibilities. The organization has well-deployed, effective, systematic processes in place to do the following:
	
	a. Organizational Governance
	
	1. Address the following key factors in the organization's governance system:
	   • Accountability for management's actions
	   • Fiscal accountability
	   • Transparency in operations and selection and disclosure policies for governance board members, as appropriate
	   • Independence in internal and external audits
	   • Protection of stakeholder and stockholder interests, as appropriate
	
	2. Evaluate the performance of senior leaders, including the chief executive and members of the governance board, as appropriate. Senior leaders and the governance board use these performance reviews to improve both their personal leadership effectiveness and that of the board and leadership system, as appropriate.
	
	b. Legal and Ethical Behavior.
	
	1. Address any adverse impacts on society of the organization's products, services, and operations. Anticipate public concerns with current and future products, services, and operations. Prepare for these concerns in a proactive manner, including using resource-sustaining processes, as appropriate. Establish key compliance processes, measures, and goals for achieving and surpassing regulatory and legal requirements, as appropriate. Establish key processes, measures, and goals for addressing risks associated with its products, services, and operations.
	
	2. Promote and ensure ethical behavior in all interactions. Establish key processes and measures or indicators for enabling and monitoring ethical behavior in the governance structure, throughout the organization, and in interactions with customers, partners, and other stakeholders. Monitor and respond to breaches of ethical behavior.
	
	c. Support of Key Communities. Actively support and strengthen key communities with which the organization interacts. Identify and define (list) key communities and determine areas of emphasis for organizational involvement and support. Senior leaders and employees contribute to improving these communities.
	
	The approach is well deployed with no significant gaps (D). There is a systematic, fact-based process in place to evaluate and improve elements of (a), (b), and (c) above with clear evidence of innovation, learning, and organizational sharing, which results in refinements and improved integration organizationwide (L). The approach is integrated and consistent with the organizational needs identified in other Criteria Items (such as strategic objectives, customer requirements, and performance-review and improvement systems (I).

2.1 Strategy Development *(40 points possible)*	
Best Fit Scoring Guidelines	**Expected Findings**
0-5% If examiners observe the applicant is not responsive to the requirements of an Item or provides no information, the score should be zero. If the applicant provides only anecdotal information, but no indication that a systematic approach has begun (even though deployment is very limited) the score should be 5%.	*0-5% Scoring Band: No Systems to Meet Requirements* *2.1 Strategy Development.* The organization has no effective processes to develop strategic plans [2.1a(1)] *(A) throughout the organization (D). Reacting to problems is the normal way of approaching work and no consistent effort is made to prevent problems (L). There is no effective alignment in the organization related to the development of strategic plans and people and/or units seem to operate independently (I).*
10-25%. If examiners observe the applicant is barely doing the things described in the 10-25% scoring band, the score should be in the lower part of this band. If they observe the applicant is doing everything in the 10-25% band, but nothing in the next higher 30-45% band, the score should be 25%.	*10-25% Scoring Band: Beginning to Meet Basic Requirements* *2.1 Strategy Development.* The organization is in the beginning stages of establishing effective processes for systematically developing strategic plans [2.1a(1)] *(A). Major gaps exist where the strategic planning process does not consider most business requirements that are key to future business success and essential to effective strategic planning (D). Reacting to problems in the planning process is widespread; working to prevent problems is in the beginning stages (L). Alignment within the planning process is enhanced primarily by the use of joint problem solving (I).*
30-45%. If examiners observe the applicant is doing everything described in the 10-25% scoring band, and a few additional things in the next higher 30-45% band, the score should be in the lower part of the 30-45% band. If they observe the applicant is doing everything in the 30-45% band, but nothing in the next higher 50-65% band, the score should be 45%.	*30-45% Scoring Band: Systematically Meeting Basic Requirements* *2.1 Strategy Development.* The organization has effective, systematic processes in place to develop its strategic plans [2.1a(1)] *(A). The planning process considers many business requirements or challenges that are key to future business success and essential to effective strategic planning (D). The organization is beginning to evaluate some of these processes and may or may not have made improvements based on the evaluation (L). The strategic development process is somewhat aligned with other Item requirements such as the values that guide the organization (1.1) and key customer requirements determined by the processes in Item in 3.1 and the requirements set forth in other Criteria Categories (I).*
50-65%. If examiners observe the applicant is doing everything described in the 30-45% scoring band, and a few additional things in the next higher 50-65% band, the score should be in the lower part of the 50-65% band. If they observe the applicant is doing everything in the 50-65% band, but nothing in the next higher 70-85% band, the score should be 65%.	*50-65% Scoring Band: Systematically Meeting Overall Requirements* *2.1 Strategy Development.* The organization has effective, systematic strategic planning processes in place to do the following: *a. Strategy Development Process.* Consider factors and challenges that are key to future business success [2.1a(1)]. *(A).* *b. Strategic Objectives.* Develop and summarize clear strategic objectives that address important business challenges (e.g., measurable, outcome-oriented that define what the organization must achieve to be successful) and related goals [2.1b(1)]. *(A)* *Some relatively minor gaps may exist in the process of planning and setting strategic objectives (D). There is a systematic, fact-based process in place to evaluate and improve some of the key elements of (a) and/or (b) above (L). The planning processes are generally aligned with organizational needs and the requirements set forth in other Criteria Categories (I).*

Continued

2.1 Strategy Development *(40 points possible)*	Continued
Best Fit Scoring Guidelines	**Expected Findings**

Best Fit Scoring Guidelines	Expected Findings
70-85% If examiners observe the applicant is doing everything described in the 50-65% Overall Requirements scoring band, and a few additional things in the 70-100% Multiple Requirements scoring band, the score should be in the lower part of the Multiple Requirements) scoring band (for example, 70-75%). If they observe the applicant is meeting many to most requirements in the 70-100% Multiple Requirements scoring band the score should be 85%. **90-100%** If examiners observe the applicant is doing nearly everything described in the 70-100% Multiple Requirements scoring band, the score should be 90-95%. If examiners observe the applicant is meeting all of the requirements in the 70-100% Multiple Requirements band, the score should be 100%. **Note**: *A score of 100% is possible only if **all** requirements are met and no Opportunities for Improvement can be identified. In addition, examiners must observe full deployment, extensive and ongoing evaluation, improvement, organizational learning, innovation, and knowledge sharing throughout the organization. Required approaches must be well integrated with organizational needs identified in response to the other Criteria Items.*	***70-85% and 90-100% Scoring Bands: Multiple Requirements*** *2.1 Strategy Development.* The organization has well-deployed, effective, systematic processes in place to do the following: *a. Strategy Development Process* 1. Conduct strategic planning, with process steps and key participants clearly defined. Identify potential blind spots. Set and address short- and longer-term planning-time horizons. 2. Ensure that strategic planning addresses the key factors listed below and collect and analyze relevant data and information pertaining to these factors as part of the strategic planning process: • Organizational strengths, weaknesses, opportunities, and threats • Early indications of major shifts in technology, markets, competition, or the regulatory environment • Long-term organizational sustainability and continuity in emergencies • The organization's ability to execute the strategic plan *b. Strategic Objectives* 1. Define key strategic objectives and the timetable for accomplishing them. Define the most important goals for these strategic objectives. 2. Ensure that strategic objectives address the challenges identified in response to P.2 in the Organizational Profile, and balance short- and longer-term challenges and opportunities, and balance the needs of all key stakeholders. *The approach is well deployed with no significant gaps (D). There is a systematic, fact-based process in place to evaluate and improve (a) and (b) above with clear evidence of innovation, learning, and organizational sharing, which results in refinements and improved integration organizationwide (L). The approach is integrated and consistent with the organizational needs identified in other Criteria Items (such as strategic objectives, customer requirements, and performance-review and improvement systems) (I).*

2.2 Strategic Deployment *(45 points possible)*	
Best Fit Scoring Guidelines	**Expected Findings**
0-5% If examiners observe the applicant is not responsive to the requirements of an Item or provides no information, the score should be zero. If the applicant provides only anecdotal information, but no indication that a systematic approach has begun (even though deployment is very limited) the score should be 5%.	***0-5% Scoring Band: No Systems to Meet Requirements*** **2.2 Strategy Deployment.** The organization has no effective processes to deploy its strategy (usually involving a process to convert its strategic objectives into action plans and implement them [2.2a(1)] *(A). Day-to-day work actions are generally ad hoc (D). Reacting to problems is the normal way of approaching work and no consistent effort is made to prevent problems (L). There is no effective alignment in the organization related to strategy deployment and people and/or units seem to operate independently (I).*
10-25%. If examiners observe the applicant is barely doing the things described in the 10-25% scoring band, the score should be in the lower part of this band. If they observe the applicant is doing everything in the 10-25% band, but nothing in the next higher 30-45% band, the score should be 25%.	***10-25% Scoring Band: Beginning to Meet Basic Requirements*** **2.2 Strategy Deployment.** The organization is in the beginning stages of establishing effective processes for systematically developing action plans to deploy its strategy (usually involving a process to convert its strategic objectives into action plans and implement them)[2.2a(1)] *(A). Major gaps exist where the action plans do not cover most elements essential to effective deployment of strategic objectives (D). Reacting to problems in deploying strategic plans and actions is widespread; working to prevent problems is in the beginning stages (L). Alignment of action plans may be enhanced somewhat by the use of joint problem solving (I).*
30-45%. If examiners observe the applicant is doing everything described in the 10-25% scoring band, and a few additional things in the next higher 30-45% band, the score should be in the lower part of the 30-45% band. If they observe the applicant is doing everything in the 30-45% band, but nothing in the next higher 50-65% band, the score should be 45%.	***30-45% Scoring Band: Systematically Meeting Basic Requirements*** **2.2 Strategy Deployment.** The organization has effective, systematic processes in place to develop action plans to deploy its strategy (usually involving a process to convert its strategic objectives into action plans and implement them) [2.2a(1)] *(A). Action plans for key elements of its strategic plan (A) have been deployed to most key areas in the organization (D). The organization is beginning to evaluate some of these processes and may or may not have made improvements based on the evaluation (L). The action plans are generally aligned with organizational mission, vision, and strategy and the requirements set forth in other Criteria Categories (I).*
50-65%. If examiners observe the applicant is doing everything described in the 30-45% scoring band, and a few additional things in the next higher 50-65% band, the score should be in the lower part of the 50-65% band. If they observe the applicant is doing everything in the 50-65% band, but nothing in the next higher 70-85% band, the score should be 65%.	***50-65% Scoring Band: Systematically Meeting Overall Requirements*** **2.2 Strategy Deployment.** The organization has effective, systematic processes in place to do the following: **a. Action Plan Development and Deployment.** Convert its strategic objectives into action plans [2.2a(1)]. Related performance measures or indicators for action plans are developed [2.2a(5)] and summarized *(A).* **b. Performance Projection.** Project the organization's future performance levels for most of the key performance measures or indicators [2.2b] *(A).* *Some relatively minor gaps may exist in the deployment of these processes in some parts of the organization (D). However, there is a systematic, fact-based process in place to evaluate and improve the efficiency/effectiveness of some of the key elements of (a) and/or (b) above (L). Action plans are generally used to align the work of the organization and the requirements set forth in other Criteria Categories (I).*

Continued

2.2 Strategic Deployment *(45 points possible)*	*Continued*
Best Fit Scoring Guidelines	**Expected Findings**

70-85% If examiners observe the applicant is doing everything described in the 50-65% Overall Requirements scoring band, and a few additional things in the 70-100% Multiple Requirements scoring band, the score should be in the lower part of the Multiple Requirements) scoring band (for example, 70-75%). If they observe the applicant is meeting many to most requirements in the 70-100% Multiple Requirements scoring band the score should be 85%.

90-100% If examiners observe the applicant is doing nearly everything described in the 70-100% Multiple Requirements scoring band, the score should be 90-95%. If examiners observe the applicant is meeting all of the requirements in the 70-100% Multiple Requirements band, the score should be 100%.

Note: *A score of 100% is possible only if **all** requirements are met and no Opportunities for Improvement can be identified. In addition, examiners must observe full deployment, extensive and ongoing evaluation, improvement, organizational learning, innovation, and knowledge sharing throughout the organization. Required approaches must be well integrated with organizational needs identified in response to the other Criteria Items.*

2.2 Strategy Deployment. The organization has well-deployed, effective, systematic processes in place to do the following:

a. Action Plan Development and Deployment
1. Develop and deploy action plans to achieve the organization's key strategic objectives. Allocate resources to ensure accomplishment of action plans. Ensure that the key changes resulting from action plans can be sustained.
2. Establish and deploy modified action plans promptly if circumstances require a shift in plans and rapid execution of new plans.
3. List key short- and longer-term action plans. Identify the key changes, if any, in the organization's products, services, customers, markets, and operations based on these action plans.
4. Develop key human resource plans that derive from (are needed to support) the short- and longer-term strategic objectives and action plans.
5. Develop and list key performance measures or indicators that are used for tracking progress in carrying out the action plans. Ensure that the organization's overall action plan measurement system reinforces organizational alignment and covers all key deployment areas and stakeholders.

b. Performance Projection. For the key performance measures or indicators identified in 2.2a(5), define performance projections for both short- and longer-term planning-time horizons. Compare the organization's projected performance with the projected performance of competitors or comparable organizations and with key benchmarks, goals, and past performance, as appropriate. Ensure that any current or projected gaps in performance, compared against competitors, comparable organizations, or benchmarks, are addressed.

The approach is well deployed with no significant gaps (D). There is a systematic, fact-based process in place to evaluate and improve (a) and (b) above with clear evidence of innovation, learning, and organizational sharing, which results in refinements and improved integration organizationwide (L). The approach is integrated and consistent with the organizational needs identified in other Criteria Items (such as strategic objectives, customer requirements, and performance-review and improvement systems) (I).

3.1 Customer and Market Knowledge *(40 points possible)*	
Best Fit Scoring Guidelines	**Expected Findings**
0-5% If examiners observe the applicant is not responsive to the requirements of an Item or provides no information, the score should be zero. If the applicant provides only anecdotal information, but no indication that a systematic approach has begun (even though deployment is very limited) the score should be 5%.	**0-5% Scoring Band: No Systems to Meet Requirements** **3.1 Customer and Market Knowledge.** The organization has no effective processes for using customer or market knowledge to identify requirements and/or expectations [3.1a(2)] *(A)*. Efforts to learn about customer and market requirements are ad hoc (D). Reacting to problems is the normal way of approaching work and no consistent effort is made to prevent problems (L). There is no effective alignment in the organization related to understanding customer and market requirements and people and/or units seem to operate independently (I).
10-25%. If examiners observe the applicant is barely doing the things described in the 10-25% scoring band, the score should be in the lower part of this band. If they observe the applicant is doing everything in the 10-25% band, but nothing in the next higher 30-45% band, the score should be 25%.	*10-25% Scoring Band: Beginning to Meet Basic Requirements* **3.1 Customer and Market Knowledge.** The organization is in the beginning stages of establishing effective processes for using customer and market knowledge to identify key requirements and/or expectations [3.1a(2)] *(A)*. *Major gaps exist where the processes to acquire knowledge about customer requirements do not cover most customer segments or groups (D). Reacting to problems related to understanding customer and market requirements is widespread; working to prevent problems is in the beginning stages (L). Alignment of customer requirements with organization priorities and work is accomplished somewhat by the use of joint problem solving (I).*
30-45%. If examiners observe the applicant is doing everything described in the 10-25% scoring band, and a few additional things in the next higher 30-45% band, the score should be in the lower part of the 30-45% band. If they observe the applicant is doing everything in the 30-45% band, but nothing in the next higher 50-65% band, the score should be 45%.	*30-45% Scoring Band: Systematically Meeting Basic Requirements* **3.1 Customer and Market Knowledge.** The organization has effective, systematic processes in place to identify customer and market requirements and/or expectations [3.1a(2)] *(A)*. *Some gaps exist where the listening and learning (knowledge acquisition) processes do not cover some customer segments or groups to effectively understand their requirements (D). The organization is beginning to evaluate some of these processes and may or may not have made improvements based on the evaluation (L). The processes to learn about customer and market requirements are generally consistent with some organizational priorities such as those in the organizational mission, vision, and strategy and the requirements set forth in other Criteria Categories (I).*
50-65%. If examiners observe the applicant is doing everything described in the 30-45% scoring band, and a few additional things in the next higher 50-65% band, the score should be in the lower part of the 50-65% band. If they observe the applicant is doing everything in the 50-65% band, but nothing in the next higher 70-85% band, the score should be 65%.	*50-65% Scoring Band: Systematically Meeting Overall Requirements* **3.1 Customer and Market Knowledge.** The organization has effective, systematic processes in place to do the following: a. **Customer and Market Knowledge.** Identify customer and market requirements, expectations, and preferences to determine their relative value; ensure the continuing relevance of products and services; and develop new business opportunities [3.1a(2)] *(A)*. *Some relatively minor gaps may exist in the use of these processes in some parts of the organization and may not fully consider all customer or market segments (D). There is a systematic, fact-based process in place to evaluate and improve the efficiency/effectiveness of some of the key elements of (a) above (L). The customer and market knowledge processes are aligned with organizational needs and the requirements set forth in other Criteria Categories (I).*

Continued

3.1 Customer and Market Knowledge *(40 points possible)*	Continued
Best Fit Scoring Guidelines	**Expected Findings**

70-85% If examiners observe the applicant is doing everything described in the 50-65% Overall Requirements scoring band, and a few additional things in the 70-100% Multiple Requirements scoring band, the score should be in the lower part of the Multiple Requirements) scoring band (for example, 70-75%). If they observe the applicant is meeting many to most requirements in the 70-100% Multiple Requirements scoring band the score should be 85%.

90-100% If examiners observe the applicant is doing nearly everything described in the 70-100% Multiple Requirements scoring band, the score should be 90-95%. If examiners observe the applicant is meeting all of the requirements in the 70-100% Multiple Requirements band, the score should be 100%.

Note: *A score of 100% is possible only if **all** requirements are met and no Opportunities for Improvement can be identified. In addition, examiners must observe full deployment, extensive and ongoing evaluation, improvement, organizational learning, innovation, and knowledge sharing throughout the organization. Required approaches must be well integrated with organizational needs identified in response to the other Criteria Items.*

3.1 Customer and Market Knowledge. The organization has well-deployed, effective, systematic processes in place to do the following:

a. Customer and Market Knowledge

1. Identify customers, customer groups, and market segments. Determine which customers, customer groups, and market segments to pursue for current and future products and services. Include customers of competitors and other potential customers and markets in this determination.
2. Listen to and learn from customers to determine their key requirements, needs, and changing expectations (including those related to product and service features). Understand the relative importance of these requirements to customers' purchasing or relationship decisions. Use different processes for determining customer requirements and preferences as needed to get accurate information from different customers or customer groups. Use relevant information and feedback from current and former customers, including marketing and sales information, customer loyalty and retention data, win/loss analysis, and complaint data for purposes of planning products and services, marketing, making process improvements, and developing new business opportunities. In addition, use this information and feedback to become more customer-focused and to better satisfy customer needs and desires.
3. Keep the processes for listening and learning (about customer requirements and preferences) current with business needs and directions, including changes in the marketplace.

The approach to understanding customer requirements and preferences is well deployed with no significant gaps (D). There is a systematic, fact-based process in place to evaluate and improve the processes in (a) above with clear evidence of innovation, learning, and organizational sharing, which results in refinements and improved integration organizationwide (L). The approach is integrated and consistent with the organizational needs identified in other Criteria Items (such as strategic objectives and performance-review and improvement systems (I).

3.2 Customer Relationships and Satisfaction *(45 points possible)*

Best Fit Scoring Guidelines	Expected Findings
0-5% If examiners observe the applicant is not responsive to the requirements of an Item or provides no information, the score should be zero. If the applicant provides only anecdotal information, but no indication that a systematic approach has begun (even though deployment is very limited) the score should be 5%.	*0-5% Scoring Band: No Systems to Meet Requirements* *3.2 Customer Relationships and Satisfaction.* The organization has no effective processes for building customer relationships, growing customer satisfaction and loyalty [3.2a(1)] or determining customer satisfaction [3.2b(1)] *(A). Efforts to build customer relationships and/or determine customer satisfaction are ad hoc (D). Reacting to problems is the normal way of approaching work and no consistent effort is made to prevent problems related to building customer relationships or determining levels of satisfaction (L). There is no effective alignment in the organization related to building customer relationships and determining levels of satisfaction; people and/or units seem to operate independently (I).*
10-25%. If examiners observe the applicant is barely doing the things described in the 10-25% scoring band, the score should be in the lower part of this band. If they observe the applicant is doing everything in the 10-25% band, but nothing in the next higher 30-45% band, the score should be 25%.	*10-25% Scoring Band: Beginning to Meet Basic Requirements* *3.2 Customer Relationships and Satisfaction.* The organization is in the beginning stages of establishing effective processes for building good relationships with customers, growing customer satisfaction and loyalty [3.2a(1)] and determining their levels of satisfaction [3.2b(1)] *(A). Major gaps exist where the relationship-building and/or satisfaction-determination processes do not cover most customer segments/groups and/or products and services (D). Reacting to problems with customer relationships and satisfaction is widespread; working to prevent problems is in the beginning stages (L). The organization generally relies on joint problem-solving teams to align activities to build relationships and understand customer-satisfaction levels (I).*
30-45%. If examiners observe the applicant is doing everything described in the 10-25% scoring band, and a few additional things in the next higher 30-45% band, the score should be in the lower part of the 30-45% band. If they observe the applicant is doing everything in the 30-45% band, but nothing in the next higher 50-65% band, the score should be 45%.	*30-45% Scoring Band: Systematically Meeting Basic Requirements* *3.2 Customer Relationships and Satisfaction.* The organization has effective, systematic processes in place to build good relationships with customers, grow customer satisfaction and loyalty [3.2a(1)] and assess their satisfaction [3.2b(1)] *(A). Some gaps exist where the relationship-building and satisfaction-determination processes do not cover many customer segments or groups (D). The organization is beginning to evaluate some of these processes and may or may not have made improvements based on the evaluation (L). The processes to build customer relationships and determine satisfaction are beginning to be aligned with basic customer-focus values and organization priorities and the requirements set forth in other Criteria Categories (I).*
50-65%. If examiners observe the applicant is doing everything described in the 30-45% scoring band, and a few additional things in the next higher 50-65% band, the score should be in the lower part of the 50-65% band. If they observe the applicant is doing everything in the 50-65% band, but nothing in the next higher 70-85% band, the score should be 65%.	*50-65% Scoring Band: Systematically Meeting Overall Requirements* *3.2 Customer Relationships and Satisfaction.* The organization has effective, systematic processes in place to do the following: *a. Customer Relationship Building.* Build relationships to acquire, satisfy, and retain customers, increase loyalty, and develop new business opportunities [3.2a(1)] *(A).* *b. Customer Satisfaction Determination.* Determine the satisfaction of customer and market segments [3.2b(1)] *(A).* *Some relatively minor gaps may exist in the use of these processes in some parts of the organization (D). There is a systematic, fact-based process in place to evaluate and improve the efficiency/effectiveness of some of the key elements of (a) and/or (b) above (L). The processes for building customer relations and assessing satisfaction are generally aligned with organizational needs such as those related to strategic plans and achieving organization mission and vision and the requirements set forth in other Criteria Categories (I).*

Continued

3.2 Customer Relationships and Satisfaction *(45 points possible)* *Continued*

Best Fit Scoring Guidelines	Expected Findings

70-85% If examiners observe the applicant is doing everything described in the 50-65% Overall Requirements scoring band, and a few additional things in the 70-100% Multiple Requirements scoring band, the score should be in the lower part of the Multiple Requirements) scoring band (for example, 70-75%). If they observe the applicant is meeting many to most requirements in the 70-100% Multiple Requirements scoring band the score should be 85%.

90-100% If examiners observe the applicant is doing nearly everything described in the 70-100% Multiple Requirements scoring band, the score should be 90-95%. If examiners observe the applicant is meeting all of the requirements in the 70-100% Multiple Requirements band, the score should be 100%.

Note: *A score of 100% is possible only if* ***all*** *requirements are met and no Opportunities for Improvement can be identified. In addition, examiners must observe full deployment, extensive and ongoing evaluation, improvement, organizational learning, innovation, and knowledge sharing throughout the organization. Required approaches must be well integrated with organizational needs identified in response to the other Criteria Items.*

3.2 Customer Relationships and Satisfaction. The organization has well-deployed, effective, systematic processes in place to do the following:

a. Customer Relationship Building

1) Build relationships to acquire customers, meet and exceed their expectations, increase loyalty and repeat business, and gain positive referrals.
2. Establish and define access mechanisms to enable customers to readily seek information, conduct business, and make complaints. Define customer contact requirements for each mode of customer access and ensure that these contact requirements are deployed to all people and processes involved in the customer-response chain.
3. Establish an effective complaint-management process to ensure that complaints are resolved effectively and promptly. Aggregate and analyze the complaints and use this information to make improvements throughout the organization and by affected partners. Use these processes to minimize customer dissatisfaction and, as appropriate, loss of repeat business.
4. Keep approaches to building relationships and providing customer access current with business needs and directions.

b. Customer Satisfaction Determination

1) Determine customer satisfaction, dissatisfaction, and loyalty and adjust these determination methods according to the needs of differing customer groups. Ensure that measurements capture actionable information for use in exceeding customers' expectations, securing their future business, and gaining positive referrals. Use customer satisfaction and dissatisfaction information to drive improvements.
2. Follow up with customers on the quality of products, services, and transactions to receive prompt and actionable feedback.
3. Obtain and use information about customers' satisfaction relative to the customers' satisfaction with competitors, other organizations providing similar products or services, and/or industry benchmarks.
4. Keep approaches to determining satisfaction current with business needs and directions.

The approach is well deployed with no significant gaps (D). There is a systematic, fact-based process in place to evaluate and improve elements of (a) and (b) above with clear evidence of innovation, learning, and organizational sharing, which results in refinements and improved integration organizationwide (L). The approach is integrated and consistent with the organizational needs identified in other Criteria Items (such as customer requirements and preferences, strategic objectives, and performance-review and improvement systems (I).

4.1 Measurement and Analysis of Organizational Performance *(45 points possible)*	
Best Fit Scoring Guidelines	**Expected Findings**
0-5% If examiners observe the applicant is not responsive to the requirements of an Item or provides no information, the score should be zero. If the applicant provides only anecdotal information, but no indication that a systematic approach has begun (even though deployment is very limited) the score should be 5%.	*0-5% Scoring Band: No Systems to Meet Requirements* *4.1 Measurement, Analysis, and Review of Organizational Performance.* The organization has no effective processes to measure, analyze, and review organizational performance *(A). Efforts to gather and use data to support decision making throughout the organization are ad hoc (D). Intuition, "gut feel," and guess work are usually used rather than data; reacting to problems is the normal way of approaching work (L). There is no effective alignment in the organization to ensure data and information are used to support decision making and organization priorities, mission, and vision and people and/or units seem to operate independently (I).*
10-25%. If examiners observe the applicant is barely doing the things described in the 10-25% scoring band, the score should be in the lower part of this band. If they observe the applicant is doing everything in the 10-25% band, but nothing in the next higher 30-45% band, the score should be 25%.	*10-25% Scoring Band: Beginning to Meet Basic Requirements* *4.1 Measurement, Analysis, and Review of Organizational Performance.* The organization is in the beginning stages of establishing effective processes for measuring [4.1a(1)], analyzing, and reviewing organizational performance [4.1b(1)] *(A). Major gaps exist where the measures and reviews do not cover many elements essential to effective organizational decision making (D). Reacting to problems with ineffective data and analyses to support decision making is widespread; working to prevent problems is in the beginning stages (L). The organization generally relies on joint problem solving to promote organization alignment of measurement, analysis, and review needs (I).*
30-45%. If examiners observe the applicant is doing everything described in the 10-25% scoring band, and a few additional things in the next higher 30-45% band, the score should be in the lower part of the 30-45% band. If they observe the applicant is doing everything in the 30-45% band, but nothing in the next higher 50-65% band, the score should be 45%.	*30-45% Scoring Band: Systematically Meeting Basic Requirements* *4.1 Measurement, Analysis, and Review of Organizational Performance.* The organization has effective, systematic processes in place for measuring [4.1a(1)], analyzing, and reviewing organizational performance [4.1b(1)] *(A). Measures, analyses, and reviews cover many to most areas essential to effective organizational decision making (D). The organization is beginning to evaluate some of these processes and may or may not have made improvements based on the evaluation (L). The processes to measure, analyze, and review organizational performance are beginning to be aligned with organization priorities and needs related to effective decision support and the requirements set forth in other Criteria Categories (I).*

50-65%. If examiners observe the applicant is doing everything described in the 30-45% scoring band, and a few additional things in the next higher 50-65% band, the score should be in the lower part of the 50-65% band. If they observe the applicant is doing everything in the 50-65% band, but nothing in the next higher 70-85% band, the score should be 65%.	*50-65% Scoring Band: Systematically Meeting Overall Requirements*
	
	4.1 Measurement, Analysis, and Review of Organizational Performance. The organization has effective, systematic processes in place to do the following:
	
	  a. *Performance Measurement.* Measure (gather), align, and improve performance data and information and ensure the data support effective decision making at all levels and parts of the organization [4.1a(1)] *(A).*
	
	  b. *Performance Analysis and Review.* Review organizational performance and analyze data to support effective decision making at all levels and in all parts of the organization [4.1b(1)] *(A).*
	
	Some relatively minor gaps may exist in the deployment or use of these processes in some parts of the organization (D). There is a systematic, fact-based process in place to evaluate and improve the efficiency/effectiveness of some of the key elements of (a) and/or (b) above. The measurement and analysis processes are generally aligned with organizational needs such as strategic objectives, action plans, vision, and mission and the requirements set forth in other Criteria Categories (I).

Continued

4.1 Measurement and Analysis of Organizational Performance *(45 points possible)* *Continued*	
Best Fit Scoring Guidelines	**Expected Findings**

Best Fit Scoring Guidelines

70-85% If examiners observe the applicant is doing everything described in the 50-65% Overall Requirements scoring band, and a few additional things in the 70-100% Multiple Requirements scoring band, the score should be in the lower part of the Multiple Requirements) scoring band (for example, 70-75%). If they observe the applicant is meeting many to most requirements in the 70-100% Multiple Requirements scoring band the score should be 85%.

90-100% If examiners observe the applicant is doing nearly everything described in the 70-100% Multiple Requirements scoring band, the score should be 90-95%. If examiners observe the applicant is meeting all of the requirements in the 70-100% Multiple Requirements band, the score should be 100%.

Note: *A score of 100% is possible only if* ***all*** *requirements are met and no Opportunities for Improvement can be identified. In addition, examiners must observe full deployment, extensive and ongoing evaluation, improvement, organizational learning, innovation, and knowledge sharing throughout the organization. Required approaches must be well integrated with organizational needs identified in response to the other Criteria Items.*

Expected Findings

4.1 Measurement, Analysis, and Review of Organizational Performance. The organization has well-deployed, effective, systematic processes in place to do the following:

a. Performance Measurement

1. Select, collect, align, and integrate data and information for tracking daily operations and for tracking overall organizational performance, including progress relative to strategic objectives and action plans. Define key organizational performance measures. Use these data and information to support organizational decision making and innovation.

2. Select and ensure the effective use of key comparative data and information to support operational and strategic decision making and innovation.

3. Keep the performance-measurement system current with business needs and directions. Ensure that the performance-measurement system is sensitive to rapid or unexpected organizational or external changes.

b. Performance Analysis

1. Review organizational performance and capabilities and ensure senior leaders participate in these reviews. Define analyses that are conducted to support these reviews and to ensure that conclusions are valid. Use these reviews to assess organizational success, competitive performance, progress relative to strategic objectives and action plans and the organization's ability to rapidly respond to changing organizational needs and challenges in its operating environment.

2. Translate organizational performance-review findings into priorities for continuous and breakthrough improvement and into opportunities for innovation. Deploy priorities and opportunities to work group- and functional-level operations throughout the organization to enable effective support for decision making. When appropriate, ensure the priorities and opportunities are deployed to suppliers, partners, and collaborators to ensure organizational alignment.

The approach is well deployed with no significant gaps (D). There is a systematic, fact-based process in place to evaluate and improve elements of (a) and (b) above with clear evidence of innovation, learning, and organizational sharing, which results in refinements and improved integration organizationwide (L). The approach is integrated and consistent with the organizational needs identified in other parts of the Criteria (such as customer requirements, strategic objectives, and performance-review and improvement systems (I).

4.2 Information and Knowledge Management *(45 points possible)*	
Best Fit Scoring Guidelines	**Expected Findings**
0-5% If examiners observe the applicant is not responsive to the requirements of an Item or provides no information, the score should be zero. If the applicant provides only anecdotal information, but no indication that a systematic approach has begun (even though deployment is very limited) the score should be 5%.	*0-5% Scoring Band: No Systems to Meet Requirements* *4.2 Information and Knowledge Management.* The organization has no effective processes to manage organizational information and knowledge [4.2a(1)] *(A). Efforts to make needed information and/or knowledge available to support organizational decision making and/or learning are ad hoc (D). Reacting to problems is the normal way of approaching work and no consistent effort is made to prevent problems (L). There is no effective alignment in the organization related to data availability and people and/or units seem to operate independently (I).*
10-25%. If examiners observe the applicant is barely doing the things described in the 10-25% scoring band, the score should be in the lower part of this band. If they observe the applicant is doing everything in the 10-25% band, but nothing in the next higher 30-45% band, the score should be 25%.	*10-25% Scoring Band: Beginning to Meet Basic Requirements* *4.2 Information and Knowledge Management.* The organization is in the beginning stages of establishing effective processes to manage organizational information and knowledge (ensuring their availability to support decision making) [4.2a(1)] *(A). Major gaps exist where the needed information and/or knowledge are not available to support organizational decision making (D). Reacting to problems related to poor data availability is widespread; working to prevent problems is in the beginning stages (L). The organization generally relies on joint problem solving to promote alignment of information-management and knowledge-management needs (I).*
30-45%. If examiners observe the applicant is doing everything described in the 10-25% scoring band, and a few additional things in the next higher 30-45% band, the score should be in the lower part of the 30-45% band. If they observe the applicant is doing everything in the 30-45% band, but nothing in the next higher 50-65% band, the score should be 45%.	*30-45% Scoring Band: Systematically Meeting Basic Requirements* *4.2 Information and Knowledge Management.* The organization has effective, systematic processes in place for managing organizational information and knowledge (ensuring their availability to support decision making [4.2a(1)] *(A). Information and knowledge are available for most areas essential to effective organizational decision making and/or learning (D). The organization is beginning to evaluate some of these processes and may or may not have made improvements based on the evaluation (L). Information- and knowledge-management processes are beginning to be aligned with organization priorities and needs related to effective decision support and the requirements set forth in other Criteria Categories (I).*
50-65%. If examiners observe the applicant is doing everything described in the 30-45% scoring band, and a few additional things in the next higher 50-65% band, the score should be in the lower part of the 50-65% band. If they observe the applicant is doing everything in the 50-65% band, but nothing in the next higher 70-85% band, the score should be 65%.	*50-65% Scoring Band: Systematically Meeting Overall Requirements* *4.2 Information and Knowledge Management.* The organization has effective, systematic processes in place to do the following: *a. Data and Information Availability.* Ensure the right data and information are available when needed by appropriate employees, suppliers and partners, collaborators. and customers to support decision making [4.2a(1)]*(A).* *b. Organizational Knowledge Management.* Build and manage knowledge assets (information systems) to effectively transfer needed knowledge [4.2b(1)] *(A).* *c. Data, Information, and Knowledge Quality.* Ensure the quality (accuracy, reliability, timeliness) of needed data and information [4.2c] *(A).* *Some relatively minor gaps may exist in the deployment of these processes in some parts of the organization (D). There is a systematic, fact-based process in place to evaluate and improve the efficiency/effectiveness of some of the key elements of (a), (b), and/or (c) above (L). Information- and knowledge-management processes are generally aligned with organizational needs as related to strategic plan, action, and organizational performance and process effectiveness and the requirements set forth in other Criteria Categories (I).*

Continued

4.2 Information and Knowledge Management *(45 points possible)*	*Continued*
Best Fit Scoring Guidelines	**Expected Findings**

70-85% If examiners observe the applicant is doing everything described in the 50-65% Overall Requirements scoring band, and a few additional things in the 70-100% Multiple Requirements scoring band, the score should be in the lower part of the Multiple Requirements) scoring band (for example, 70-75%). If they observe the applicant is meeting many to most requirements in the 70-100% Multiple Requirements scoring band the score should be 85%.

90-100% If examiners observe the applicant is doing nearly everything described in the 70-100% Multiple Requirements scoring band, the score should be 90-95%. If examiners observe the applicant is meeting all of the requirements in the 70-100% Multiple Requirements band, the score should be 100%.

Note: *A score of 100% is possible only if **all** requirements are met and no Opportunities for Improvement can be identified. In addition, examiners must observe full deployment, extensive and ongoing evaluation, improvement, organizational learning, innovation, and knowledge sharing throughout the organization. Required approaches must be well integrated with organizational needs identified in response to the other Criteria Items.*

4.2 Information and Knowledge Management. The organization has well-deployed, effective, systematic processes in place to do the following:

a. Data and Information Availability
1. Make needed data and information available and accessible to employees, suppliers, partners, collaborators, and customers, as appropriate.
2. Ensure that hardware and software are reliable, secure, and user-friendly.
3. Ensure the continued availability of data and information, including the availability of hardware and software systems, in the event of an emergency.
4. Keep data and information-availability mechanisms, including software and hardware systems, current with business needs and directions and with technological changes in the operating environment.

b. Organizational Knowledge
1. Manage organizational knowledge to accomplish:
   - The collection and transfer of employee knowledge
   - The transfer of relevant knowledge from and to customers, suppliers, partners, and collaborators
   - The rapid identification, sharing, and implementation of best practices
2. Ensure data, information, and organizational knowledge have the following properties:
   - Accuracy (correct)
   - Integrity (complete) and reliability (consistent)
   - Timeliness (available when needed)
   - Security (free from attack) and confidentiality (free from inappropriate release)

The approach is well deployed with no significant gaps (D). There is a systematic, fact-based process in place to evaluate and improve elements of (a), (b), and (c) above with clear evidence of innovation, learning, and organizational sharing, which results in refinements and improved integration organizationwide (L). The approach is integrated and consistent with the organizational needs identified in other Criteria Items (such as strategic objectives and performance-review and improvement systems (I).

5.1 Work Systems *(35 points possible)*	
Best Fit Scoring Guidelines	**Expected Findings**
0-5% If examiners observe the applicant is not responsive to the requirements of an Item or provides no information, the score should be zero. If the applicant provides only anecdotal information, but no indication that a systematic approach has begun (even though deployment is very limited) the score should be 5%.	*0-5% Scoring Band: No Systems to Meet Requirements* **5.1 Work Systems.** The organization has no effective processes to enable employees to accomplish the work of the organization (which are usually defined by strategic objectives and related action plans) [5.1a(1) and b] *(A). Efforts to ensure work is designed to achieve high levels of performance are ad hoc (D). Reacting to problems is the normal way of approaching work (L). There is no effective alignment of work systems with organization priorities and people and/or units seem to operate independently (I).*
10-25%. If examiners observe the applicant is barely doing the things described in the 10-25% scoring band, the score should be in the lower part of this band. If they observe the applicant is doing everything in the 10-25% band, but nothing in the next higher 30-45% band, the score should be 25%.	*10-25% Scoring Band: Beginning to Meet Basic Requirements* **5.1 Work Systems.** The organization is in the beginning stages of establishing effective processes to enable employees to manage work and jobs (which are usually defined by strategic objectives and related action plans) [5.1a(1) and b] *(A). Major gaps exist where the work systems do not help most employees to achieve high-performance objectives (D). Reacting to employee performance problems is widespread; working to prevent problems is in the beginning stages (L). The organization generally relies on joint problem solving to promote alignment of key work systems (I).*
30-45%. If examiners observe the applicant is doing everything described in the 10-25% scoring band, and a few additional things in the next higher 30-45% band, the score should be in the lower part of the 30-45% band. If they observe the applicant is doing everything in the 30-45% band, but nothing in the next higher 50-65% band, the score should be 45%.	*30-45% Scoring Band: Systematically Meeting Basic Requirements* **5.1 Work Systems.** The organization has effective, systematic processes in place to enable employees to manage work and jobs (which are usually defined by strategic objectives and related action plans) [5.1a(1) and b] *(A). Work and jobs in some parts of the organization support (or are beginning to support) performance objectives (D). The organization is beginning to evaluate some of these processes and may or may not have made improvements based on the evaluation (L). Work systems are beginning to be aligned with some organization priorities and the requirements set forth in other Criteria Categories (I).*
50-65%. If examiners observe the applicant is doing everything described in the 30-45% scoring band, and a few additional things in the next higher 50-65% band, the score should be in the lower part of the 50-65% band. If they observe the applicant is doing everything in the 50-65% band, but nothing in the next higher 70-85% band, the score should be 65%.	*50-65% Scoring Band: Systematically Meeting Overall Requirements* **5.1 Work Systems.** The organization has effective, systematic processes in place to do the following: a. *Organization and Management of Work.* Ensure that work and jobs enable employees and the organization to achieve high performance objectives [5.1a(1)] *(A).* b. *Employee Performance Management System.* Ensure compensation and related workforce and practices (such as employee feedback, recognition, and rewards) enable employees and the organization to achieve high-performance objectives [5.1b] *(A).* c. *Hiring and Career Progression.* Ensure career progression opportunities and related workforce practices; support achievement of high-performance objectives [5.1c] *(A).* *Some relatively minor gaps may exist in the deployment of these processes in some parts of the organization (D). There is a systematic, fact-based process in place to evaluate and improve the efficiency/effectiveness of some of the key elements of (a), (b), and/or (c) above (L). The processes of managing work and reinforcing and recognizing employee performance are generally aligned with organizational needs such as those defined by organization mission, vision, strategic plans, and action plans and the requirements set forth in other Criteria Categories (I).*

Continued

5.1 Work Systems *(35 points possible)*	*Continued*
Best Fit Scoring Guidelines	**Expected Findings**

Best Fit Scoring Guidelines	Expected Findings
70-85% If examiners observe the applicant is doing everything described in the 50-65% Overall Requirements scoring band, and a few additional things in the 70-100% Multiple Requirements scoring band, the score should be in the lower part of the Multiple Requirements) scoring band (for example, 70-75%). If they observe the applicant is meeting many to most requirements in the 70-100% Multiple Requirements scoring band the score should be 85%. **90-100%** If examiners observe the applicant is doing nearly everything described in the 70-100% Multiple Requirements scoring band, the score should be 90-95%. If examiners observe the applicant is meeting all of the requirements in the 70-100% Multiple Requirements band, the score should be 100%. **Note**: *A score of 100% is possible only if **all** requirements are met and no Opportunities for Improvement can be identified. In addition, examiners must observe full deployment, extensive and ongoing evaluation, improvement, organizational learning, innovation, and knowledge sharing throughout the organization. Required approaches must be well integrated with organizational needs identified in response to the other Criteria Items.*	*70-85% and 90-100% Scoring Bands: Multiple Requirements* *5.1 Work Systems.* The organization has well-deployed, effective, systematic processes in place to do the following: *a. Organization and Management of Work* 1. Organize and manage work and jobs, including skills, to promote cooperation, initiative, empowerment, innovation, the organizational culture. Organize and manage work and jobs, including skills, to achieve the agility to keep current with business needs and to achieve action plans. 2. Ensure work systems capitalize on the diverse ideas, cultures, and thinking of employees and the communities with which the organization interacts (the employee-hiring and customer communities). 3. Achieve effective communication and skill sharing across work units, jobs, and locations. *b. Employee Performance Management System* Ensure the employee performance management system, including feedback to employees, supports high-performance work, contributes to the achievement of action plans, and supports a customer and business focus. Ensure compensation, recognition, and related reward and incentive practices reinforce high-performance work and a customer and business focus. *c. Hiring and Career Progression* 1. Identify characteristics and skills needed by potential employees. 2. Recruit, hire, and retain new employees and ensure employees represent the diverse ideas, cultures, and thinking of the organization's hiring community. 3. Ensure effective succession planning for leadership and management positions and manage the effective career progression for all employees throughout the organization. *The approach is well deployed with no significant gaps (D). There is a systematic, fact-based process in place to evaluate and improve elements of (a), (b), and (c) above with clear evidence of innovation, learning, and organizational sharing, which results in refinements and improved integration organizationwide (L). The approach is integrated and consistent with the organizational needs identified in other Criteria Items (such as customer requirements, strategic objectives, and performance-review and improvement systems (I).*

5.2 Employee Learning and Motivation *(25 points possible)*	
Best Fit Scoring Guidelines	**Expected Findings**
0-5% If examiners observe the applicant is not responsive to the requirements of an Item or provides no information, the score should be zero. If the applicant provides only anecdotal information, but no indication that a systematic approach has begun (even though deployment is very limited) the score should be 5%.	*0-5% Scoring Band: No Systems to Meet Requirements* **5.2 Employee Learning and Motivation.** The organization has no effective processes to contribute to employee learning [5.2a(1)] and motivation [5.2b] (which typically includes encouraging skill and career development) to help employees achieve high-performance objectives *(A). Employee learning and motivation efforts are ad hoc (D). Reacting to problems is the normal way of approaching employee learning and motivation (L). There is no effective alignment between learning processes and employee needs in the organization and people and/or units seem to operate independently (I).*
10-25%. If examiners observe the applicant is barely doing the things described in the 10-25% scoring band, the score should be in the lower part of this band. If they observe the applicant is doing everything in the 10-25% band, but nothing in the next higher 30-45% band, the score should be 25%.	*10-25% Scoring Band: Beginning to Meet Basic Requirements* **5.2 Employee Learning and Motivation.** The organization is in the beginning stages of establishing effective processes to contribute to employee learning [5.2a(1)] and motivation [5.2b] (which typically includes encouraging skill and career development) to help employees achieve high-performance objectives (such as those defined by strategic objectives and related action plans) *(A). Major gaps exist where the employee learning and motivation processes do not help most employees acquire the knowledge and skills needed to achieve performance objectives (D). Reacting to employee learning and motivation problems is widespread; working to prevent problems is in the beginning stages (L). The organization generally relies on joint problem solving to promote alignment of employee learning and motivation with other organization needs (I).*
30-45%. If examiners observe the applicant is doing everything described in the 10-25% scoring band, and a few additional things in the next higher 30-45% band, the score should be in the lower part of the 30-45% band. If they observe the applicant is doing everything in the 30-45% band, but nothing in the next higher 50-65% band, the score should be 45%.	*30-45% Scoring Band: Systematically Meeting Basic Requirements* **5.2 Employee Learning and Motivation.** The organization has effective, systematic, education and training processes in place to contribute to employee learning [5.2a(1)] and motivation [5.2b] (which typically includes encouraging skill and career development) to help employees achieve high-performance objectives (such as those defined by strategic objectives and related action plans) *(A). Employee learning and motivation processes in some parts of the organization support (or are just beginning to support) performance objectives (D). The organization is beginning to evaluate some of these processes and may or may not have made improvements based on the evaluation (L). Employee learning and motivation processes are beginning to be aligned with organization priorities and the requirements set forth in other Criteria Categories (I).*
50-65%. If examiners observe the applicant is doing everything described in the 30-45% scoring band, and a few additional things in the next higher 50-65% band, the score should be in the lower part of the 50-65% band. If they observe the applicant is doing everything in the 50-65% band, but nothing in the next higher 70-85% band, the score should be 65%.	*50-65% Scoring Band: Systematically Meeting Overall Requirements* **5.2 Employee Learning and Motivation.** The organization has effective, systematic processes in place to do the following: **a. Employee Education, Training, and Development.** Build employee knowledge, skills, and capabilities through education and training to help them achieve overall organizational objectives and contribute to high performance [5.2a(1)] *(A).* **b. Motivation and Career Development.** Build employee knowledge, skills, and capabilities to help them achieve overall career development and organizational high-performance objectives [5.2b] *(A).* *Some relatively minor gaps may exist in the deployment of these processes in some parts of the organization (D). There is a systematic, fact-based process in place to evaluate and improve the efficiency/effectiveness of some of the key elements of (a) and/or (b) above (L). Employee learning and motivation processes are generally aligned with organizational needs such as those set forth in strategic plans, action plans, vision, and mission and the requirements set forth in other Criteria Categories (I).*

Continued

5.2 Employee Learning and Motivation *(25 points possible)*	*Continued*
Best Fit Scoring Guidelines	**Expected Findings**

70-85% If examiners observe the applicant is doing everything described in the 50-65% Overall Requirements scoring band, and a few additional things in the 70-100% Multiple Requirements scoring band, the score should be in the lower part of the Multiple Requirements) scoring band (for example, 70-75%). If they observe the applicant is meeting many to most requirements in the 70-100% Multiple Requirements scoring band the score should be 85%.

90-100% If examiners observe the applicant is doing nearly everything described in the 70-100% Multiple Requirements scoring band, the score should be 90-95%. If examiners observe the applicant is meeting all of the requirements in the 70-100% Multiple Requirements band, the score should be 100%.

Note: *A score of 100% is possible only if all requirements are met and no Opportunities for Improvement can be identified. In addition, examiners must observe full deployment, extensive and ongoing evaluation, improvement, organizational learning, innovation, and knowledge sharing throughout the organization. Required approaches must be well integrated with organizational needs identified in response to the other Criteria Items.*

70-85% and 90-100% Scoring Bands: Multiple Requirements

5.2 Employee Learning and Motivation. The organization has well-deployed, effective, systematic processes in place to do the following:

a. Employee Education, Training, and Development

1. Employee education and training contribute to the achievement of the organization's action plans. Employee education, training, and development address key needs associated with organizational performance measurement, performance improvement, and technological change. Education and training approach balance short- and longer-term organizational objectives with employee needs for development, ongoing learning, and career progression.

2. Employee education, training, and development address key organizational needs associated with new-employee orientation, diversity, ethical business practices, management and leadership development and employee, workplace, and environmental safety.

3. The organization seeks and uses input from employees and their supervisors and managers to help determine education, training, and development needs. The organization incorporates its learning and knowledge assets into its education and training.

4. Seek and use input from employees and their supervisors and managers in determining approaches to deliver education and training. Use both formal and informal approaches, including mentoring and other approaches, as appropriate to deliver education and training.

5. Reinforce the use of new knowledge and skills on the job and retain this knowledge for long-term organizational use. Systematically transfer knowledge from departing or retiring employees.

6. Evaluate the effectiveness of education and training, taking into account individual and organizational performance.

b. Motivation and Career Development

Motivate employees to develop and utilize their full potential. Use formal and informal mechanisms to help employees attain job- and career-related development and learning objectives. Ensure managers and supervisors help employees attain job- and career-related development and learning objectives.

The approach is well deployed with no significant gaps (D). There is a systematic, fact-based process in place to evaluate and improve elements of (a), (b), and (c) above with clear evidence of innovation, learning, and organizational sharing, which results in refinements and improved integration organizationwide (L). The approach is integrated and consistent with the organizational needs identified in other Criteria Items (such as strategic objectives, action plans, and performance-review and improvement systems (I).

5.3 Employee Well-Being and Satisfaction *(25 points possible)*	
Best Fit Scoring Guidelines	**Expected Findings**
0-5% If examiners observe the applicant is not responsive to the requirements of an Item or provides no information, the score should be zero. If the applicant provides only anecdotal information, but no indication that a systematic approach has begun (even though deployment is very limited) the score should be 5%.	*0-5% Scoring Band: No Systems to Meet Requirements* **5.3 Employee Well-Being and Satisfaction.** The organization has no effective processes to contribute to the well-being [5.3a(1)] and satisfaction [5.3b(2)] of employees *(A)*. *Efforts to promote the well-being and satisfaction of employees are ad hoc (D). Reacting to problems is the normal way of approaching issues related to employee well-being and satisfaction (L). There is no effective alignment related to well-being and organization priorities and people and/or units seem to operate independently (I).*
10-25%. If examiners observe the applicant is barely doing the things described in the 10-25% scoring band, the score should be in the lower part of this band. If they observe the applicant is doing everything in the 10-25% band, but nothing in the next higher 30-45% band, the score should be 25%.	*10-25% Scoring Band: Beginning to Meet Basic Requirements* **5.3 Employee Well-Being and Satisfaction.** The organization is in the beginning stages of establishing effective processes that contribute to the well-being [5.3a(1)] and satisfaction [5.3b(2)] of employees *(A). Major gaps exist where the organization has not created a work environment to promote employee well-being and satisfaction in most parts of the organization or for most employee groups (D). Reacting to employee well-being and satisfaction problems is widespread; working to prevent problems is in the beginning stages (L). The organization generally relies on joint problem solving to promote alignment of employee well-being and satisfaction with organization priorities (I).*
30-45%. If examiners observe the applicant is doing everything described in the 10-25% scoring band, and a few additional things in the next higher 30-45% band, the score should be in the lower part of the 30-45% band. If they observe the applicant is doing everything in the 30-45% band, but nothing in the next higher 50-65% band, the score should be 45%.	*30-45% Scoring Band: Systematically Meeting Basic Requirements* **5.3 Employee Well-Being and Satisfaction.** The organization has effective, systematic processes in place that contribute to the well-being [5.3a(1)] and satisfaction [5.3b(2)] of employees *(A). These processes in some parts of the organization may be just beginning to support employee well-being and satisfaction (D). The organization is beginning to evaluate some of these processes and may or may not have made improvements based on the evaluation (L). The processes to build employee well-being and satisfaction are beginning to be aligned with organization priorities and the requirements set forth in other Criteria Categories (I).*
50-65%. If examiners observe the applicant is doing everything described in the 30-45% scoring band, and a few additional things in the next higher 50-65% band, the score should be in the lower part of the 50-65% band. If they observe the applicant is doing everything in the 50-65% band, but nothing in the next higher 70-85% band, the score should be 65%.	*50-65% Scoring Band: Systematically Meeting Overall Requirements* **5.3 Employee Well-Being and Satisfaction.** The organization has effective, systematic processes in place to do the following: **a. Work Environment.** Maintain a work environment that contributes to the well-being, satisfaction, and motivation of all employees [5.3a(1)] *(A)*. **b. Employee Support and Satisfaction.** Maintain a support climate that contributes to the well-being, satisfaction, and motivation of all employees [5.3b(2)] *(A)*. *Some relatively minor gaps may exist in some parts of the organization to maintain a work environment and support climate that inhibit the achievement of employee well-being, satisfaction, and motivation (D). There is a systematic, fact-based process in place to evaluate and improve the efficiency/effectiveness of some of the key elements of (a) and/or (b) above (L). The processes to promote employee well-being and satisfaction are generally aligned with organizational needs and the requirements set forth in other Criteria Categories (I).*

Continued

5.3 Employee Well-Being and Satisfaction *(25 points possible)*	*Continued*
Best Fit Scoring Guidelines	**Expected Findings**

70-85% If examiners observe the applicant is doing everything described in the 50-65% Overall Requirements scoring band, and a few additional things in the 70-100% Multiple Requirements scoring band, the score should be in the lower part of the Multiple Requirements) scoring band (for example, 70-75%). If they observe the applicant is meeting many to most requirements in the 70-100% Multiple Requirements scoring band the score should be 85%.

90-100% If examiners observe the applicant is doing nearly everything described in the 70-100% Multiple Requirements scoring band, the score should be 90-95%. If examiners observe the applicant is meeting all of the requirements in the 70-100% Multiple Requirements band, the score should be 100%.

Note: *A score of 100% is possible only if **all** requirements are met and no Opportunities for Improvement can be identified. In addition, examiners must observe full deployment, extensive and ongoing evaluation, improvement, organizational learning, innovation, and knowledge sharing throughout the organization. Required approaches must be well integrated with organizational needs identified in response to the other Criteria Items.*

70-85% and 90-100% Scoring Bands: Multiple Requirements

5.3 Employee Well-Being and Satisfaction. The organization has well-deployed, effective, systematic processes in place to do the following:

a. Work Environment

1. Ensure and improve workplace health, safety, security, and ergonomics in a proactive manner, involving employees in the improvement efforts. Define performance measures or improvement goals for each of the key workplace factors related to health, safety, security, and ergonomics. Identify any significant differences in these workplace factors and performance measures or targets if different employee groups and work units have different work environments.
2. Ensure workplace preparedness for disasters or emergencies.

b. Employee Support and Satisfaction

1. Determine the key factors that affect employee well-being, satisfaction, and motivation. Segment these factors for a diverse workforce and for different categories and types of employees.
2. Provide appropriate support for employees via services, benefits, and policies. Tailor this support to address the needs of a diverse workforce and different categories and types of employees as appropriate.
3. Implement formal and informal assessment methods and measures to determine employee well-being, satisfaction, and motivation. Use different assessment methods and measures as needed across a diverse workforce and different categories and types of employees. Use these and other indicators, such as employee retention, absenteeism, grievances, safety, and productivity to assess and improve employee well-being, satisfaction, and motivation.
4. Relate assessment findings to key business results to identify priorities for improving the work environment and employee support climate.

The approach is well deployed with no significant gaps (D). There is a systematic, fact-based process in place to evaluate and improve elements of (a) and (b) above with clear evidence of innovation, learning, and organizational sharing, which results in refinements and improved integration organizationwide (L). The approach is integrated and consistent with the organizational needs identified in other Criteria Items (such as strategic objectives and performance-review and improvement systems (I).

6.1 Value Creation Processes *(50 points possible)*	
Best Fit Scoring Guidelines	**Expected Findings**
0-5% If examiners observe the applicant is not responsive to the requirements of an Item or provides no information, the score should be zero. If the applicant provides only anecdotal information, but no indication that a systematic approach has begun (even though deployment is very limited) the score should be 5%.	*0-5% Scoring Band: No Systems to Meet Requirements* **6.1 Value Creation Processes.** The organization has no effective processes to identify and manage its key value creation processes (such as designing [6.1a(3)] and delivering [6.1a(4)] core products and services) *(A)*. *Efforts to design products and services to deliver value are ad hoc (D). Reacting to problems is the normal way of approaching work (L). There is no effective alignment of value creation and key business processes in the organization and people and/or units seem to operate independently (I).*
10-25%. If examiners observe the applicant is barely doing the things described in the 10-25% scoring band, the score should be in the lower part of this band. If they observe the applicant is doing everything in the 10-25% band, but nothing in the next higher 30-45% band, the score should be 25%.	*10-25% Scoring Band: Beginning to Meet Basic Requirements* **6.1 Value Creation Processes.** The organization is in the beginning stages of establishing effective processes to identify and manage its key value creation processes (such as designing [6.1a(3)] and delivering [6.1a(4)] core products and services important to creating value) *(A)*. *Major gaps exist where key value creation processes essential to business success and growth have not been developed (D). Reacting to problems with design and delivery of value creation processes is widespread; working to prevent problems is in the beginning stages (L). The organization generally relies on joint problem solving to promote alignment of key value creation processes with organization priorities (I).*
30-45%. If examiners observe the applicant is doing everything described in the 10-25% scoring band, and a few additional things in the next higher 30-45% band, the score should be in the lower part of the 30-45% band. If they observe the applicant is doing everything in the 30-45% band, but nothing in the next higher 50-65% band, the score should be 45%.	*30-45% Scoring Band: Systematically Meeting Basic Requirements* **6.1 Value Creation Processes.** The organization has effective, systematic value creation processes in place to manage its key processes (such as designing [6.1a(3)] and delivering [6.1a(4)] core products and services important to creating customer value and achieving business success and growth) *(A)*. *Value creation processes in some parts of the organization may be just beginning to support customer requirements and key business needs (D). The organization is beginning to evaluate some of these processes and may or may not have made improvements based on the evaluation (L). Key value creation processes are beginning to be aligned with organization priorities and the requirements set forth in other Criteria Categories (I).*
50-65%. If examiners observe the applicant is doing everything described in the 30-45% scoring band, and a few additional things in the next higher 50-65% band, the score should be in the lower part of the 50-65% band. If they observe the applicant is doing everything in the 50-65% band, but nothing in the next higher 70-85% band, the score should be 65%.	*50-65% Scoring Band: Systematically Meeting Overall Requirements* **6.1 Value Creation Processes.** The organization has effective, systematic processes in place to do the following: **a. Value Creation Processes.** Identify and manage key work processes to deliver customer value and achieve business success and growth (which typically involve effective design and management of these processes. The design [6.1a(3)] of value creation processes should ensure key customer requirements are met. The management [6.1a(4)] of value creation processes should ensure that process steps are effectively monitored and controlled to ensure required products and services are consistently delivered.) *(A)* *Some relatively minor gaps may exist in the deployment of these processes in some parts of the organization (D). There is a systematic, fact-based process in place to evaluate and improve the efficiency/effectiveness of some of the key elements of (a) above (L). The value creation processes are generally aligned with organizational needs and the requirements set forth in other Criteria Categories (I).*

Continued

6.1 Value Creation Processes *(50 points possible)* — *Continued*

Best Fit Scoring Guidelines	Expected Findings
70-85% If examiners observe the applicant is doing everything described in the 50-65% Overall Requirements scoring band, and a few additional things in the 70-100% Multiple Requirements scoring band, the score should be in the lower part of the Multiple Requirements) scoring band (for example, 70-75%). If they observe the applicant is meeting many to most requirements in the 70-100% Multiple Requirements scoring band the score should be 85%.	*70-85% and 90-100% Scoring Bands: Multiple Requirements*

70-85% and 90-100% Scoring Bands: Multiple Requirements

6.1 Value Creation Processes. The organization has well-deployed, effective, systematic processes in place to do the following:

a. Value Creation Processes

1. Determine its key value creation processes. Define its key product, service, and business processes for creating or adding value. Ensure value creation processes contribute to profitability, sustainability, and organizational success.
2. Determine and list the key value creation process requirements, incorporating input from customers, suppliers, partners, and collaborators, as appropriate.
3. Design value creation processes to meet all the key requirements, incorporating new technology, organizational knowledge, and the potential need for agility into the design of these processes. Incorporate cycle time, productivity, cost control, and other efficiency and effectiveness factors into the design of these processes. Implement these processes to ensure they meet design requirements.
4. Define key performance measures or indicators used for the control and improvement of value creation processes. Ensure the day-to-day operation of these processes meet key process requirements. Use in-process measures and, as appropriate, customer, supplier, partner, and collaborator input to manage these processes.
5. Minimize overall costs associated with inspections, tests, and process or performance audits, as appropriate. Prevent defects, service errors, and rework, and minimize warranty costs, as appropriate.
6. Improve value creation processes to achieve better performance, reduce variability, improve products and services, and keep the processes current with business needs and directions. Share improvements and lessons learned with other organizational units and processes to drive organizational learning and innovation.

90-100% If examiners observe the applicant is doing nearly everything described in the 70-100% Multiple Requirements scoring band, the score should be 90-95%. If examiners observe the applicant is meeting all of the requirements in the 70-100% Multiple Requirements band, the score should be 100%.

Note: *A score of 100% is possible only if* ***all*** *requirements are met and no Opportunities for Improvement can be identified. In addition, examiners must observe full deployment, extensive and ongoing evaluation, improvement, organizational learning, innovation, and knowledge sharing throughout the organization. Required approaches must be well integrated with organizational needs identified in response to the other Criteria Items.*

The approach is well deployed with no significant gaps (D). There is a systematic, fact-based process in place to evaluate and improve elements of (a) above with clear evidence of innovation, learning, and organizational sharing, which results in refinements and improved integration organizationwide (L). The approach is integrated and consistent with the organizational needs identified in other Criteria Items (such as customer requirements, strategic objectives, and performance-review and improvement systems (I).

6.2 Support Processes *(35 points possible)*	
Best Fit Scoring Guidelines	**Expected Findings**
0-5% If examiners observe the applicant is not responsive to the requirements of an Item or provides no information, the score should be zero. If the applicant provides only anecdotal information, but no indication that a systematic approach has begun (even though deployment is very limited) the score should be 5%.	*0-5% Scoring Band: No Systems to Meet Requirements* *6.2 Support Processes and Operational Planning.* The organization has no effective processes to identify and manage its support processes [6.2a(3) and 6.2a(4)] or accomplish operational planning [6.2b(1)] *(A). Efforts to design and deliver processes to support value creation and operational planning are ad hoc (D). Reacting to problems is the normal way of approaching these processes (L). There is no alignment of key support and operational planning processes in the organization and people and/or units seem to operate independently (I).*
10-25%. If examiners observe the applicant is barely doing the things described in the 10-25% scoring band, the score should be in the lower part of this band. If they observe the applicant is doing everything in the 10-25% band, but nothing in the next higher 30-45% band, the score should be 25%.	*10-25% Scoring Band: Beginning to Meet Basic Requirements* *6.2 Support Processes and Operational Planning.* The organization is in the beginning stages of establishing effective processes to identify and manage its support processes (such as designing [6.2a(3)] and delivering [6.2a(4)] support services and accomplishing operational planning to ensure resources are available to support business requirements [6.2b(1)] *(A). Major gaps exist where key support processes essential to business success and growth have not been developed (D). Reacting to problems with design and delivery of support processes is widespread; working to prevent problems is in the beginning stages (L). The organization generally relies on joint problem solving to promote alignment of key support processes (I).*
30-45%. If examiners observe the applicant is doing everything described in the 10-25% scoring band, and a few additional things in the next higher 30-45% band, the score should be in the lower part of the 30-45% band. If they observe the applicant is doing everything in the 30-45% band, but nothing in the next higher 50-65% band, the score should be 45%.	*30-45% Scoring Band: Systematically Meeting Basic Requirements* *6.2 Support Processes and Operational Planning.* The organization has effective, systematic processes in place to identify and manage its support processes (typically involving the design [6.2a(3)] and delivery [6.2a(4)] of these support services) and accomplish operational planning [6.2b(1)] *(A). Support and operational planning processes in some parts of the organization may be just beginning to support customer requirements and key business needs (D). The organization is beginning to evaluate some of these processes and may or may not have made improvements based on the evaluation (L). Key Support and operational planning processes are beginning to be aligned with organization priorities and the requirements set forth in other Criteria Categories (I).*
50-65%. If examiners observe the applicant is doing everything described in the 30-45% scoring band, and a few additional things in the next higher 50-65% band, the score should be in the lower part of the 50-65% band. If they observe the applicant is doing everything in the 50-65% band, but nothing in the next higher 70-85% band, the score should be 65%.	*50-65% Scoring Band: Systematically Meeting Overall Requirements* *6.2 Support Processes.* The organization has effective, systematic processes in place to do the following: a. *Support Processes.* Manage key processes that support customer value and business success and growth (which typically involve the effective design and management of these processes). (The design [6.2a(3)] of support processes should ensure key customer requirements are met. The management [6.1a(4)] of support processes should ensure that process steps are effectively monitored and controlled to ensure required support products and services are consistently delivered.) *(A).* b. *Operational Planning.* Provide for financial management (to ensure, for example, that financial resources are available as needed[6.2b(1)]; and ensure continuity of operations in an emergency [6.2b(2)] *(A).* *Some relatively minor gaps may exist in the deployment of these processes in some parts of the organization (D). There is a systematic, fact-based process in place to evaluate and improve the efficiency/effectiveness of some of the key elements of (a) and/or (b) above (L). The support processes are generally aligned with organizational and value creation needs and the requirements set forth in other Criteria Categories (I).*

Continued

6.2 Support Processes *(35 points possible)*	*Continued*
Best Fit Scoring Guidelines	**Expected Findings**

70-85% If examiners observe the applicant is doing everything described in the 50-65% Overall Requirements scoring band, and a few additional things in the 70-100% Multiple Requirements scoring band, the score should be in the lower part of the Multiple Requirements) scoring band (for example, 70-75%). If they observe the applicant is meeting many to most requirements in the 70-100% Multiple Requirements scoring band the score should be 85%.

90-100% If examiners observe the applicant is doing nearly everything described in the 70-100% Multiple Requirements scoring band, the score should be 90-95%. If examiners observe the applicant is meeting all of the requirements in the 70-100% Multiple Requirements band, the score should be 100%.

Note: *A score of 100% is possible only if **all** requirements are met and no Opportunities for Improvement can be identified. In addition, examiners must observe full deployment, extensive and ongoing evaluation, improvement, organizational learning, innovation, and knowledge sharing throughout the organization. Required approaches must be well integrated with organizational needs identified in response to the other Criteria Items.*

70-85% and 90-100% Scoring Bands: Multiple Requirements

6.2 Support Processes. The organization has well-deployed, effective, systematic processes in place to do the following:

a. Support Processes
1. Determine and define its key processes for supporting value creation processes.
2. Determine and define key support-process requirements, incorporating input from internal and external customers, suppliers, partners, and collaborators, as appropriate.
3. Design these support processes to meet all the key requirements, incorporating new technology, organizational knowledge, and the potential need for agility into the design of these processes. Incorporate cycle time, productivity, cost control, and other efficiency and effectiveness factors into the design of these processes. Implement these processes to ensure they meet design requirements.
4. Define and use key performance measures or indicators for the control and improvement of support processes. Ensure day-to-day operation of key support processes meets key performance requirements. Use in-process measures and, as appropriate customer, supplier, partner, and collaborator input to manage these processes.
5. Minimize overall costs associated with inspections, tests, and process or performance audits, as appropriate. Prevent defects, service errors, and rework.
6. Improve support processes to achieve better performance, to reduce variability, and to keep the processes current with business needs and directions. Share improvements and lessons learned with other organizational units and processes to drive organizational learning and innovation.

b. Operational Planning
1. Determine the resources needed to meet current financial obligations. Ensure adequate financial resources are available to support operations. Assess the financial risks associated with current operations and major new business investments. Ensure adequate resources are available to support major new business investments.
2. Ensure continuity of operations in the event of an emergency.

The approach is well deployed with no significant gaps (D). There is a systematic, fact-based process in place to evaluate and improve elements of (a) and (b) above with clear evidence of innovation, learning, and organizational sharing, which results in refinements and improved integration organizationwide (L). The approach is integrated and consistent with the organizational needs identified in other Criteria Items (such as customer requirements, strategic objectives, and performance-review and improvement systems and value creation process requirements (I).

Category 7 - Results Overall Item Requirements

7.1 Product and Service Outcomes *(100 points possible)*

7.1 Performance outcomes are provided for the organization's key product and service performance results. Results are segmented by appropriate customer groups and markets. Appropriate comparative data are provided.

a. Product and Service Results

Provide data showing current levels and trends in key measures or indicators of product and service performance that are important to customers.

For the measures or indicators above, provide comparative data that demonstrate how well the organization's results compare with the performance of competitors' and other organizations providing similar products and services.

7.2 Customer-Focused Outcomes *(70 points possible)*

7.2 Performance outcomes are provided for the organization's key customer-focused results, including customer satisfaction and customer-perceived value. Results are segmented by appropriate customer groups and markets. Appropriate comparative data are provided.

a. Customer-Focused Results

1. Current levels and trends in key measures or indicators of customer satisfaction and dissatisfaction are provided. The results with the customer satisfaction levels of competitors and other organizations providing similar products and services are compared.

2. Current levels and trends in key measures or indicators of customer-perceived value are provided, such as customer loyalty and retention, positive referral, and other aspects of building relationships with customers, as appropriate.

For the measures or indicators above, provide comparative data that demonstrate how well the organization's results compare with competitors' performance, including competitors' levels of customer satisfaction.

7.3 Financial and Market Outcomes *(70 points possible)*

7.3 Performance outcomes are provided for the organization's key financial and marketplace performance results. These results are broken out by appropriate customer and market segments. Appropriate comparative data are provided.

a. Financial and Market Results

1. Provide data showing current levels and trends in key measures or indicators of financial performance, including aggregate measures of financial return and economic value or budgetary measures, as appropriate.

2. Provide data showing current levels and trends in key measures or indicators of marketplace performance, including market share or position, growth, and new markets entered, as appropriate.

For the measures or indicators above, provide comparative data that demonstrate how well the organization's results compare with competitors' performance.

Continued

Category 7 - Results Overall Item Requirements *Continued*

7.4 Human Resource Outcomes *(70 points possible)*

7.4 Performance outcomes are provided for the organization's key human resource results, including work system performance, and employee learning, development, well-being, and satisfaction. Results are segmented as appropriate to reflect the diversity of the workforce and the different types and categories of employees. Appropriate comparative data are provided.

a. Human Resource Results

1. Provide data showing current levels and trends in key measures or indicators of work system performance and effectiveness.

2. Provide data showing current levels and trends in key measures of employee learning and development.

3. Provide data showing current levels and trends in key measures or indicators of employee well-being, satisfaction, and dissatisfaction.

For the measures or indicators above, provide comparative data that demonstrate how well the organization's results compare with competitors' performance.

7.5 Organizational Effectiveness Outcomes *(70 points possible)*

7.5 Performance outcomes are provided for the organization's key operational performance results that contribute to the achievement of organizational effectiveness. These results are broken out by product groups and market segments, as appropriate. Appropriate comparative data are provided.

a. Organizational Effectiveness Results

1. Provide data showing current levels and trends in key measures or indicators of the operational performance of key value creation processes. Include productivity, cycle time, supplier and partner performance, and other appropriate measures of effectiveness and efficiency.

2. Provide data showing current levels and trends in key measures or indicators of the operational performance of other key processes. Include productivity, cycle time, supplier and partner performance, and other appropriate measures of effectiveness and efficiency.

For the measures or indicators above, provide comparative data that demonstrate how well the organization's results compare with competitors' performance.

7.6 Social Responsibility Outcomes *(70 points possible)*

7.6 Performance outcomes are provided for the organization's key governance and social responsibility results, including evidence of fiscal accountability ethical behavior, legal compliance, and organizational citizenship. These results are broken out by business units, as appropriate. Appropriate comparative data are provided.

a. Governance and Social Responsibility Results

1. Provide data showing key current findings and trends in key measures or indicators of organizational strategy and action plans.

2. Provide data showing key measures or indicators ethical behavior and of stakeholder trust in the senior leaders and governance of the organization. In addition, provide results for key measures or indicators of breaches of ethical behavior.

3. Provide data showing key current findings and trends in key measures or indicators of fiscal accountability, both internal and external, as appropriate.

4. Provide data showing key measures or indicators of regulatory and legal compliance.

5. Provide data showing key measures or indicators of organizational citizenship in support of key communities.

For the measures or indicators above, provide comparative data that demonstrate how well the organization's results compare with competitors' performance.

Scoring Calibration Statement	Actual Scoring Guidelines
0 or 5% If the examiners observe there are no business results or only poor results in areas reported, the score should be zero. If any trend data are reported that are positive, the score should be at least 5%. Comparative information is not expected. Results are not reported for any areas of importance to the organization's key business requirements.	• There are no business results or poor results in areas reported. • Trend data are either not reported or show mainly adverse trends. • Comparative information is not reported. • Results are not reported for any areas of importance to your organization's key business requirements.
10 - 25% If no comparative data and only a few results are reported with some improvements and/or early good performance levels in a few areas the score should be at the bottom of this band. If, in addition, comparative data and/or trend data are reported for a few areas of importance to the organization's key business requirements the score should be in the upper part of this band.	• A few business results are reported; there are some improvements and/or early good performance levels in a few areas. • Little or no trend data are reported. • Little or no comparative information is reported. • Results are reported for a few areas of importance to your organization's key business requirements.
30 - 45% If all of the requirements of the 10-25% scoring band have been met, and if some trend data and/or good performance levels are reported for many areas of importance to the organization's key business requirements, the score should be at least 30%. If, in addition to these trend data, comparative data are reported that show a few good levels of performance, the score should be in the higher part of this band (40–45%).	• Improvements and/or good performance levels are reported in many areas addressed in the Item requirements. • Early stages of developing trends are evident. • Early stages of obtaining comparative information are evident. • Results are reported in many areas of importance to your organization's key business requirements.
50 - 65% If all of the requirements of the 30-45% scoring band have been met, and if improvement trends and/or good performance levels are reported for most areas of importance to the organization's key business requirements, the score should be at least 50%. If , in addition, there is no pattern of adverse trends and no poor performance levels reported, the score should be higher (55%). Furthermore, if some trends and/or current performance levels—evaluated against relevant comparisons and/or benchmarks—show areas of good to very good relative performance the score should be in the upper part of the band (60-65%).	• Improvement trends and/or good performance levels are reported for most areas addressed in the Item requirements. • No pattern of adverse trends and no poor performance levels are evident in areas of importance to your organization's key business requirements. • Some trends and/or current performance levels—evaluated against relevant comparisons and/or benchmarks—show areas of good to very good relative performance. • Business results address most key customer, market, and process requirements.
70 - 85% If all of the requirements of the 50-65% scoring band have been met and if current performance is good to excellent in most areas of importance to the Item requirements the score should be at least 70-75%. If, in addition, data show that most improvement trends and/or current performance levels are sustained, and many to most reported trends and/or current performance levels—evaluated against relevant comparisons and/or benchmarks—show areas of leadership and very good relative performance the score should be higher 80-85%).	• Current performance is good to excellent in most areas of importance to the Item requirements. • Most improvement trends and/or current performance levels are sustained. • Many to most reported trends and/or current performance levels—evaluated against relevant comparisons and/or benchmarks—show areas of leadership and very good relative performance. • Business results address most key customer, market, process, and action plan requirements.
90 - 100% If all of the requirements of the 70-85% scoring band have been met and if current performance is excellent in most areas of importance to the Item requirements the score should be at least 90%. If, in addition, excellent improvement trends and/or sustained excellent performance levels are reported in most areas the score should be higher (95%). Finally, if there is also evidence of industry and benchmark leadership demonstrated in many areas important to business success the score could be higher.	• Current performance is excellent in most areas of importance to the Item requirements. • Excellent improvement trends and/or sustained excellent performance levels are reported in most areas. • Evidence of industry and benchmark leadership is demonstrated in many areas. • Business results fully address key customer, market, process, and action plan requirements.

Self-Assessments of Organizations and Management Systems

Baldrige-based self-assessments of organization performance and management systems take several forms, ranging from rigorous and time-intensive to simple and somewhat superficial. This section discusses the various approaches to organizational self-assessment and the pros and cons of each. Curt Reimann, the first director of the Malcolm Baldrige National Quality Award Office and the closing speaker for the 10th Quest for Excellence Conference, spoke of the need to streamline assessments to get a good sense of strengths, opportunities for improvement, and the vital few areas to focus leadership and drive organizational change. Three distinct types of self-assessment will be examined: the written narrative, the Likert-scale survey, and the behaviorally anchored survey.

Full-Length Written Narrative

The Baldrige application development process is the most time-consuming organizational self-assessment process. To apply for the Baldrige Award, applicants must prepare a 50-page written narrative to address the requirements of the performance excellence Criteria. In the written self-assessment, the applicant is expected to describe the processes and programs it has in place to drive performance excellence. The Baldrige application process serves as the vehicle for self-assessment in most state-level quality awards. The process has not changed since the national quality award program was created in 1987 (except for reducing the maximum page limit from 85 pages to 50 pages). (Author's note: *The CD-ROM attached to the back cover of this book contains a document designed to facilitate the collection of information within an organization to serve as a basis for a complete and thorough written application.*)

Over the years, three methods have been used to prepare the full-length, comprehensive written narrative self-assessment.

1. The most widely used technique involves gathering a team of people to prepare the application. The team members are usually assigned one of the seven Categories and asked to develop a narrative to address the Criteria requirements of that Category. The Category writing teams are frequently subdivided to prepare responses Item by Item. After the initial draft is complete, an oversight team consolidates the narrative and tries to ensure processes are linked and integrated throughout. Finally, top leaders review and *scrub* the written narrative to put the best spin on the systems, processes, and results reported.

2. Another technique is similar to that described previously. However, instead of subdividing the writing team according to the Baldrige Categories, the team remains together to write the entire application. In this way, the application may be more coherent and the linkages between business processes are easier to understand. This approach also helps to ensure consistency and integrity of the review processes. With fewer people involved, however, the natural *blind spots* of the team may prevent a full and accurate analysis of the management system. Finally, as with the method described previously, top leaders review and scrub the written narrative.

3. The third method of preparing the written narrative is the least common and involves one person writing for several days to produce the application. Considering the immense amount of knowledge and work involved, it is easy to understand why the third method is used so rarely.

With all three methods, external experts are usually involved. Nearly all Baldrige Award recipients reported they hired consultants to help them finalize their application by sharpening its focus and clarifying linkages.

Pros:

- Baldrige Award-winning organizations report that the discipline of producing a full-length written self-assessment (Baldrige application) helped them learn about their organization and identify opportunities for improvement before the site-visit team arrived. The written narrative self-assessment process clearly helped focus leaders on their organization's strengths and opportunities for improvement—provided that a complete and honest assessment was made.

- The written narrative self-assessment also provides rich information to help examiners conduct a site visit (the purpose of which is to verify and clarify the information contained in the written self-assessment).

Cons:

- Written narrative self-assessments are extremely time and labor intensive. Organizations that use this approach for Baldrige or state applications or for internal organizational review report that it requires between approximately 2000 and 4000 person-hours of effort—sometimes much more. People working on the self-assessment are diverted from other tasks during this period.

- Because the application is closely scrutinized and carefully scrubbed, and because of page limits, it may not fully and accurately describe the actual management processes and systems of the organization. Decisions based on misleading or incomplete information may take the organization down the wrong path.

- Although the written self-assessment provides information to help guide a site visit, examiners cannot determine the depth of deployment because only a few points of view are represented in the narrative.

- Finally, and perhaps most importantly, the discipline and knowledge required to write a meaningful narrative self-assessment is usually far greater than that possessed within the vast majority of organizations. Even the four 1997 Baldrige Award winners hired expert consultants to help them prepare and refine their written narrative.

Short Written Narrative

Two of the most significant obstacles to writing a useful full-length written narrative self-assessment are poor knowledge of the performance excellence Criteria and the time required to produce a meaningful assessment. If people do not understand the Criteria, it takes significantly longer to prepare a written self-assessment. In fact, the amount of time required to write an application/assessment is inversely related to the writers' knowledge of the Criteria. The difficulty associated with writing a full-length narrative has prevented many organizations from participating in state, local, or national award programs.

To encourage more organizations to begin the performance improvement journey, many state award programs developed progressively higher levels of recognition, ranging, for example, from *commitment* at the low end, through *demonstrated progress,* to *achieving excellence* at the top of the range. Even with progressive levels of recognition, however, the obstacle of preparing a 50-page written narrative discouraged many from engaging in the process. To help resolve this problem, several state programs permit applicants who seek recognition at the lower levels to submit a 7- to 20-page *short* written narrative self-assessment. The short form ranges from requiring a one-page description per Category to one page per Item (hence the 7- to 20-page range in length). The very short (one page per Category) applications have not provided sufficient detail for examiners, and many states now require longer applications.

Pros:

- It clearly takes less time to prepare the short form.

- Because of the reduced effort required to complete the self-assessment, more organizations are beginning the process of assessing and improving their performance.

Cons:

- The short form provides significantly less information to help examiners prepare for the site visit. In some cases, the very short, seven-page version provides examiners with no useful information.

- The short form is usually as closely scrutinized and carefully scrubbed as its full-length cousin.

This reduces accuracy and value to both the organization and examiners.

- The knowledge required to write even a short narrative prevents organizations in the beginning stages from preparing an accurate and meaningful assessment.

- Finally, there is not enough information presented in the short form to understand the extent of deployment of the systems and processes covered by the Criteria.

The Survey Approach

Just about everyone is familiar with a Likert-scale survey. These surveys typically ask respondents to rate, on a scale of one to five, the extent to which they strongly disagree or strongly agree with a comment. The following is an example of a simple Likert-scale survey item from the *Are We Making Progress as Leaders* survey released in February 2004 by the Baldrige Award Office of NIST:

Our leadership team shares information about the organization				
1	2	3	4	5
Strongly Disagree				Strongly Agree

A variation on the simple Likert-scale survey item has been developed in an attempt to improve consistency among respondents. Brief descriptors have been added at each level as shown in this descriptive Likert-scale survey item:

Senior leaders effectively share information about the organization				
1	2	3	4	5
Strongly Disagree				Strongly Agree

Pros:

- The Likert-scale survey is quick and easy to administer. People from all functions and levels within the organization can provide their opinion.

Cons:

- Both the simple and the descriptive Likert-scale survey items are subject to wide ranges of interpretation. One person's rating of *two* and another

person's rating of *four* may actually describe the same systems or behaviors. This problem of scoring reliability raises serious questions about the usefulness of both the simple and the word-descriptor survey techniques for conducting accurate organizational self-assessments. After all, a quick and easy survey that produces inaccurate data still has low value. That is the main reason why states have not adopted the brief Likert-scale survey as a tool for conducting the self-assessments, even for organizations in the beginning stages of the quality journey.

The Behaviorally Anchored Survey

A behaviorally anchored survey contains elements of a written narrative and a survey approach to conducting a self-assessment. The method is simple. Instead of brief descriptors such as *strongly agree/strongly disagree* or *none–few–some–many–most,* a more complete behavioral description is presented for each level of the survey scale. Respondents simply identify the behavioral description that most closely fits the activities in the organization. In addition, by asking the respondent to describe briefly the processes used by the organization to do what the Baldrige Criteria require, we can simulate the kind of information collected on a site visit, checking deployment and process integration. A sample is shown on the next page.

Since the behavioral descriptions in the survey combine the requirements of the Criteria with the standards from the scoring guidelines, it is possible to produce accurate Baldrige-based scores for Items and Categories for the entire organization and for any subgroup or division.

Figure 37 provides sample scores for the entire organization. The chart shows the percent scores, on a zero to 100 scale, for each Item. This helps users determine, at a glance, the relative strengths and weaknesses.

Figure 38 shows the ratings by job-classification subgroup, in this case, positions of senior leaders and employees. In Figure 37, Item 1.1, Leadership System reflected a rating of 50 percent. According to the breakout in Figure 38, however, senior leaders believe the processes are much stronger (more than 60 percent) than employees (less than 35 percent).

Improving Leadership Effectiveness throughout the Organization [1.2a(2)]

How well do senior leaders, managers, and supervisors at all levels evaluate and improve their effectiveness?

1 **Not Evident** ☐	Effective processes are not in place to ensure management and fiscal accountability in organization operations. The governing board is not well informed or involved in important fiscal and policy matters. They may be a rubber stamp for management and/or may have significant conflicts of interest that prevent effective oversight of management.
2 **Beginning** ☐	The governing board is beginning to set up systems to hold leaders and managers accountable for the organization's actions. The processes are not very effective since they are not used consistently. The processes are not evaluated to check effectiveness or see how they could be improved.
3 **Basically** **Effective** ☐	The governing board is involved in occasional reviews to hold managers accountable for the organization's actions and protect stakeholder interests against serious problems. They are starting to gather data about the effectiveness of some of these processes.
4 **Mature** ☐	Effective processes are in place to ensure management and fiscal accountability. Independent audits help ensure stakeholder interests are protected. The board sometimes checks the effectiveness of its governance processes and the board and/or senior leaders may have made some changes as a result.
5 **Advanced** ☐	Effective processes are in place to ensure management and fiscal accountability and transparency in most governing board operations. Independent audits provide information to support effective governance and help ensure stakeholder interests are protected. The performance of most senior leaders (including the chief executive) and the governance board is occasionally evaluated based on organizational performance results and/or other feedback (such as peer and subordinate reviews). The governing board, and many senior leaders and managers throughout the leadership system use this information to improve their personal effectiveness and governance/leadership-system processes. Some refinements are made to the processes as a result.
6 **Role Model** ☐	Effective processes are in place to ensure management and fiscal accountability and transparency in nearly all governing board and organization operations. Independent audits provide complete and accurate information to support effective governance and help ensure stakeholder interests are protected. The performance of nearly all senior leaders (including the chief executive) and the governance board is regularly evaluated based on organizational performance results and other feedback (such as peer and subordinate reviews). The governing board, and most senior leaders and managers and supervisors throughout the leadership system use this information to improve their personal effectiveness and governance and leadership-system processes. Ongoing refinements are made to the processes as a result. Innovative processes have been developed and shared as appropriate.
? or Not **Applicable** ☐	I do not have enough information to answer this question or it is not applicable to my organization.

Describe how the governance system ensures leaders and managers are held accountable for the organization's actions. Describe how independent audits or other processes are used to support effective governance and help ensure stakeholder interests are protected. Describe how the performance of senior leaders (including the chief executive) and the governance board is evaluated. Describe how these evaluations and feedback are used to improve the personal effectiveness of leaders, governance, and leadership-system processes. How widely is this done? Describe improvements and/or innovations to these processes, if any.

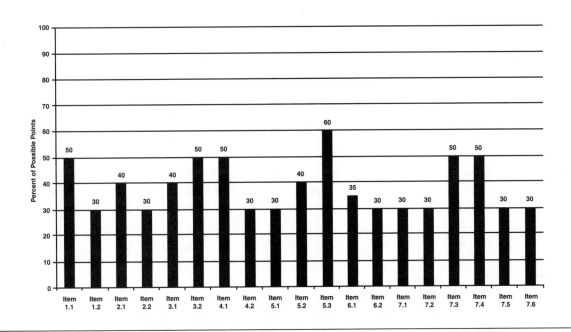

Figure 37 Sample organization overall percent scores by item.

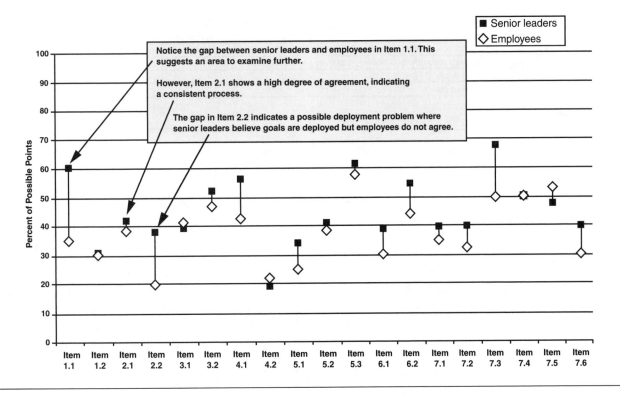

Figure 38 Sample organization position percent scores by item and job classification.

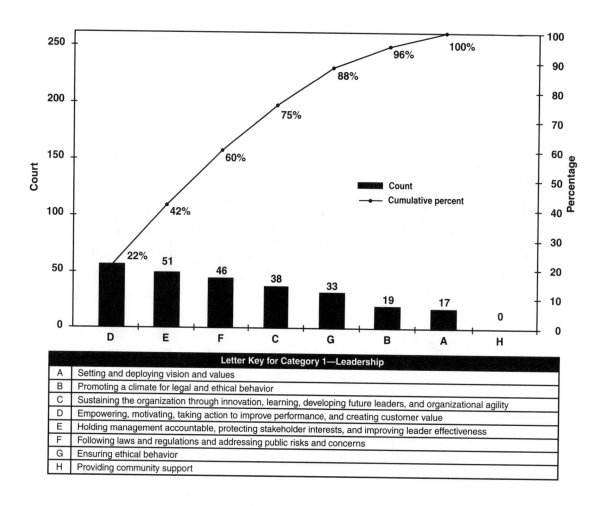

Figure 39 Category 1—Leadership: analysis of areas most needing improvement.

This typically indicates incomplete systems development or poor deployment of existing systems and processes required by the Item.

The Pareto diagram in Figure 39 presents data reflecting the areas respondents believed were most in need of improvement. Continuing with the leadership example, it is clear that respondents believe that leaders need to do a better job of empowerment, motivation, taking action to improve performance, creating customer value (theme D), management accountability, protecting stakeholder interests, improving leader effectiveness (theme E), and following laws and regulations and addressing public risks and concerns (theme F). This helps examiners focus on which areas

in leadership may present the most important opportunities for improvement.

Figure 40 allows examiners to determine what type of employee identified the various improvement priorities. Look at *D* in Figure 40 and you will see that employees identified the need to improve *D* by more than a 2 to 1 margin over managers/supervisors. This tends to indicate a deployment gap.

Finally, a complete report of the comments and explanations of the respondents can be prepared and used by examiners and organization leaders for improvement planning.

1. Leadership

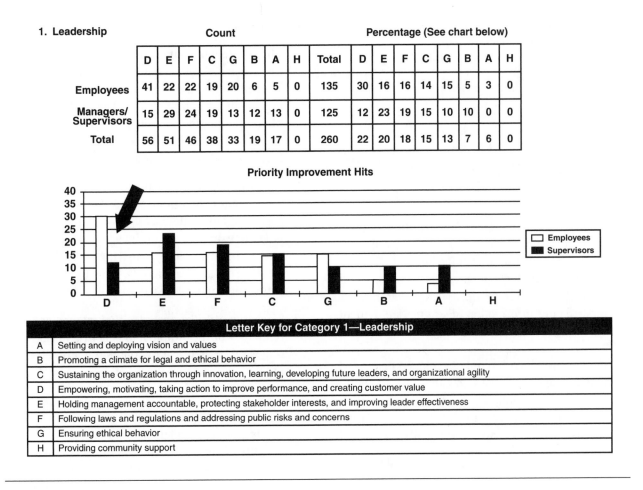

	D	E	F	C	G	B	A	H	Total	D	E	F	C	G	B	A	H
				Count								Percentage (See chart below)					
Employees	41	22	22	19	20	6	5	0	135	30	16	16	14	15	5	3	0
Managers/ Supervisors	15	29	24	19	13	12	13	0	125	12	23	19	15	10	10	0	0
Total	56	51	46	38	33	19	17	0	260	22	20	18	15	13	7	6	0

Priority Improvement Hits

	Letter Key for Category 1—Leadership
A	Setting and deploying vision and values
B	Promoting a climate for legal and ethical behavior
C	Sustaining the organization through innovation, learning, developing future leaders, and organizational agility
D	Empowering, motivating, taking action to improve performance, and creating customer value
E	Holding management accountable, protecting stakeholder interests, and improving leader effectiveness
F	Following laws and regulations and addressing public risks and concerns
G	Ensuring ethical behavior
H	Providing community support

Figure 40 Priority improvement counts and percentages—by position for the Leadership Category.

Pros:

- Descriptive behavioral anchors increase the consistency of rating. That is, one respondent's rating of *two* is likely to reflect the same observed behaviors as another respondent's rating of *two*.

- Although completing a behaviorally anchored survey requires more reading than a Likert-scale survey, the amount of time and cost required to complete it is still less than 10 percent of the time and cost required to prepare a written narrative.

- Because it is easy and simple to use, the behaviorally anchored survey does not impose a barrier to participation as does the written narrative. States and companies that use surveys with properly written behavioral anchors find the accuracy of the assessment to be as good and in many cases better than that achieved by the full-length narrative self-assessment, and significantly better than Likert-scale or short-narrative assessments. By obtaining input from a cross section of functions, locations, and grade levels throughout the organization, a performance profile can be developed, which not only identifies strengths and opportunities for improvement, but deployment gaps as well—something the written-narrative assessments rarely provide.

- For organizations doing business throughout the world, the behaviorally anchored survey—translated into the native language of respondents—permits far greater input than the written narrative.

- Modern techniques involving surveying through Internet access have created an easy way to survey a large, global company.

- Accurate survey data, based on behavioral anchors, can be used to compare or benchmark organizations within and among industries, and can also support longitudinal performance studies.

- Finally, examiners report that the effort required to analyze survey data and plan a site visit is about 50 percent less than the amount of effort required to analyze and prepare for a site visit based on a written narrative. Moreover, they report better information regarding deployment.

Cons:

- Organizations with highly developed performance management systems that seek to apply for top state or national recognition may prefer to practice developing the full-length narrative self-assessment because it is usually required.

- Examiners who are comfortable with the Baldrige application review process, which requires 25 to 40 or more hours to conduct an individual review of a full-length narrative self-assessment, initially find it disconcerting to develop comments and plan a site visit based on data gathered from a survey. Different training for examiners is required to develop skills at using survey data to prepare feedback and plan site visits.

Note: The preceding report summary is of a behaviorally anchored organizational self-assessment administered by the National Council for Performance Excellence. Readers may contact them by calling 802-655-1922 or by writing to NCPE, 480 Hercules Drive, Colchester, VT 05446. Several state quality awards and many private-sector organizations are using this type of assessment instead of the written-narrative form of evaluation. NCPE is the only organization authorized to administer this assessment tool. Any other use is not permitted.

In conclusion:

- The full-length written-narrative self-assessment is costly. It provides useful information both to examiners and the organizations completing it. The process of completing the written self-assessment can help more advanced organizations to focus and work together as a team.

- The usefulness of the short-form written self-assessment is marginal, especially for beginning organizations; little useful information is provided to examiners and managers/employees of the organization. Because the short-form written self-assessment takes less time to complete, one barrier to participation is lowered.

- Concerns over the accuracy and inter-rater reliability of the simple and descriptive Likert scales make their use in conducting effective organizational assessments of management systems marginal.

- The behaviorally anchored survey with comments from respondents combines the benefits of survey speed with the accuracy and completeness of a well-developed written-narrative self-assessment. In addition, the behaviorally anchored survey can identify gaps in deployment unlike the written-narrative self-assessment and is less costly and faster to administer than the written narrative.

In addition to the business assessment presented in this book, NCPE administers organizational self-assessments in education, health care, and nonprofit organizations including government agencies. More information about business, education, and health care surveys can be obtained from the National Council for Performance Excellence, 480 Hercules Drive, Colchester, VT 05446, (802-655-1922). Its Web site is: http://www.PerformanceExcellence.com.

Following is a sample of a behaviorally anchored survey originally developed by Mark Blazey in 1992 and revised each year since then.

2006 Baldrige Business

Organizational Self-Assessment, Behaviorally Anchored Version

Customized Demographic Profile

Each participating organization completes a customized demographic profile (a generic sample follows). In this way, survey data can be analyzed by these variables to help pinpoint specific areas needing improvement. This allows the extent of use (deployment) of management systems to be examined.

Please circle one selection from each column below to indicate your position within the organization.

Position	Location	Function	Org.	Years of Service
• Executive	• North	• Engineering	• 1	• 0 < 1
• Manager	• South	• Sales	• 2	• 1 < 3
• Supervisor	• East	• Human Resources	• 3	• 3 < 5
• Technician	• West	• Finance	• 4	• 5 < 10
• Individual Contributor	• HQ	Marketing	• 5	• 10 +
		• Manufacturing	Other	
		• Supply Management		
		• Info Technology		
		• Other		

BALDRIGE IN-DEPTH FOR BUSINESS INSTRUCTIONS

This survey consists of 49 themes or questions that relate to the 2006 Baldrige Performance Excellence Criteria. It is organized into seven *sections*, one for each of the seven Performance Excellence Criteria Categories.

- To the best of your knowledge, select a rating (1 to 6) that describes the level of development in your organization. Note that *all* of the elements of a statement must be true before you can select that level. If one or more is not true, you must go to a lower level. After you have selected the

rating level, please enter the value in the empty box to the right of the row of statements.

˝ Accuracy tip: The rating scale involves your assessment about the extent of use of the required management processes. The following definitions should help you rate this consistently:

4	Few	less than 15%
4	Some	15% to less than 30%
4	Many	30% to less than 50%
4	Most	50% to less than 80%
4	Nearly All	80% to less than 99%
4	All	100%

(Time-saving tip: Start reading at level 3. If all parts of the statement are true, go to level 4, if not, drop back to read level 2. After a few answers, save even more time by starting at the number you select most often. Don't waste time by reading from row 1 each time (unless most of your answers are 1).

- If you do not know an answer, enter NA (Not Applicable/Does Not Apply) or ? (Don't Know). If you are unsure of the meaning of a word or phrase, please check the glossary at the end of this booklet.

- After all statements in each Category have been rated, you will be directed to identify two areas you believe are the most important to improve in your organization now. Then, go back to the space below each row of statements you identified as vital to improve and describe briefly the activities your organization conducts that relate to the topic. Also, please suggest steps that your organization or its leaders could take to improve the processes. Your thoughtful comments are as helpful as the rating itself. If you want to comment on more themes, please do so.

- Continue in the same way to complete all seven Categories.

SUMMARY OF CATEGORY 1: LEADERSHIP

This sample assessment looks at one question in the Leadership Category (see sample question at Figure 41). The full-length assessment of Leadership contains eight themes: The first part (four questions—1A through 1D) looks at how senior leaders guide and sustain the organization by setting organizational vision and values and deploying these through the organization to all employees, and key suppliers and partners. Senior leaders need to communicate openly with employees and set high-performance expectations. Their personal actions must reflect the values they communicate. In addition, they must promote an environment that fosters legal and ethical behavior as well as one where accomplishment of strategic objec-

tives, innovation, and organizational agility will lead to performance improvement. Senior leaders must empower employees to achieve high performance through customer and business focus.

- You are asked to comment on the extent to which senior leaders guide and sustain the organization through clear values, vision, and setting of high-performance expectations. This includes how leaders create an environment for innovation, learning, knowledge sharing, and organizational agility. You are asked how senior leaders create an environment that fosters legal and ethical behavior. You are also asked how senior leaders personally participate in succession planning and develop future leaders.

- You are asked how senior leaders communicate with, empower, and motivate employees while encouraging frank, two-way communications. This includes taking an active role in reward and recognition to encourage high performance. You are asked how they focus on creating and balancing value for customers and other stakeholders.

The second part (four questions—1E through 1H) looks at how well the organization's governance system works to address its responsibilities to the public.

- You are asked to comment on management accountability and governance-system effectiveness in protecting interests of stakeholders and stockholders, and how senior leaders and members of the governance board are evaluated and how the system has improved.

- You are asked to comment on how well the organization ensures its behavior addresses impacts on the public and complies with legal and other regulatory requirements, as well as acts ethically in business interactions.

- Finally, you are asked to comment on the organization's support for its communities.

Communication and Organizational Performance: Empowerment, Motivation, Taking Action to Improve Performance, and Creating Customer Value
[Baldrige reference: 1.1b(1 and 2)]

1D. How well do senior leaders empower and motivate employees? To what extent do they encourage frank, two-way communication and personally take an active role in supporting employee reward and recognition to emphasize the importance of high performance and a customer and business focus? To what extent do leaders create a focus on action to accomplish objectives, improve performance, and attain the organization's vision? To what extent do leaders ensure a focus on creating and balancing value for customers and other stakeholders?

Not Evident

1. Top leaders do not effectively communicate with, empower, and motivate employees. They do not encourage two-way communication or actively participate in reward and recognition. Leaders usually wait and react to problems after they become serious.

Beginning

2. A few top leaders have started to communicate systematically with a few employees to reinforce organizational direction. The process is not very effective. The process is not evaluated to see how it could be improved.

Basically Effective

3. Top leaders communicate with some employees to reinforce organizational direction. They are starting to check the effectiveness of some of these processes.

Mature

4. Top leaders effectively motivate and communicate with many employees in many parts of the organization to encourage high performance and a customer focus by their actions, not just words. They sometimes check to see if their efforts in these areas are effective and may have made some changes as a result.

Advanced

5. Top leaders effectively communicate with, empower, and motivate most employees throughout the organization. Most leaders make sure that frank, two-way communication occurs most the time. They actively participate in reward and recognition and reinforce high performance and a customer and business focus. They emphasize taking action to achieve objectives and vision, including creating and balancing value for customers. They regularly check the effectiveness of these processes and sometimes make improvements. Some sharing of effective practices in this area occurs within the organization.

Role Model

6. Top leaders effectively communicate with, empower, and motivate nearly all employees throughout the organization. Nearly all leaders make sure that frank, two-way communication occurs nearly all the time. They actively participate in reward and recognition and reinforce high performance and a customer and business focus. They consistently emphasize taking action to achieve objectives and vision, including creating and balancing value for customers and other stakeholders. They regularly check the effectiveness of these processes and make ongoing improvements. They have developed innovative approaches in these areas and share best practices across the organization.

Figure 41 Sample Leadership question.

SUMMARY OF CATEGORY 2: STRATEGIC PLANNING

This sample assessment looks at one question in the Strategic Planning Category (see sample question at Figure 42). The full-length assessment of Strategic Planning contains six themes.

The first part (three questions—2A through 2C) looks at how the organization develops its strategic plans. The Category stresses that customer-driven quality and operational-performance excellence are key strategic challenges that need to be integral parts of the organization's overall planning. Specifically:

- Customer-driven quality is a strategic view of quality. The focus is on the drivers of customer satisfaction, customer retention, new markets, and market share—key factors in competitiveness, profitability, and business success; and

- Operational-performance improvement contributes to short-term and longer-term productivity, growth, and cost/price competitiveness. Building operational capability—including speed, responsiveness, and flexibility—represents an investment in strengthening your competitive fitness.

The second part (three questions—2D through 2F) looks at the way the organization converts its strategic objectives into action to align work to support the organization's strategic directions, and make sure that priorities are carried out.

• The organization must translate its strategic objectives into action plans to accomplish the objectives. The organization must also be able to assess the progress of action plans. The aim is to ensure that strategies are understood and followed by everyone in the organization to help achieve goals.

Strategy Development Process: Developing Strategic Plans Based on Business Data [Baldrige Reference: 2.1a(1 and 2)]

2A. How well do leaders develop strategic plans based on business-related data (such as customer and market needs, new opportunities for products and services, competition, world/national economy, technology, financial risks or societal threats, resource availability, ethical issues, and human resource, operational, and partner capabilities)?

Not Evident

1. The organization does not use a systematic strategic planning process. Leaders' opinion seems to drive plans or no plans exist. It usually waits and reacts to problems with its planning process after they become serious.

Beginning

2. The organization is beginning to plan consistently. Leaders use very little business-related data to help plan. The process is not very effective. The planning process is not evaluated to see how it could be improved.

Basically Effective

3. An effective strategic planning process is in place that considers some business requirements and challenges that are key to future business success, such as customer requirements; competition; organizational strengths and weaknesses; and human resource capabilities. The organization has started to gather data about the effectiveness of the planning process.

Mature

4. A clear, effective strategic planning process is in place to identify what the organization must accomplish to be successful in the future. The strategic planning process considers organizational strengths, weaknesses, opportunities, and threats that cover most business requirements and challenges that are key to future business success. The organization sometimes checks the accuracy of its planning assumptions and the effectiveness of its planning processes and may have made some changes as a result.

Advanced

5. A clear, effective strategic planning process is in place to identify what the organization must accomplish to be successful in the short and long term. The planning

---

process considers most of the following areas: organizational strengths, weaknesses, opportunities, and threats (SWOT analysis—including areas such as customer/market expectations, human resource capabilities, financial, societal, ethical, or other potential risks); major shifts in technology, markets, competition, or the regulatory environment; long-term sustainability and business continuity in emergencies; and its ability to execute the strategic plan. The organization regularly checks the accuracy of its planning assumptions and the effectiveness of its planning process and sometimes makes improvements. Some sharing of effective practices within the organization is done.

Role Model

6. A clear, effective strategic planning process is in place to identify what the organization must accomplish to be successful in the short and long term. The planning process considers nearly all of the following areas: organizational strengths, weaknesses, opportunities, and threats (SWOT analysis—including areas such as customer/market expectations, human resource capabilities, financial, societal, ethical, or other potential risks); major shifts in technology, markets, competition, or the regulatory environment; long-term sustainability and business continuity in emergencies; and its ability to execute the strategic plan. The organization regularly checks the accuracy of its planning assumptions and the effectiveness of its planning process and makes ongoing improvements. It has developed innovative approaches to strategic planning and shares best practices across the organization.

Figure 42   Sample Strategic Planning question.

SUMMARY OF CATEGORY 3: CUSTOMER AND MARKET FOCUS

This sample assessment looks at one question in the Customer and Market Focus Category (see sample question at Figure 43). The full-length assessment of Customer and Market Focus contains seven themes.

The first part (three questions—3A through 3C) looks at how the organization tries to understand what the customers and the marketplace want. The organization must learn about customers and markets to understand new customer requirements, offer the right products and services, and keep pace with changing customer demands and increasing competition.

- You are asked how the organization determines key customer groups and how it segments the markets.

- You are asked how the organization determines the most important product/service features.

- Also, you are asked how the organization improves the way it listens and learns from customers so that it keeps current with changing business needs, including changes in the marketplace.

The second part (four questions—3D through 3G) looks at how well the organization builds good relationships with customers to get repeat business and positive referrals. You are also asked how the organization gets data on customer satisfaction and dissatisfaction for customers and competitors' customers.

- You are asked how the organization makes it easy for customers and potential customers to access information or assistance and/or to comment and complain.

- You are asked how the organization gathers, analyzes, and learns from complaint information to increase customer satisfaction and loyalty.

- You are asked how the organization builds relationships with customers, since success depends on maintaining close relationships with customers.

- You are asked how the organization determines the satisfaction and dissatisfaction for different customer groups because satisfied customers are necessary for loyalty, repeat business, and positive referrals.

- Finally, you are asked how the organization follows up with customers, and how it determines customer satisfaction relative to competitors so that it may improve future performance.

Customer and Market Knowledge: Determining Customer Groupings and Segments [Baldrige Reference: 3.1a(1)]

3A. How well does the organization understand its customers and markets? Does the organization group its customers and markets into different categories to determine which to pursue for current and future business? How are the appropriate requirements and needs of all parts of the customer chain considered (such as products and services that are sold or delivered to end-users through retail stores, dealers, or other service providers)?To what extent does the organization include customers of competitors and other potential customers and markets in this determination?

Not Evident

1. The organization does not have an effective process in place to identify which customers and markets would be best to pursue. Leaders and managers usually wait and react to customer problems when they become serious.

Beginning

2. The organization has developed the beginnings of a process to identify appropriate customer groups and market segments for the purpose of determining their different requirements. The process is not very effective and not used consistently. The process is not evaluated to see how it could be improved.

Basically Effective

3. An effective process is in place to identify customer groups and market segments to understand their differing needs in order to identify some of the best groups to pursue to market current products and services. The organization has started to evaluate the effectiveness of its process to define customer groups and segments.

Mature

4. An effective process is in place to identify customer groups and market segments to understand their differing needs in order to identify many of the best groups to pursue to market current and future products and services. The organization sometimes evaluates the effectiveness of processes to define customer groups and may have made some changes as a result.

Advanced

5. An effective process is in place to identify customer groups and market segments to understand their differing needs in order to identify most of the best groups to pursue for current and future products and services. Most customers in the chain from immediate customer (such as dealer or retail store) to end users are defined. The process is regularly checked for accuracy. It is sometimes improved. Some sharing of improved practices within the organization takes place.

Continued

Figure 43 Sample Customer and Market Focus question.

Continued

Role Model

6. An effective process is in place to identify customer groups and market segments to understand their differing needs in order to identify nearly all of the best groups to pursue for current and future products and services. When deciding how to group its customers and markets the organization considers customers of competitors and potential customers. Nearly all customers in the chain from immediate customer (such as dealer or retail store) to end users are defined. The organization regularly checks the process for accuracy and ongoing improvements are made. It has put in place innovative approaches to customer segmentation and shares these approaches across the organization.

Figure 43 Sample Customer and Market Focus question.

SUMMARY OF CATEGORY 4: MEASUREMENT, ANALYSIS, AND KNOWLEDGE MANAGEMENT

This sample assessment looks at one question in the Measurement, Analysis, and Knowledge Management Category (see sample question at Figure 44). The full-length assessment of Measurement, Analysis, and Knowledge Management contains seven themes.

Measurement, Analysis, and Knowledge Management is the *brain center* of an effective management system. Appropriate information and analysis are used to improve decision making at all levels to achieve high levels of performance. Effective measures, properly deployed, help align the organization's operations to achieve its strategic goals as well as protect organizational knowledge.

The first part (four questions—4A through 4D) looks at the selection, collection, alignment, review, and integration of data and information to support effective decision making at all levels. Data and information guide decision making to help the organization achieve key business results and strategic objectives. Measurement, Analysis, and Knowledge systems serve as a key foundation for achieving innovation and sustaining peak performance.

- The organization must build an effective performance measurement system. It must select, collect, align, and integrate the right measures for tracking daily operations and use those measures for monitoring overall organizational performance. The organization must also make sure that data and information are accurate and reliable.

- Competitive comparisons and benchmarking (best practices) information should be used to help drive innovation and performance improvement.

- The organization should evaluate and improve the performance measurement system to keep it current with changing business needs and be able to respond to rapid changes.

- Data and information concerning processes and results (outcomes) from all parts of the organization must be analyzed to support the senior leaders' assessment of overall organizational health, organizational planning, and daily operations.

- Performance-review findings must support identification of priorities to support decision making and strategic planning at all levels of the organization and when appropriate, to suppliers and partners.

- Analyses must be communicated to support decision making and strategic planning at all levels of the organization.

The second part (three questions—4E through 4G) looks at how the organization ensures the quality and availability of data and information to support effective decision making for employees and appropriate suppliers, partners, and customers. It also examines building and managing knowledge assets.

- The organization must ensure integrity (completeness) of data and information as well as ensuring they are available, accessible, reliable, accurate, timely, confidential, and secure.

- The organization must identify, manage, collect, and transfer relevant knowledge and best practices.

- For data that are captured, stored, analyzed, and/or accessed through electronic means, the organization must ensure hardware and software reliability, security, and user friendliness.

All of these systems must be evaluated and enhanced to ensure they remain current with changing business needs and directions.

Performance Analysis and Review: Translate Performance Review Findings into Priorities for Improvement and Innovation. Communicate the Priorities to Support Decision Making [Baldrige Reference: 4.1b(2)]

4D. How well are priorities resulting from data analyses deployed to work groups and functional-level operations to support innovation, improvements, and effective decision making in all parts of the organization?

Not Evident

1. The organization does not systematically use the results of organizational performance reviews to support effective decision making. It usually waits and then reacts to problems when they become serious.

Beginning

2. The organization uses a few results of organizational performance reviews to support decision making of a few work groups or functions. The process is not very effective since it is not used consistently. The process is not evaluated to see how it could be improved.

Basically Effective

3. The organization uses some results of organizational performance review to support decision making of some work groups or functional levels. The organization has started to evaluate the effectiveness of some of these processes.

Mature

4. The organization translates its performance review analyses and findings to help prioritize action, align work, and support decision making for many work groups and functional levels. These priorities and targets for improvement are communicated to many leaders, managers, and employees. The organization sometimes evaluates the effectiveness of these processes and may have made some changes as a result.

Advanced

5. The organization translates its performance review analyses and findings to help prioritize action, align work, and support decision making for most work groups and functional levels. These priorities and targets for improvement are communicated to most leaders, managers, and employees. The organization regularly checks the process and sometimes makes improvements. Some sharing of improved data analysis translation within the organization takes place.

Role Model

6. The organization translates its performance review analyses and findings to help prioritize action, align work, and support decision making for nearly all work groups and functional levels. These priorities and targets for improvement are communicated to nearly all leaders, managers, employees, and when appropriate, suppliers and partners. The organization regularly checks the effectiveness of the process and makes ongoing improvements. Some innovations to the processes for identifying and communicating priorities have been made and best practices are shared across the organization.

Figure 44 Sample Measurement, Analysis, and Knowledge Management question.

SUMMARY OF CATEGORY 5: HUMAN RESOURCE FOCUS

This sample assessment looks at one question in the Human Resource Focus Category (see sample question at Figure 45). The full-length assessment of Human Resource Focus contains nine themes.

The first part (three questions—5A through 5C) looks at how well the organization's systems for work and job design, compensation, motivation, recognition, and hiring help all employees reach peak performance.

- You are asked how the organization designs work and jobs to empower employees to develop work skills, exercise initiative, innovation, and decision making, resulting in high performance.

- You are asked how the organization compensates, recognizes, and rewards employees to promote cooperation and support its high-performance objectives (strategic objectives) as well as ensuring a customer and business focus.

- Finally, you are asked how the organization recruits and hires employees who will meet its expectations and needs. The right workforce is an enabler of high performance.

The second part (three questions—5D through 5F) looks at how well education, training, and career development support high performance.

- You are asked how education and training are designed, delivered, reinforced on the job, and evaluated.

- You are also asked about how well the organization provides training in different areas of performance excellence, which includes leadership development.

- In addition, you are asked how employees are motivated to reach their full potential.

The third part (three questions—5G through 5I) examines the organization's work environment, its employee-support climate, and how the organization determines employee satisfaction, with the aim of fostering the well-being, satisfaction, and motivation of all employees.

- You are asked how the organization's work environment for all employees is safe, secure, and healthful and how well the organization is prepared to deal with emergencies and disasters to ensure the business continues to function.

- You are asked how the organization provides benefits and services to enhance employee well-being, satisfaction, and motivation for all employee groups.

- Finally, you are asked how the organization assesses employee well-being, satisfaction, and motivation, and how it relates assessment findings to key business results to set improvement priorities.

Employee Performance Management System: Providing Feedback, Compensation, and Recognition to Support High-Performance Goals and a Customer and Business Focus [Baldrige Reference: 5.1b]

5B. How well do managers and supervisors at all levels provide feedback to employees and make sure pay, reward, and recognition support high performance and a customer and business focus? [Note: compensation and recognition might include promotions and bonuses based on performance, skills acquired, and other factors contributing to high-performance goals. Recognition may be provided to individuals and/or groups and includes monetary and nonmonetary and formal and informal techniques.]

Not Evident

1. The organization does not systematically provide effective feedback or recognition to employees to enable them to achieve high-performance objectives. Managers and supervisors usually wait and then react to performance problems when they become serious.

Beginning

2. The organization is beginning to provide effective feedback and recognition to a few employees to enable them to achieve high-performance objectives. The process is not very effective since it is not used consistently. The process is not evaluated to see how it could be improved.

Basically Effective

3. The organization provides effective feedback and recognition to some employees to enable them to achieve high-performance objectives. The organization has started to evaluate the effectiveness of some of these processes.

Mature

4. The organization provides effective feedback, recognition, compensation, and rewards to enable many employees to achieve high-performance objectives. The organization sometimes evaluates the effectiveness of these processes and may have made some changes as a result.

Advanced

5. The organization provides effective feedback about performance to most employees. It ties compensation and recognition to most high performance, customer focus, and business goals and strategies. The organization regularly checks its feedback and compensation processes and improvements are sometimes made. Some sharing of improved reward and recognition practices within the organization takes place.

Role Model

6. The organization provides effective feedback about performance to nearly all employees. It ties compensation and recognition to nearly all high performance, customer focus, and business goals and strategies, consistent with organizational needs. The organization regularly checks its feedback and compensation processes and makes ongoing improvements. Some innovations to these processes have been made and the best reward and recognition practices are shared across the organization.

Figure 45 Sample Human Resource Focus question.

SUMMARY OF CATEGORY 6: PROCESS MANAGEMENT

This sample assessment looks at one question in the Process Management Category (see sample question at Figure 46). The full-length assessment of Process Management contains six themes.

Process Management is the focal point for all key work processes. The first part (three questions—6A through 6C) looks at the organization's key processes for creating customer value, business success, and growth.

- You are asked how key value creation processes are determined using input from customers and suppliers/partners as appropriate and how they contribute to profitability and success.

- You are asked how all key requirements are addressed in the design process. You are also asked how cost control, cycle time, and other efficiency and effectiveness factors are considered. You should make sure that design processes actually work as expected.

- You are asked how the organization makes sure that value creation processes work consistently and how performance measures are used to get an early alert of potential problems so you can take prompt corrective action.

- You are asked how well the overall costs associated with inspections, tests, and audits are minimized while preventing defects and rework. and minimizing warranty costs.

- In addition, you are asked how the organization improves its value creation processes to achieve better performance, shares these lessons learned, reduces variability, and keeps processes current with changing business needs.

The second part (three questions—6D through 6F) examines the organization's key support processes, with the aim of improving overall operational performance

- You are asked how key support processes are designed to meet all the requirements of internal and external customers and suppliers/partners as appropriate, incorporating cycle time, productiv-

ity, cost control, and other efficiency and effectiveness measures.

- The day-to-day operation of key support processes should meet the key requirements. In-process measures and internal customer feedback should be used to get an early alert of problems.

- You are asked how well the overall costs associated with inspections, tests, and audits are minimized while preventing defects and rework.

- You are asked how the organization improves its key support processes to achieve better performance and shares lessons learned.

- Finally, you are asked how the organization's operational planning ensures financial obligations will be met and risks assessed and addressed and how it ensures its operations will continue in an emergency.

Value Creation Processes: Managing and Improving Value Creation and Business Processes to Consistently Meet Requirements and Preventing Errors and Rework While Reducing Costs of Inspections, Tests, and Process/Performance Audits [Baldrige Reference: 6.1a(4, 5, and 6)

6C. How well do all parts of the organization involved in value creation use measures of process performance and customer input to control and improve these processes? How well does the organization reduce costs of inspections, tests, and process/performance audits and/or rework costs for value creation processes? What prevention-based processes does the organization use to reduce tests and inspection? How effectively are process improvements and lessons learned shared with other units in the organization and with appropriate suppliers/partners?

Not Evident

1. The organization does not have measures or other control mechanisms to ensure value creation processes consistently deliver desired results. Managers and supervisors usually wait and then react to problems when they become serious.

Continued

Figure 46 Sample Process Management question.

Continued

Beginning

2. The organization is starting to use measures or other control mechanisms to ensure a few value creation processes consistently produce or deliver desired results. The process is not very effective since it is not used consistently. The process is not evaluated to see how it could be improved.

Basically Effective

3. The organization effectively controls some value creation processes to ensure they usually deliver desired results. These measures are taken during the production cycle to check for consistency and make adjustments. The organization has started to gather data about the effectiveness of some of these processes.

Mature

4. The organization effectively monitors and controls many value creation processes to ensure they usually deliver desired results. These measures are taken during the production cycle to check for consistency and make adjustments. The organization sometimes gathers data to evaluate the effectiveness of these control mechanisms and may have made some changes as a result.

Advanced

5. The organization effectively uses measures or other control mechanisms to ensure most value creation processes usually deliver desired results. These measures are taken during the production cycle to check for consistency and make adjustments. The organization also uses customer and key supplier/partner input to ensure production and delivery processes consistently meet requirements. The organization regularly checks the effectiveness of these processes and sometimes makes improvements. Some sharing of improved practices within the organization takes place.

Role Model

6. The organization effectively uses measures or other control mechanisms to ensure nearly all value creation processes consistently deliver desired results. These measures are taken during the production cycle to check for consistency and make adjustments. The organization also uses customer and key supplier/partner input to ensure production and delivery processes consistently meet requirements. Effective systems are in place to prevent defects, rework, reduce inspections, tests, warranty, and rework costs. The organization regularly checks the effectiveness of these processes and makes ongoing improvements. Some innovations to these processes have been made and best practices are shared across the organization.

Figure 46 Sample Process Management question.

SUMMARY OF CATEGORY 7: RESULTS

This sample assessment looks at one theme in the Results Category (see sample question at Figure 47). The full-length assessment of the Results Category contains six themes.

The Results Category looks for the results produced by the management systems described in Categories 1 through 6. Results range from lagging performance outcomes such as product and service performance, customer satisfaction, market share, and financial performance to predictive or leading outcomes such as internal operating measures and human resource results. Together, these lagging and leading results create a set of balanced indicators of organizational health, commonly called a *balanced scorecard*.

- Question 7A looks at looks at product and service quality that lead to customer satisfaction, loyalty, and positive referral such as on-time delivery.

- Question 7B looks at how well the organization has been satisfying customers and achieving better customer-focused results

- Question 7C looks at the strength of the organization's financial and market results.

- Question 7D looks at how well the organization has been creating and maintaining a positive, productive, learning, and caring work environment.

- Question 7E looks at the organization's key operational (internal) performance results with the aim of achieving organizational effectiveness.

- Question 7F looks at key results in the areas of leadership, governance, and social responsibilities; accomplishment of strategy and action plans, organizational citizenship, ethical behavior, and compliance with applicable laws and regulations.

Customer-Focused Outcomes [Baldrige Reference: 7.2a(1 and 2)]

7B. What are the trends and results for customer satisfaction and dissatisfaction? These include customer relationship and loyalty indicators and measures of customer-perceived value including retention and positive referral. How does your level of performance compare with that of competitors or similar organizations? [Results data may come from internal measures as well as data from customers and independent organizations such as Consumer Reports, J.D. Powers, and so on.]

Not Evident

1. No results or poor results exist.

Beginning

2. Performance levels are good in a few areas that are important to the business.

Basically Effective

3. Performance levels are good in many areas important to the business. The organization is beginning to demonstrate improvement trends and get comparison data.

Mature

4. Performance levels are good in most areas of importance to the organization's key business requirements (such as customer satisfaction, dissatisfaction, and loyalty indicators, measures of customer-perceived value, customer retention, and positive referral) when compared to industry average. Some trends in areas of importance to the organization's key business requirements show growth.

Advanced

5. Performance levels are very good in most areas of importance to the organization's key business requirements (such as customer satisfaction, dissatisfaction, and loyalty indicators, measures of customer-perceived value, customer retention, and positive referral) when compared to top-performing competitors or benchmarks. Unless the actual level of performance is already at the top levels, many to most trends in areas of importance to the organization's key business requirements continue to improve and show sustained growth. No pattern of adverse trends and no poor performance levels are evident in areas of importance to the organization's key business requirements.

Role Model

6. Performance levels are excellent in most areas of importance to the organization's key business requirements (such as customer satisfaction, dissatisfaction, and loyalty indicators, measures of customer-perceived value, customer retention, and positive referral) when compared to top-performing competitors or benchmarks. Unless the actual level of performance is already at the top levels, most trends in areas of importance to the organization's key business requirements continue to improve and show sustained growth. No pattern of adverse trends and no poor performance levels are evident in areas of importance to the organization's key business requirements.

Figure 47   Sample Results question.

The Site Visit

INTRODUCTION

Many people and organizations have asked about how to prepare for site visits. This section is intended to help answer those questions and prepare the organization for an on-site examination. It includes rules of the game for examiners and what they are taught to look for. As we all know, the best preparation for this type of examination is to see things through the eyes of the trained examiner.

Before an organization can be recommended to receive the Malcolm Baldrige National Quality Award, it must receive a visit from a team of organizational assessment experts from the National Board of Examiners. Approximately 25 percent to 30 percent of organizations applying for the Baldrige Award in recent years have received these site visits. Although the panel of judges does not have a predetermined scoring minimum for site-visit candidates, generally a score of 550 points or more is needed.

The Baldrige Award site-visit team usually includes two to five senior examiners—one of whom is designated as team leader—and three to eight other examiners. In addition, the team is accompanied by a representative of the National Quality Award Office and a representative of the American Society for Quality (ASQ), which provides administrative services to the Baldrige Award Office under contract.

The site-visit team usually gathers at a hotel near the organization's headquarters on the Sunday immediately preceding the site visit. During the day, the team makes final preparations and plans for the visit.

Each examiner is assigned lead responsibility for one or more categories of the Award Criteria. Each examiner is usually teamed with one other examiner for most interviews during the site visit. These examiners usually conduct the visit in pairs to ensure the accurate interpretation and recording of information.

Site visits usually begin on a Monday morning and last one week. By Wednesday afternoon or Thursday morning, most site-visit teams will have completed their on-site review. (Geographically diverse organizations may require more time.) They retire to the nearby hotel to confer and write their reports. By the end of the week, the team must reach consensus on the findings and prepare a final report for the panel of judges.

Purpose of Site Visits

Site visits help clarify uncertain points and verify self-assessment (that is, application) accuracy. During the site visit, examiners investigate areas most difficult to understand from self-assessments, such as the following:

- Deployment: How widely a process is used throughout the organization

- Integration: Whether processes fit together to support performance excellence

- Process ownership: Whether processes are broadly owned, simply directed, or micromanaged

- Employee involvement: The extent to which employees' participation in managing processes of all types is optimized

- Continuous improvement maturity (learning): The number and extent of improvement cycles and resulting refinements in all areas of the organization and at all levels

Characteristics of Site-Visit Issues

Examiners look at issues that are an essential component of scoring and role-model determination. They have a responsibility to:

- Clarify information that is missing or vague and verify significant strengths identified from the self-assessment

- Verify deployment of the practices described in the self-assessment

Examiners will:

- Concentrate on cross-cutting issues

- Examine data, reports, and documents

- Interview individuals and teams

- Receive presentations from the applicant organization

Examiners may not conduct their own focus groups or surveys with customers, suppliers, or dealers. Conducting focus groups or surveys would violate confidentiality agreements as well as be statistically unsound.

Discussions with the Applicant Prior to the Site Visit

Prior to the official Baldrige Award site visit, all communication between the applicant organization and its team must be routed through their respective single points of contact. Only the team leader may contact the applicant on behalf of the site-visit team prior to the site visit. This helps ensure consistency of message and communication for both parties. It prevents confusion and misunderstandings. The team leader should provide the applicant organization with basic information about the process. This includes schedules, arrival times, and equipment and meeting room needs.

Applicant organizations usually provide the following information prior to the site-visit team's final planning meeting at the hotel on the day before the site visit starts:

TYPICALLY IMPORTANT SITE VISIT ISSUES

- Role of senior management in leading and serving as a role model
- Independence of governance system to protect stakeholder interests and hold managers accountable
- Degree of involvement and self-direction of employees below upper management
- Comprehensiveness and accessibility of the information system
- Extent that facts and data are used in decision making
- Degree of emphasis on customer satisfaction
- Extent of systematic approaches to work processes
- Training effectiveness
- Use of compensation, recognition, and rewards to promote key values
- Extent that strategic plans align organizational work
- Extent of the use of measurable goals at all levels in the organization
- Evidence of evaluation and improvement cycles in all work processes and in system effectiveness
- Improvements in cycle times and other operating processes
- Extent of integration of all processes—operational and support
- Extent of benchmarking effort

- List of key contacts

- Organization chart

- Facility layout

- Performance data requested by examiners

The team leader, on behalf of team members, will ask for supplementary documentation to be compiled (such as results data brought up to date) to avoid placing an undue burden on the organization at the time of the site visit. The team will select sites that allow them to examine key issues and check deployment in key areas. This information may or may not be discussed with the applicant prior to the site visit. Examiners will need access to all areas of the organization.

Conduct of Site-Visit Team Members (Examiners)

Examiners are not allowed to discuss findings with anyone but team members. Examiners may not disclose the following to the applicant:

- Personal or team observations and findings

- Conclusions and decisions

- Observations about the applicant's performance systems, whether complimentary or critical

Examiners may not discuss the following with anyone:

- Observations about other applicants

- Names of other award program applicants

Examiners may not accept trinkets, gifts, or gratuities of any kind (coffee, cookies, rolls, breakfast, and lunch are okay), so applicant organizations should not offer them. At the conclusion of the site visit, examiners are not permitted to leave with any of the applicant's materials including logo items or catalogs—not even items usually given to visitors. Examiners will dress in appropriate business attire unless instructed otherwise by the applicant organization.

Opening Meeting

An opening meeting will be scheduled to introduce all parties and set the structure for the site visit. The meeting is usually attended by senior executives and the self-assessment writing team. The opening meeting usually is scheduled first on the initial day of the site visit (8:30 AM or 9:00 AM). The team leader generally starts the meeting, introduces the team, and opens the site visit. Overhead slides and formal presentations are usually unnecessary.

The applicant organization usually has one hour to present any information it believes important for the examiners to know. This includes time for a tour, if necessary.

Immediately after the meeting, examiners usually meet with senior leaders and those responsible for preparing sections of the self-assessment (application), since those people are likely to be at the opening meeting.

Conducting the Site Visit

The team will follow the site-visit plan, subject to periodic adjustments according to its findings. The site-visit team will need a private room to conduct frequent caucuses. Applicant representatives are not present at these caucuses. The team will also conduct evening meetings at the hotel to review the findings of the day, reach consensus, write comments, and revise the site-visit report.

If, during the course of the site visit, someone from the applicant organization believes the team or any of its members are missing the point, the designated point of contact should inform the team leader or the Baldrige Award Office monitor. Also, someone who believes an examiner behaved inappropriately should inform the designated point of contact, who will inform the team leader or the award office monitor.

Employees should be instructed to mark every document given to examiners with the name and work location of the person providing the document. This will ensure that it is returned to the proper person. Records should be made of all material given to team members. Organizational personnel may not ask examiners for opinions and advice. Examiners are not permitted to provide any information of this type during the site visit.

GENERIC SITE-VISIT QUESTIONS

Examiners must verify or clarify the information contained in an application, whether they have determined a process to be a strength or an opportunity for improvement. Examiners must verify the existence of strengths as well as clarify the nature of each opportunity for improvement in the final feedback report.

Before and during the site-visit review process, examiners formulate a series of questions based on the Baldrige Criteria. It is possible to identify a series of generic questions that examiners are likely to ask during the site-visit process, based only on the Baldrige Criteria. Of course, all questions should be tailored to the specific key factors of the organization to be most relevant. The questions in the following section are presented to help prepare applicants and examiners for the site-visit process.

Many times, leaders and employees become focused on the process they have in place today. They often fail to describe how they systematically refined the process and show how it evolved to the process of today. Therefore, after learning how the process works today, *all examiners should ask the following questions: "Have you always done it this way? How did you do it before? Why did you change? Do you have additional improvements in the works?" If examiners do not ask these questions, each employee should offer the answer as if they were asked.*

Category 1—Leadership

1. (To top leaders) How do you set vision and values to guide the organization? Please share with us the values of your organization. [1.1a(1)]

    - What are your top priorities to achieve vision?

    - How do you ensure that all your employees know these priorities?

    - How do you know how effective you are at communicating these values to employees, customers, partners, and suppliers?

    - How you know your messages to employees are understood as you intended?

2. (To leaders) What behavior do you exhibit that proves to employees, customers, and suppliers that you fully embrace the values you mentioned?

    - (To employees) What does your leader do to show you that he or she actually believes these values are important? [1.1a(1)]

3. What does two-way communication mean to you (the leader)? Give me some examples. How widely is the process actually used? [1.1b(1)] Ask employees about how this two-way communication works to check deployment.

4. What do you do to make sure everyone in the organization behaves in a legal and ethical manner? What are your ethical rules that must not be violated (zero tolerance)? What happens when someone—a senior manager—breaks these rules? Ask employees the same question. [1.1a(2)]

    - What are some of the most important ethical principles? What processes have you put in place to achieve the desired ethical behavior? How well do these processes work? How do you know? What has been done to improve them?

5. What does it mean to you (senior leader) to create a *sustainable* organization? How do you make sure that your organization will continue to excel even after you or your key staff leave? (Note: "I do not plan to leave" is not an acceptable answer. Follow this answer with "What might happen if you were hit by a bus or incapacitated?" [1.1a(3)]

6. What do you do to increase continuous improvement throughout the organization, with all units and employees? What are some examples of new knowledge they have acquired?

7. What techniques have you put in place to make sure the strategic goals or objectives are achieved? [1.1a(3)]

8. What does *innovation* mean for you? For your employees? For your organization? What process have you put in place to encourage innovation? What innovative approaches have you personally implemented? Your employees? [1.1a(3)]

    - What do employees do differently to achieve the high-performance objectives of the organization? (Ask employers the same question.)

- What does organizational agility mean to you? What are the barriers to this agility you have identified in the organization? Pick some barriers and ask, what have you done to overcome this barrier?

- What processes have you put in place to ensure that innovations and other knowledge are effectively shared throughout the organization to appropriate managers and employees? How well do these processes work? How do you know? What has been done to improve them? [1.1a(3)]

9. Please describe the methods you use to program people for leadership roles. What is your role in this effort? How do you know this process is working? What improvements have you made in it? [1.1a(3)]

10. What are the ways you communicate throughout the organization and to key partners and suppliers? What kind of information do you communicate? When do you do this? [1.1b(1)]

   - What kinds of communication or feedback do you receive from employees and partners/suppliers? What do you do with this information? How well do these processes work? How do you know? What has been done to improve them? [1.1b(1)]

11. What is your role in supporting processes to ensure performance excellence (high-performance)? [1.1b(1)]

   - How do you encourage innovation and employee empowerment? Give me some examples of improved empowerment throughout the organization as a result of your efforts. (Follow up on these examples with other employees.) [1.1b(1)]

   - How do you ensure that middle managers and other subordinates promote employee empowerment and innovation throughout the organization? [1.1b(1)]

12. How independent is your board of directors? [1.2a]

- What percentage of the board is not affiliated with your organization in any way (other than being a board member)?

- How does your audit function ensure objectivity and independence?

- Have problems existed in the past where stakeholder interests were threatened? If so, what was done to prevent the possibility of those problems recurring?

- How does the board make sure managers behave properly and account for their actions in the organization?

- How would you rate the board's climate of trust? To what extent are distention and disagreement among board members tolerated? Encouraged?

- What policies are in place to ensure the board remains alert to management problems in the organization?

- What type of fiscal oversight does the board provide? What problems or issues have emerged in the past three to five years? Pick some and ask, what was the board's reaction to this issue? How was it resolved? What steps were taken to prevent the problem from happening again?

- What processes have you put in place to ensure the board effectively protects stockholder and shareholder value? How well do these processes work? How do you know? What has been done to improve them?

13. What are your key customer or stakeholder segments? [3.1a(1), 1.1a(1)], 1.1b(2)]

   - Pick one and ask, what does this customer/stakeholder group value?

   - Are the requirements or value expected of this customer group different from any other group? If so, what are the differences, and how have you ensured that the different or competing interests of these groups are addressed by your organization? [1.1b(2)]

14. What is your process for evaluating the effectiveness of the leadership system? [1.2a(2)]

    - How do you include or use employee feedback from the two-way communication (if done) in the evaluation?

    - Please identify specific examples where the senior leadership improved the leadership system as a result of these evaluations. How do managers evaluate and improve their personal leadership effectiveness? How are data from organizational performance reviews used here?

15. What are the criteria for promoting and rewarding managers within the organization? [1.2a(2); 5.1b]

    - How are you making managers accountable for performance-improvement, employee-involvement, and customer-satisfaction objectives? (Look at some samples of managers' evaluations [chosen at random] and check to see if they reflect refinements based on organizational performance review findings and employee feedback.)

    - How have you improved the process of evaluating managers over the years?

    - What processes have been put in place to evaluate and improve the effectiveness of the board of directors as a whole and individual board members? How well do these processes work? How do you know? What has been done to improve them?

16. What do you do to anticipate public concerns over the possible impact of your organization? How do you determine what risks the public faces because of your current and/or future products, services, and operations? What are some examples of risks you have identified? Pick some risks at random and ask, what have you done to reduce the risk or threat to the public? How do you know you are successful in these areas? How do you measure progress? [1.2b(1)]

    - What goals have been developed to identify and reduce risks?

    - What are the biggest environmental issues your organization faces? As a corporate citizen, what is your process for contributing to and improving the environment and society?

    - How do you know that your processes for protecting the public from risks associated with your products, services, and programs are effective? How have you improved these processes?

17. What are some ways your organization ensures that employees and key partners act in an ethical manner in all business and stakeholder transactions? How is this measured and monitored to ensure compliance? [1.2b(2)]

18. What support does your organization provide to local communities? Why do you provide this support? How does this support align with organizational priorities and the strategy? [1.2c]

    - How do you know that the processes you have in place for identifying and supporting key communities are appropriate?

    - How do you know the resource issues allocated for these purposes are appropriately used? Have you always provided this type of support?

    - What has been done to improve your efforts to support these communities?

Category 2—Strategic Planning

1. When was the last time the strategic plan was updated? Were you involved in the strategic planning process? What was your role? Who else was involved and what did each contribute? [2.1a(1)]

    - How far out does your planning look? Why? Why not shorter or longer?

    - How does the overall process for developing strategy work? (If people were involved in the planning process, ask them to recite how the process works without referring to written documentation. We must determine whether a consistent planning process is in place that meets the requirements of the Criteria—we are not testing the ability of senior leaders to read a written document.)

2. Please give some examples of how your planning process has helped you to identify problems, trouble areas, or threats that you might not have known about otherwise. [2.1a(1)]

3. What factors do you consider when you analyze organizational strengths, weaknesses, opportunities, and threats? Please show the data you use to help you understand the issues. [2.1a(2)]

4. What data, information, and other factors did you consider in the development of your strategic plan? [2.1a(2)]

   - Does your organization depend on key suppliers or partners to be successful? If so, which ones? Examiners should pick some from their list and ask, how did you consider the needs and capabilities of these suppliers/partners during the process of developing your strategic plan?

   - Does your organization have key competitors that affect your ability to be successful? Which ones? Pick some and ask, what abilities does this competitor possess that may create a problem for your organization? How did you consider the threats posed by this key competitor during the process of developing your strategic plan? How has your plan addressed these potential problems or threats?

   - Is your organization helped or hurt by new technologies? Which ones? Pick some and ask, how did you consider these new technologies during the process of developing your strategic plan?

   - How do you consider the needs of all key customers (or other appropriate stakeholders) in the development of the strategic plan? How do you balance the requirements and preferences of these customers when they are conflicting?

   - What future regulatory, legal, financial, economic, or ethical risks does your organization face? Pick some and ask, how did you determine this was a risk? How did your planning process consider the potential problems presented by this risk when developing your plan?

   - Were you or are you likely to be affected by changes in the national or global economy? If so, in what ways? Help me understand how you considered the likely impact of these problems in your planning process.

   - How has your planning process helped you identify opportunities to redirect resources to more productive uses, such as higher-priority products, services, and programs? Please give some examples of new opportunities and how you capitalized on them as a result of your planning.

   - What have you done to check the accuracy of planning assumptions and projections you used in the past to develop your strategic plan? How accurate have your past planning assumptions been? What have you done to improve the accuracy and effectiveness of your planning process? What refinements have you made during the past few years?

5. How often do you review progress of your key strategic objectives? Please show me the time lines or projections for achieving each objective. How did you develop the projected or expected levels of future performance for each strategic objective (also called time lines)? [2.1b(1)]

6. Review the list of strategic challenges the organization provided in P2. Pick one, then ask: Please show me how you check your objectives to be sure this strategic challenge was addressed. Then repeat the process for another challenge. [2.1b(2)]

   - Can you tell from this information where you expect to be on each objective when you review performance the next time? Next quarter? Next year? In two years? (Note: the frequency of review should be consistent with the review processes described in Item 4.1b(1). For example, if progress toward achieving the customer-satisfaction objectives is reviewed quarterly by the senior leadership team, then quarterly time lines or milestones should be defined to permit effective review. In addition, the time lines reported under 2.1b(1) should identify the measurable, outcome-based levels of performance that are expected during these reviews, not just a list of activities.)

- How did you determine the appropriate frequency or period to review progress for these objectives?

7. What is the process you use to identify the actions that need to be taken throughout the organization in order to meet your goals or strategic objectives? [2.2a(1)]

- How do you break the strategic objectives into actions that drive work at all levels of the organization?

- How do you make sure that every employee knows what work he or she must do to achieve his or her part of the plan?

- What process is used to figure out what resources are needed to do this work? How are resources allocated to make sure the actions can be completed on schedule? How effective are these processes? How do you know? What improvements in the processes of converting plans to actions and assigning resources have been made in the past few years?

- How do you determine what people and skills you will need to carry out your strategic objectives and related action plans? What changes have been made in your human resource plan during the past few years to help you achieve your strategic objectives and related action plans? How effective and accurate have your human resource plans been?

8. Another way of examining the issues outlined in No. 7 is as follows: How do you make sure that goals, objectives, and action plans are understood and used throughout the organization to drive and align work? [2.2a(1)]

- How do you ensure that organizational, work unit, and individual actions and

resources are aligned at all levels? (Pick a strategy that the leader has indicated is important to organizational success. Then ask the leader what actions they have determined are critical to achieve the strategy. From the list of actions, pick one or two and ask the leader to explain specifically how resources were allocated to ensure these plans would be accomplished. Then ask how the leader checks to determine if appropriate resources were allocated. Ask if any improvements have been made in this process over the past few years. Repeat this line of questioning at different levels in the organization to check alignment.)

- Ask to see an old plan. Pick an action that drove improvement. Determine the extent to which the changes that were put in place have been sustained. If the change was not sustained, determine what process changes were made to ensure that future changes can be sustained. In other words, determine what they learned from the failure and what they did with that knowledge.

9. Have circumstances changed in your organization that required a change of action plans? If yes, ask how did you make sure that everyone involved understood and took appropriate action to make the change. If no, ask what process they have in place to make sure that everyone involved understood and took appropriate action to make the change. [2.2a(2)]

10. Have any changes been made in key products, services, customers, markets, or operations since the Baldrige application was submitted? If no, go to the next issue. If yes, how were actions required by these changes identified and deployed to appropriate units and people to implement? Follow the action trail to determine if those who need to take action know about the changes, how they learned about them, when, and what action they are taking. [2.2a(3)]

11. Describe your long- and short-term plans to make sure that any changes in actions meet the recruitment, recognition, safety and security,

motivation, development, education, and training needs of the organization that are necessary to carry out the strategic plans. What are the measures of progress to meet these human resource plans? [2.2a(4)]

12. Summarize the organization's human resource plans that are needed to carry out the strategic objectives and related action plans. How do these human resource plans ensure sufficient human resources? [2.2a(4)]

    • What are examples of changes to the human resource plans based on inputs from the strategic planning in the following areas: recruitment, training, compensation, rewards, incentives, fringe benefits, and other programs, as appropriate?

13. What is (summarize) your process for evaluation and improvement of the strategic planning and plan deployment processes, including human resource planning?

    • What are examples of improvements made as a result of these evaluation processes? Where and when did they occur?

    • Why did you decide to focus on these improvements? What facts helped with your decisions on what to improve and how to improve the planning process?

14. How did you determine that the goals or objectives you set were appropriate? How do you know that achieving this goal will make you a leader in the industry or sector? [2.2b]

15. Who do you consider to be your top competitors, and how does your planned performance (goals) compare to theirs and/or similar providers? How did you determine who your top competitors are? [2.2b]

    • At what level do you expect your key competitors or other similar providers to perform during the same period as your plan covers?

    • How did you figure this out?

    • How accurate have your past estimates of your competitor's future performance been?

What have you done to make these projections more accurate?

    • What gaps have you identified where the competitor is ahead? What are you doing to close the gap?

Category 3—Customer and Market Focus

1. Who are your key customers, customer groups, or market segments? [3.1a(1); 3.1a(2)]

    • What was your reason for grouping them this way?

    • How did you figure out what your customers expect of you?

    • How does your organization determine short- and long-term customer requirements for each of the customer groups or segments? Do you use the same techniques for all customer groups? Why or why not?

    • How do you know what the customers of competitors (your potential customers) are getting or want? How have you used this knowledge?

    • How do you use information you learned from customers, including data such as retention rates, complaints, and loyalty to plan products and services, market them, make improvements in them, or develop new business?

2. Which customers/groups/market segments do you want to attract for future business? How did you make this determination? What data or decision process did you use? Have you always done it this way? Why or why not? [3.1a(1)]

3. What are the key requirements of your customers (break out by segment or group)? Are the requirements of potential customers different from the requirements of the customers you presently serve? [3.1a(2)]

    • What is most important or valuable to the different customer groups you serve or want to serve? What features of products and services are most important to getting them and keeping them happy? How did you determine this? How do you separate the most important customer requirements from less important requirements? [3.1a(2)]

- How do you anticipate new or emerging customer requirements? What do you do with this information? How do you use customer feedback? Help me understand how customer data and feedback are used to better satisfy their needs.

- How do you evaluate and improve processes for determining customer requirements? What role has new technology or changing business needs played in deciding what improvements to make? Provide some examples of improvements that you have made in the past few years. [3.1a(3)]

4. How do you make it easy for your customers to contact you, get information and assistance, or complain? What do you expect to learn from customer complaints? What have you learned? Please provide examples. [3.2a(2 and 3)]

- What are the customer-contact requirements or service standards? How were they determined? How do you make sure that every employee who comes in contact with customers understands and works to these standards? How do you know the customer-contact requirements (standards) are consistently met for all customers throughout the organization? [3.2a(2)]

- Describe your process for handling customer complaints? What do you do with the complaint or comment data? (Ask to see some sample complaints and follow the data trail. Determine how the data are analyzed and used to drive improvements.) [3.2a(3)]

- What occurs between receiving the complaint and resolving the complaint? [3.2a(3)]

- What does *prompt and effective resolution of a complaint* mean to your organization?

- What processes do you have in place to ensure complaints are resolved by the first person in your organization to receive the complaint?

What skills and authority do your customer contact employees need to resolve complaints promptly and effectively? How do you check to determine if your complaint-resolution processes are effective or not? [3.2a(3)] What improvements have you made in these processes over the past few years? [3.2a(4)]

5. How do you evaluate and improve the customer-relationship process? What are some improvements you've made to the way you strengthen customer relationships and loyalty? How did you decide they were important to make, and when were they made? [3.2a(4)]

6. What are your key measures for customer satisfaction and dissatisfaction? How do these measures provide information on likely future market behavior such as loyalty, repurchase, and referrals? [3.2b(1)]

- What tools and techniques do you use to measure customer satisfaction and dissatisfaction?

- Do you measure satisfaction/dissatisfaction for all key customer groups/segments? What do you do with the information?

7. Describe your process for follow-up with customers after the customer has had contact with the organization or used its products and services? What do you do with feedback you solicit from customers regarding products and services? What triggers follow-up action? [3.2b(2)]

8. What customer-satisfaction information do you have about your competitors or benchmarks? What do you do with this information? How do employees use this information in their regular work? What action do they take as a result? Please provide some examples. [3.2b(3)]

9. How do you go about checking and improving the way you determine customer satisfaction and dissatisfaction? Please provide some examples of how you have improved these techniques over the past several years. [3.2b(3)]

- How do you know appropriate action is taken in response to customer satisfaction data at all levels of the organization?

- How do you know you are asking customers and right questions when trying to determine satisfaction and dissatisfaction? [3.2b(4)]

Category 4—Measurement, Analysis, and Knowledge Management

1. What kind of decisions do you have to make in your job? Show me the data that you collect to help you make these decisions. [4.1a(1)]

   - What are the major performance indicators critical to running your organization?

2. How do you determine whether the information you collect and use for decision making is appropriate for tracking your daily work and the performance of the entire organization? [4.1a(1)]

   - What criteria do you use for data selection? How do you ensure that all data collected meet these criteria?

3. What is the process you use to determine the relevance of the information to organizational goals and strategic planning? [4.1a(1)]

   - What information or data do you use to check if adequate progress in achieving strategic objectives is being made? [4.1a(1)]

   - Describe how you obtain feedback from the users of the information, the employees, suppliers, and customers who use this information to support their decision making. How is this feedback used to make improvements in the data and information you collect and analyze?

4. You have told us what your top priorities are. How do you benchmark against these? [4.1a(2)]

   - Please describe how needs and priorities for selecting comparisons and benchmarking are determined.

   - Show us samples of comparative studies and how the resulting information was used to

support innovation throughout the organization. Picking some at random, determine:

   - Why was the area selected for benchmarking?

   - How did you use competitive or comparative performance data?

   - How are the results of your benchmarking efforts used to set appropriate goals, make better decisions about work, and set priorities for improvement or innovation?

   - How are the results of your benchmarking efforts used to improve work processes?

   - How do you evaluate and improve your benchmarking processes to make them more efficient and useful?

5. Please share with us an example of analysis of information important to organizational performance review and strategic planning. [4.1b(1)]

   - How are data analyzed to determine relationships between customer information and financial performance; operational data and financial performance; or operational data and human resource requirements and/or performance?

   - What data and analyses do you use to understand your people, your customers, and your market to help with strategic planning?

   - How widely are these analyses used for decision making throughout the organization at both functional or work-group levels?

   - What are you doing to improve the analysis process and make it more useful for organizational and operational decision making?

6. How do you make sure that the analysis needed to support decision making at all levels of the organization is effectively communicated (made available)? Show how the following types of analyses are used to support decision making and innovation or improvements: [4.1b(2)]

   - Technology projections

   - Cause–effect relationships

- Root-cause analysis

- Descriptive analyses such as statistical process control, central tendencies, Pareto analysis, histograms

- Other statistical tools such as correlation analysis, regression and factor analyses, and tests of significance (t-tests, f-tests)

7. What is the process used to monitor the performance of your organization? How does it relate to the organization's strategic business plan? [4.1b(1)]

    - What measurable goals exist? How are they monitored? How often? How well do these monitoring processes work? How do you know? Have you always done it this way? What has been done to improve them?

    - What are the key success factors (or key result areas, critical success factors, key business drivers) for your organization, and how do you use them to drive performance excellence?

    - What percentage of your time is spent on performance review and improvement activities? How do you review performance to assess the organization's health, competitive performance, and progress against key objectives? What key performance measures do you and other senior leaders regularly review?

8. How do top priorities and opportunities for innovation reflect organizational review findings? Have you set or changed priorities for innovation and resource allocation? Please give examples of how this is done. [4.1b(2)]

    - How do you ensure that these priorities and opportunities for innovation are understood and used throughout the organization to align work? (After you identify a top priority for innovation, ask the leader to provide specific examples of how they ensure these priorities are implemented and aligned throughout the organization, as appropriate.) To what extent do these priorities and innovation opportuni-

ties involve support from key suppliers and/or partners? (Pick one example of a priority and ask the leader to help you understand how the organization works with affected suppliers or partners.) [4.1b(2)]

9. How do you make sure that data, information, and analysis needed to support decision making at all levels of the organization are available, timely, and accurate? [4.2a(1)]

10. How do you make sure that your hardware and software systems meet the needs of all users? How do you determine whether the software and hardware are *user friendly*? (Ask what groups use the hardware/software system. Randomly pick a group and ask how the organization makes sure these people can easily use the hardware and software. Then randomly ask some people in a group how their *user-friendliness* requirements were identified and met.) [4.2a(2)]

11. Please walk me through the process you use to make sure data and information systems (both hardware and software) will continue to be available during an emergency. [4.2a(3)]

12. Please show how you ensure software and hardware are correct. What drives decisions to change or upgrade systems? [4.2a(4)]

13. What are the data-security requirements you believe are critical to your system? (For example, certain statutes and regulations, such as the Family and Education Rights and Privacy Act, may require certain levels of security and data protection.) How do you guarantee data and system security and confidentiality? [4.2a(2); 4.2c]

14. How do you make sure relevant knowledge and information are appropriately shared throughout the organization and with appropriate suppliers, partners, and customers? [4.2a(1); 4.2b]

    - How are worthy processes and work practices shared among all appropriate employees quickly and effectively? (These processes and practices are also known as best practices, exemplary practices, role-model practices or, in Minnesota, pretty good practices.)

15. What do you do to make sure the data that support decision making are complete, tell the whole story (data integrity)? [4.2c]

16. What kind of reliability problems have you experienced with your hardware and software? How have you resolved them? What have you done to prevent these types of problems from happening again? [4.2c]

Category 5—Human Resource Focus

1. What authority do employees have to direct their own actions and make decisions about their work? [5.1a(1)]

   • (To employees) What authority do you have to make decisions about your work, such as resolving problems and improving work processes? What have managers done to encourage innovation within the workforce?

   • (To all) To what extent do leaders, managers, and supervisors make it easy to change and keep pace with changing business and customer requirements? If extremely agile and flexible were a 10 and slow-moving, bureaucratic, and bound in *red tape* were a one, where would you rate the organization as a whole? Why? Where would you rate your unit? Why?

   • (To managers) How do you empower employees? What do you do to encourage initiative and self-directed responsibility among employees in their regular work and jobs? What are some examples of processes you have used to evaluate and enhance opportunities for employees to take individual initiative and demonstrate self-directed responsibility in designing and managing their work? What have you done to increase employee innovation, where employees actually make improvements, not just suggestions? Show examples of actions taken and improvements made. When were they made?

2. What different cultural groups do you employ? What have you done to draw out and use ideas and thinking of these diverse cultures and types of employees? [5.1a(2)]

3. What do you do to ensure effective communication and knowledge sharing among employees and work units (not top-down)? [5.1a(3)]

   • How do you break down barriers to effective sharing and communication?

   • How do you know the communication among employees and work units is understood correctly?

4. Describe your approach to employee recognition and compensation. [5.1b]

   • What specific reward and recognition programs are in place? Is the reward and recognition the same for all employees? Why are they the same (or different)?

   • How does the organization link recognition, reward, and compensation to achieve high-performance objectives (which are usually stated as strategic objectives or goals)?

   • How do compensation, recognition, and related reward and incentive systems reinforce, strengthen, or support customer-focus objectives (for example, customer satisfaction)?

   • (General question for employees) What do you get rewarded for around here? What recognition is offered and why? Are the reward and recognition systems consistent? Fair?

5. How do you figure out what skills will be needed by future (potential) employees? [5.1c(1)]

   • How do you attract employees with the right skills your organization needs to be successful? How do you make sure that employees represent the diversity of the general community from which you hire? What diverse employees do you recruit and why? How does this recruitment help you get the right mix of diverse ideas, culture, and thinking? [5.1c(2)]

- How do you make sure these skills, diverse ideas, and cultures are used to maximum advantage within your organization? [5.1c(2)]

6. What development and/or replacement strategy or process do you have in place for key leaders and employees/ employee groups throughout the organization? (For example, if the organization knows key senior leaders or a group of engineers/technicians are scheduled to retire, determine what it is doing to fill the gap this retirement makes.) [5.1c(3)]

7. What training is provided for your employees? [5.2a(1)]

- (From the action plans identified in 2.2, pick some and ask) What training and education are provided to support the achievement of (the selected action plan)?

8. After you determine the key groups or segments of employees within the organization, ask the following question: What training and education do you provide to ensure that you meet the education and training needs of all categories of employees? [5.2a(1)]

- What training does a new employee receive to obtain the knowledge and skills necessary for success and high performance, including leadership development, performance measurement, improvement, and technology changes? [5.2a(1)]

9. What is included in new-employee orientation? How do you address key training needs, such as environmental safety, ethical business practices, and diversity? [5.2a(2)]

- If applicable, how do employees in remote locations participate in training programs? What kinds? When? [5.2a]

10. How do you integrate employee, supervisor, and manager feedback into the design and delivery of your training program? (Ask related follow-up questions to supervisors, managers, and employees to determine the extent to which their needs for development, learning, and career progression were identified

and considered when designing the education and training approach.) [5.2a(3)]

11. How is your training curriculum designed and delivered? What methods are used to determine what training should be offered and how it should be delivered? [5.2a(4)]

12. How do you make sure that the knowledge and skills acquired during training are actually used and reinforced on the job? Provide some examples (then select from this list and follow up with employees and their supervisors to determine how skills are reinforced on the job). [5.2a(5)]

13. How does your training program affect operational-performance goals? How do you know your training improves your business results? What evaluation of training effectiveness has been done? How often? What improvements were made as a result? Show examples. [5.2a(6)]

14. What is your system for improving training? Please give us some examples of improvements made and when they were made. [5.2a(6)]

15. To what extent is training provided to enhance employee motivation, career development, and progression? What do you (senior leaders, managers, and supervisors) do to develop the full potential of employees? Give examples. [5.2b]

16. What are your standards, performance measures, and targets for employee health, ergonomics, security, and safety? [5.3a(1)]

- How were they derived?

- How do you make sure that your approach to health and safety addresses the needs of all employee groups?

17. How do you determine that you have a safe and healthy work environment? How do you measure this? [5.3a(1)]

- What are your procedures for systematic evaluation and improvement of workplace health, safety, and ergonomics?

- What have you done to improve workplace health, safety, and ergonomics?

18. What processes or systems have you put in place to prepare for emergencies or disasters that may affect your workplace? [5.3a(2)]

    - How do you know these systems work as intended? What kinds of disruptions have you faced in the past? What was the impact on the workplace and your customers and employees? What have you put in place to reduce the possible impact of such disasters or emergencies?

19. What services, facilities, activities, and benefits are most important to your workforce? [5.3b(1)]

    - How did you determine these were the most important? Are they the same for all groups or segments of the workforce? If not, how have the services and benefits been modified or tailored to meet the needs of different groups or categories of employees?

20. What are the key elements, conditions, or factors that help or hurt employee well-being, satisfaction, and motivation? [5.3b(1)]

    - How did do you determine that these were the key elements? Are the elements the same for all groups of employees? If not, how do they differ?

21. What are the benefits and services you provide for employees to enhance motivation and satisfaction? [5.3b(2)]

    - To what extent are these customized for different employee types or groups? How did you determine what changes in the benefits and services should be offered?

22. How is employee satisfaction measured? (If a survey is used, ask how they know they are asking the right questions on the survey. Unless they have already told you, ask for some specific examples about how they use other information such as employee retention, absenteeism, grievances, safety, and productivity data to assess and improve employee well-being, satisfaction, and motivation.) [5.3b(3)]

- What do you do with the information? Provide examples.

- Please show us how your employee-assessment tools (for example, surveys) reflect the key factors you identified that affect employee well-being, satisfaction, and motivation.

23. What do you do to actually improve employee well-being, satisfaction, and motivation systematically? [5.3b(3)]

    - Describe the process you use to analyze employee-satisfaction data and other indicators to determine what problems exist that may disrupt or hurt employee well-being, satisfaction, and motivation?

    - How quickly or effectively do you use this information to drive improvements to employee well-being, satisfaction, and motivation?

24. How do you ensure that managers throughout the organization work to improve the climate for employee well-being, satisfaction, and motivation? [5.3b(3)] [Links to 1.1b(1)]

25. When you identify the priorities for improving the work environment to promote employee well-being, satisfaction, and motivation, what factors do you consider? [5.3b(4)]

    - What are the top three or four improvement priorities? (Pick one and ask the leader.) What specific finding from the employee-satisfaction survey or other assessment tool did the organization use to identify this priority action? How is this priority for improving work environment likely to affect key business results? How did you determine the potential impact on business results?

26. What improvements have you made in the process of determining employee satisfaction, well-being, and motivation, and then actually improving the work climate? [Scoring Guidelines].

Category 6—Process Management

1. What new program, product, or service have you designed in the past few years? (Pick one from their list and ask.) What is your process for designing this new or revised product or service to ensure that customer requirements are met and value is created for the customers, the organization, or other stakeholders? Please walk us through the steps. [6.1a(1); 6.1a(2)]

2. What new design technologies, including e-technology, have you used in recent product/service and production/delivery or support-service projects? [6.1a(3) and 6.2a(3)]

3. How do you test new products or services before they are introduced to be sure they perform as expected and meet all customer and operational requirements? What have you done to prevent errors in the design process? What have you done to consider speed and agility in designing these processes? Provide examples of increased speed, flexibility, or agility as a result. [6.1a(3)] What kinds of problems or troubles have you had with past introductions of new products and services? Provide examples of how you have learned from these problems and prevented them in subsequent product/service designs. [6.1a(3); 6.2]

4. What are your key production and delivery [6.1a(4)] or support service [6.2a(4)] processes and their requirements for creating value, including quality and performance indicators?

   - What steps have you taken to improve the effectiveness/efficiency of key work processes, including cycle time?

   - Once you determine that a process may not be meeting measurement goals or performing according to expectations, what process do you use to determine root cause and to bring about process improvement?

   - Please give an example of how a customer request or complaint resulted in an improvement of a current process or the establishment of a new process. How often do customers change their requirements? How do you respond to these changes? How has this process been refined to respond more quickly, especially when customer requirements change more often?

5. Please share with us your list of key business/support processes, requirements, and associated performance measures, including in-process measures. (Remember that key business processes include critical processes that support value creation and are necessary for business growth and success.) For example, if supply-chain management is designated as a key business process, the following series of questions may be useful: What process is in place for managing your supplier chain? Who are your most important [key] suppliers? How do you establish and communicate to your key suppliers the key requirements they must meet so your needs are met? What are the key performance requirements? Please explain how you measure your suppliers' performance and provide feedback to help them improve. [6.1a(1); 6.1a(4); 6.2a(1); 6.2a(4)]

   - What are the steps you have taken to design your key business processes to ensure they meet all performance requirements? How do you determine the types of services and outputs needed? How do your key business processes add value to enhance business growth and success?

6. What kinds of tests, audits, or inspections do you routinely conduct to ensure products and services are defect-free and require no rework? Show how you have reduced the need for these tests, audits, or inspections and still eliminated defects and rework. [6.1a(5); 6.2a(5)]

   - What are the steps you have taken to design your key support processes? How do you determine the types of services needed? How do your support services interact with and add value to your operational processes? [6.2a(2)]

• How does your organization maintain the performance of key support services? Share some examples of processes used to determine root causes of support problems and how you prevent recurrence of problems. How do you monitor costs of these processes? How have you reduced costs? Please give examples. [6.2a(4)]

7. How do you evaluate and improve the process for designing and delivering new value-creating business and support processes, and make improvements in cycle time, cost control, productivity, and other effectiveness or efficiency factors? Please provide some examples of improvements and when they were made. [6.1a(6); 6.2a(6)]

   • What process do you have in place to make sure that lessons learned in one part of the organization (or from past improvement efforts) are transferred to others in the organization to save time and prevent rework?

8. When strategic objectives (including new business ventures) and related action plans are developed and deployed throughout the organization, how do you make sure that adequate financial resources are available to carry out the plans and achieve the desired outcomes? Who or what unit is responsible for these activities? [6.2b]

   • What unit is responsible for assessing or uncovering any financial risks that may arise with business activities or investments? What problems or surprises have been experienced in this area? What was done to

prevent this type of problem from happening again? [6.2b(1)]

9. What kinds of emergencies or disasters have occurred in your area? What are you doing to make sure these kinds of things do not disrupt your operations? That customer needs continue to be met? [6.2b]

Category 7—Results

Normally, applicants are eager to display *good* results and sometimes neglect to report results that are not as good. The scoring guidelines penalize applicants for failing to provide results that are important to the organization's key business requirements.

To score accurately, examiners must be able to determine what results should be reported in the application that are important to the organization's success. To evaluate Category 7 properly, examiners first develop a list of the results that they *expect* to be provided in Category 7 based on what the organization reported was important to its success. Then, by comparing the list of *expected* results to the results actually provided in the application, examiners can determine what important results are missing.

Usually a description of important results can be found in the Organizational Profile, strategic goals [Item 2.1b], the list of actions required to achieve strategic objectives [Item 2.2a(1)], the priority customer requirements [Item 3.1a(2)], or other places in the application.

Figure 48 represents the type of information that might be presented by an applicant in the Organizational Profile [P.1b(2)], listing Customer Segments and Requirements. Note that three cus-

Customer Segments (As Reported by the Applicant)	Key Customer Requirements (As Reported by the Applicant)
Individual End Users	Reliability, prompt repair, friendly service, value
Dealers	Reliable vehicles, order accuracy, parts availability, billing accuracy
Commercial/Fleet users	Speedy access to service, reliability, value, loaner vehicles

Figure 48 Example of applicant customer segments and corresponding key requirements provided in the Organizational Profile.

tomer segments were identified, each with multiple requirements. This information serves as a basis for *expecting* results related to the satisfaction of these customers with the important product and service features. Accordingly, note that in Figure 49, the first column identifies where these results should be reported [Item 7.2]. The second column lists the customer segments and the specific requirements of each segment as found in the Organizational Profile (Figure 49). The third column simply identifies the place in the application that the examiner found the reference to expected results. (In case another examiner on the team did not find the expected requirement, little time will be wasted searching for it.) The fourth column indicates whether results were actually reported in 7.2, where they can be found (figure reference), and whether results are improving or not. Column five indicates whether benchmark/comparative data were reported (as required) and how favor-

ably the applicant's performance compares with the benchmark data.

In this way, examiners can easily determine if few, some, many, or most important results were reported. Similarly, applicants should prepare a similar table to make sure the actual results are aligned with the important results.

Most of the site-visit work for Category 7 involves studying reports containing raw data as well as trend and comparison data. All relevant results that were reported in the application should be updated to reflect current conditions.

Comparison data and the rationale for offering the comparison data should be examined to determine if the comparisons are appropriate and relevant. Comparisons are relevant if the applicant is able to present a plausible explanation or link between the comparison data and the data the applicant has reported.

Expected Results Matrix *(Figure 49)*

Prepare a List of Critical Organizational Results

When examiners review an application for a Baldrige or State quality award, they typically develop a list of the most critical organizational results that they expect to find in Category 7. The Expected Results Matrix on the opposite page is an example of such a list. The first three columns in the matrix are completed by examiners as they read the Organizational Profile, strategic objectives, and action plans and learn about factors important to organizational success. The first column describes a name of the expected result, such as *End User Customer Satisfaction.* The second column identifies the location in the application where the expected result was described, such as a section in the Organizational Profile [P1b(2)]. The third column lists the area in Category 7 where the result is expected to be reported.

The remaining nine columns describe the results that were actually reported in Category 7 that related to the expected result.

- The *Time Frame* column identifies the time period for which data are reported.
- *Segmentation* identifies any subdivisions of the data that were reported. Such subdivisions may also be identified as an expected result in column 1.
- The *Level/Trend* column identifies whether the applicant provided current levels and/or trend data.
- The *Direction* column identifies whether the level and or trend is favorable (+), flat (=), uneven (^), or unfavorable (U).
- The *Comparison* column identifies what type of comparison data have been presented by the applicant. Comparison data may be best in class (B), a Baldrige recipient (D), an industry average (A), a key competitor (K), or no data (N).
- The *Performance Against Comparison* column identifies the strength of the applicant's data against the comparisons mentioned in the previous column. For example the applicant could be leading (L) (better than) the performance of a Baldrige recipient. The applicant could be strong (S) relative to an industry average (for example, top quartile), *good* (about average). The applicant could be lagging (L) a key competitor.

Some examiners may use other headings for the columns in the Expected Results Matrix, but these are the most common.

If applicants prepare their own Expected Results Matrix they can make certain that the results contained in Category 7 completely align with areas of importance described in the Organizational Profile and Categories 1 through 6.

Name of Expected Result	Source Reference	Cat 7 Reference	Results found in Fig. #	Time Frame	Segmentation	Level/Trend	Direction: + favorable = flat ^ uneven U unfavorable	Comparison: Best in class, BalDrige, Industry Average, Key Competitor, None	Performance Against Comparison: Leading Strong Good LAgging	Process Item Linkages	Gaps
End User Customers											
End User Customer Satisfaction (Overall)	P1b(2)	7.2a(1)	7.2-3	2001-2005	By vehicle type	Current Level & Trend	+	D	S	2.1b(1) 3.2b(1) 3.2b(2) 3.2b(3) 6.1a(4)	None
Vehicle Reliability/ Safety							+	A	L		
Prompt Repair							+	B	L	3.2a(3) 6.1a(4)	
Friendly, Knowledgeable Service Techs							=	A	G		
Value / Economy							=	A	G		
Dealer Customers											
Dealer Customer Satisfaction (Overall)	P1b(2)	7.2a(1)	7.2-4	2001-2005	By dealer size (small, medium, large)	Current Level & Trend	=	A/K	A	6.1a(4)	None
Vehicle Reliability							+	A/K	G		
Order Accuracy							+	A/K	G		
Parts Availability							=	A/K	G		
Service Support							=	B	A		
Commercial/Fleet Customers											
Commercial/Fleet Customer Satisfaction	P1b(2)	7.2a(1)	7.2-5	2001-2005	By vehicle type (full size car, premium car, small truck)	Trend	+	None	NA	6.1a(4) 3.2b(1) 3.2b(2)	Comp Data Missing
Speedy Access to Service							+	None			
Value							=	None			
Loaner Vehicles							+	None			

Figure 49   Table of expected results.

1. What are the product/service performance levels at this time? [Links to P.1b and Items 3.1, 3.2, and 6.1] [7.1]

   • Please show a breakout of data by customer group or segment.

   • What are your current levels and trends for how customers perceive your products and service performance?

   • What are the performance results for key products and services that are most critical to customer satisfaction?

   • Please bring your results up to date and close any information gaps that may have been noted in your application.

   • How do these trends and levels compare with those of your competitors or similar providers?

2. What are the customer-satisfaction and dissatisfaction trends at this time? [Links to P.1b and Items 3.1 and 3.2] [7.2]

   • Please show a breakout of data by customer group or segment.

   • What are your current levels and trends for customer loyalty, positive referral, customer-perceived value, and relationship building?

   • Please bring your customer satisfaction, dissatisfaction, and related results up to date and close any information gaps that may have been noted in your application.

   • How do these customer-satisfaction and dissatisfaction trends and levels compare with those of your competitors or similar providers?

3. What are the current levels and trends showing financial and marketplace performance or economic value? [7.3]

   • Please provide data on key financial measures, such as return on investment (ROI), operating profits (or budget reductions as appropriate), or economic value added.

   • Please provide data on market share or business growth, as appropriate. Identify new markets entered and the level of performance in those markets.

   • Please show a breakout of data by customer and market group or segment.

   • Please bring your financial and marketplace performance results up to date and close any information gaps that may have been noted in your application.

   • Show how these trends and levels compare with those of your competitors or similar providers.

4. What are the current levels and trends showing the effectiveness of your human resource practices? [Links to processes in Category 5] [7.4]

   • Please provide data on key indicators, such as safety/accident record, absenteeism, turnover by category and type of employee/manager, and grievances and related litigation.

   • Please bring your human resource results up to date and close any information gaps that may have been noted in your application.

   • How does performance on these key indicators compare to your competitors, other providers, or benchmarks?

5. What are the current levels and trends showing the effectiveness of your value creation and support processes? [Links to Items 6.1 and 6.2] [7.5]

   • What are current levels and trends for key design, production, delivery, and business process performance?

   • What are current levels and trends for production and cycle time for design, delivery, and production?

   • Please show us your supplier/partner performance data trends and current levels for each key indicator, such as on-time delivery, error rate, and reducing costs. [Links to supply chain issues in Item 6.1 or 6.2 as appropriate]

   • Please bring your data about organizational effectiveness up to date and close any information gaps that may have been noted in your application.

- How does your performance on these key indicators compare to your competitors, other providers, or benchmarks?

6. What are the current levels and trends showing the effectiveness of your governance and social responsibility processes? [Links to processes in P.1, P.2, and Items 1.2] [7.6]

- Please show us your performance data related to fiscal accountability such as financial statement issues and risks and questioned accounting practices, auditor findings and recommendations, and management's response to these issues. [Links to Item 1.2b(1)]

- Please show us your performance data related to effective governance, holding managers accountable for their actions, and ethical behavior, such as percentages of independent members of the board of directors and results of ethics reviews and audits. [Links to Item 1.2b(1)]

- What are your results for regulatory/legal compliance? [Links to Item 1.1a(2)]

- What are your results for organizational citizenship? [Links to Item 1.2c]

- Please bring your governance and social responsibility results up to date and close any information gaps that may have been noted in your application.

- How does your performance on these key indicators compare to your competitors, other providers, or benchmarks?

- Please show us results data that demonstrate the extent to which you accomplished your organizational strategy or strategic objectives. [Links to 2.1b(1) and 2.2a]

General Cross-Cutting Questions to Ask Employees

- Who are your customers and what do they want? [Links to 1.1a(1) and 3.1a(1)]

- What are the organization's mission, vision, and values? [Links to 1.1a(1)]

- What is the strategic plan for the organization? What are the organization's goals, and what role do you play in helping to achieve the goals? [Links to 2.1b(1) and 2.2a]

- What kind of training have you received? Was it useful? Who decided what training you should receive? What kind of on-the-job support did you get for using the new skills you learned during training? [Links to 5.2]

- What kinds of decisions do you usually make about your work and the work of the organization? What data or information do you use to help make these decisions? Is this information easily available to help make decisions easier? [Links to 1.1b(1), 4.2a, and 5.1a]

- What activities or work are recognized or rewarded? Is achieving customer satisfaction a critical part of your job? Are your rewards and/or recognition determined in part on achieving certain customer-satisfaction levels? If so, explain how this works. [Links to 5.1b]

- Remember to ask the employee how processes are improved. Are improvements based on evaluation or are they random? Be sure to ask if the process you are examining has been improved. Ask how the improvement was identified. Ask what steps are being taken to continue to evaluate and improve the process.

Clarifying Confusing Terms

Comparative Information versus Benchmarking

Comparative information includes benchmarking and competitive comparisons. Benchmarking refers to collecting information and data about processes and performance results that represent the best practices and performance for similar activities inside or outside the organization's business or industry. Competitive comparisons refer to collecting information and data on performance relative to direct competitors or similar providers.

For example, a personal computer manufacturer, ABC Micro, must store, retrieve, pack, and ship computers and replacement parts. ABC Micro is concerned about shipping response time, errors in shipping, and damage during shipping. To determine the level of performance of its competitors in these areas, and to set reasonable improvement goals, ABC Micro would gather competitive comparison data from similar providers (competitors). However, these performance levels may not reflect best practices for storage, retrieval, packing, and shipping.

Benchmarking would require ABC Micro to find organizations that execute these processes better than any other organization and examine both their processes and performance levels, such as the catalog company L.L. Bean.

Benchmarking seeks best-practices information. Competitive comparisons look at competitors, whether or not they are the best.

Customer-Contact Employees

Customer-contact employees are any employees who are in direct contact with customers. They may be direct-service providers or answer complaint calls. Whenever a customer makes contact with an organi-zation, either in person or by phone or other electronic means, that customer forms an opinion about the organization and its employees. Employees who come in contact with customers are in a critical position to influence customers for the good of the organization, or to its detriment.

Customer Satisfaction versus Customer Dissatisfaction

One is not the inverse of the other. The lack of complaints does not indicate satisfaction, although the presence of complaints can be a partial indicator of dissatisfaction. Measures of customer dissatisfaction can include direct measures through surveys as well as complaints, product returns, and warranty claims.

Customer satisfaction and dissatisfaction are complex areas to assess. Customers are rarely *thoroughly* dissatisfied, although they may dislike a feature of a product or an aspect of service. There are usually degrees of satisfaction and dissatisfaction.

Data versus Information

Information can be qualitative and quantitative. Data lend themselves to quantification and statistical analysis. For example, an incoming inspection might produce a count of the number of units accepted, rejected, and total shipped. This count is considered data. These counts add to the base of information about supplier quality.

Education versus Training

Training refers to learning about and acquiring job-specific skills and knowledge. Education refers to the general development of individuals. An organization might provide training in equipment maintenance for its workers, as well as support the education of workers through an associate degree program at a local community college.

Empowerment and Involvement

Empowerment generally refers to processes and procedures designed to provide individuals and teams the tools, skills, and authority to make decisions that affect their work—decisions traditionally reserved for managers and supervisors.

Empowerment as a concept has been misused in many organizations. For example, managers may appear to extend decision-making authority under the guise of chartering teams and individuals to make recommendations about their work, while continuing to reserve decision-making authority for themselves.

This practice has given rise to another term—involvement—which describes the role of employees who are asked to become involved in decision making, without necessarily making decisions. Involvement is a practice that many agree is better than not involving employees at all, but still does not optimize their contribution to initiative, flexibility, and fast response.

Measures and Indicators

The Award Criteria do not make a distinction between measures and indicators. However, some users of these terms prefer the term indicator: 1) when the measurement relates to performance but is not a direct or exclusive measure of such performance, for example, the number of complaints is an indicator of dissatisfaction, but not a direct or exclusive measure of it; and 2) when the measurement is a predictor (leading indicator) of some more significant performance, for example, gain in customer satisfaction might be a leading indicator of market share gain.

Operational Performance and Predictors of Customer Satisfaction

Operational performance processes and predictors of customer satisfaction are related but not always the same. Operational performance measures can reflect issues that concern customers as well as those that do not. Operational-performance measures are used by the organization to assess effectiveness and efficiency, as well as predict customer satisfaction.

In the example of the coffee shop, freshness is a key customer requirement. One predictor of customer satisfaction might be the length of time, in minutes, between brewing and serving to guarantee freshness and good aroma. The standard might be 10 minutes or less to ensure satisfaction. Coffee more than 10 minutes old would be discarded.

A measure of operational effectiveness might be how many cups were discarded (waste) because the coffee was too old. The customer does not care if the coffee shop pours out stale coffee, and therefore, that measure is not a predictor of satisfaction. However, pouring out coffee does affect profitability and should be measured and minimized.

Ideally, an organization should be able to identify enough measures of product and service quality to predict customer satisfaction accurately and monitor operating effectiveness and efficiency.

Performance Requirements versus Performance Measures

Performance requirements are an expression of customer requirements and expectations. Sometimes performance requirements are expressed as design requirements or engineering requirements. They are viewed as a basis for developing measures to enable the organization to determine, generally without asking the customer, whether the customer is likely to be satisfied.

Performance measures can also be used to assess efficiency, effectiveness, and productivity of a work process. Process-performance measures might include cycle time, error rate, or throughput.

Support Services

Support services are those services that support the organization's product and service delivery core operating processes. Support services might include finance and accounting, management-information services, software support, marketing, public relations, personnel administration (job posting, recruitment, and payroll), facilities maintenance and management, secretarial support, and other administration services.

Of course, if an organization is in business to provide a traditional support service such as accounting, then accounting services provided to its external customers become its core work/operating process and are no longer considered a support service. Internal accounting services would continue to be considered a support service.

In the human resources area (Category 5), the Criteria require organizations to manage their human resource assets to optimize performance. However, many human resources support services might also exist such as payroll, travel, position control, recruitment, and employee services. These processes must be designed, delivered, and refined systematically according to the requirements of Item 6.2.

Teams and Natural Work Units

Natural work units reflect the people who normally work together because they are a part of a formal work unit. For example, on an assembly line, three or four people may naturally work together to install a motor in a new car. Hotel employees who prepare food in the kitchen might constitute another natural work unit.

Teams may be formed of people within a natural work unit or may cross existing (natural) organization boundaries. To improve room service in a hotel, for example, certain members of several natural work units, such as the switchboard, kitchen workers, and waiters, may form a special team. This team would not be considered a natural work unit. It might be called a cross-functional work team because its members come from different functions within the organization.

Glossary

This glossary defines and briefly describes key terms used throughout the Criteria that are important to performance management and assessment.

action plans—the term *action plans* refers to specific actions that respond to short- and longer-term strategic objectives. Action plans include details of resource commitments and time horizons for accomplishment. Action plan development represents the critical stage in planning when strategic objectives and goals are made specific so that effective, organization-wide understanding and deployment are possible. In the Criteria, deployment of action plans includes creating aligned measures for all departments and work units. Deployment also might require specialized training for some employees or recruitment of personnel.

An example of a strategic objective for a supplier in a highly competitive industry might be to develop and maintain a price-leadership position. Action plans could entail designing efficient processes and creating an accounting system that tracks activity-level costs, aligned for the organization as a whole. Deployment requirements might include unit and/or team training in setting priorities based upon costs and benefits. Organizational-level analysis and review likely would emphasize productivity growth, cost control, and quality. See the definition of *strategic objectives* for the description of this related term.

alignment—the term *alignment* refers to consistency of plans, processes, information, resource decisions, actions, results, and analysis to support key organization-wide goals. Effective alignment requires a common understanding of purposes and goals. It also requires the use of complementary measures and information for planning, tracking, analysis, and improvement at three levels: the organizational level, the key process level, and the work-unit level. See the definition of *integration* for the description of this related term.

analysis—the term *analysis* refers to assessments performed by an organization or its work units to provide a basis for effective decisions. Every organization must analyze data to support effective decision making. The types and amount of analysis depend on the complexity and decision needs of the organization, its leaders, and employees. Overall organizational analysis guides process management toward achieving key business results and toward attaining strategic objectives.

Despite their importance, individual facts and data do not usually provide an effective basis for actions or setting priorities. Actions depend upon understanding cause/effect relationships. Understanding such relationships comes from analysis of facts and data. Examples of these analyses include, but are not limited to the following:

- How product and service-quality improvement correlates with key customer indicators such as customer satisfaction, customer retention, and market share

- Cost/revenue implications of customer-related problems and problem-resolution effectiveness

- interpretation of market-share changes in terms of customer gains and losses and changes in customer satisfaction

- Improvement trends in key operational performance indicators such as productivity, cycle time, waste reduction, new-product introduction, and defect levels

- Relationships between employee/organizational learning and value added per employee

- Financial benefits derived from improvements in employee safety, absenteeism, and turnover

- Benefits and costs associated with education and training

- Benefits and costs associated with improved organizational-knowledge management and sharing

- How the ability to identify and meet employee requirements correlates with employee retention, motivation, and productivity

- Cost/revenue implications of employee-related problems and effective problem resolution

- Individual or aggregate measures of productivity and quality relative to competitors

- Cost trends relative to competitors

- Relationships between product/service quality, operational-performance indicators, and overall financial-performance trends as reflected in indicators such as operating costs, revenues, asset utilization, and value added per employee

- Allocation of resources among alternative improvement projects based on cost/revenue implications and improvement potential

- Net earnings derived from quality/operational/ human resource performance improvements

- Comparisons among business units showing how quality and operational-performance improvement affect financial performance

- Contributions of improvement activities to cash flow, working-capital use, and shareholder value

- Profit impacts of customer retention

- Cost/revenue implications of new-market entry, including global-market entry or expansion

- Cost/revenue, customer, and productivity implications of engaging in and/or expanding e-commerce

- Market share versus profits

- Trends in economic, market, and shareholder indicators of value

anecdotal—the term *anecdotal* refers to process information that lacks specific methods, measures, deployment mechanisms, and evaluation/improvement/learning factors. Anecdotal information frequently uses examples and describes individual activities rather than systematic processes.

An anecdotal response to how senior leaders deploy performance expectations might describe a specific occasion when a senior leader visited all company facilities. On the other hand, a systematic process might describe the communication methods used by all senior leaders to deliver performance expectations on a regular basis to all employee locations, the measures used to assess effectiveness of the methods, and the tools and techniques used to evaluate and improve the communication methods.

analytical tools—the term *analytical tools* refers to tools for analyzing data may include brainstorming, Pareto charts, cause-and-effect diagrams, scatter diagrams, correlation and regression analysis, and histograms, to name a few.

approach—the term *approach* refers to the methods used by an organization to address the Baldrige Criteria Item requirements. Approach includes the appropriateness of the methods to the Item requirements and the effectiveness of their use. Approach is one of the dimensions considered in evaluating Process Items.

basic requirements—the term *basic requirements* refers to the topic Criteria users need to address when responding to the most central concept of an Item. Basic requirements are the fundamental theme of that Item. In the Criteria, the basic requirements of each item are presented as the Item title question. If you are an examiner, see the *Clarifying Baldrige Scoring Requirements* chapter in this book that provides a detailed explanation of basic, overall, and multiple requirements.

benchmarks—the term *benchmarks* refers to processes and results that represent best practices and performance for similar activities, inside or outside an organization's industry. Organizations engage in benchmarking as an approach to understand the current dimensions of world-class performance and to achieve discontinuous (nonincremental) or breakthrough improvement.

Benchmarks are one form of comparative data. Other comparative data organizations might use include industry data collected by a third party (frequently industry averages), data on competitors' performance, and comparisons with similar organizations in the same geographic area or that provide similar products and services in other geographic areas.

continuous improvement—the term *continuous improvement* refers to the ongoing improvement of products, programs, services, or processes by small increments or major breakthroughs, including reengineering.

cross purposes—the term *cross purposes* refers to actions taken by different people or units in an organization that do not support the overall mission and objectives of the organization. For example, to improve customer contact and satisfaction, one the Information Technology unit installs a new phone system but neglects to work with the Training unit to ensure everyone understands and can use the system. Customers become angry when their calls go unanswered, resulting in lower customer satisfaction and loyalty than with the old system.

customer—the term *customer* refers to actual and potential users of the organization's products, programs, or services. Customers include the end users of the organization's products or services, as well as others who might be the immediate purchasers or users of its products, programs, or services, such as wholesale distributors, agents, or organizations that further process the product as a component of their product. The Criteria address customers broadly, referencing current and future customers, as well as customers of competitors.

See the definition of *stakeholders* for the relationship between customers and others who might be affected by the organization's products, programs, or services.

customer-driven excellence—the term *customer-driven excellence* refers to the Baldrige core value embedded in the beliefs and behaviors of high-performance organizations. Customer focus impacts

and integrates an organization's strategic directions, its value creation processes, and its business results.

customer chain—the term *customer chain* refers usually to several entities that are involved as customers at different stages of the life of a program, product, or service. In the example of the automobiles (see definition of *end-user*), the original equipment manufacturer (car maker) sells to dealers, the first segment of the customer chain. When the dealer resells the car to a cab company, that company becomes the next customer in the chain as *car owner*. Finally, the ultimate users of the car, the cab driver and passengers, become the users. Customer chains can be considered to extend through the life cycle of the product. In the case of automobiles, the secondary market of used cars begins and used-car dealers and their customers may extend the customer chain. Each customer in the chain may have different requirements that must be met.

customer-interaction process—the term *customer-interaction process* refers to the process by which an organization approaches, responds to, and follows up with customers. It builds ongoing business and learns about customer needs and expectations. The process of interacting with an organization can be by many methods including phone, fax, e-mail, and face-to-face meetings. Attending to these interactions is important because customers frequently make decisions about the organization based on one interaction.

customer-contact requirement (service or performance standard)—the term *customer-contact requirement* refers to a set, measurable level of performance. A customer-contact requirement or service level defines in measurable terms expected performance levels once the customer contacts the organization with a question, comment, or complaint. For example, an objective of an organization might be *prompt customer service* but that term does not define a service level. Three examples of customer-contact requirements (service standards) follow: (1) a courteous, knowledgeable, easy-to-understand technician will be available to solve the customer's problem within ten minutes; (2) the problem will be resolved to the customer's satisfaction by the first person who comes in contact with the customer or (3) repair service will be provided within 24 hours of the customer's request. Some refer to customer-contact requirements as service after the sale, rather than the basic requirements of the product, program, or service.

cycle time—the term *cycle time* refers to the amount of time required to complete a defined process from end to end. For example, the time required from the beginning of design to the delivery of product can be measured as the *design-to-delivery cycle time*. Additionally, each component of this cycle can be also measured. The design phase can have one cycle time, the production phase can have another, and the delivery phase a third. Organizations are responsible for defining work cycles in meaningful terms. These defined cycles must make sense to the organization and help its workers to measure and monitor the processes in the cycles in order to drive improvements. Time measurements play a major role in the assessment because of the great importance of time performance to improving competitiveness and overall performance. Time-related terms in common use are setup time, lead-time, changeover time, delivery time, order-fulfillment time, time to market, and other key process times.

data validity and utility—data are numerical information. They are used as a basis for reasoning, discussion, determining status, decision making, and analysis. Data proven to measure a particular construct or characteristic are valid data. Data utility (usefulness) is determined by the customers of the data—the people who must use them.

deployment—the term *deployment* refers to the extent to which an organization's approach is applied to the requirements of a Baldrige Criteria Item. Deployment is evaluated on the basis of the breadth and depth of application of the approach to relevant work units throughout the organization. Deployment is one of the dimensions considered in evaluating Process items.

diversity—the term *diversity* refers to valuing and benefiting from personal differences. These differences address many variables including race, religion, color, gender, national origin, disability, sexual orientation, age, education, geographic origin, and skill characteristics, as well as differences in ideas, thinking, academic disciplines, and perspectives.

The Baldrige Criteria refer to the diversity of employee-hiring and customer communities. Capitalizing on both provides enhanced opportunities for high performance; customer, employee, and community satisfaction; and customer and employee loyalty.

effective—the term *effective* refers to how well a process or a measure addresses its intended purpose. Determining effectiveness requires the evaluation of how well a need is met by the approach taken and its deployment or by the outcome of the measure used.

employee—the term *employee* refers to all people who contribute to the delivery of an organization's products and services, including paid employees (such as permanent, part-time, and temporary and contract employees supervised by the organization). Employees include team leaders, supervisors, and managers at all levels. For purposes of Baldrige review, employees may include volunteers who provide essential services to the organization. Contract employees supervised by a contractor are covered by the requirements of business or support processes in Category 6.

empowerment—the term *empowerment* refers to giving employees the authority and responsibility to make decisions and take actions. Empowerment results in decisions being made closest to the *front line*, where work-related knowledge and understanding reside.

Empowerment is aimed at enabling employees to satisfy customers on first contact, to improve processes and increase productivity, and to improve the organization's performance results. Empowered employees require information to make appropriate decisions; thus, an organizational requirement is to provide that information in a timely and useful way.

end-user—the term *end-user* refers to the ultimate user of the programs, products, or services an organization produces and delivers. For example, a manufacturer of automobiles sells to a network of dealers. However, except for the cars the dealer actually uses, it is not considered an end-user. The end-user is the person at the end of the customer chain actually using the car (see definition of *customer chain*). A dealer may resell the car to a taxi company. The taxi company (car owner) hires people to drive the car. The cab driver and passengers may be considered end users until the car is resold.

ethical behavior—the term *ethical behavior* refers to how an organization ensures that all its decisions, actions, and stakeholder interactions conform to the organization's moral and professional principles. These principles should support all applicable laws and regulations. They are the foundation for the organization's culture and values and define *right* from *wrong*.

Senior leaders should act as role models for these principles of behavior. The principles apply to all individuals involved in the organization, from employees to members of the board of directors, and need to be communicated and reinforced on a regular basis. Although there is no universal model for ethical behavior, senior leaders should ensure that the organization's mission and vision are aligned with its ethical principles. Ethical behavior should be practiced with all stakeholders, including employees, shareholders, customers, partners, suppliers, and the organization's local community.

While some organizations may view their ethical principles as boundary conditions restricting behavior, well-designed and clearly articulated ethical principles should empower people to make effective decisions with great confidence.

goals—the term *goals* refers to a future condition or performance level that one intends to attain. Goals can be both short-term and longer-term. Goals are ends that guide actions. Quantitative goals, frequently referred to as *targets*, include a numerical point or range. Targets might be projections based on comparative data and/or competitive data. The term *stretch goals* refers to desired major, discontinuous (nonincremental) or breakthrough improvements, usually in areas most critical to the organization's future success.

Goals can serve many purposes, including clarifying strategic objectives and action plans to indicate how success will be measured, fostering teamwork by focusing on a common end, encouraging *out-of-the-box* thinking to achieve a stretch goal, and providing a basis for measuring and accelerating progress.

governance—the term *governance* refers to the system of management and controls exercised in the stewardship of the organization. It includes the responsibilities of the organization's owners/shareholders, board of directors, and senior leaders. Corporate or organizational charters, bylaws, and policies document the rights and responsibilities of each of the parties and describe how the organization will be directed and controlled to ensure accountability to owners/shareholders and other stakeholders, transparency of operations, and fair treatment of all stakeholders. Governance processes may include approving strategic direction, monitoring and evaluating CEO performance, succession planning, financial auditing, establishing executive compensation and benefits, managing risk, disclosure, and reporting to shareholders. Ensuring effective governance is important to stakeholders' and the larger society's trust and to organizational effectiveness.

groupings and segments—the term *groupings and segments* refers to ways in which the organization clusters or subdivides various people and organizations with which it interacts. Groupings are formed for the convenience of the organization and are defined by the organization. Sometimes the organization will group or segment customers with similar requests, such as high volume, low volume, high risk, or geographical regions. Employees and staff may be grouped as well for the convenience of the organization (for example, hourly, salary, manufacturing, technical, physicians, nurses, technicians, and so on).

high-performance work—the term *high-performance work* refers to work processes used to systematically pursue ever-higher levels of overall organizational and individual performance, including quality, productivity, innovation rate, and cycle-time performance. High-performance work results in improved service for customers and other stakeholders.

Approaches to high-performance work vary in form, function, and incentive systems. High-performance work frequently includes cooperation between management and the workforce, which may involve workforce bargaining units; cooperation among work units, often involving teams; self-directed responsibility and employee empowerment; employee input to planning; individual and organizational skill building and learning; learning from other organizations; flexibility in job design and work assignments; a flattened organizational structure, where decision making is decentralized and decisions are made closest to the *front line*; and effective use of performance measures, including comparisons. Many high-performance work systems use monetary and nonmonetary incentives based upon factors such as organizational performance, team and/or individual contributions, and skill building. Also, high-performance work processes usually seek to align the organization's structure, work, jobs, employee development, and incentives.

how—the term *how* refers to the processes that an organization uses to accomplish its mission requirements. In responding to *how* questions in the Process Item requirements, process descriptions should include information such as approach (methods and measures), deployment, learning, and integration factors.

innovation—the term *innovation* refers to making meaningful change to improve products, programs, services, processes, or organizational effectiveness, and to create new value for stakeholders. Innovation involves the adoption of an idea, process, technology, or product that is either new or new to its proposed application.

Successful organizational innovation is a multistep process that involves development and knowledge sharing, a decision to implement, implementation, evaluation, and learning. Although innovation is often associated with technological innovation, it is applicable to all key organizational processes that would benefit from change, whether through breakthrough improvement or change in approach or outputs. It could include fundamental changes in organizational structure to more effectively accomplish the organization's work.

indicators and measures—the term *indicators and measures* is relevant when two or more measurements are required to provide a more complete picture of performance. Indicators (measures) are input, output, and performance dimensions of processes, products, programs, services, and the overall organization. Indicators and measures might be simple (derived from one measurement) or composite. Some users of these terms prefer the term indicator: (1) when the measurement relates to performance, but is not a direct or exclusive measure of such performance (for example, the number of complaints is an indicator of dissatisfaction, but not a direct or exclusive measure of it); and (2) when the measurement is a predictor (*leading indicator*) of some more significant performance, for example, gain in customer satisfaction might be a leading indicator of market-share gain.

inspection and testing—the term *inspection* typically refers to assessments of product or service suitability, checks to determine if requirements are met, or whether defects exist. Counting the number of bubbles in a glass lens is an end-process inspection since it is conducted after the glass is made. The term *testing* refers to determining whether the product or service works as intended. The same lens might be tested by shining a light through it and measuring the refraction or distortion of the light. The components of a computer can be inspected to ensure they are all in place. The computer is tested by turning it on and performing calculations. In the education sector testing is used to assess levels of education progress, student achievement, or knowledge mastery.

integration—the term *integration* refers to the harmonization of plans, processes, information, resource decisions, actions, results, analysis, and learning to support key organization-wide goals. Effective integration goes beyond alignment and is achieved when the individual components of a performance management system operate as a fully interconnected unit. See the definition of *alignment* for the description of this related term. Integration is one of the dimensions considered in evaluating Process Items.

key—the term *key* refers to the major or most important elements or factors, those that are critical to achieving the intended outcome. The Baldrige Criteria, for example, refer to key challenges, key plans, key processes, key measures—those that are most important to the organization's success. They are the essential elements for pursuing or monitoring a desired outcome.

key communities—*key communities* are defined by the organization. The term *key communities* refers to elements of the public that may be affected by the work of the organization. Key communities for a local public school may include organizations such as the local library, volunteer organizations, and education/professional associations. Key communities for a large corporate manufacturer may include organizations in local areas where the company maintains facilities or conducts business. Key communities may include schools, colleges, healthcare organizations, charitable organizations, or any group the organization believes key to its business objectives. A key community may also include individuals who are affected by the process, products, services, and processes of the organization. Residents in the vicinity of an industrial facility might be considered a key community since they may impact the organization and its ability to expand or conduct business.

knowledge assets—the term *knowledge assets* refers to the accumulated intellectual resources of the organization. It is the knowledge possessed by the organization and its employees in the form of information, ideas, learning, understanding, memory, insights, cognitive and technical skills, and capabilities. Employees, software, patents, databases, documents, guides, policies and procedures, and technical drawings are repositories of an organization's knowledge assets.

Knowledge assets are held not only by an organization but reside within its customers, suppliers, and partners as well. Knowledge assets are the *know-how* that the organization has available to use, to invest, and to grow. Building and managing its knowledge assets are key components for the organization to create value for its stakeholders and to help sustain competitive advantage.

leadership system—the term *leadership system* refers to how leadership is exercised, formally and informally, throughout the organization—the basis for and the way key decisions are made, communicated, and carried out. It includes structures and mechanisms for decision making; selection and development of leaders and managers; and reinforcement of values, ethical behavior, directions, and performance expectations.

An effective leadership system respects the capabilities and requirements of employees and other stakeholders, and it sets high expectations for performance and performance improvement. It builds loyalties and teamwork based on the organization's vision and values and the pursuit of shared goals. It encourages and supports initiative and appropriate risk taking, subordinates organization structure to purpose and function, and avoids chains of command that require long, cumbersome decision paths. An effective leadership system includes mechanisms for the leaders to conduct self-examination, receive feedback, and improve.

learning—the term *learning* refers to new knowledge or skills acquired through evaluation, study, experience, and innovation. The Baldrige Criteria include two distinct kinds of learning: organizational and personal. Organizational learning is achieved through research and development, evaluation and improvement cycles, employee and stakeholder ideas and input, best-practice sharing, and benchmarking. Personal learning is achieved through education, training, and developmental opportunities that further individual growth.

To be effective, learning should be embedded in the way an organization operates. Learning contributes to a competitive advantage for the organization and its employees. For further description of organizational and personal learning, see the related Core Value and Concept on page 30 of this book.

Learning is one of the dimensions considered in evaluating Process Items.

levels—the term *levels* refers to numerical information that places or positions an organization's results and performance on a meaningful measurement scale. Performance levels permit evaluation relative to past performance, projections, goals, and appropriate comparisons.

measures and indicators—the term *measures and indicators* refers to numerical information that quantifies input, output, and performance dimensions of processes, products, programs, projects, services, and the overall organization (outcomes). Measures and indicators might be simple (derived from one measurement) or composite.

The Criteria do not make a distinction between measures and indicators. However, some users of these terms prefer the term indicator: 1) when the measurement relates to performance but is not a direct measure of such performance (for example, the number of complaints is an indicator of dissatisfaction but not a direct measure of it), and 2) when the measurement is a predictor (*leading indicator*) of some more significant performance (for example, increased customer satisfaction might be a leading indicator of market-share gain).

mission—the term *mission* refers to the overall function of an organization. The mission answers the question, "What is this organization attempting to accomplish?" The mission might define customers or markets served, distinctive competencies, or technologies used.

multiple requirements—the term *multiple requirements* refers to the individual questions Criteria users need to answer within each Area to Address. These questions constitute the details of an Item's requirements. Multiple requirements are presented in black text under each Item's Area(s) to Address. If you are an examiner, see the *Clarifying Baldrige Scoring Requirements* chapter in this book that provides a detailed explanation of basic, overall, and multiple requirements.

objective—*objectives* are usually considered to be subsets of goals. A goal may relate to financial success. One of the short-term objectives needed to meet this goal may be a monthly sales target. (See outcome-based strategic objectives)

organization—the term *organization* refers to a group of people with common goals and mission.

The group may be any size, formal or informal, ad hoc or permanent.

organizational agility—the term *organizational agility* refers to the ability of the organization to act quickly or change quickly. Speed of response of all aspects of organizational operations is increasingly important as organizations experience less tolerance from customers and stakeholders for slow, plodding service and bureaucratic inefficiency. Organizational agility, like the agility demonstrated by an Olympic gymnast, suggests the ability to move quickly and bend the organization to adapt to changing requirements and environmental constraints.

organization leaders and senior leaders—this refers to the leaders—executives and top managers—in the applying organization or the organization under review. At a bank, senior leaders could include the president, vice presidents, branch managers, and staff managers. For a company, senior leaders could include the chief executive officer and his or her direct reports. If the unit under review is a division of a larger organization, the division manager and direct reports are considered *senior leaders*. If the unit under review is a government organization or subdivision, the leaders might include top officials, members of policy boards, workforce-development boards, and city or county commissions.

outcome-based strategic objectives—the term *outcome-based strategic objectives* (also called *results-oriented* or *results-based* strategic objectives) defines in measurable terms the outcomes or results that the organization must achieve to be successful in the future. To achieve Outcome-Based Strategic Objectives the organization must engage in activities but it should be outcome achievement not activity completion that is used to measure success. Since it is possible to carry out the assigned activity and still fail to achieve the desired outcome, strategic objectives define the outcome required for success, not the activities to be carried out.

overall requirements—the term *overall requirements* refers to the topics Criteria users need to address when responding to the central theme of an

Item. Overall requirements address the most significant features of the Item requirements. In the Criteria, the overall requirements of each Item are presented as an introductory sentence(s) printed in bold. If you are an examiner, see the *Clarifying Baldrige Scoring Requirements* chapter in this book that provides a detailed explanation of basic, overall, and multiple requirements.

partners—the term *partners* refers to those key organizations or individuals who are working in concert with the organization to achieve a common goal or to improve performance. Typically, partnerships are formal arrangements for a specific aim or purpose, such as to achieve a strategic objective or to deliver a specific product or service.

Formal partnerships are usually for extended periods of time and involve a clear understanding of the individual and mutual roles and benefits for the partners.

performance—the term *performance* refers to output results and their outcomes obtained from processes, products, and services that permit evaluation and comparison relative to goals, standards, past results, and other organizations. Performance might be expressed in nonfinancial and financial terms. The Baldrige Criteria address four types of performance: 1) product and service, 2) customer-focused, 3) financial and marketplace, and 4) operational.

Customer-focused performance refers to performance relative to measures and indicators of customers' perceptions, reactions, and behaviors. Examples include customer retention, complaints, and customer-survey results. These are considered *direct* measures of customer satisfaction since they are *telling* organizations directly about their levels of satisfaction or dissatisfaction. In the Criteria these results are reported in Item 7.2.

Product and service performance refers to performance relative to measures and indicators of product and service characteristics important to customers. Examples include product reliability, on-time delivery, customer-experienced defect levels, and service-response time. These are considered *indirect* measures of customer satisfaction since the organizations are using measures or indicators of product and service quality to *predict* what the customer is likely to think without actually asking the customer or waiting for the customer to leave. For nonprofit organizations, *product and service performance* examples might include program and project performance in areas of rapid response to emergencies, at-home services, or multilingual services. In the Criteria these results are reported in Item 7.1.

Financial and marketplace performance refers to performance relative to measures of cost, revenue, and market position, including asset utilization, asset growth, and market share. Examples include returns on investments, value added per employee, debt-to-equity ratio, returns on assets, operating margins, performance to budget, amount of reserve funds, cash-to-cash cycle time, other profitability and liquidity measures, and market gains. In the Criteria these results are reported in Item 7.3.

Operational performance refers to human resource, organizational, and ethical performance relative to effectiveness, efficiency, and accountability measures and indicators. Examples include cycle time, productivity, waste reduction, employee turnover, employee cross-training rates, regulatory compliance, fiscal accountability, and community involvement. Operational performance might be measured at the work-unit level, key-process level, and organizational level. In the Criteria these results are reported in Items 7.4, 7.5, and 7.6.

performance excellence—the term *performance excellence* refers to an integrated approach to organizational-performance management that results in: 1) delivery of ever-improving value to customers, contributing to organizational sustainability; 2) improvement of overall organizational effectiveness and capabilities; and 3) organizational and personal learning. The Baldrige Criteria for Performance Excellence provide a framework and an assessment tool for understanding organizational strengths and opportunities for improvement and thus for guiding planning efforts.

performance projections—the term *performance projections* refers to estimates of future performance or goals for future results. Projections may be inferred from past performance, may be based on competitors' or similar organizations' performance that must be met or exceeded, may be predicted based on changes in a dynamic environment, or may be goals for future performance. Projections integrate estimates of the organization's rate of improvement and change, and they may be used to indicate where breakthrough improvement or change is needed. Thus, performance projections serve as a key management-planning tool.

prevention-based intervention—the term *prevention-based intervention* refers to determining the root cause of a problem and preventing its recurrence rather than just solving the problem and waiting for it to happen again (reactive posture).

process—the term *process* refers to linked activities with the purpose of producing a product or service for a customer (user) within or outside the organization. Generally, processes involve combinations of people, machines, tools, techniques, and materials in a defined series of steps or actions. In some situations, processes might require adherence to a specific sequence of steps, with documentation (sometimes formal) of procedures and requirements, including well-defined measurement and control steps.

In many service situations, particularly when customers are directly involved in the service, process is used in a more general way, that is, to spell out what must be done, possibly including a preferred or expected sequence. If a sequence is critical, the service needs to include information to help customers understand and follow the sequence. Service processes involving customers also require guidance to the providers of those services on handling contingencies related to customers' likely or possible actions or behaviors.

In knowledge work such as strategic planning, research, development, and analysis, process does not necessarily imply formal sequences of steps. Rather, process implies general understandings regarding competent performance such as timing, options to be included, evaluation, and reporting. Sequences might arise as part of these understandings.

In the Baldrige Scoring System, process-achievement level is assessed. This achievement level is based on four factors that can be evaluated for each of an organization's key processes: Approach, Deployment, Learning, and Integration.

productivity—the term *productivity* refers to measures of the efficiency of resource use. Although the term often is applied to single factors such as staffing (labor productivity), machines, materials, energy, and capital, the productivity concept applies as well to the total resources used in producing outputs. The use of an aggregate measure of overall productivity allows a determination of whether the net effect of overall changes in a process—possibly involving resource trade-offs—is beneficial.

purpose—the term *purpose* refers to the fundamental reason that an organization exists. The primary role of purpose is to inspire an organization and guide its setting of values. Purpose is generally broad and enduring. Two organizations in different businesses could have similar purposes, and two organizations in the same business could have different purposes.

results—the term *results* refers to outputs and outcomes achieved by an organization in addressing the requirements of a Baldrige Criteria Item. Results are evaluated on the basis of current performance; performance relative to appropriate comparisons; the rate, breadth, and importance of performance improvements; and the relationship of results measures to key organizational performance requirements.

rework and defects—the terms *rework* and *defects* refer to problems associated with not doing things right the first time. In manufacturing, rework (doing the job again) typically results when the inspector notices that a product has flaws (is defective or contains defects). This forces the organization to make the product again. Since the work must be done again, it is considered re-work. Other examples of rework caused by defective processes might include remedial education, rewriting a sentence to correct typographical or grammatical errors, repealing faulty legislation and passing new or replacement legislation, or repairing an incisional hernia caused by faulty (or defective) surgical procedures. The list of defects, which causes work to be done again, is virtually endless.

root cause—the term *root cause* refers to the original or basic cause or reason for a condition. The root cause of a condition is that cause which, if eliminated, ensures that the condition will not recur.

segment—the term *segment* refers to a part of an organization's overall customer, market, product line or employee base. Segments typically have common characteristics that can be logically grouped. In Results Items, the term refers to disaggregating results data in a way that allows for meaningful analysis of an organization's performance. It is up to each organization to determine the specific factors that it uses to segment its customers, markets, products, services, and employees.

Understanding segments is critical to identifying the distinct needs and expectations of different customer, market, and employee groups and to tailoring products, services, and programs to meet their needs and expectations. As an example, market segmentation might be based on geography, distribution channels, business volume, or technologies employed. Employee segmentation might be based on geography, skills, needs, work assignments, or job classification.

senior leaders—the term *senior leaders* refers to an organization's senior management group or team. In many organizations, this consists of the head of the organization and his or her direct reports.

societal risk—the term *societal risk* refers to potential dangers to the community and society at large that must be considered. For example, speculative investing by a bank may pose a risk to the public as well as the customers of the bank.

stakeholders—the term *stakeholders* refers to all groups that are or might be affected by an organization's actions and success. Examples of key stakeholders include customers, employees, partners, governing boards, stockholders, donors, suppliers, taxpayers, policy makers, funders, and local and professional communities.

strategic challenges—the term *strategic challenges* refers to those pressures that exert a decisive influence on an organization's likelihood of future success. These challenges frequently are driven by an organization's future competitive position relative to other providers of similar products or services. While not exclusively so, strategic challenges generally are externally driven. However, in responding to externally driven strategic challenges, an organization may face internal strategic challenges.

External strategic challenges may relate to customer or market needs or expectations; product, service, or technological changes; or financial, societal, and other risks or needs. Internal strategic challenges may relate to an organization's capabilities or its human and other resources.

See the definition of *strategic objectives* for the relationship between strategic challenges and the strategic objectives organizations create to address key challenges.

strategic objectives—the term *strategic objectives* refers to an organization's articulated aims or responses to address major change or improvement, competitiveness, social issues, or business advantages. Strategic objectives generally are focused externally and relate to significant customer, market, product, service, or technological opportunities and challenges (strategic challenges). Broadly stated, they are what an organization must achieve to remain or become competitive and ensure the organization's long-term sustainability. Strategic objectives set an organization's longer-term directions and guide resource allocations and redistributions.

See the definition of *action plans* for the relationship between strategic objectives and action plans and for an example of each.

supplier and partner capability—the term *supplier and partner capability* refers to the ability of suppliers and partners to provide products and services as required. If an organization fails to consider the capability of its key suppliers and partners when planning or designing new products or services, the ability of that organization to deliver may be threatened.

sustainability—the term *sustainability* refers to an organization's ability to address current business needs and to have the agility and strategic management to prepare successfully for future business, market, and operating environments. Both external and internal factors need to be considered. The specific combination of factors might include industry-wide and organization-specific components.

In addition to responding to changes in the business, market, and operating environment, sustainability also has a component related to preparedness for real-time or short-term emergencies.

system versus process—a system is a set of disciplined, consistent, well-defined, and well-designed processes for meeting the organization's quality and performance requirements. For example, the Leadership System refers to how leadership is exercised throughout the organization and includes all people exercising leadership, from top executives to managers, to supervisors. Everything done in an organization is a process but not all processes are part of a system and not all processes are systematic.

systematic—the term *systematic* refers to approaches that are repeatable and use data and information so that improvement and learning are possible. In other words, approaches are systematic if they build in the opportunity for evaluation, improvement, and sharing, thereby permitting a gain in maturity. For use of the term, see the Scoring Guidelines.

timetable—a *timetable* for accomplishing strategic objectives sets forth the expected levels of achievement that leaders use to monitor progress toward achieving the outcome-based strategic objectives. To be aligned with strategic objectives, each objective should have a corresponding set of milestones to track progress. To be well-integrated, the timetable should be aligned and the intervals in the timetable should match the review cycle of the leaders. For example, if leaders review progress each quarter, then milestones should be developed that identify the level of progress that is expected to be made each quarter. Without timetables that predict the desired level of achievement,

it is difficult for leaders to know if progress is on track or adjustments need to be made.

trends—the term *trends* refers to numerical information that shows the direction and rate of change for an organization's results. Trends provide a time sequence of organizational performance.

A minimum of three data points generally is needed to begin to ascertain a trend. More data points are needed to define a statistically valid trend. The time period for a trend is determined by the cycle time of the process being measured. Shorter cycle times demand more frequent measurement, while longer cycle times might require longer periods before meaningful trends can be determined.

Examples of trends called for by the Criteria include data related to product and service performance, customer and employee satisfaction and dissatisfaction results, financial performance, marketplace performance, and operational performance, such as cycle time and productivity.

value—the term *value* refers to the perceived worth of a product, service, process, asset, or function relative to cost and to possible alternatives.

Organizations frequently use value considerations to determine the benefits of various options relative to their costs, such as the value of various product and service combinations to customers. Organizations need to understand what different stakeholder groups value and then deliver value to each group. This frequently requires balancing value for customers and other stakeholders, such as stockholders, employees, and the community.

value creation—the term *value creation* refers to processes that produce benefit for the organization's customers and for the organization. They are the processes most important to *running the business*—those that involve the majority of employees and generate products, services, and positive business results for stockholders and other key stakeholders.

values—the term *values* refers to the guiding principles and behaviors that embody how the organization and its people are expected to operate. Values reflect and reinforce the desired culture of the organization. Values support and guide the decision making of every employee, helping the organization to accomplish its mission and attain its vision in an appropriate manner.

Examples of values might include ensuring integrity and fairness in all interactions, exceeding customer expectations, valuing employees and diversity, protecting the environment, and demonstrating performance excellence every day.

vision—the term *vision* refers to the desired future state of the organization. The vision describes where the organization is headed, what it intends to be, or how it wishes to be perceived.

work systems—the term *work systems* refers to how employees are organized into formal or informal units to accomplish the mission and strategic objectives; how job responsibilities are managed; and the processes for compensation, employee performance management, recognition, communication, hiring, and succession planning. Organizations design work systems to align their components to enable and encourage all employees to contribute effectively and to the best of their ability.

About the Author

Mark L. Blazey, EdD

Mark Blazey is the president of Quantum Performance Group, a management consulting and training firm specializing in organization assessment and high-performance systems development. Dr. Blazey has an extensive background in quality systems. For five years he served as a senior examiner for the Malcolm Baldrige National Quality Award. He also served as the lead judge for Baldrige-based awards for New York State, Vermont, Delaware, and Aruba, and a judge for the Wisconsin Forward Award. Dr. Blazey has participated on and led numerous site-visit teams for national, state, and company quality awards and audits over the past 15 years.

Dr. Blazey has trained thousands of quality award examiners and judges for state and national quality programs including the Alabama Quality Award, Delaware Quality Award, Illinois Lincoln Award for Excellence, Kentucky Quality Award, Minnesota Quality Award, New York State Quality Award, Pennsylvania Quality Leadership Awards, Nebraska Quality Award, Vermont Quality Award, Wisconsin Forward Award, Aruba Quality Award, Costa Rica Quality Award, the Army Community of Excellence Award, the Army Performance Excellence Award, and the national Workforce Excellence Network Award, as well as managers and examiners for schools, healthcare organizations, major businesses, and government agencies. He has set up numerous Baldrige-based programs to enhance and assess performance excellence for all sectors and types of organizations, many of which have subsequently received State and Baldrige recognition.

Dr. Blazey has written many books and articles on quality, including the ASQ Quality Press best-seller *Insights to Performance Excellence,* and co-authored *Insights to Performance Excellence in Education, Insights to Performance Excellence in Health Care,* and *Baldrige in Brief: A Guide to the Baldrige Performance Excellence Criteria.* He is a member and a certified quality auditor of the American Society for Quality.

Dr. Blazey may be contacted via e-mail at authors@asq.org or Blazey@QuantumPerformance.com, or by telephone at 585-394-3700. He encourages feedback, recommendations, and questions about this book.

Index